INDIRA GANDHI: A LIFE IN NATURE

INDIRA GANDHI

A Life in Nature

Jairam Ramesh

SIMON &
SCHUSTER

London · New York · Sydney · Toronto · New Delhi

A CBS COMPANY

Contents

A Note on Names   *ix*

I.   A First Word   1

II.   The Wellsprings (1917–c1943)   9

III. The Companionship Years (1950–1964)   31

IV.   The Naturalist Prime Minister–I (1966–1977)   53

V.   Out of Office (1977–79)   245

VI.   The Naturalist Prime Minister–II (1980–1984)   265

VII. A Final Word   411

A Note on Sources   418

A Note of Thanks   420

Bibliography   424

Index   429

All the birds have flown up and gone;
A lonely cloud floats leisurely by.
We never tire of looking at each other—
Only the mountain and I.

—Li Po, 'Alone Looking at the Mountain'*

For oft, when on my couch I lie
In vacant or in pensive mood,
They flash upon that inward eye
Which is the bliss of solitude;
And then my heart with pleasure fills,
And dances with the daffodils.

—William Wordsworth, 'I Wandered Lonely on a Cloud'*

It was the Rainbow gave thee birth,
And left thee all her lovely hues; […]
Thou hast no proud, ambitious mind;
I also love a quiet place
That's green, away from all mankind;
A lonely pool, and let a tree
Sigh with her bosom over me.

—William Henry Davies, 'The Kingfisher'*

---

*These were some of Indira Gandhi's favourite poems.

A Note on Names

I HAVE MAINTAINED THE NAMES AS THEY EXISTED DURING INDIRA GANDHI'S time although they were changed subsequently.

Old Name	New Name
Simla	Shimla
Poona	Pune
Bombay	Mumbai
Calcutta	Kolkata
Orissa	Odisha
Bangalore	Bengaluru
Baroda	Vadodara
Trivandrum	Thiruvananthapuram
New Delhi Municipal Committee (NDMC)	New Delhi Municipal Council (NDMC)
Madras	Chennai
Trichur	Thrissur
Dum Dum Airport	Netaji Subhas Chandra Bose International Airport
Ceylon	Sri Lanka
Giridhar Gomango	Giridhar Gamang
Rs (Rupees)	₹

I. A First Word

It was the night of 26 October 1984. Five days later she was to be brutally gunned down by her own security guards.

But that was later. For now, she wanted to fulfill a life's ambition—and said so.

For almost half a century, she had been going to the land of her ancestors—a land she loved as nature's paradise. It came with mountains, flowers, gardens, streams and, most of all, trees—particularly chinars that over autumn explode into a spray of colours—from a deep vermilion to tones of burnt sienna to pale amber.

She had never seen this gorgeous sight and, after years of putting it off, she desperately wanted to experience it first-hand. The governor of the state advised her against visiting because of the prevailing political situation. But she ignored what he had to say.

Off she went early the next morning, accompanied by her grandchildren, to see the chinar trees in all their glory. She also visited her favourite Dachigam National Park—literally walking on a carpet of leaves. A strange sense of satisfaction engulfed her.

She came back to Delhi on 28 October and wrote a foreword for a book authored by a ministerial colleague. It happened to be a book on her abiding love—the environment. She then left for Orissa the next morning. On the 30th, she made her very last speech in Bhubaneswar in which, famously, she seemed to have a premonition of a violent ending to her life soon.

Her premonition turned out to be right. The very next morning at around 9 a.m. she was walking briskly from her home to her adjoining office to record an interview for the BBC. Within a few minutes, however, she was assassinated in a most ghastly manner, at point-blank range, by two men assigned to protect her.

Her funeral was on 3 November. It drew mourners from across the globe. High-powered delegations from numerous countries came as a mark of respect to her. The American team had a world-famous ornithologist who had been in touch with her for over three decades.

As the funeral procession moved to its destination, the naval band played 'Flowers of the Forest', both of which were very much part of her life. Eight days after her body was consigned to the flames, in keeping with her last wish, Indira Gandhi's ashes were sprinkled over the Himalayas with which she had had a special bond, first over Gomukh and Gangotri, and later over Nun Kun and the sacred cave of Amarnath.

Thus passed into history Indira Gandhi, daughter of Jawaharlal Nehru, the prime architect of the modern Indian nation-state.

Thus passed into history Indira Gandhi who herself had been prime minister across two terms for sixteen years and who continues to inspire awe and admiration, draw hostility and criticism.

This is an unconventional biography of Indira Gandhi—for it deals with only one aspect of her personality and her record in office.

Why focus on Indira Gandhi's life as a naturalist when she was quintessentially a politician?

The answer is simple.

A naturalist is who Indira Gandhi really was, who she *thought* she was. She got sucked into the whirlpool of politics but the real Indira Gandhi was the person who loved the mountains, cared deeply for wildlife, was passionate about birds, stones, trees and forests, and was worried deeply about the environmental consequences of urbanization and industrialization.

She was the only head of government, other than the host prime minister, to speak at the first-ever United Nations (UN) Conference on the Human Environment in Stockholm in June 1972. Her speech there has reverberated down the decades.

She was singularly responsible not just for India's best-known wildlife conservation programme—namely, Project Tiger—but also for less high-profile initiatives for the protection of crocodiles, lions, hanguls, cranes, bustards, flamingos, deer and other endangered species.

She almost single-handedly pushed through two laws—one for the protection of wildlife and another for the conservation of forests, which continue to hold sway. Today's laws for dealing with water and air pollution were enacted during her tenure.

Indira Gandhi used her political authority to save ecologically sensitive areas from destruction like the Andaman and Nicobar Islands, the entire northeast and the rainforests in the Western Ghats.

She repeatedly drew the attention of chief ministers and other political colleagues to issues concerning wildlife, forests, pollution, resettlement, and for the need to always maintain what she called 'ecological balance'.

She highlighted, time and again, the inextricable link between India's natural and built heritage. Indeed, she was one of the very few—perhaps, the only one—to see nature and culture as two sides of the same coin.

It is because of these accomplishments, among several others, that Indira Gandhi deserves to be looked at with a fresh 'green' lens. While her politics and economics changed over the years, all through she remained steadfast to conservation. This passion survived the vicissitudes in her life.

Indira Gandhi had a large network of friends in the conservation community across the world. She kept in touch with them. They had easy access to her. They would write to her directly and she would find time to respond.

On matters related to the environment, she was open-minded and deeply engaged all the time. She listened, consulted and reached out. She responded to what she was being told. She was both active and proactive. She gave political space to different points of view; she offered time, often at short notice, to those who would not normally have been able to reach individuals at the helm of decision-making. She took courageous positions that had no immediate electoral payoffs.

The environmentalist in her has never got the acknowledgement it warrants from her biographers[1]—none of whom has done justice to her avatar as the ecology's champion, or considered her passion for conservation in a balance sheet of her successes and failures. While some of her aides have written their memoirs, they have mostly dwelt on her political activities.[2] Indira Gandhi figures in some books by conservationists but mostly through anecdotes or through her published speeches. A cohesive ecological narrative extending right through her life based on written records has been missing.[3]

5

That is the unabashed reason for this book. It is an exploration of a relatively under-appreciated dimension of Indira Gandhi's personality and of her achievements in public life as an ecologist.

Where did she get her love and concern for nature from? How did it develop? How did it get reflected in what she thought, spoke, wrote and did? Who influenced her when she took far-reaching decisions on the nation's ecological well-being? What is the relevance of her work today?

These are some of the questions I wish to explore.

I have maintained a chronological sequence particularly in the sections that deal with her prime ministerial years. This is to convey how Indira Gandhi was dealing with nature conservation issues even as she was grappling with serious political, economic, social and foreign policy matters. So, in a way, the book is a diary of her environmental activities—a diary not maintained by her obviously but reconstructed with the help of archival material.

To build the narrative, I have used the letters she wrote, the speeches she delivered, the articles she penned, the forewords she provided, the memos she dispatched, the notes she scribbled and the messages she sent. Most of these are not part of her official compendium of writings and are not easily available. In addition, I have used her observations on files put up to her. The idea is to have a biography which allows Indira Gandhi herself to do much of the talking.

∾

19 November 2017 marks the centenary of Indira Gandhi's birth. It is an appropriate occasion to explore her tryst with nature.

I myself was dimly aware of Indira Gandhi as nature's champion—that is, until I became the environment and forests minister in May 2009. I remained in that post for twenty-six months.

During this period, I got transformed from being a zealot for rapid economic growth at all costs to someone who came to insist that such rapid economic growth must be anchored in ecological sustainability.[4] A large part of this shift occurred because of my deeper understanding of India's third prime minister and how she tried her best to make ecological issues an integral part of the political discourse. It was at this point that I came to appreciate more fully the environmental facet of Indira Gandhi—the causes she promoted, the decisions she took, the directions she gave, the legacy she bequeathed.

This country cannot afford to follow a blind 'grow now, pay later' model. We are already a nation of around 1.24 billion and we will add a third of that number by the middle of the century. Climate change is a devastating reality, and is affecting our monsoon patterns, glaciers and mean sea levels. Pollution and chemical contamination are having very substantial public health consequences.

Our forests—the absorbers of greenhouse gases that cause global warming—are under threat as we extract more coal, iron ore and other minerals, and as we build more irrigation projects and power plants to fuel our economic growth.

Livelihoods across the country are under threat as we give over-riding primacy to faster GDP growth. India certainly needs accelerated economic advance. But, at the same time, it cannot afford to pollute its way to prosperity, deforest its way to affluence, endanger its valuable biodiversity to become a global economic dynamo.

Whatever the judgement regarding her politics or economics, Indira Gandhi is still relevant as far as India's search for ecological security in its pursuit of high economic growth is concerned.

On more than one occasion Indira Gandhi had said that she was no feminist. By the same token, she was no narrow, one-dimensional environmentalist either. She was always acutely aware and deeply conscious that she was the prime minister of a country burdened by deprivation and poverty, a country where malnutrition and disease were widely prevalent, a country where the main challenge was to educate a growing population and provide it with expanding employment opportunities.

Her entire effort, therefore, was to arrive at a *balance* between ecology[5] and economic growth. This meant that, at times, she would align herself with the ecology and on other occasions, with the forces of growth and industrialization, while insisting on ecological safeguards. As a result, environmentalists bemoan the fact that she did not go far enough with her intent to conserve natural ecosystems, while the growth supremacists feel that she paid far too much attention to conservation. This, of course, is the inherent hazard in pursing the middle path.

But Indira Gandhi persisted and persevered. This then is a story of such persistence and perseverance.

Notes

1. Notable of them are Mohan (1967), Vasudev (1974), Bhatia (1974), Masani (1975), Moraes (1980), Gupte (1992), Jayakar (1992), Frank (2001) and Malhotra (2014)

2. These include Alexander (1991), Dhar (2000), Alexander (2004) and Bhagat (2005).

3. Rangarajan (2015) is the only such scholarly narrative in the form of a long essay which looks at her entire life. The best example of a book by a conservationist in which she figures somewhat prominently is Thapar (2010).

4. I have described this transformation from an 'eco-hawk' to an 'enviro-dove' as it were in Ramesh (2015a)

5. 'Ecology' carries connotations of living resources, nature, biogeochemical cycles and life support systems. 'Environment' is, in some senses, slightly bigger in that it includes ecology but addresses the physical phenomena too—pollution, noise, waste, settlements, and the nuances of the interaction between people and machines. Both terms carry the idea of complex systems, fragility, and indeed resilience—if biology underpins the former, physics, chemistry and engineering underpin the latter. Indira Gandhi liked to use the word 'ecology', although over her long prime ministerial innings she used the two terms interchangeably. I owe this distinction to Ashok Khosla.

II. The Wellsprings
(1917–c1943)

Where did Indira Gandhi get her empathy for nature from? Who and what influenced her? How did she become so sensitive to what are today called 'environmental' issues? The conviction, courage and consistency she demonstrated on matters concerning the conservation of biodiversity must have had their foundations somewhere. In this chapter I explore that 'somewhere'.

Indira Nehru in Santiniketan with her friends; 1934–35.

ON 10 APRIL 1917, MAHATMA GANDHI'S FIRST GRASSROOTS ASSAULT ON British rule in India began at Champaran, Bihar where he helped poor farmers protest against the forced cultivation of indigo. All at once, India's independence movement began shifting from debates amongst lawyers and a small English-speaking class to mass mobilization and popular agitation.

A little over seven months later—and eleven days after Lenin had triggered the Bolshevik revolution in Russia[1]—on 19 November 1917, Indira was born in Allahabad, into a family immersed in India's freedom movement. Both her grandfather and father, although ideologically dissimilar, were leading lights of the Indian National Congress.

Indira was an only child. Her childhood was tough. Her mother suffered from tuberculosis, while her father was in and out of jail. Between December 1921 and June 1945, Nehru was in prison for approximately nine years—or for almost 40 per cent of the time.

Indira herself was quite sickly. Her schooling was thus unsettled. She studied in Switzerland, Poona, Santiniketan and England. Two of these places—Switzerland and Santiniketan—left a deep imprint on her as a person sensitive to the environment.

All through, Indira had an excellent tutor and mentor who educated her and expanded her intellectual horizons. This was her father—Jawaharlal Nehru. She had another teacher and that was history itself unfolding before her eyes. Her home in Allahabad—Anand Bhawan—was frequented by all the leading figures of the independence movement. It was where several milestones of the freedom struggle were etched.

One consequence of Indira's mother's illness, as well of her own, was that she spent many days in a year in 'hill stations' like Mussoorie, Dehra Dun, Almora, Matheran and Panchgani, not to be speak of her ancestral land, Kashmir. These places further reinforced her affinity for nature.

There can be no doubt that the most profound intellectual influence on Indira during her teens and youth was that of her father. Such influence was largely exerted through the extraordinarily large number of letters he wrote to her, contained in three books—*Letters from a Father to His Daughter*, *Glimpses of World History*, and *Two Alone, Two Together*. Two of these are key to understanding the evolution of Indira, the naturalist.

Letters from a Father to His Daughter has thirty letters written when Nehru was in Allahabad and Indira, in Mussoorie and about to turn eleven. Five letters were expositions on natural history, with the very first one being 'The Book of Nature'. Decades later in a foreword to an edition reprinted in 1973, Indira Gandhi had this to say about these letters:

> The letters in this book [...] deal with the beginnings of the earth and of man's awareness of himself. They were not merely letters to be read and put away. They brought a fresh outlook and aroused a feeling of concern for people and interest in the world around. They taught one to treat nature as a book. I spent absorbing hours studying stones and plants, the lives of insects and at night, the stars.

It wouldn't be a stretch to infer that she had these letters at the back of her mind when she started her most famous speech on 14 June 1972 at the UN Conference on the Human Environment at Stockholm:

> I have had the good fortune of growing up with a sense of kinship with nature in all its manifestations. Birds, plants, stones were companions

and, sleeping under a star-strewn sky, I became familiar with the names and movements of the constellations.

Two Alone, Two Together contains 535 father–daughter letters exchanged between 1922 and 1964,[2] and have an 'informal intimacy'[3] about them 'that suggests they were not intended for publication'. Of these, 263 letters are from daughter to father, which make this exchange an even-handed one, contrary to the popular belief that Nehru out-wrote Indira by a huge margin. I will be making use of this anthology[4] to show how deeply interested Indira Gandhi became in bird watching in the 1940s and how evocatively she described the natural world to her father from Srinagar and other hill stations.[5]

Nehru influenced Indira's love for nature not just through the letters he wrote, but also by the books he gifted her when she was very young, among them *The Life of the Bee* by Maurice Maeterlinck—the well-known Belgian writer on entomological subjects who had received the Nobel Prize for Literature in 1911. Nehru's inscription in Hindi read:

Indira Priyadarshini
Papu ka Bahut, Bahut Pyaar [Lots and lots of love from Daddy]
Naini Jail
10 December 1930

Indira loved *The Life of the Bee* enough to mention it in one of the earliest letters she wrote to her father (December 1930; date unknown) from Calcutta:

[…] I have enjoyed reading *The Life of the Bee*. […] I have also begun *The Life of the Ant* [also by Maurice Maeterlinck]. But as I have read only a few pages I have not formed my opinion about it […]

That these books stayed in Indira's mind is evident from a comment she was to make very much later to an American lady:

Entirely different types of books, for instance, the *Faber Book of Insects* and Maeterlinck's books on bees, ants […] also contributed to the shaping of my personality. They inculcated the habit of close observations of everything around and reinforced what my mother used to tell me of the links between all creatures. My father's letters had explained how rocks, stones, and trees told not only their own story but those of the people and creatures who lived amongst them. Very early I became a conservationist with a strong feeling of companionship and kinship with all living things.[6]

Indira Gandhi's private library sometimes throws light on the books she grew up reading—such as, *The Book of Baby Birds* by E.J. Detmold—with a handwritten inscription on the opening page:

Indira Nehru, Calcutta, 5/1/29.

Correspondence between daughter and father further suggests what Indira voraciously pored over in 1932. There were some sixty books, both in English and French, that included several classics such as *What Dare I Think* by Julian Huxley, spanning both biology and religion; *The Life of a Butterfly* by Friedrich Schnack, examining the life cycle of the peacock butterfly; the *Swallows and Amazons* series by Arthur Ransome, which engaged with children camping, fishing and exploring; and *Far Away and Long Ago* by William Henry Hudson—an autobiography of a well-known naturalist of those times who spent the first eighteen years of his life in the Argentinian Pampas.

A letter from Indira to her father on 13 April 1940 from Leysin in Switzerland—where she was undergoing treatment for pleurisy—gives a glimpse not only of her wide reading preferences, but also of the policies she was to later adopt as prime minister:

I have been reading, in the *Reader's Digest*, a condensation from the book *Flowering Earth* by D.C. Peattie. I am sure it would fascinate you, as it did me. It is a story of green life—the plant kingdom—upon the earth. Is it not wonderful, the oneness of life? It is ever a source of marvel to me how intrinsically the fates of all living things are bound together and how dependent on one another they are.

This must be the only book of that time that Indira read without her father suggesting it. In fact, it was one that her father himself hadn't read. In a letter dated 25 April 1940, written from Bombay, with an addition made the next day, Nehru admitted to his daughter that he found her account of D.C. Peattie's book 'fascinating' and that he would try and get the book—a rare biblio-victory for Indira over her father.

∾

Kamala Nehru had, by Indira Gandhi's own admission, a deep impact on her daughter's personality. But it was Kamala Nehru's youngest brother who helped deepen her interest in and concern for nature. While describing her holidays at her maternal grandmother's house in Old Delhi, Indira Gandhi recalled:

> My mother's youngest brother was passionately keen on botany and zoology and finally took his degree in those subjects and he was very keen on snakes. So anything you opened in the house you found a snake in it, much to my grandmother's horror. But it made me friendly with snakes and animals.[7]

The uncle, twelve years older than her, was Kailas Nath Kaul, a brilliant student of botany who had studied under one of India's greatest botanists Birbal Sahni at Lucknow University. He later trained at London's famed Royal Botanic Gardens at Kew, becoming the first Indian to serve there as a scientist in 1939. On his return to India in 1944 he worked to develop and expand the botanical gardens originally established by the Nawabs of Oudh in Lucknow. These gardens became a part of the National Botanical Gardens, and were later incorporated into the newly established National Botanical Research Institute (NBRI).

Unlike Nehru who had only studied botany at Cambridge as part of his natural sciences tripos,[8] Kaul was a professional botanist with a fine reputation. He went on to become the first vice chancellor of the Chandra Shekhar Azad University of Agricultural Sciences and Technology in Kanpur. His ideas for solving the water problems of the erstwhile princely state of Jodhpur and for reclaiming alkaline soils using non-chemical methods earned him acclaim.[9] Just before his death, he contributed significantly to Indira Gandhi's policy on forestry management in the hill areas of Uttar Pradesh.

Kailas Nath Kaul and Indira Gandhi did not actually spend much time together but, as in many Indian families, the mother's brother had a special place in her life. We are offered a glimpse of this in Indira Gandhi's own words, when she responded on 25 February 1983 to her paternal aunt Vijaya Lakshmi Pandit's condolence letter soon after her beloved 'Mamu' had passed away:

> Thank you for your letter of sympathy on Mamu's death. He had been ill for a long time but somehow one finds it difficult to accept death and Mamu was full of life and following up so many interests up to the very last.

Later that year, Indira Gandhi recalled him fondly in a speech she delivered at the centenary celebrations of the Bombay Natural History Society (BNHS) on 15 September 1983:

> Sitting here, I was also reminded that one of my earliest associations with animals was with snakes because my mother's brother was not only a keen botanist but had a passion for snakes. When I was, I suppose, not more than six or so, we used to come to Delhi and stay with my grandmother. Anything you opened out popped a snake. It might be a cigarette box, it might be a drawer or it might be out of the pipe in the bathroom, much, of course, to the distress of my grandmother. And later when he was grown up, he kept two pythons, almost as large as the one we saw here, in his garden as pets. Unfortunately, on his marriage he had to give them away.

While Nehru had an overarching influence on Indira, her fondness for nature was nurtured through her formal schooling, too. At the age of nine, Indira joined L'Ecole Nouvelle in Bex near Geneva. She was there since her mother was undergoing treatment for tuberculosis. Much later, she was to reminisce about this phase of her life:[10]

> Even as a small child, I was very keen on nature. At the International School they attached great importance to the study of nature: we studied leaves, insects and everything in detail. I think that also had a life-long influence.

On the evening of 6 July 1934, Indira reached Santiniketan, the home of Visva-Bharati, started by Rabindranath Tagore. There, she spent nine months, before cutting short her stay because of her mother's worsening health. While there is nothing in her correspondence at that time with her father to suggest any special link between Santiniketan and her affinity with nature, it will not be far-fetched to assume that by its very character, Tagore's university did indeed have some influence. As Indira Gandhi herself much later confirmed:

> Santiniketan was most of all permeated with Gurudeva's personality. I was so interested in all the aspects in general. So many things that are fashionable today but were unheard of in those days were all there in Gurudeva. For example, the environment and concern for the environment are so fashionable today but Gurudeva was working for it in Santiniketan and Sriniketan. I was absorbing all those things when living there. They became a part of me. Now whether they were already in me and the place helped to bring them out or whether I had got them from the place itself I cannot tell.[11]

Still later, in a radio interview broadcast just about a year before her death, Indira Gandhi, when asked how her life transformed at Santiniketan, had this to say:

> Before [Santiniketan] there was absolutely no music in our home [...] At Santiniketan, my relationship with all these things grew [...] We also went closer to nature.[12]

It is also almost certain that Santiniketan stirred in her a love for gardening. Only a day after she had arrived, she wrote to her father:

> And I had better give you my opinion of the place [...] Everything is so artistic & beautiful & wild [...]
>
> Gurudev suggested that I do some gardening in my free time. He seems to be very fond of it and was complaining that so few girls take it up.

Gardening was to remain a central element of Indira Gandhi's life to the end.

While Indira Gandhi's childhood and teenage years were unsettled, they were not unprivileged. Holidays in hill stations were a regular feature. Indira was eleven when she first went to Mussoorie with Kamala Nehru. Two years later, at her grandfather's behest, she spent time with a relative in Nainital. In late 1931, father, mother and daughter spent a month in Ceylon. In March 1932, mother and daughter went to Panchgani and Mahabaleshwar, both hill stations near Poona.

May and June 1934 found Indira in Kashmir with her mother. This was her very first visit to her ancestral land, and on 11 June she wrote to her father from Srinagar:

> In this wonderful land, no matter where you are you get a lovely view
> of the snow-covered peaks which surround it and the beautiful springs.
> I don't think the waters of Kashmir can be compared to those of any
> other country. They have a standard of their own [...]
> Ever since I first saw the chenar [*sic*], I have been lost in admiration.
> It is a magnificent tree.

Indira's admiration for chinar trees would only grow with time, and as I described earlier she was to soak in their beauty mere days before she was gunned down.

In October 1934, mother and daughter were in Bhowali in the Himalayan foothills—a land of lakes as well—and a young Indira was reminded most compellingly of Switzerland. Till her mother's death in February 1936, these trips could certainly not be called 'holidays' since most of her time was spent looking after an ailing Kamala Nehru. Very soon, Indira herself became a patient of pleurisy.

1939 began with a letter to her friend Kathleen Davis; on 6 January, Indira wrote: 'I have been packed off to Almora because it is very dry and cold and quiet'. The next day, she wrote to another friend Rajni Patel asking for forgiveness for not replying to his letters for a long time: 'I suppose it was sheer laziness, lying in the sun or under the pines with the magnificent Nanda Devi and her sister peaks towering above me.' On 15 July 1939, with war about to break out in Europe, she penned a letter to her father from Bürgenstock near Lucerne:

Feroze's holidays have begun and just before I left Stansstad he came over to Switzerland. We did two trips together—to Trubsee (just above Stansstad) from whence we climbed to the "Joch Pass" and further to "Jochstockli", a peak above the pass. It was a climb of 1,403 feet. The Joch Pass is 7,303 feet above sea-level. It was an enjoyable climb for we found many lovely Alpine spring flowers. I thought of you and wanted to send you some but they would only arrive withered.

Clearly, by now, Indira had become bit of an outdoors woman. She kept alive her interest in mountains—viewing them not just as places to relax and unwind but also as places where she could exert herself.

Kashmir continued to hold a special fascination for her—as it did for her father—and, I believe, was crucial to her evolution as a naturalist.[13] On 5 July 1942 she wrote to Nehru from Srinagar:

Truly if there is a heaven, it is this. There is nothing in Switzerland to compare with these flower-filled slopes, the sweet-scented breezes. Maybe there are other things besides running water that pour over the soul the anodyne of forgetfulness and peace.

A few years down the road, on 23 May 1945, she wrote to her father again from Srinagar:

Srinagar is really lovely. After a whole night's rain, the sky was clear and cloudless and studded with stars, and the mountain ranges glistening silver with the freshly fallen snow [...]

I should like to do at least one small trek. In one of the guidebooks there is such a lovely description of the road to Tragbal Pass near the Nanga Parbat, that I cannot resist the temptation to go and see for myself [...]

Through the 1940s, the locations chosen for Indira's annual holidays had therapeutic value, and they were all, without exception, delights of nature.

May–June 1941	Mussoorie
July 1942	Kashmir
July 1943	Panchgani
March–April 1944	Matheran

May 1944	Mahabaleswar
May–June 1945	Murree, Kashmir
May 1946	Nainital
June 1946	Almora
May 1948	Kashmir

Mountains remained a common thread running through her life:

> We went to the mountains every summer. We went to different places.
> My grandmother often said to my grandfather: "Why don't you get them
> a house in the hills as they go every year?" He would reply: "But they will
> then go to the same place. That is why I don't want to have a house in
> the hills." One of the nicest trips I remember was to Chamba. In those
> days it was very lovely and beautiful.[14]

As prime minister, Indira Gandhi was to be known for her fierce
determination to protect India's forests. Her conversation with Pupul
Jayakar tells us something about the genesis of this stance:

> I have always loved trees, trees more than flowers. And animals, I have
> always had animals. Even as a child I looked upon a tree as a life-giving
> thing. I also looked upon it as a refuge [...] I liked climbing trees. I liked
> it as an exercise but also because I could hide there. I had my little places
> where I could take my books and sit up and nobody would disturb me.
> I did that till quite late. Even when I was in school in Pune, I used to go
> up a favourite tree. I would hear people shouting: "Where is she, where
> is she?" but I would not come down until I chose.[15]

When, in February 1976, a Bombay-based organization, Friends of Trees,[16]
asked her for a message to give wider public exposure to its activities, she
reiterated her love affair with trees:

> I have always regarded myself as a friend of trees and have experienced
> a sense of companionship with them—the-easy-to-climb ones so dear
> to all active children seeking occasional haven from the adult world; the
> spreading ones which give protection from the glare and heat of the Indian

sun; the flowering ones, bursting into colourful bloom; the gnarled old ones, mute witnesses of history.

❧

That Salim Ali, India's best known ornithologist, had a pronounced influence on Indira Gandhi, the prime minister, is proven by a letter she wrote to him on 3 August 1980—this was in response to his note of condolence on the death of her younger son Sanjay:

> I am grateful for your message of sympathy.
> Sanjay was so full of fun and so vibrantly alive it is difficult to realize that he isn't there any more.
> You will have noticed that I am referring all issues concerned with ecology to you. I hope it is not too much of a burden and that you will help us to find amicable solutions. As you know, the State Governments are very persistent with their demands.

This was obviously no routine letter of acknowledgement.

Indira Gandhi got to know of Salim Ali before she actually met him, through his book which had been brought to her attention by her father. In his autobiography,[17] Salim Ali writes that he met Nehru in Dehra Dun, where he had been jailed, and autographed his recently released book *The Book of Indian Birds*. This would have been between August 1941 when the book came out and 3 December 1941 when Nehru left that prison.

The beginnings of Indira Gandhi's direct connection with Salim Ali's classic is best recounted in her own words, contained in a foreword she wrote in 1959 to a book on Indian birds:[18]

> [...] Like most Indians I took birds for granted until my father sent me Dr. Salim Ali's delightful book from Dehra Dun jail and opened my eyes to an entirely new world. Only then, did I realize how much I had been missing.
> Bird watching is one of the most absorbing and rewarding activities. First, one learns to distinguish the different species, their nesting habits and their calls. Then gradually one realizes that birds are also little individuals each with his own characteristics.

21

[…] We are fortunate still to be able to live amongst birds even in our cities. In other countries you will have to go deep into the countryside to see any.

Twenty-three years later, in the same speech at the BNHS's centenary function, in which she had recalled the influence of her maternal uncle, she reminisced about Salim Ali's classic yet again:

Dr. Salim Ali's *Book of Indian Birds* and Prater's *Book of Indian Animals* opened out a whole new world to many Indians. I had always loved animals. But I did not know much about birds until the high walls of Naini prison shut us off from them and for the first time I paid attention to bird songs. I noted the sounds and later on after my release my father sent me Dr. Salim Ali's book and I was able to identify the birds from the book.

Indira Gandhi was incarcerated from 11 September 1942 to 13 May 1943 in Naini Central Prison, Allahabad, where she developed a life-long interest in birdwatching. Between April 1943 and May 1945, she wrote eleven letters on her arboreal and ornithological interests to Jawaharlal Nehru, and each of them is a delight, revealing a little-known aspect of her personality.

On 23 March 1943, she wrote from her prison to her father who also was in jail—this time in Ahmednagar:

[…] We have only three large shady trees. Or rather had, for one of them, a stately gnarled old neem, fell with such a tremendous thud the other day. It looked so strong and one would have thought it would last forever. Its roots had all been eaten away by the white ants and it was rotten to the core. There was majesty in its every branch even as it lay prostrate, but almost immediately it was chopped up for firewood and removed. Only a stump now remains. Remember—

The potent bear whose hug
Was feared by all, is now a rug.

Vivid descriptions of birds followed from her on 6 April 1943:

Often we have visitors in the night. Bartholomew Bat is the one I dislike most. In the days when Knights were bold, they used to give names to their swords. Following that charming custom, I have given names to all the animals and insects & lots of other things besides, which come here. Among our nightly visitors are Minto & Morley Musk-rat (their predecessor Montague was killed by Mehitabel the cat) and Marmaduke, who is the husband of Mehitabel. Marmaduke is an errant coward and is most unbeautiful, though he has a marked resemblance to Mr. Gladstone. He only comes at night. On the other hand, Mehitabel is very pretty and is our constant companion as also her kittens Kanhaiya, Moti and Parvati.

I wonder how the British censors, who examined each letter of high-profile political prisoners, allowed the allusions to leading UK politicians of the day to go through unscathed! Perhaps they just smiled at Indira Gandhi's characterizations and let them pass.

Just before her release nineteen days later, she wrote once again showing her fondness for nature in its myriad forms. It is worth quoting at some length for what it reveals of the letter writer:

We have a peepul in our yard, a tree which, had it depended on human praise and approbation, would have withered away long since. However, it ignored our derision and went on its lordly way. And now that *phagun* is come again, the few remaining shreds of last year's garment, yellow with age, are being shed off and its bare limbs are being clothed in glorious sunset pink. It looks as if a deep blush were spreading along the branches which gives it a rather coy look. Amazingly beautiful it is. Over the walls we have glimpses of the tops of some mahua trees—a balm for sore eyes.

Beautiful things attract other beautiful things. Our solitary peepul provides our only opportunity of watching birds, other than the ever-present sparrows, babblers, crows, pigeons and parrots which are numerous and extremely rowdy. Unfortunately the peepul is in such a spot that by the time one hears the call of a bird and rushes round one can just see it disappearing into the sky. In this way, I failed to identify a most peculiar specimen. It happened in the evening. It was singing on a warbling, whistling note. It took me quite a while to locate the sound as coming out of the peepul (this is a feat, the sound being thrown back and forth by the high walls). Just as I got under the trees, the bird gave an extra loud whistle and away he flew. All I saw a bit of beige, a bright tail in two dazzling shades of blue, a long dull red curved beak. Can you tell us what it is?

Mehitabel the cat is getting increasingly vicious and quite adept at catching and devouring pigeons and sparrows. She has recently produced more kittens. The latest family to join us is the Cuthbert centipedes […]

On 14 May 1943, Nehru replied to this letter in which he endearingly ticked off his daughter a bit:

You give me a vague description of a new bird you saw and want me to name it from here! This faith in my extensive knowledge is very touching but it has not justification. But surely you have a kind of an expert on birds with you. Nora fancies herself that way and sent me a book on Indian birds when I was in Dehra Dun jail.

Nora, Indira Gandhi's fellow-inmate at Naini, was Purnima Banerjee from Allahabad. Sister of the heroine of the Quit India movement Aruna Asaf Ali, she was later to become a member of the Constituent Assembly but died very young in 1950.

On 14 July 1943, Indira Gandhi wrote to her father from Panchgani:

I am vastly intrigued by a little bird. It appears to be the only bird in Panchgani apart from the babblers. It goes 'Ferdi', 'Ferdi'—'tweet-tweet', rather like an insolent schoolboy. I haven't managed to get a glimpse of it yet.

Three days later from the same place, she told her father that, while cleaning a room for her husband[19] who had joined her there on his release from prison, she had found a book of common Indian birds:

Looking at the pictures, I was just wondering whether 'Ferdi', the bird, was a grey tit or nuthatch, for I had a glimpse of its blackhead and greyish body—when he called out again and we rushed out for another glimpse. We saw a bright red patch under the tail. So everybody says it must be the red-vented bulbul. Also in the book, I was able to identify the lovely brown and blue creature Nora and I saw in Naini—it is the white-breasted kingfisher.

Roughly two months later, on 13 September 1943, she gave her father news about Agatha Harrison who had been with her while she was undergoing treatment in Switzerland and concluded the letter thus:

> Re. bird watching—I have spotted two very regular visitors and hope to make friends with them soon: a lovely vivid oriole and a perky little robin. There are a lot of blue jays too and in the afternoon just as I am settling down to a nap, I hear the call of a coppersmith—tuk, tuk. But I haven't seen it yet.

Each time a bird was spotted—and even when none were to be found—Nehru was on Indira's mind. The frequent separations were beginning to take their emotional toll. Acute nostalgia was very much in the air. A month later, writing from Allahabad itself, she confessed:[20]

> Sometimes when I see a new bird or something I feel like rushing in to call you to have a look and then of course I remember you are somewhere in India, but definitely not in Anand Bhawan.

Then, in another letter dated 21 October 1943, along with describing her daily schedule and giving Nehru information on how Anand Bhawan was being spruced up in his absence, she wrote:

> The winter birds are coming in. I saw a redstart yesterday. Rather an amusing little fellow, the way he shivers his tail all the time. His call is exactly like the squeak of an unoiled bicycle wheel. There is even a slight pause between one squeak and the next, just enough for one revolution of the wheel! This morning a blue jay caught a baby mouse and sat and devoured it on our porch [...]

By the last week of March 1944, a pregnant Indira Gandhi had come to Bombay to stay with her younger paternal aunt. She spent a couple of days in Matheran and wrote to her father from there on 28 March:

> Matheran is very very quiet. I think I am going to like it. It is very woody and full of shady but rather small trees. Just outside our rooms, a white-whiskered bulbul has its nest. I spotted him as soon as I arrived. He had a cheerful song. A grouchy old Englishman told Rajabhai[21] that

there are all sorts of lovely birds here, including the paradise flycatcher.
I am all excited to see him.

Jawaharlal Nehru was transferred from Ahmednagar Fort Prison to Bareilly
Central Prison on 30 March 1945. En route, he spent a day at Naini Central
Prison where Indira Gandhi had a brief glimpse of her father at the prison
gate. This led to an emotional letter from her on 31 March 1945 which
had a long and colourful postscript:

> It was wonderful to see you even for that brief while […]
> PS.
>
> Did you notice the moonlit Jumna last evening?
>
> Our peepul tree has been invaded by crowds of interesting mynas.
> The Bark Myna, the Brahmini Myna and the Pied Myna which is the
> most elegant of the lot. What a noise these little things can make! There
> are also the rose-coloured starlings also known as the 'Rosy Pastor'. This is
> the first time I have seen them. I wonder if they are migrating to Central
> Asia for that is where they are said to live most of the year, coming to
> India only for the winter.

Her concern for the protection of migratory birds, particularly the Siberian
cranes, was to reveal itself in a series of actions she was to take as prime
minister in the early 1980s.

She went to Kashmir in early May 1945 with her baby boy to escape
the 'rather unpleasant months in Allahabad, full of illness and insect bites'.
Writing to her father on 19 May, she said:

> Coming from the plains—the dry, dusty roads, the scorching sun—you
> can imagine what a relief it was to the eyes to see miles and miles of
> fresh green. […]
>
> Half the joy of being here is that there are no crows and no babblers.
> There are mynas but they are not as noisy as in the plains. The birds that
> are constantly in the garden are the white-whiskered bulbuls, shrikes,
> golden orioles and different kinds of tits. All such lovely creatures. I am
> longing to see the paradise flycatchers—they say there are lots here. It is
> truly a heavenly bird.

By the mid-1940s, it is abundantly clear that Indira Gandhi had become knowledgeable about birds and was extremely fond of the mountains. The books she read, the schools in which she studied, the places she holidayed in, and the people she was close to had all combined to give her a special affinity for nature. This affinity was to blossom when she herself became prime minister in January 1966. But before that, there was to be a fourteen-year period when she was to be her father—the prime minister's—constant companion. It is this period that I now turn to.

Notes

1. Reckoned by the Gregorian calendar.
2. Actually, over 80 per cent of these letters are between 1922 and 1947.
3. The phrase and the later description is that of S. Gopal in Raghavan (2013).
4. There are two books with the same name, both edited by Sonia Gandhi. One has letters between 1940 and 1964 and was published in 1989 by Hodder and Stoughton. The other has letters between 1922 and 1964 and was published by Penguin in 2004. I make use of the latter mostly, except for portions of one letter which is drawn from the former.
5. Her speech writer and confidante all through her prime ministership, H.Y. Sharada Prasad, wrote in 2003: 'There is a widespread tendency to underrate Indira Gandhi's mind […] Those who have read *Two Alone, Two Together* […] will rid themselves of such condescension' (Sharada Prasad, 2003).
6. In a letter dated 24 September 1972 to J.R. Davis responding to a query about the books that shaped her thinking. She also mentioned the lasting influence of the Ramayana and the Mahabharata, of books on Joan of Arc, William Tell, Garibaldi, Juarez and others, of the works of Oscar Wilde and Victor Hugo, and Tagore's poetry.
7. Indira Gandhi Memorial Trust (1985). Just before her assassination, Indira Gandhi recorded a number of conversations with her close friend Pupul Jayakar. The conversations were wide-ranging and at times philosophical. But there were vignettes that provide some valuable clues to how Indira Gandhi came to be fond of nature.
8. In a letter to Indira Gandhi from Dehradun Jail dated 3 April 1933, Nehru had written: '[…] I am glad you are doing Chemistry. Chemistry was one

of my special subjects in which I took my degree at Cambridge. The other subjects were Geology and Botany [...]'

9. Indira Gandhi was to write on 5 March 1981: 'Prof. Kaul has demonstrated in a very practical manner that his method [for the reclamation of alkaline soils] can succeed and has succeeded. Therefore, his views need urgent and serious consideration.'

10. These long conversations were published in a book 'by' Indira Gandhi, *My Truth* (Vision Books; 1982). In a letter to Dorothy Norman dated 23 August 1983 Indira Gandhi wrote: 'Another book has appeared in my name with the ridiculous title "My Truth". This is based on two long interviews with Mr Pouchpadas. He has added extracts from my writings, speeches and other interviews. So far as I know the words are mine but the book is actually brought out by him. Mr Pouchpadas now lives in France' (Norman, 1985). Jacques Pouchepadass, the author's son now living in Bordeaux, confirmed to me in an email dated 5 August 2016 that Indira Gandhi and his father knew each other well and had first met each other in 1938 in Paris. He had subsequently worked for the Indian Embassy in Tokyo and at UNESCO in Paris and had many interactions with her in both places, apart from having a close common friend in the French journalist Louise Moran.

11. Interview with Uma Dasgupta, 12 April 1982, as published in *Indira Gandhi: Selected Speeches and Writings, Volume V, 1982–84*, Ministry of Information and Broadcasting, 1986.

12. Interview in Hindi with Uma Chakbast, All India Radio, 14 November 1983. Transcript in the original, Nehru Memorial Library and Museum Manuscripts Section, Miscellaneous Collection.

13. Short holidays, at least twice or thrice a year, especially in the hills of what is now Uttarakhand, Himachal Pradesh and, most of all, Kashmir were to be a regular feature of Indira Gandhi's life till her death.

14. Indira Gandhi Memorial Trust (1986).

15. Ibid.

16. The organization had been started in 1957 and her good friend J.J. Bhabha, brother of Homi Bhabha, was then its president.

17. Ali (1985).

18. Sinha (1959). This book had been published first in 1958 in Hindi with a foreword by Jawaharlal Nehru.

19. Indira Gandhi had married Feroze Gandhi on 26 March 1942. There is a delightful account of how they first met when she was thirteen years old in Gundevia (1992). The two had spent time together in Switzerland, France and England in the 1930s. By Indira's own admission, it was Feroze who brought an appreciation of music and all things mechanical into the Nehru household.
20. Date not given in the original.
21. Raja Hutheesing, husband of Nehru's youngest sister Krishna.

III. The Companionship Years
(1950–1964)

By Indira's own admission, her entire life revolved around India's first prime minister. But this does not mean she did not have a mind of her own and even a life of her own. She took a keen interest in children and social welfare. She travelled extensively both in India and abroad speaking about a country in transformation. She had her own experiences with nature in its different forms. And when she plunged into a political career around the mid-1950s, she showed that she could stay with her father, yet differ with—and not defer to—him.

The era has been described by some as Indira's 'apprentice years'. This is not only unfair to father and daughter, but also misleading since it conveys the impression that Indira was being deliberately trained for something bigger. Others have used the word 'chatelaine' to describe Indira during this time. This, too, does not do full justice to her role and activities.

Maybe—and especially for the purposes of this book—it's best to describe the time between 1950 and 1964 as 'the companionship years'.

❧

Indira Gandhi with a tiger, Teen Murti House; 1956/57.

FOR FOURTEEN YEARS, INDIRA GANDHI LIVED IN TEEN MURTI HOUSE, THE prime minister's official residence in a lush green 65-acre complex with peacocks and various other birds. This sprawling colonial-era bungalow was originally built for the British commander-in-chief who started living there in 1930. When Mahatma Gandhi was assassinated on 30 January 1948, there was concern that Nehru might be the next target. A reluctant Nehru was persuaded by his cabinet to move into the bungalow, which he did on 2 August 1948. Indira Gandhi shuttled back and forth between Lucknow and New Delhi, before moving in full-time with her father in early 1950.

The prime minister's residence was a mini-zoo of sorts—as graphically described by Indira Gandhi herself seven years into her stay there:

> We always had dogs, the good kind with long pedigrees and others rescued off the streets that were just as devoted—also parrots, pigeons, squirrels and practically every small creature common to the Indian scene. And we thought life was pretty full, looking after them on top of all the older [*sic*] chores. Then in Assam, we were presented with a baby cat-bear (or

red Himalayan panda), although we did not know what it was until we reached Agartala and were able to study the book of Indian animals in the Commissioner's library [...] Much later we got him a mate [...] and now they have the most adorable little cubs—the first, I believe, to be bred in captivity. My father calls on the panda family morning and evening. They miss him when he is out of station [...]

Two years ago, we received our first tiger cubs—there were three named Bhim, Bhairav and Hidamba. A man came from Lucknow Zoo to teach us how to look after them [...After a while] we sent them off to the Lucknow Zoo where you can still meet Bhim and Hidimba; magnificent beasts, their muscles rippling with power and grace. [Marshal Tito] asked for one of them and Bhairav now resides in Belgrade.[1]

The Keoladeo Ghana Bird Sanctuary at Bharatpur, Rajasthan was to play an important role in Indira Gandhi's life as prime minister. But it had already become a matter of concern to her father in the 1950s. On 8 September 1953 Nehru recorded this note to his principal private secretary:

Mr. Horace Alexander came to see me today. He told me that there is a famous bird preserve (heronry) in Bharatpur State. He himself went to see it but to his surprise found that the place was deserted and the herons were not there. Something had happened to prevent them from following their usual practice. There was some suspicion that some people had deliberately done this to prevent the birds from coming. Possibly the water supply has been diverted.

2. This matter has been referred both to the Rajasthan Government and to the Inspector General of Forests here. I enclose a note by Mr. Horace Alexander.

3. I should like you to write to the Rajasthan Government about this and also to the Food and Agriculture Ministry. There is just a possibility that they might not pay attention to this matter and that would be a tragedy and this famous preserve will be spoiled as the birds will then go elsewhere. In fact, the Rajasthan Government has declared this preserve as a bird sanctuary. But it can only remain a bird sanctuary if it is looked after properly. I want you to write in order to make both the Rajasthan Government and our Food and Agriculture Ministry aware that we attach importance to this.

It is inconceivable that Nehru would not have spoken about Bharatpur to his bird-loving daughter—but admittedly, there is no paper trail I could locate. Twenty-three years later, Indira Gandhi was to visit this waterfowl resort with her family and subsequently have it declared as a national park in 1982—thereby ensuring the highest level of legal and administrative protection.

❧

On 23 April 1950, Indira Gandhi sent a three-page handwritten letter to Horace Alexander, giving him a swift account of the preceding weeks. She began by saying:

> I have been having a dreadfully busy time and on top of that I got flu, then my son was in bed with a serious attack of dysentery and finally I had to go to Dehra Dun from where I returned only late last evening thereby missing all the bird watching too.

A few days later, the Delhi Bird Watching Society was formed.[2] This announcement appeared in the journal of the BNHS in December 1950, and included a reference to Dillon Ripley.[3]

ANNOUNCEMENT

I. THE DELHI BIRD WATCHING SOCIETY

At the beginning of 1950 the Delhi Bird Watching Society was started. Its main purpose is to encourage the study of birds in and around the capital city [...]

Expeditions to local bird-haunts are being arranged once or twice a month and a first lecture by Dr. Dillon Ripley on the Birds of Nepal was given to an appreciative audience of nearly fifty in the Prime Minister's House on August 7th, 1950.

The present officers of the Society are:-

Mr. Horace Alexander (Chairman); Captain H.C. Ranald, R.N. (Hon. Treasurer); Mrs W.F. Rivers (Hon Secretary); *Mrs Indira Gandhi* [emphasis mine], Mr. F.C. Badhwar, Rev. J. Bishop, Mr. C.J.L. Stokoe and Maj-Gen H. Williams (Committee Members).

As Mrs. Rivers is leaving Delhi her place as Honorary Secretary is to be taken by Mr. L.J. Wallach.

Indira's fondness for nature was, of course, not missed by her father. When R.S. Dharmakumar Sinhji—a well-respected naturalist and a member of the Indian Board for Wildlife—wrote to Nehru in July 1955, the latter replied soon after:

> Thank you for your letter and for the lovely book on the "Birds of Saurashtra" that you have sent me. It is a good production. I am happy to see more and more interest is being taken in wild birds in India, and suitable books are being produced. *I am interested in this but even more so my daughter, Indira Gandhi, is interested in birds. We shall both enjoy this book* [emphasis mine].

Like Nehru, visitors to Teen Murti House, too, grew acquainted with Indira's fondness for birds. Malcolm MacDonald, a pillar of the British establishment and son of a former prime minister, who had been sent as a high commissioner to India in 1955, was an avid birdwatcher. Quite often, he would be found sitting with Indira Gandhi 'quietly observing birds in the back garden of the Prime Minister's home'.[4] On 27 June 1958, she wrote to him:

> Thank you so much for sending me a copy of your delightful speech.[5] I read it with my boys and we enjoyed the bird stories.
>
> The first part of it reminded me of a conversation I overheard in Mahatma Gandhi's hut in Wardha. Someone—it could have been Horace Alexander—remarked, "But life is fast disappearing from your jungles." "But it is increasing in our cities," replied the Mahatma.[6]

By 1960, Malcolm MacDonald had published a book, *Birds in My Indian Garden*, that became a classic. Nehru wrote to him on 15 December 1960:

> I have just received your letter and your new book "Birds in my Indian Garden". Thank you for it. I have been looking at the photographs. They are delightful. Altogether, the book is very welcome and I am grateful to you for sending it to us.
>
> Indira is still in Paris attending the UNESCO meeting. She is expected back here on the 18th of December, *and I shall pass on your book to her* [emphasis mine].

As a part of the letter dated 27 June 1958 to Malcolm MacDonald, Indira Gandhi had written:

> Yesterday we had a visit from a three-member team of the Women's Himalayan Expedition.[7] Aren't they charming. My father produced various maps and for a whole hour we all squatted around them on the carpet. How I wish I could have accompanied the expedition! Stephen Spender is so right when he says that "different living is not living in different places". But occasionally one does long to get away.

Propelled by the desire to travel and 'get away', Indira Gandhi visited Kashmir almost every year through the 1950s with her sons Rajiv and Sanjay. On 18 June 1960, she wrote to her father from a houseboat on Nagin Lake in Srinagar:

> Today is the first clear day since our arrival & it is truly a magnificent sight. In Kashmir there is always an element of sadness or is it melancholy. Perhaps it is due to willows & their droopy look reminding one of Davies's poem on the kingfisher:
>
> *So runs it in thy blood to choose*
> *For haunts the lovely pools, & keep*
> *In company with trees that weep.*
>
> The boys are busy. Sanjay swims, rows & takes photographs. He is very independent & loves this life close to nature, observing dragonflies and kingfishers. Yesterday, a kingfisher came right into our sitting room—a swift perched on Rajiv's shoulder.

Of course, Kashmir offered more than just birds. Indira Gandhi wrote to her aide Usha Bhagat on 26 June 1963:

> We have had a wonderful trek to the Kolahoi glacier. Refreshing. The magnificence and grandeur of the mountains gives quite a different perspective to life.

The mountains called Indira often. In April 1951, she went to Dehra Dun; in October 1950 and June 1954 to Mashobra; and in January 1955 to Simla.

From time to time, Indira Gandhi would express her desire to have a place for herself in the hills. This wish would continue to get expressed even after she became prime minister. One of the earliest occasions she spoke of this was on 20 January 1955; expectedly, the desire was articulated in a letter to her father from Simla while on a short holiday with her two sons:

> You always accuse me of the possessive instinct when I talk about acquiring a small place in the hills but I feel that life would be much pleasanter if there was a tiny small house where one could go for a weekend or longer without upsetting governmental machinery and a lot of fuss and bother. As Justice Khosla says, "The Himalayas are essential to my emotional existence". I read his book almost at a single setting.

The reference in her letter was to the book *Himalayan Circuit* by G.D. Khosla,[8] a chief justice of the Punjab High Court who, upon retirement, settled down in Manali.

Interestingly, just three years later, Indira Gandhi recalled a visit to Manali in an article she published for the *Sunday Statesman* on 13 July 1958 with the title 'Manali: A Place for Contemplation'. Alongside another article by one of India's best-known naturalists, M. Krishnan, she wrote:

> [...] A year ago I took a two-day holiday in Manali in the midst of a most tiring, hot and dusty tour of our welfare projects in Himachal and the Kullu and Kangra Valleys [...] It is not a place to escape from life but to become more poignantly aware of its many facets.
>
> A deputation came to me requesting a visit from my father. I knew my father would love the place [...] And yet at the back of my mind there was a lurking fear too. [...] Is there no way of improving the economy and bringing in better education, health and transport services without also introducing the restlessness of the plains which might cause a weakening of their vital touch with nature?
>
> I find in some of our officials a deplorable tendency to try and make every place look like the better-known hill-stations. For those who want urban comforts, tarred roads and organized entertainment there are many hill-stations to go to—Simla, Mussoorie, Darjeeling, Ootacamund and Mahabaleswar to give only a few examples. Let the Kullu Valley attract a different type—those who are young at heart and eager for adventure, those who yearn to conquer the peaks and those who seek quiet contemplation, those who can appreciate the beauty of nature and draw from it spiritual, mental and physical vigour.

In this article, she encapsulated the themes that were to dominate her concerns as prime minister: the balance between economic advancement and environmental protection, the preservation of the finest traditions of living in harmony with nature even while aspiring for a higher standard of living, and the need to pay attention to the special challenges faced by the people living in the hill areas.

On 17 April 1958, when Indira Gandhi wrote to her closest epistolary friend Dorothy Norman, she, once more, spoke of the urge to move away from the noise and chaos of a capital city:

> I myself am feeling very unsettled—is it age do you think? [...] anyhow I get a tremendous urge to leave everything and retire to a far far place high in the mountains [...]

It was in this letter that she also first mentioned Buckminster Fuller.

> We have had two interesting Americans—Charles Eames and Buckminster Fuller. The latter was only passing through but managed to give me nearly five hours of higher mathematics. Quite exhausting but so stimulating.

Buckminster 'Bucky' Fuller was an American designer, architect and a futurist thinker. Today he may be little remembered but in the 1960s and 1970s he was quite a rage and commanded attention across the globe, especially for propagating the concept of a geodesic dome. In his biography, authored by Alden Hatch,[9] his meeting with Indira Gandhi and her father is mentioned in somewhat dramatic terms:

> In 1958, on his first trip around the world, Bucky stopped off in India where he had numerous speaking engagements. One day he made three speeches in New Delhi [...] At all three meetings he noticed a striking woman dressed in exquisite saris, who usually sat in or near the front row listening intently, her large dark eyes refulgent with intellectual excitement.
>
> At the evening lecture, Bucky used a little tensegrity sphere model, only about six inches in diameter, made of string and small turnbuckles. After the lecture he was presented to the lady, Mrs. Indira Gandhi, Prime Minister Nehru's daughter. Mrs. Gandhi asked him if he would come on Saturday to meet her father at their house. Bucky says, "I did meet

him and we had a very extraordinary time" [...] At the end of an hour and a half Bucky stopped talking [...] Nehru bowed with folded hands and left the room. He had not spoken a word.

Was it for real—Nehru not speaking a word for ninety minutes in a meeting? Alas, Nehru's published works have no record of this encounter. So we will have to take Fuller on his word for having accomplished a minor miracle! Buckminster Fuller was to re-enter Indira Gandhi's life in 1969 and remain a constant presence in her speeches to the very end.

Nehru was scheduled to visit Tibet in September 1958. But, at the last moment, the trip did not materialize. So, it was decided—at the suggestion of a lowly deputy secretary in the Ministry of External Affairs, Jagat Mehta, who was to rise to greater heights later—that Nehru would visit Bhutan instead. Mehta has described this historic visit in colourful detail in his book *Negotiating for India*. He considered it a diplomatic watershed, the results of which have stood India in good stead for almost six decades.

Nehru decided to trek to Bhutan. He was soon to be sixty-nine. Indira Gandhi was about to turn forty-one. Both loved the outdoors and were more than comfortable with the mountains; they weren't strangers to snow. Thus it was that the prime ministerial entourage flew to Bagdogra—the nearest airport to the capital of Sikkim, Gangtok, which was then a protectorate of India. From Gangtok, the party drove to Sherathang which is at an altitude of approximately 12,000 feet, and from there, they climbed to Nathu La Pass at roughly 14,000 feet.

At Nathu La, which is at the border with Tibet, Nehru, Indira and the others were met with a dozen yaks, several ponies and a pack of over a hundred animals. The trek into Paro in Bhutan via Yadong in Tibet lasted five days and there were times when the altitude touched 15,500 feet. This meant that, all told, father and daughter trekked something like 105 kilometres for almost ten days.

On 12 October 1958, Nehru wrote to his sister Vijaya Lakshmi Pandit who was then India's high commissioner to the UK:

I returned from Bhutan just ten days ago today. This visit to Bhutan and incidentally to a little corner of Tibet, was an exhilarating experience. I confess that I was not quite sure in my mind as to how I would be able to stand it. On the first day I did not feel too well. Possibly this was due to the altitude or, perhaps, to my getting tired after a long trek: partly also, it might have been due to my unsuccessful attempt at sleeping in a sleeping bag, which was a novel experience for me. But from the next day, I improved and acclimatized myself. It was tough work. This was not only because of the heights involved, but also the long and tiring treks [...] with six, seven, eight or even nine hours of trekking at high altitudes. But it was thoroughly enjoyable or, at any rate, I enjoyed it and so did Indu.

Sixteen years later, on 5 January 1974, Indira Gandhi was to write a foreword to diplomat Apa Pant's memoir *A Moment in Time.* Pant had accompanied Nehru and her on the Bhutan trek and she wrote:[10]

Our trip to Bhutan is an indelible experience, reasserting that the joy of being in the mountains, the pleasure of companionship and good conversation are heightened rather than diminished by physical effort or the lack of what some might consider essential comforts.

Nari Rustomji, who was then dewan of Sikkim, had also accompanied them on this trek. Thirteen years later, he was to write about his experience and concluded by saying:

I later sent Indira, as a memento, some photographs we had taken during the trip—not the usual, formal VIP photographs of tape-cutting, but the little incidents that are so endearing to recollect in after years—the swallowing of a hot potato, being caught off-guard, [a] quizzical look. I cannot say I was not elated—I was thrilled to high heaven!—to receive her reply, not a bread and butter 'Thank You' affair from the Prime Minister's Office, but a letter in her own hand which expressed so neatly my own imaginings of the trials of her existence.[11]

Indira Gandhi had indeed written to Rustomji on 3 January 1959:

The journey to Bhutan was a mental adventure, no less than a physical one. As such it has a permanent place in my memory book. [...]

I am rather ashamed of myself for not writing earlier and thanking you for the snapshots. They are good. If you had a crystal & could glimpse how we race against time and fit the day's work into the meagre twenty-four hours allotted for the purpose, you would surely forgive me [...]

Papa and I are off to Nagpur—the annual Congress Session is quite the most interesting event of the year [...]

Indira Gandhi would go on to demonstrate great commitment to the cause of mountaineering when she became prime minister. The Himalayas were very dear to her and all through her tenure she worried about them. It was perhaps in recognition of this special bond that after her cremation her ashes were sprinkled over the Himalayas.

Besides spending time in the hills, Indira devoted time to the country's natural parks—among them Gir in Gujarat which was and still is, the only home of the Asiatic lion. Beginning 1948, Nehru had taken keen personal interest in the protection of the lion. On 13 January 1948, the duke of Devonshire—also the president of the Society for the Preservation of the Wild Fauna of the Empire—had written to the high commissioner of India in London appealing for a sanctuary for lions in the Gir forest; he had wanted this matter to be brought to the prime minister's notice. Nehru sent a note to his officials on 5 February 1948.

> I have long been interested in the preservation of lions in India. They exist only in Kathiawar now in the Gir Forest and it would be a great pity if they were allowed to be shot or otherwise to suffer extinction. I trust that the Regional Commissioner of Kathiawar and the Administrator of Junagadh will be specially asked to issue such directions as may be considered necessary for the protection of lions and that no shooting of them should be permitted.

Along with his daughter, Nehru visited Gir in November 1955. They spent close to eight hours in its thick jungles on the night of 3 November 1955. The morning after, following another visit before dawn, Nehru said in a public meeting at Keshod,

I met some of your lions. The lions kept watching me. I kept watching them. Both of us seemed to have liked it.

On 13 November 1955 Nehru wrote to Edwina Mountbatten:

[…] I have recently been to Saurashtra. This is the one part of India which neither you nor Dickie visited […] I went to Saurashtra for a number of functions but as I wrote to you what interested me most was a visit to the lions of the Gir forest. We had a good deal of luck. We only went to the Gir forest in the afternoon, spent the night in a Rest House there and returned early the next morning. During this period we saw a number of lions and lionesses. Probably because killing them is prohibited, they are not afraid of human beings and we can approach them in our cars to within fifty feet or so sometimes. We also saw wild boar in that forest and were told that that is the one animal the lion does not like at all.

The fact is, much had unfolded behind the scenes to give the prime minister and his daughter a good sighting of lions. This is best described by the noted conservationist-author Divyabhanusinh:

The Prime Minister naturally had limited time, and the lions had to be shown to him. The shikaris […] resorted to the age-old practice of localizing the lions by regular baiting of male buffalo calves which are virtually of no use to humans in that area as they are not used as draught animals. […] It appears that hundreds of baits were fed to the lions for six months prior to the prime ministerial visit in several locations of the Gir. Be that as it may, in the event Jawaharlal Nehru and Indira Gandhi did meet up with the lions. The Forest Department saw it fit to make them wear khaki overcoats before taking them on foot close to the lions, in order not to alarm the animals.[12]

Sadly, the baiting system continued in Gir till 2001 when it was finally abandoned. But the damage it did was noted by Indira Gandhi herself years later. During her second visit to Gir on 21 January 1981 she was to record her impressions in the visitor's book:

To be in a game sanctuary is one of the most pleasurable of experiences. The lion is very special. But the lions now are much more tame, having got used to staring visitors! Last time I was here with my father, it was more exciting. However, it is good to see how well looked after the place is and the growth of ecology consciousness. We have much to do to catch up with negligence of centuries.

❧

Lions alone weren't 'special' to Indira; so were rhinos. In 1956, she visited the famed Kaziranga Sanctuary in Assam twice. The first was on 29 February 1956, and she recounted her experience a few days later to her elder son Rajiv:

> The Kaziranga Sanctuary is a bigger one than Manas and it is easier to meet animals. Here we started on time in great style. There was a regular howdah on the elephant. In this jungle, there are hardly any trees—there are mostly tall reeds, over 12 feet high, so that it is difficult to see an animal until you come right upon it or unless it is an open ditch.
>
> We saw 15 rhinos which included some baby ones which are called calves. When almost any animal is running the mother leads the way and the baby follows, but the rhinos do the opposite. Here the baby leads and the mother follows. The rhino lives about 100 years and really looks like an old prehistoric monster. If there is only one elephant they may attack but we were 5 or 6 and so they did not dare do anything except stop and snort and try to frighten us that way!

This was a future prime minister educating her son and a future prime minister himself on the behaviour of rhinos!

On Indira Gandhi's second visit to Kaziranga on 19 October 1956, her husband was with her, as also her father. Nehru had also asked Lieutenant General K.S. Thimayya, who was in charge of the Indian army's operations against the Naga rebels, to join them. What followed is described by British naturalist E.P. Gee:

> I was glad that I had been invited for the occasion, for I knew that Mr. Nehru was personally interested in animals and birds and here was a chance to bring to his notice the seriousness of the situation in which India's wildlife now finds itself. […] We talked about the sanctuary and its animals […]

It was characteristic of the "world's busiest Prime Minister" that, near the end of the visit, he left the throng of Ministers and Officers which surrounded him and came over to where I stood on the fringe of the crowd to thank me for showing him some wild life. "I have always been struck," he said, "by the unique combination of sub-tropical vegetation of this valley with the alpine or Himalayan snow-capped mountains."[13]

Of all the jungle's magnificent creatures, Indira was unarguably most committed to the tiger. She had read Jim Corbett, of course, but perhaps the first time she actually saw the beast in the wild was on 19 October 1955 on the way to Jog Falls in Karnataka. That day, she wrote to her father:

Here I am after all. And truly it's a sight worth seeing. The scenery all along the road was very lovely too, although the road itself was deplorable.

Just as I was being told that there is no likelihood of seeing any wild animal at that time of the forenoon and in this season when water is plentiful throughout the forest, a tiger, magnificent creature, sauntered across the road just in front of our car.

The sight was permanently etched in her mind—and twenty-seven years later she recalled it vividly in a foreword to a book of wildlife photographs by one of her senior colleagues from Karnataka.

Consequently, if there's one environmental cause Indira is forever associated with, it is tiger conservation. Intriguingly, throughout the 1950s, the Indian Board for Wild Life (IBWL), set up in April 1952, never recommended a ban on shooting tigers. In fact, in its very first meeting in Mysore in November–December 1952, it identified fourteen animals that required urgent protection, but failed to mention the grand beast! A ban on hunting tigers came to be initiated only in 1970, four years after Indira became prime minister.

But that Indira thoroughly disapproved of the practice is revealed by a letter dated 7 September 1956 that she wrote to her son Rajiv:

We have received a huge tiger's skin. The tiger was shot by the Maharaja of Rewa only two months ago. The skin is lying in the ballroom. Every time I pass it I feel very sad that instead of lying here he might have been roaming and roaring in the jungle. Our tigers are such beautiful creatures, so graceful. You can see their muscles rippling under their skins. Such a short time ago he must have been King of the Jungle—striking terror in the hearts of other animals.

I am so glad that nowadays more and more people prefer to go into the jungles with their cameras instead of guns. It seems such a shame to deprive anything of the joy of living just for our pleasure.

It was perhaps on account of her firm love for conservation that Humayun Abdulali made the first formal effort on the part of the BNHS—an organization that Indira would be closely associated with as prime minister—to establish a connection with her in 1962.

Abdulali has not got the kind of public recognition that his cousin Salim Ali, and another relation, Zafar Futehally, have won. But, by all accounts, he was exceptionally talented, as Salim Ali himself admitted in his autobiography. In fact, he was one the architects of the Bombay Wild Birds and Wild Animals Protection Act, 1951 which was to serve as a model for the landmark wildlife protection law passed during Indira Gandhi's tenure. But that was years later. On 18 May 1962, Abdulali wrote to Nehru's private secretary:

> On the 3rd of March I wrote to Pundit Jawaharlal Nehru in connection with a matter relating to Wild Life Protection and also sent him a copy of our Journal in which was included a review of a foreigner's book on shikar in India.
>
> I would be grateful if you dropped me a line confirming receipt of this Journal. If it is possible *I would also appreciate your handing over the enclosed prospectus to Smt. Indira Gandhi who may also perhaps be interested in this Society and its work* [emphasis mine].

Exactly a month later came the confirmation from M.L. Bazaz, the private secretary to the prime minister, that the prospectus has indeed 'been passed on to Shrimati Indira Gandhi'.

Indira Gandhi wrote to her sons every now and then. While I was unable to obtain her letters to her younger son Sanjay—his widow told me that 'deemaks [termites] have eaten them away over the years'—I have been able to get some of her letters to her elder son. I have already quoted from two of them. There were some others as well. On 14 February 1955, she wrote to him:

> Your cassia tree is laden with pink blossoms and is looking very lovely. Isn't it a wonderful thing that we have these beautiful flowers as our best friend when it is hot and uncomfortable?

In a letter dated 7 May 1955, she wrote:

> A film called "The Living Desert" has come to Delhi. We think of a desert as a dead place and that nothing can live there but that is not true. If only you have the patience to sit and look at the sands, you will find them teeming with all kinds of insects, snakes and rodents. I saw one such film in Russia but I believe "The Living Desert", which is made by Walt Disney is really wonderful. I hope you will be able to see it when you come home.

Some months later, on 26 February 1956, she wrote to Rajiv from the Manas Sanctuary in Assam:

> It is pitch dark, so I can't see anything except two huge rather frightening forest fires. And I can hear the lovely sound of a waterfall, or maybe it is a rushing torrent.
>
> Tomorrow, we start at 5 am to try and see wild rhinos and elephants.

Throughout, Indira tried to give her sons a flavour of her fondness for nature—a fondness she wished to inculcate in them. She wrote to Rajiv again on 9 April 1957:

> Bhimsa and Pema (the new little panda—Pema is a Tibetan name and means 'Lotus') and the two little tigers have left for Lucknow. One of the tigers had some skin trouble and he was not getting any better here [...]
>
> When you were here I wanted to point out the peepul tree that grows just outside our bathroom. At that time it did not have a single leaf and looked as if it was covered with pimples; then one day the pimples became

stiff little green thorns—now the thorns have grown even longer and the top one of each twig has opened into a leaf which looks like a flag. It is really quite fascinating to watch.

Then, there were letters recommending hill stations, among them Darjeeling. In a missive from Allahabad to him (date unknown), she revealed why it was one of her favourite places:

> From Darjeeling one gets what is said to be the most significant view of the Himalayas—the Kanchenjunga Range. Some miles from Darjeeling is Tiger Hill from where one can have a glimpse of the Everest if there are no clouds. There are clouds most of the time. The only time one can see the Everest, if one is lucky, is at sunrise.

Indira Gandhi became the Congress president on 1 February 1959. Five days later she wrote to her friend Phyllis Mehrotra, an Englishwoman married to an Indian and settled in Allahabad, expressing unhappiness with her new political role.

> I wish I were happy too, but I am not. In fact, I am quite miserable over this whole thing. This heavy responsibility and hard work has descended on me just when I was planning for a quiet and peaceful year. There must be some such thing as fate.

Phyllis Mehrotra was completely non-political and so there was no need for Indira Gandhi to present a façade or be hypocritical before her.

On 8 February 1959 her conversation with Bhadra Desai appeared in *The Times of India*, in which she said:

> Whatever experiences I might share with ladies in other lands, I wonder how many of them have had to chase a panda through their living-room or to sit up nights with a sick tiger […] There are golden moments too. I love birds and mountains and music and pictures and yet all these cannot vie with the deep joy of bringing some small measure of happiness to a human being.

In August 1961, Nehru sent Indira Gandhi to Kenya as his personal representative to establish contact with Jomo Kenyatta who had just been released from prison. On 25 August 1961, she reported to her father:

> We returned this morning from the Amboseli National Park [...] what a perfectly entrancing place it is. It was fun to drive around and come across herds of that comic, supercilious creature, the giraffe, the prosperous and plump zebra, fleet-footed gazelles of different kinds and the lordly and kindly (looking at least) lion and his family. But the best part was the unexpected frolic that took place right in front my hut in the pale hours of dawn—elephants, giraffes, zebras, gazelles were thoroughly enjoying themselves. Earlier, we had seen a most captivating lion family: two lionesses and four cubs. Just a short distance away was the lion with his latest and most favourite wife [...]

If she had not been her father's daughter and got sucked into a political career, she would undoubtedly have been a first-class commentator on nature and wildlife. The letter captivates both for the language and for her powers of observation, bringing back memories of a letter she had written to her father from jail in 1943 in which she had compared the creatures she saw to well-known British political figures.

Dehra Dun figured prominently in the loves of both father and daughter. Nehru had spent a little over two years in jail there in four different spells between June 1932 and December 1941. Both Indira Gandhi and he regularly holidayed there and in nearby Mussoorie. Indira's sons, too, had studied in Dehra Dun.

By early 1964, Nehru's health had begun to worsen. Indira Gandhi and he decided to spend a few days in that city in May. On 25 May, Nehru wrote in the visitor's book in the Dehra Dun gardens:

> I have come here for rest and quiet along with my daughter. The gardens continue to be attractive and well looked after. It is a pleasure to stay here.

What was unusual about this page was not just the fact that Indira Gandhi also entered her remarks in the visitor's book below her father's, but that it was also substantially longer.

Familiarity bred of countless visits has not dimmed my joy in this garden. Each time my heart leaps up, as Wordsworth would say, to behold the wonder of this setting in the delicate loveliness of the flowering cassia against the imposing background of the Mussoorie Hills. I must confess, however, that the attraction of the garden lies in its setting and its magnificent trees. The pot plants are good but the layout of the flower beds leave much room for improvement.

Just two days later Nehru died. The companionship years came to an end. A new life was beginning for Indira Gandhi.

On 9 June 1964, Lal Bahadur Shastri was sworn in as India's second prime minister. Indira Gandhi was the minister of information and broadcasting in his cabinet. Her tryst with nature was not evident during this interregnum except when she was in the news briefly in May 1965 congratulating members of India's first successful Everest expedition.

However, this period is important because two people, who became part of her close circle then,[14] were to play a crucial role on environmental issues during her prime ministerial tenure—Pitambar Pant and H.Y. Sharada Prasad. The former laid the foundations of environmental appraisal of development projects before passing away in February 1973, while the latter was to be her speechwriter from the day she became prime minister till the day she was killed. But Sharada Prasad was actually more than a speechwriter—he was actually her sounding board and confidante on various matters, especially those concerning nature and culture.

Shastri passed away on 11 January 1966—and Indira Gandhi succeeded him. It is to her prime ministerial tenure that I now turn.

Notes

1. In August 1957, Indira Gandhi herself wrote about her place of stay in a little-known publication out of Bombay called *The International*. This was reproduced in Indira Gandhi Memorial Trust (1987).
2. The Delhi Bird Watching Society was started in May 1950. Usha Ganguli joined in September 1950. She is widely acknowledged as having been

one of India's finest ornithologists but she died young in November 1970. Her husband had been the vice chancellor of Delhi University and, in 1967, Indira Gandhi opened a school started by Usha Ganguli in the university campus. Ganguli's *A Guide to the Birds of the Delhi Area* appeared posthumously in May 1975 with a foreword by Salim Ali and is considered to be the earliest authoritative work of its kind.

3.   On 21 November 1950 Ripley was to receive a letter from the governor of Assam, Jairamdas Daulatram, asking him to leave the Naga Hills immediately. These hills were then a part of Assam, and Ripley was there on an ornithological expedition. There were suspicions that he had CIA links based on a profile of his that had appeared in the magazine *New Yorker*. Horace Alexander interceded on his behalf; Nehru was quite relaxed about the whole affair and had no objections to Ripley continuing with his ornithological work.

4.   Bhagat (2005).

5.   This was a speech at the inaugural meeting of the Nature Study Society, University of Jammu and Kashmir, Srinagar, delivered on 19 June 1958, available in the Malcolm MacDonald archives at Durham University, UK.

6.   As regards the reference to the Mahatma in the letter, in a speech she gave on 24 November 1969, Indira Gandhi was to repeat his quip but this time with certainty about the identity of the Englishman involved—not Horace Alexander but the noted author and friend of Rabindranath Tagore, Edward Thompson.

7.   The Women's Himalayan Expedition Indira Gandhi wrote to MacDonald about was a remarkable overland journey (by Land Rover and on foot) from France to Zaskar undertaken by three British housewives in 1958. Two of them, Anne Davies and Antonia Deacock, wrote about their adventures, including their encounter with Nehru and his daughter in Davies (1959) and Deacock (1960).

8.   The book carried a foreword by Jawaharlal Nehru which revealed the reasons behind Nehru's fascination for mountains. Many years later, in 1974, Khosla was to write a pictorial biography of Indira Gandhi.

9.   Alden Hatch also collaborated with Nehru's sister Krishna Hutheesing for her book *We Nehrus* published in 1967.

10.   Pant (1974).

11.   Rustomji (1971).

12. Divyabhanusinh (2005).
13. Just three months before he passed away on 27 May 1964, Nehru was to write a foreword to E.P. Gee's masterpiece *The Wild Life of India*, a book that has educated generations of Indians. It was among the first books I read as a boy of eleven. It opened a whole new world to which I was to return forty-four years later when I became minister of environment and forests.
14. There was a third person who came into contact with Indira Gandhi in August 1965, joined her secretariat as an adviser in November 1970, and became her secretary a few years later. He was P.N. Dhar but he had no role whatsoever in her activities concerning the environment. He has written about his association with Indira Gandhi in Dhar (2000).

IV. The Naturalist Prime Minister–I
(1966–1977)

Indira Gandhi became India's third prime minister on 24 January 1966. She was to remain in this position for slightly over eleven years. The first three were lean and uneventful as far as nature conservation was concerned, preoccupied as she was with other burning issues, including her own political survival. Her top-most priority in that period was agriculture so as to make India self-reliant in wheat and rice in the quickest time possible. Nothing else really mattered. The other issue that she spoke about frequently in 1966, 1967 and 1968 was the need for family planning and India's population policy acquired heightened importance with the formation of a Cabinet Committee on Family Planning. But 1969 was the take-off year for Indira Gandhi the naturalist prime minister. In July, as banks were being nationalized, she was moving decisively on wildlife protection. In November, as she was being expelled from her own party, she emerged as a forceful global champion of nature conservation. There was to be no looking back thereafter.

CENTRAL SAVE RICE FOR KERALA COMMITTEE.

17, Barakhamba Road,
New Delhi.1.
~~January~~ 1966.
FEBRUARY 3.

RICE PLEDGE.

I pledge to surrender my rice ration for the people of Kerala, and authorise the Central Save Rice for Kerala Committee to send my pledge to the rationing authorities. My ration of rice may be utilised to meet rice shortage in Kerala.

I also pledge not to eat rice or serve rice till food situation in Kerala is normal.

Name: INDIRA GANDHI
(In block letters)
Address: PRIME MINISTER'S HOUSE, NO.1, SAFDARJANG ROAD, NEW DELHI.

.... Signature.

RATION CARD NO: 23/5/ND 526685

Please sign and send this to the above address.

Photostat copy of the Rice Pledge taken by the Prime Minister, Mrs. Indira Gandhi, in New Delhi on February 3, 1966 whereunder she surrendered her rice ration for the people of Kerala

Indira Gandhi's pledge to surrender rice rations for Kerala; February 1966.

Indira Gandhi became prime minister on 24 January following almost ten days of intense political activities. Tragically, on that very day, India's most distinguished nuclear scientist-administrator and her friend Homi Bhabha had died in an air crash on Mont Blanc on his way to Geneva.

Three issues were to dominate Indira Gandhi's very first year as prime minister—food imports, devaluation of the rupee and the reorganization of Punjab. Twelve days of her being sworn in, Indira Gandhi wrote a long letter to all chief ministers spelling out what she considered the pressing national issues. She said, 'Of problems today there is no dearth. Undoubtedly the most important of them is the food problem. We have had an unprecedented drought and the crops have failed [...] I have been greatly distressed by the situation in Kerala.' She talked of the Tashkent declaration of January 1966 in which both India and Pakistan 'have resolved to live as peaceful neighbours despite the irreconcilability of their positions on Jammu and Kashmir'. She added, '[...] It is important that communal forces should not be allowed to become active again'.

But the bulk of the letter was on what she called the 'food problem'. Indira Gandhi soon realized that the key was self-sufficiency in the production of rice and wheat at the earliest. She first announced this as her policy on 1 March in a speech in the Lok Sabha and followed it up with a conference of chief ministers on 9 April.

She visited the USA and France in March and the USSR a few months later. Her meetings with Lyndon Johnson have become the stuff of history. De Gaulle is supposed to have confided to Andre Malraux after meeting Indira Gandhi: 'Women do not succeed in politics, but this one will.' That she spoke French fluently must have impressed the French president.

The devaluation of the rupee had been under discussion for almost a year. Most were opposed to it. She bit the bullet finally on 6 June with the hefty devaluation being accompanied by a significant liberalization of the economy. Less than a week before this courageous decision, on 30 May she had written to her personal friend T.N. Kaul, India's ambassador to the USSR, revealing her state of mind then:

> Our economic situation is as bad as it can be [...] With starvation, stoppage of industry, rising unemployment and so on staring us in the face, we have no recourse but to give top priority to the economic situation. A weak nation cannot resist foreign influence but I am convinced that with aid now, we can become strong and stand on our own feet. What is the alternative, especially because of the lack of discipline and support? [...] If I am unable to put through what I consider necessary for salvaging the situation, I must resign. I simply cannot remain and watch the country drifting down and down [...]

During the year, Indira Gandhi also confronted head-on the reorganization of Punjab—an idea that her father had steadfastly rejected, convinced that this *was nothing but yet another division based on religion. But having looked at the issue in some detail when she had been a member of Lal Bahadur Shastri's cabinet, she gave the go-ahead for the creation of Haryana and an expanded Himachal Pradesh; Sikhs were now a majority in Punjab.*

Just four days after she had become prime minister, *Time* magazine had her on its cover and ran a long and positive profile, describing her family background; her experience, such as it was, in party politics; her varied interests; her friends; and what the world could expect from her. Contained in the profile was this hark-back to her living in the mini-zoo with her father:

> As India's first First Lady, Indira ran the Prime Minister's rambling mansion on Teen Murti Marg with impeccable efficiency, inspected every menu, and made sure that her father took time off to romp with his grandsons and play with the family's menagerie of baby tigers, monkeys and assorted reptiles. "I once had a baby crocodile," remembers Sanjay, now an apprentice at a Rolls-Royce plant near Manchester. "It bit everybody except me. But when it bit Mother, it had to go."

Sanjay Gandhi would soon return to India and thereafter become hugely controversial. As for crocodiles, nine years later Indira Gandhi was to personally get involved in the launch of a conservation programme which proved to be very successful!

1966 also reinforced Indira Gandhi's association with environmentalists, among them Horace Alexander, who always had had easy access to Nehru. But the Quaker had also provoked her occasionally with his statements on Nagaland (where he had been birdwatching in the 1950s), Kashmir and China. He wrote a note of congratulations on her becoming prime minister, and she replied on 26 February:

> Thank you for your letter of good wishes. I am sorry for the delay in acknowledging it. You can imagine how rushed I have been.

There must have been some misunderstanding about the Bird Watching Club. What I said was that I was one of the first members of the Delhi Bird Watching Club. Actually, my interest in birds began in prison. There were no trees for birds to sit on. I began to note down birdcalls and on my release identified them from Salim Ali's book.

There would be a few more letters to Horace Alexander in the years to come on birdwatching. But this particular letter is important, not only because it records the first exchange Indira had with him on becoming prime minister, but also because it calls into question a claim made by the noted historian Ramachandra Guha that Horace Alexander *introduced* Indira Gandhi to birdwatching.[1] By her own admission, she got interested while in prison, because of her past interactions with Salim Ali, and also on account of—as evidenced from the letters exchanged between them—Nehru.

It was significant that as soon as she became prime minister, Indira Gandhi spoke boldly on the importance of family planning. Her very first speech in the Lok Sabha on 1 March understandably focused on attaining self-sufficiency in foodgrains. But she took personal interest in adding a few paragraphs on India's population policy.

On 26 June, Indira Gandhi returned to this theme at the SNDT (Shreemati Nathibai Damodar Thackersey) University in Bombay. She said that family planning required the same zeal and dedication that an earlier generation of social reformers like Ishwar Chandra Vidyasagar and Maharshi Karve had brought to the upliftment of widows and the education of girls. Later that year, while speaking at a conference of the International Union of Family Organizations in New Delhi on 11 December, she expressed her preference for the phrase 'family planning' over 'population control':

> This year we have crossed the five hundred million mark; we are a 150 million more people now than when India became independent. It is time for us to think about its implications. [...] If India is to get out of poverty within our generation [...] it will only be possible with a stable population. To plan when population growth is unchecked is like building

a house where the ground is flooded [...] Family planning in our country
is an essential part of our whole strategy of enlarging welfare.

༄

On 6 September 1963, the All India Services Act, 1951 was amended to
create an Indian Forest Service (IFS). Matters had got delayed because the
powerful home minister, Govind Ballabh Pant (who passed away in 1961),
felt forests were best managed by states themselves and did not require a
national cadre.

On 1 July, about six months after Indira Gandhi became prime
minister, the IFS was formally launched. The management of forests was
to become Indira's major preoccupation. That the IFS came to adore her
was evidenced by the resolution that the IFS Association passed following
her assassination. She, in turn, respected individual foresters but was quite
critical of the way foresters as a collective entity dealt with wildlife and
larger ecological and social concerns.

In the first two years of her prime ministership, Indira Gandhi also
organized round tables on subjects she considered important. While the
first, on 14 June, was devoted to the public sector, the second on 28 October
was concerned with international tourism which she described as the
'world's largest "export" industry [that] enjoys the highest rate of growth'.

If the second conclave is particularly relevant to this book, it is because
it came to be among the very few occasions in Indira's first three years in
office when she spoke publicly on subjects pertaining to the environment.
First, she said that 'the tourist wants to see the ancient monuments [...]
eat Indian specialties, go to shikar—preferable with a camera, climb in
the Himalayas'. Second, she announced that there was great need for the
'beautification of the surroundings and new constructions harmonizing with
the environment.' Both these themes were to engage her attention very soon.

༄

Less than a fortnight after taking the hugely controversial step of devaluing
the Indian rupee and opening up the economy, Indira Gandhi embarked
on a four-day tour of the hill districts of Uttar Pradesh. After landing by

59

helicopter in Uttarkashi on 16 June, she was received by the twenty-nine-year-old district magistrate Manmohan 'Moni' Malhoutra. They drove to the rest house where Indira Gandhi's political colleagues were waiting. There, she talked to them, after which Malhoutra and Indira Gandhi had a conversation on administrative issues in the district, which began thus—as recalled to me by Malhoutra:

> Indira Gandhi: Well, my people tell me you are not being very helpful to them.
>
> Moni Malhoutra: Madam, you mean helpful or pliant?
>
> Sucheta Kripalani (chief minister of UP): Indiraji, he is one of our finest officers.

Despite a demanding schedule, Indira Gandhi made time to visit the newly established Nehru Institute of Mountaineering and speak to its first batch of trainees, along with the principal, Brigadier Gyan Singh who had led the unsuccessful Indian expedition to the Everest in 1960.

A month later, on 20 July, she visited Uttarkashi again—but this time with no entourage and without any fanfare whatsoever. She had come with her sons for a four-day private holiday at Harsil, a remote village that had no telephone and telegraph facilities. As protocol demanded, Malhoutra was in attendance. In this desolate place, the prime minister and he conversed about life in the mountains, trekking and books.

Indira Gandhi flew back to New Delhi on 23 July. Three months later Malhoutra was told that he had to move to the prime minister's secretariat as an under secretary—the lowest position in the Indian Administrative Service (IAS) hierarchy in the Government of India. There was no formal office order regarding what exactly he was supposed to do but, as it turned out, Malhoutra was to assist the prime minister *directly* on environmental subjects for seven years. This shows the non-hierarchical manner in which Indira Gandhi ran her secretariat for the first five–six years.

The Ninth General Assembly of the International Union for the Conservation of Nature and Natural Resources (IUCN) took place at

Lucerne in Switzerland between 25 June and 2 July. With Indira Gandhi's approval, Hari Singh, the inspector general of forests, presented an official invitation for holding the IUCN's next General Assembly in 1969 in New Delhi. Along with Zafar Futehally, a well-respected naturalist who happened to be part of Salim Ali's extended family, he canvassed India's case. This was accepted with acclamation.

The Tenth General Assembly was to become a milestone for everyone concerned—for the IUCN, for Indira Gandhi, and for the country as a whole.

ॐ

The monsoon had failed miserably in 1965 and 1966 and India was forced to be a supplicant for wheat especially from the USA. This had contributed to Indira Gandhi's determination to make India self-sufficient in the production of foodgrains at the earliest. Much has been written about this in her biographies and in the histories of the bilateral relationship between India and the USA.

But two successive monsoon failures also led to top-secret environmental diplomacy which has not been written about by anyone, except American historian Kristine Harper.[2] With Indira Gandhi's approval in late 1966, the USA was to launch Project Gromet—a cloud seeding venture by the US military in Bihar and eastern Uttar Pradesh—in the early months of 1967. President Lyndon Johnson and Defence Secretary Robert McNamara were its greatest champions.

Gromet was not as innocent and straightforward as it appeared. It was very much part of the Cold War and linked with the use of the 'weather weapon' by the US military in Laos and Vietnam.[3] It is inconceivable that Indira Gandhi would have been unaware of this, but whatever objections she may have had would have found counter-arguments by key advisers like Vikram Sarabhai who had been appointed as the chairman of the Atomic Energy Commission in May; L.K. Jha, her secretary; and B.K. Nehru, India's ambassador in the USA. It is a measure of how weak she was politically and how desperate the situation was agriculturally that she allowed herself to be persuaded to go along with Gromet, even though ultimately it amounted to nothing.

As it turned out, the monsoon revived in 1967 and 1968 without this project. Besides, by then, new high-yielding crop varieties had started generating enthusiasm among farmers in Punjab and Haryana. The moment of extreme danger had passed.

∾

Towards the end of 1966, Indira—now as prime minister and chancellor of Visva-Bharati University—returned to her alma mater Santiniketan. During her convocation address on 24 December, she said:

> As I wear the scarf of Acharya, my mind goes back thirty years when I first arrived here with my mother and came under the enchantment of the wonderful man who brought this institution into being and breathed life and purpose into it [...]
>
> What gives Visva-Bharati its distinctive character? [...] It is situated in idyllic surroundings which make a difference, evoking a feeling of communion with nature.

Indira Gandhi was to come back to Santiniketan regularly thereafter renewing her association with a place which had played a vital role in deepening her affinity to nature.

Notes

1. He makes this assertion in Guha (2005) and bases it on Horace Alexander's papers at the Quaker Archives in London. Unfortunately, in spite of my best efforts and those of the librarians as well, these papers could not be located.
2. Harper (2017).
3. In fact, Operation Popeye was a highly classified American weather modification programme during the Vietnam War that aimed to extend the monsoon season and deny the 'Vietnamese enemy' the use of roads.

1967

Indira Gandhi with an all-women mountaineering expedition
from Calcutta; September 1967.

The biggest event of 1967 was undoubtedly the elections held between 17 and 21 February. These polls were momentous. The Congress lost power in six states for the very first time and got a slim majority at the centre. Indira Gandhi was sworn in again as prime minister on 13 March. She brought in non-politicians in positions that she considered important. These included V.K.R.V. Rao a distinguished economist, Triguna Sen and K.L. Rao, eminent engineers, and S. Chandrasekhar, a well-known demographer. She also inducted Karan Singh who was to play a crucial role in wildlife conservation. India's first two prime ministers had only a minister of health. Indira Gandhi appointed Chandrasekhar as minister of health and family planning and set up a Cabinet

Committee on Family Planning. This showed that she was well aware of the need to give a political thrust to India's population policy.

On 7 May P.N. Haksar joined her secretariat as secretary. He had first met Feroze Gandhi in London in the late 1930s and through him came into contact with Indira Gandhi. The three of them then became acolytes of Krishna Menon in the India League in London. Later, he was inducted into the Foreign Service. Each of her stellar achievements during May 1967–December 1972 for which history applauds her—the nationalization of banks, the abolition of privy purses and privileges for the princes, the huge emphasis on science and technology, the massive win in the 1971 mid-term elections, the standing up to President Nixon and the mobilization of international opinion on the Bangladesh issue, the Indo-Soviet Treaty of August 1971, the victorious war with Pakistan in December 1971 and finally, the unusual act of statesmanship that resulted in the Simla Accord between India and Pakistan in July 1972—all bore Haksar's imprimatur. But on environmental issues, she did not need his hand-holding or back-seat driving. She more than held her own—indeed she was always at the steering wheel.

A few months after Haksar joined her, a violent uprising of landless labour and sharecroppers took place in Naxalbari in north Bengal. This gave birth to what has come to be known as the Naxalite movement and was soon to spread to other states as well. In August as the nation celebrated the twentieth anniversary of India's independence, the Films Division released a twenty-minute film called I Am Twenty *based on conversations with youth born in 1947. The star of the film was T.N. Subramaniam, a student at the Indian Institute of Technology (IIT) Bombay where he was quite a legend as I can personally testify. Out of the blue, Indira Gandhi wrote to 'TN' as he was known:*

> *Recently I saw the film "I am Twenty". I was impressed by your self-confidence. I thought to myself—here is a young man capable of effort and achievement, a young man of whom India may well be proud of one day. But each thing has its price and the price for quality is always higher. So your responsibility will be the more. Never be discouraged. Life is a constant challenge. Meet it with courage, good humour and humility. Even defects and mistakes have much to teach and often lay the foundation for future victory.*

∾

Indira Gandhi had already written to Horace Alexander the previous year, recalling how her interest in birds began. On 29 March, she wrote to him again in response to a letter he had sent, congratulating her on becoming prime minister a second time:

> [...] How long ago it is since I could bird-watch. It may interest you that in my constituency, which is out of the way and rather unfrequented, I found some 'jheels' teeming with bird life.

The Keoladeo Ghana Bird Sanctuary in Bharatpur in Rajasthan would be a recurring headache for Indira Gandhi right up to the early 1980s. In July 1967, General Harold Williams, who was known to her both as a keen birdwatcher and a distinguished engineer, had met her and had complained about constant poaching in the sanctuary. He was particularly critical of the activities of the Maharaja of Bharatpur who considered the sanctuary his private fiefdom. An upset Indira Gandhi spoke to the Maharaja, who issued counter-allegations against local forest officials. Finally, Indira Gandhi asked her aide Natwar Singh, who was from Bharatpur and had links with the princely family there, to follow up. On 24 July, he sent her a note:

> I am afraid the chief culprit in this regard is the Maharaja of Bharatpur himself. The former rulers were given certain exclusive shooting rights and one hopes that in the not too distant future the situation will correct itself once these privileges are withdrawn.

It would take four years for these privileges to be abrogated.

In July–August an all-women expedition from Calcutta was facing some hurdles in its plans to climb Nanda Ghunti in Chamoli district of what is now Uttarakhand. The Indian Mountaineering Foundation felt that at almost 21,000 feet, the peak was not one that the women were equipped to handle. Deepali Sinha, the leader of team, met the former West Bengal chief minister, P.C. Sen, and through him was able to reach Indira Gandhi. The prime minister was obviously impressed with Sinha and the team, and spoke to H.C. Sarin, president of the foundation. Initially, he was reluctant to attend to the matter, but when a second phone call came from the prime minister, he personally sat with the women and selected a lower peak for them to climb—Ronti at about 19,900 feet in Garhwal district. Swapna Mitra, accompanied by two sherpas, scaled the peak on 28 October.

Indira Gandhi had visited the newly established Nehru Institute of Mountaineering in her first trip to Uttarkashi in June the previous year. On 10 November 1967, she wrote to Brigadier Gyan Singh conveying her delight at the graduation of the youngsters she had met there, and added, 'I need hardly tell you of the great hopes I have of the Institute.' Her hopes were to be finally fulfilled a few months before she died when, on 23 May 1984, Bachendri Pal, an alumnus of the institute, became the first Indian woman to scale Mount Everest.[1]

Indira Gandhi revamped the Planning Commission in August–September. The respected economist D.R. Gadgil—an avid birdwatcher, whose son Madhav Gadgil was to play a key role in the Silent Valley episode in the early 1980s—became its deputy chairman. Indira Gandhi also selected Pitambar Pant—who had been a close aide of Nehru—as one of the members. In the mid-1950s, he had almost single-handedly prepared a detailed design for India's adoption of the metric system and spearheaded the changeover. He had also pioneered perspective planning in the country.

After discussions with her, Pant articulated Indira Gandhi's thoughts on the environment and development in the Fourth Five-Year Plan document that would be released two years later. This would be the first time that protection of the environment would be recognized as an integral part of the development process—an obvious stance today, but unheard of in the late 1960s when India was confronted by numerous other challenges. The relevant paragraph read:

> Most countries face in varying degrees problems of pollution of air and water, erosion of soil, waste of natural resources, derelict lands, loss of wildlife, ugly landscape, urban sprawl and city slums—generally a progressive deterioration in the quality of environment. There is growing concern about the matter in India also [...] The physical environment is a dynamic, complex and inter-connected system in which any action

in one part affects others. There is also the inter-dependence of living things and their relationships with land, air, and water. Planning for harmonious development recognizes this unity of nature and man [...] There are instances in which timely specialised advice on environmental aspects could have helped in project design and in averting subsequent adverse effects on the environment, leading to loss of invested resources. It is necessary, therefore, to introduce the environmental aspect into our planning and development [...]

As prime minister, Indira Gandhi was to engage with the problems of India's greatest cities, particularly Delhi and Bombay. She began with the nation's capital. On 25 September she sent a note to Karan Singh:

> I understand that the NDMC [New Delhi Municipal Committee] have a 'plan' to improve the Lodhi Gardens in Delhi presumably to develop them as a greater tourist attraction. I hope the Tourism Department has been consulted by the local authorities and nothing will be done to spoil this beautiful oasis in the capital. Today's editorial on this subject in the *Hindustan Times* makes me apprehensive. Could you look into the matter? We have committees for the Buddha Jayanti Park, the Shanti Vana, etc. Could we not have a similar committee which could screen proposals like the one regarding the Lodhi Gardens and also prepare schemes with due regards to aesthetic values?

The newspaper editorial that the prime minister was referring to expressed grave apprehensions regarding the plans afoot that would destroy 'the best example in the country of a natural, well-wooded park that served as "lungs of fresh air".' The prime minister's note to the minister demonstrated the seriousness with which she took media reports on environmental issues. This pattern of sending notes to her ministers based on something that she had read that very day was to continue in the years ahead.[2]

7 November 1966 had seen a most unusual attack on Parliament. Thousands of sadhus—many clad in saffron robes, others naked—staged an assault

demanding a national law to ban cow slaughter immediately. Police had to resort to firing and a few of the protesters were killed. Indira Gandhi quickly secured the resignation of Home Minister Gulzarilal Nanda, who was widely seen to be sympathetic to the agitationists.

On 29 June, she set up a high power committee to examine the entire issue of a national law to ban cow slaughter. It was headed by A.K. Sarkar, a former chief justice of India, and had, as its members, chief ministers, political leaders, religious figures, cow protection activists, animal husbandry experts like Dr V. Kurien,[3] and the then chairman of the Agricultural Prices Commission, Ashok Mitra.[4] The high power committee was given six months to submit its report.

Meanwhile, conservationists got involved in the debate and, at the behest of Zafar Futehally, Dillon Ripley wrote to Indira Gandhi on 3 October suggesting a study be conducted by the BNHS and the Smithsonian Institution on India's cattle issue from the point of view environmental management. He wrote:

> I personally believe that one of the most important studies that might be undertaken today is an ecological approach to the age-old problem of the impact of cattle on lands in India.
>
> I write at this time with some sense of urgency because of the recent developments which have led, I am informed, to the appointment of a committee which will report to your Government on the issue of imposing a ban on the slaughter of cows throughout India.

To ensure that his letter got the prime minister's personal attention, Ripley added a postscript:

> I hope to come to Delhi soon and have a chance to speak once more to the Delhi Bird Watching Society. Salim Ali took me along with him to Bhutan this spring. Peter Jackson joined us. We had a marvelous time and had wonderful birding.

The letter was acknowledged a week later by an official in the prime minister's secretariat. But the next month, on 7 November, India's US Ambassador Chester Bowles reprimanded Dillon Ripley:

At my request, my deputy Mr. Greene, found an opportunity the other day to sound out Mrs. Gandhi's right-hand man, P.N. Haksar, about your letter. Haksar readily confirmed that it had been received […] and as much said he thought it better to leave the complexities of the cow problem to the Government of India. Mr. Greene asked whether the Prime Minister had replied to your letter and was told that she had not; we infer that she probably will not.

[…] It would help to get acceptance of projects in which you are interested if you would forward them to us for comment and/or discussion with the Government of India, rather than directly.

From then on, Ripley was to make sure that Salim Ali approved all his letters to Indira Gandhi. As for the study, it never did take off and the cow protection committee itself was to keep meeting for twelve years till it was disbanded in 1979 by Indira Gandhi's successor. It never submitted its report.[5]

On 13 December, the deputy head of the Swedish mission at the UN, Borje Billner, spoke in the general assembly, and proposed a UN conference on the human environment. It has been long believed that this was done because Sweden was very concerned about the serious environmental problem of acid rain caused by emissions of sulphur dioxide and nitrogen oxide. But some years back it was revealed that there was a far more pressing political motivation. Given its strong opposition to anything to do with nuclear energy, Sweden wanted to counter a proposal, which enjoyed the backing of the US and USSR, for a conference on the peaceful uses of atomic energy.[6]

This Swedish initiative was to play a crucial role in Indira Gandhi's environmental life. Almost a year later, on 3 December 1968, the UN general assembly formally adopted a resolution accepting the Swedish idea. Subsequently, the conference—scheduled to be in Stockholm in 1972—came under attack from some developing countries like Brazil, but India, no doubt at the prime minister's bidding, supported it strongly.

Notes

1. Indira Gandhi and Bachendri Pal were to meet at the former's office at 1, Akbar Road, New Delhi on 10 June 1984.

2. On 5 July 1983, for instance, she was to get one of her officers, Arvind Pande, to send the agriculture secretary copies of news items critical of India's social forestry programme—these had appeared in *The Guardian* of 3 July 1983 and *The Indian Express* of 4 July 1983. Comments were asked for 'within a week' (the timeline underlined was her instruction).

3. In his autobiography (Kurien, 2005) Dr V. Kurien, known popularly as the Amul man, has left a hilarious account of his experience in the committee which kept meeting for twelve years and never submitted a report. In the same book, he provides telling examples of how Indira Gandhi gave him unstinted support, in the face of opposition from some of her ministerial colleagues, to make India's White Revolution a reality.

4. Ashok Mitra, too, has provided an amusing account of the committee in his *A Prattler's Tale* (2006).

5. I have written about this in *The Hindu*, 9 November 2016.

6. The authoritative account of the motivations of Sweden is in Engfeldt (2009).

1968

Indira Gandhi with a koala, Taronga Zoo, Sydney; May 1968.

In the previous two years, Indira Gandhi had visited ten countries—1968 was to see her travel to twelve nations in Asia and Central and South America. In one of these visits she took time off to indulge herself in her love of animals. On 22 May she went to the Taronga Zoo in Sydney and this is where two iconic photographs of hers—cuddling a koala and having her legs nibbled at by a wombat—were to be taken. Her foreign visits in 1968 are well known. But less known is that in February 1968 she became the first prime minister to visit the Andaman and Nicobar Islands whose ecological challenges were to concern her till a few months before her death.[1]

She had her usual quota of political problems—dealing with non-Congress governments, agitations in the northeast for the formation of a hill state out of Assam and continuing friction with her senior-most cabinet colleague and finance minister. Her relationship with her party bosses kept deteriorating to the point of moves being made to oust her but what gave her strength was the rise of a vocal, younger group within the Congress committed to a progressive economic agenda. Although not strongly ideological herself, she encouraged these colleagues as a way of bolstering her own position.

On 23 July she wrote to her friend Lucile Kyle who lived near New York:

> I am writing from Parliament—such boring speeches. What threatened to
> be a big united roar of the opposition parties has turned out to be a mousy
> squeak. I don't often admit that I am tired but now I am. Such hectic pace
> and no holiday at all. Even the few days in Srinagar were not relaxing because
> there were so many visitors.
>
> All the family is together [...] Sanjay is very busy with his car.

After a stint as a special student apprentice at Rolls Royce Motors in the UK, Sanjay Gandhi had returned home by late 1967 with the ambition of building a low-cost, people's car that was given the name Maruti. On 11 December, he formally applied for a licence to manufacture such a car. His efforts were written about in the media as the aspirations of a young man with a spirit of daring and enterprise. The controversy was still two years away.

Early in her tenure, Indira Gandhi was confronted with an environmental disaster in the town of Monghyr, Bihar. A government-owned petroleum refinery at Barauni had discharged untreated effluent into the Ganga which, in turn, resulted in the contamination of water supply to the town. Parliament was agitated by what had happened and the prime minister, taking cognizance of these sentiments, sent a note to Minister of Health Satyanarayan Singh on 20 February:

> The recent contamination of the Ganga, leading to water supply
> difficulties at Monghyr, has highlighted the necessity of regulatory
> measures to control the discharge of industrial waste and effluents into
> rivers and other water sources.

While Indira Gandhi wanted the minister to come forward with legislation, the problem was a constitutional one—both rivers and water were subjects dealt with by states. This stymied the central government from passing laws dealing with water pollution. According to the Constitution, however, there was a way out. If two or more states gave their consent, the centre could legislate. In this instance, only one state had given its approval—Gujarat. Indira Gandhi wanted the minister to chase his counterparts in other states to ensure they followed Gujarat's example. But the minister, himself from Bihar, seemed to be unfazed by what had happened in Monghyr.

Not surprisingly, it would take six more years for such a law to be enacted by Parliament.

The Keoladeo Ghana Bird Sanctuary in Bharatpur continued to concern Indira Gandhi.

Horace Alexander had approached Jawaharlal Nehru fifteen years earlier to save the sanctuary and the prime minister had intervened. Salim Ali who had been closely involved with Alexander's efforts again took up the issue with Indira Gandhi on 4 March:

> I hesitate to bother you, but this is a matter in which no one else will do. I had occasion to resort to similar pleading with your father [...]
>
> However in the last few months ugly rumours have revived [...] that plans are afoot for draining the Ghana for cultivation or of 'de-sanctuarizing' it [...]
>
> I am writing this letter to request that you will please make known your personal interest and concern for the preservation of this unique natural monument to the Rajasthan Government upon whom the fate of the sanctuary presently rests.

The response from the prime minister was quick and on 12 March, she replied:

> Thank you for your letter of the 4th March regarding the Bird Sanctuary at Bharatpur. I am asking for an urgent report on the subject from the Rajasthan Government. Natwar Singh spoke to the Chief Secretary on

the telephone and the Chief Secretary assured him that there is no truth in the rumours that you have heard.

In his letter to the prime minister, Salim Ali had also suggested that the sanctuary should be converted into a natural park under the direct control of the central government. Natwar Singh supported this move in a note he put up a few days later to her but she cooled his enthusiasm by observing on the note:

I agree but tact and caution are necessary.

Four months later, Salim Ali sent Indira Gandhi a copy of the first volume of the *Handbook of Birds of India and Pakistan* which he had authored along with Dillon Ripley. The prime minister acknowledged the book more than perfunctorily on 3 August:

I have not given up my interest in bird watching, so I was delighted to receive your new book. How thoughtful of you to send it to me.

News of this interest had travelled to Australia and New Zealand ahead of me and I was presented with two very lovely books there.

There would be nine more volumes by Salim Ali over the next seven years.

Mountaineering continued to hold the prime minister's interest. On 21 March, in a foreword to *Nine atop Everest* by Captain M.S. Kohli—who had led India's first successful expedition to the world's highest peak in 1965—Indira Gandhi recalled:[2]

Through the ages, India's thinkers have been inspired by the beauty and majesty of the Himalayas and by their sacred associations. But mountaineering as an adventure and sport is of recent origin. In India specially it is a young calling, although one of the fastest growing and most exacting. Within a few years we have scaled many forbidding peaks of the world's greatest mountains. One of the most exclusive groups in the world must surely be of those who have stood on top of Everest. Nearly half of them are from our country. Is this not a tribute to the courage and capacity of our young people [...]?

Indira Gandhi termed the Kohli-led expedition 'a masterpiece of planning, organization, team-work, individual effort and leadership' and believed that it would serve as an inspiration to the youth of the country.

On 15 May, Indira Gandhi inaugurated the tenth anniversary celebrations of the Indian Mountaineering Foundation. The 1966 devaluation had made her allergic to one IMF—the International Monetary Fund—but this IMF she related to warmly. At the celebrations, Indira Gandhi spoke about the story of Indian mountaineering:

> The Himalayas have shaped our history: they have moulded our philosophy; they have inspired our saints and poets. They influence our weather. Once they defended us; now we must defend them.

Decades later, in the context of climate change, India began to appreciate the crucial role of Himalayan ecosystems; how fragile they have become; and the urgent need to restore them to health.

On 2 November, the prime minister visited the drought-affected areas of Barmer and Jaisalmer—a desert city of considerable architectural and historical value—in Rajasthan. This was her second trip to Jaisalmer, having been there last in October 1965 during a tour of the border districts of the state. On her return to the capital, she wrote on 14 November to her two ministerial colleagues, Dr Karan Singh who was in charge of tourism and civil aviation and Dr Triguna Sen who looked after education and culture:

> When I was there [in Jaisalmer] a few days ago, I was told that portions of the city are in an advanced state of decay [...]
>
> I should, therefore, like you to instruct the Department of Archaeology to depute a team within the next week or two to make a quick, preliminary survey of Jaisalmer [...] I should like to have the preliminary report by the middle of December. After that we can work out the details of declaring portions of the city of Jaisalmer as "protected monuments".
>
> I am anxious that the character of the old town be preserved before Municipal righteousness ruins the city. Perhaps we could urgently devise

a sort of a Master Plan for a new Jaisalmer city and try and preserve some of the old portions, particularly the Fort Area.

Dr Sen followed her directions and sent her the preliminary plan she had asked for. In response, Indira Gandhi wrote to him on 20 December, highlighting the fact that she had read the report carefully:

> Your letter confirms my own view that Jaisalmer Fort is in a very poor state of repair and is being encroached upon by squatters and tradesmen. I also note that there is some difficulty in arriving at a suitable Agreement between the Maharawal and the ASI [Archaeological Survey of India] for the better preservation of the monuments [...]
>
> According to the Report, action by the ASI will depend [on] whether or not the other monuments are more than hundred years old. Even if some of these monuments are disqualified under this clause some other means must be found to preserve them.
>
> [...] It is also for consideration whether the 'hundred years clause' that at present governs eligibility for protection by the ASI needs to be amended [...]
>
> [An] immediate plan should be drawn up for Jaisalmer [...]

Going by the speeches she made in the initial years of her prime ministership, it was clear that agriculture and family planning, or—as she herself put it—'the peasant and the parent' were Indira Gandhi's two urgent priorities. She drew the link between the two when she addressed the Sixth All India Conference on Family Planning in Chandigarh on 30 November:

> Family planning is an accepted official policy in India. But our programme will not succeed if it remains only an official programme. [...] Recently in agriculture we have seen that the people's willingness to adopt new methods has overtaken official effort. This might possibly happen in the family planning programme also. It should be proved to every village and to every family that a smaller, more compact family makes for better health and greater happiness for the family and hence for more prosperity for the village. [...] Simultaneous progress in programmes of intensive agriculture and family planning can give us the chance of conquering rural poverty.

At the same time, Indira Gandhi was candid enough to confess that the 'biggest enemy of family planning in India is the lassitude of our people'. Ironically, she also spoke of the dangers of fixing targets, something she would seemingly forget some years later in the high noon of the Emergency in late 1975 and 1976.

Notes

1. She spent two nights on *INS Mysore* going from Madras to Port Blair. The second night she revealed to the naval personnel a side of her personality that still remains largely unknown. At their request she sang 'Oh Susannah' one of the most popular American minstrel songs ever written. This evidently left a deep impression on Lieutenant Premvir Das who had been assigned 'flunky duty' with her. The reward for that duty was a hand-written invitation from the prime minister for the wedding of her elder son. He was to write about that memorable experience many years later (*Times of India*, 5 June 1998).
2. Kohli (1969).

1969

Indira Gandhi at the first meeting of the reconstituted Indian Board of Wildlife, with Karan Singh (left) and Jagjivan Ram (right); July 1969.

1969 was truly a watershed year and saw the emergence of a whole new Indira Gandhi. Gone was the caution and tentativeness that had marked the previous two years in office. A transformed Indira Gandhi emerged. The agitation to create a separate state of Telangana out of Andhra Pradesh reached a peak and it required all of her political skills to contain this agitation.[1] July was to see the nationalization of banks which she saw not just in economic but in broader social and political terms as well. Much has been written about this but the only book that has an insider account of Indira Gandhi's role is D.N. Ghosh's No Regrets. *Ghosh had worked closely with Haksar to make this historic decision happen. August 1969 saw a bitterly contested presidential election in which an independent candidate for whom she canvassed on grounds of 'conscience voting' emerged victorious, defeating the 'official' Congress candidate. This was to lead to convulsions in her party with Indira Gandhi more than convinced that her party's bosses were hell-bent on removing her as prime minister.*

On 3 September she wrote to Dorothy Norman while flying in to Delhi from Srinagar after a holiday in Gulmarg:

> *[...] Need I assure you that I am not closer to the communists or dictatorship of any kind [...] Unfortunately, the institution of bossism created a clash [...] Each state boss came to believe that he was the state [...] Perhaps because I have tried to be accommodating, they all thought I was weak. The last two years have been of tremendous pressure and difficulty. If it had been a question of myself or my position, it would not have mattered but the manner in which I was being pushed around, with a view to finally pushing me out of office, would have not only split the Congress but weakened it along the line [...]*

But the split did take place. The party bosses expelled her from the party on 12 November and a formal break-up into two separate parties happened four days thereafter. Subsequently, she needed the support of left and regional parties in Parliament which was forthcoming.

This was undoubtedly a year in which Indira Gandhi finally established herself as the undisputed leader of the country with a clear ideological stance in both politics and economics. This is also the year in which Indira Gandhi, the lover of nature, came into her own and there was to be no looking back thereafter. Amidst all the political hurly-burly, in October she became the first prime minister to visit another area of India that symbolized its ecological diversity—the remote, lagoon-ringed coral-reefed Laccadives, Aminidivi and Minicoy group of islands off the Kerala coast that were to be renamed Lakshadweep four years later.[2]

National parks, and their security, continued to preoccupy Indira Gandhi— among them, the Keoladeo Ghana Bird Sanctuary, Bharatpur. Salim Ali was her main source of ground information.

On 7 February, Indira Gandhi sent a note to Cabinet Secretary B. Sivaraman, who earlier, as agriculture secretary, had played an important role in the Green Revolution:

> From time to time I receive complaints regarding the unsatisfactory manner in which the Bharatpur Bird Sanctuary is run. My office has

been in touch with the Rajasthan Government in this connection. On one or two occasions I have also spoken to the Maharaja of Bharatpur in this matter.

Some time ago Shri Salim Ali wrote to me suggesting that the Bird sanctuary be converted into a national park under the Central Government. His proposal was forwarded to the Rajasthan government who have now agreed to offer the sanctuary to the Central government for a period of ten years in the first instance.

Would Cabinet Secretary please examine the proposal of the Rajasthan government urgently and let me know?

Salim Ali's suggestion was novel. Its acceptance by the state was most surprising and was at the behest of Chief Minister Mohanlal Sukhadia. But it went against the Constitution—so, two weeks later the cabinet secretary informed Indira Gandhi that Salim Ali's proposal was a non-starter; and that it was the state government that had to declare Bharatpur a national park because the central government did not control such parks. The idea died for the time being, only to be revived four years later.

Meanwhile, there was the tiger reserve in Sariska in Alwar district of Rajasthan that also called for Indira Gandhi's attention. To most of us, it is common knowledge that in 2005, there were precisely zero tigers left in Sariska. All tigers had been poached by a well-organized gang. The catastrophe forced the then prime minister, Dr Manmohan Singh, to order an inquiry by the Central Bureau of Investigation (CBI) and also set up an expert group to revisit the entire question of the protection of India's national animal. A couple of years later, Sariska was again in the news when a tiger translocation programme to repopulate the reserve was launched—this would go on to become very successful.

But what has not been known is the threat Sariska faced very early on during Indira Gandhi's prime ministership. That she got to know of the threat is proof of the many informal channels she had for feedback; what she did about it reveals her approach to wildlife management.

Here's what happened. Jai Singh, a local forester, knew somebody who, in turn, was acquainted with N.K. Seshan, Indira Gandhi's private secretary. On 14 February, Seshan was alerted to the fact that a huge contingent of the Central Reserve Police Force (CRPF) was about to make its home in the old palace in the middle of the sanctuary. He brought this to his boss's attention right away. Indira Gandhi, after making inquiries with the state government, got her aide Natwar Singh to send a note to Home Secretary L.P. Singh on 1 March:

> A few days ago it was reported to PM that a Training centre for the CRP [Central Reserve Police] had been established at the Sariska Palace in the Sariska Game Sanctuary in Alwar [...] It will eventually have 1200 men in residence. They will also have firing ranges.
>
> PM would like HS [Home Secretary] to kindly look into the matter and explore possibilities of locating another house to the CRP outside the Sariska Sanctuary.

The note had its desired impact and Sariska was saved for the moment.

On 20 February, Indira Gandhi received a two-page letter from someone she did not know at all. The letterhead simply read: 'Alvin P. Adams, PanAm Building, New York'. Today thanks to Google search, one can confirm that Alvin P. Adams was a well-known airline executive, a bon vivant and a big-game hunter—so popular that his death in 1996 merited a longish obituary in the *New York Times*.[3] But such information was unavailable to Indira Gandhi or her aides in February 1969—in fact, nobody from Indira Gandhi's circle seemed to be even remotely aware of Alvin P. Adams.

Adams conveyed to the prime minister:

> [...] Having visited India and it neighbouring boundaries of Nepal and Bhutan on ten different hunting trips, I have been deeply alarmed at the rapidly depleting big game population. Even this past month hunting in the best Indian blocks, although I saw certain signs—I never saw a tiger. This is the second consecutive year this has happened.
>
> I have been convinced for some time that the cause of this condition lies in the apparently uncontrolled slaughtering by the natives of these magnificent tigers and leopards. The purpose is to sell to local dealers who are currently paying from $ 200 for a tiger skin and $ 150 for a leopard skin [...]
>
> The usual method employed is poisoning [...]

I am certain that the only solution to this tragic problem is for the country in question to pass legislation which would make it illegal, punishable by severe fine and prison for anyone to buy or sell tiger or leopard skin [...]

Adams continued in this strain and ended by expressing the hope that the prime minister would take an interest in what he had said. She required no prompting and noted on his letter:

I am deeply concerned about this matter. We must take it up in a big way.

She got Natwar Singh to acknowledge Alvin Adams' communication on 28 February and to reassure him that 'we are exploring the possibilities of controlling the indiscriminate killing of precious wild life in the country.'

Adams' letter was the trigger for a whole sequence of events that were to follow. On 30 April, she wrote to Agriculture Minister Jagjivan Ram, who was looking after forests and wildlife:

I have been greatly concerned at the progressive decimation of our wild life. From all that I read and hear, the situation appears to be much more serious than official circles are prepared to admit.

I enclose a copy of a letter which I received some time ago from Mr. Alvin P. Adams. In their latest publication, the International Union for the Conservation of Nature and Natural Resources have also placed a disconcertingly large number of our animals in the danger-list. I am most anxious for if we continue to lose ground, the loss will be irretrievable.

The enclosed note I have received suggests certain measures which might help to turn the tide. I shall be grateful if you would have them urgently examined [...] In the midst of our many pre-occupations, it would be tragic indeed if we lost sight of this precious but dwindling heritage.

Jagjivan Ram was an old and experienced war-horse, having been a cabinet minister since 1947. He replied to the prime minister on 19 May, only to get her even more frustrated as she noted on his letter:

This is a routine ministerial answer. The question needs to be gone into more deeply.

In May, Indira Gandhi began to think seriously about the Indian Board for Wildlife (IBWL), which had not met for four years. Its chairman, the Maharaja of Mysore, was an outstanding musicologist of world renown. But he had been ill for several years.

Indira Gandhi looked around for replacements. One obvious choice was Jagjivan Ram who was administratively in charge of the IBWL. But she knew instinctively that his heart would not be in the job. Largely on the advice of her close friend and fellow nature-lover Padmaja Naidu, she finally settled on her thirty-nine-year old colleague, the Minister of Tourism and Civil Aviation Dr Karan Singh. She knew him exceedingly well, not least because he had been a protégé of her father since he was eighteen. His appointment as the chairman of the IBWL was announced on 3 June.

Karan Singh immediately swung into action. The first meeting of the reconstituted IBWL was called a month later, in July 1969—eleven days before the historic decision to nationalize banks was announced. Indira Gandhi had it conveyed to Karan Singh that she would attend and inaugurate the meeting.

In her opening speech on 8 July, the prime minister covered a wide canvas. She was highly critical of the indiscriminate felling of trees in the name of development, pointing out that in some places landslides were the direct consequence of deforestation. Presaging the ban that was soon to come, she boldly declared that the 'need for foreign exchange does not justify the killing of tigers, leopards and other animals in a manner they become extinct'. She chided engineers, administrators and dam-builders for not having any reverence for nature.

This meeting of the IBWL was historic because it called for national legislation 'to ensure uniformity and cogency' in the wildlife law of the country. Clearly, it found the existing situation in which each state had its own law unsatisfactory. It was historic also because the IBWL formally decided to make the lion, so far the national symbol, the national animal as well. This decision taken on 9 July was guided by three reasons—the lion had a long association with Indian mythology, culture and history; it decorated the national symbol; and the existence of this rare animal was threatened.[4]

Indira Gandhi was quite pleased with the IBWL meeting. On 22 July, she wrote to Karan Singh:

> From all accounts the recent meeting of the IBWL was more lively and promising than ever before. I have heard much praise of the manner in which you conducted it.
>
> I understand that the Board will have an Executive Committee as well as a small ad hoc committee for the specific purpose of conducting an All India survey of wildlife [...] In determining the composition of these committees I hope you will ensure that at least some of the members are young and active field workers [...] like Futehally, Hari Dang, Krishnan and Sankhala.
>
> I am especially concerned about the blackbuck for which no sanctuary exists at present. Could not something be done for this animal, whose numbers have diminished so greatly over the past few years?
>
> I hope the Board will produce a journal and perhaps also a film on the wildlife of India.

Even as she dispatched this letter to Karan Singh, she wrote to all the chief ministers. This was the first of such communications. Over the next fifteen years, there would be many more such letters to chief ministers as a group on environmental issues.

Indira Gandhi started her letter to the chief ministers by expressing her great concern with the 'progressive decimation of our wildlife' and by recalling the discussions at the recently concluded meeting of the IBWL. She acknowledged that the conservation of wildlife and forests are the responsibility of states but she also pointed out that they are an Indian national heritage. She went on to say:

> I am writing to you to enlist your active cooperation because it is only when leaders take a personal interest that things get done [...]
>
> [...] The carnage of recent years can be ended only if wild life legislation, on the pattern of the Maharashtra Wild Birds and Animals Protection Act is passed in each State [...] To implement this legislation and to enforce it in the field, each State Forest Department should have within it, a Wild Life Department [...] Specialists should be trained and retained [...]

> I think it would be useful for a State Wild Life (Advisory) Board to be constituted on the pattern of the Indian Board for Wild Life [...]
>
> Poaching has become a lucrative profession in many states. To curb this all commercial transactions in game meat, the netting and snaring of birds, and the poaching of animals for furs, meat and skins must be stopped [...]

She went on to make a number of other suggestions and ended by saying:

> I have written to you at some length, not only because I love animals, but also because our parks and sanctuaries could, in the long run, become tourist attractions and thus more than repay the care and investment which they now demand.

Indira Gandhi told her aides that economic arguments were key to political saleability especially to less-than-convinced chief ministers.

Buckminster Fuller came to India twice in 1969. After his first visit, Indira Gandhi wrote to Dorothy Norman on 26 May:

> Guess who turned up here the other day? Our old friend Bucky Fuller. He has paid me the biggest compliment and I must share it with you. On one of his maps, he has inscribed as follows: "To Indira, in whose integrity God is entrusting much of the evolutionary success of humanity and with utter safety." I must say I was deeply touched and also somewhat embarrassed.

A day after the Congress split on 12 November, Indira Gandhi welcomed 'our old friend' to deliver the third Jawaharlal Nehru Memorial Lecture in the capital. She was fulsome in her praise for him:

> Mr. Fuller is described as an architect. He is that because of his intense concern with living space. But he is something more than an architect because his obsession is with the architecture of the universe. We all have heard of Mr. Fuller's invention, the geodesic dome which is known and seen all over the world. It is a brilliant use of space and material. Then there is the world map and other items. But what is important is that

> Mr. Fuller has shown how to get the maximum from minimum material
> by making intelligent use of the resources available on earth [...]

Buckminster Fuller spoke on 'Planetary Planning' for over two hours. His printed lecture is at least ten times the length of the essays of others who have delivered the lecture before or after. He thanked Indira Gandhi describing her as a 'clear headed planetary housekeeper of humanity'. Immediately thereafter,[5] Fuller was engaged to develop designs for international airports at Delhi, Bombay and Madras. There was undoubtedly a risk as Indira Gandhi herself recognized in her letter of 12 August 1970 to Karan Singh. But the risk was taken and by November 1972, at Karan Singh's suggestion, the Srinagar airport was also proposed to be added to Fuller's list of assignments.

However, things began to fall apart soon after. Both Habib Rahman—the chief architect of the Central Public Works Department (CPWD)—and Malhoutra convinced Indira Gandhi that the Fuller experiment wasn't wholly successful and that he had not come up with any great technological suggestion. Thus Indira Gandhi was to write to Karan Singh on 1 March 1973:

> I understand Habib Rahman has written to the Chairman of the
> International Airport Authority of India expressing his disappointment
> with Dr. Buckminster Fuller's architectural concept for our new airport
> terminals. You have no doubt seen his letter. Have you looked into the
> matter personally? I hope no irrevocable commitments are being made
> without giving careful consideration to the points Rahman has urged.
> Please let me know the position. Meanwhile, your proposal to ask Fuller
> to design a building for the Srinagar Terminal should be kept in abeyance.

While the Fuller experiment came to an inglorious end, Indira Gandhi continued to quote the eminently quotable architect in her speeches till the very end.[6]

A day after Fuller's lecture, Kailash Sankhala—then director of the Delhi zoo—was awarded the prestigious Jawaharlal Nehru Fellowship by the Jawaharlal Nehru Fund for his project 'The Controversial Tiger: A Study of Ecology, Behaviour and Status'. He was the second conservationist to have been recognized in this manner. The inaugural list announced on 27 May 1968 had named M. Krishnan for this award for his project 'Ecological Survey of the Mammals in the Peninsular Region'. While Sankhala was to become the first director of Project Tiger, Krishnan would continue to be a member of the IBWL, a loner but one whose voice was respected.[7]

Indira Gandhi turned fifty-two on 19 November. Five days later, she inaugurated the Tenth General Assembly of the IUCN. The same morning *The Times of India* brought out a special supplement with this message from the prime minister:

> Man has lived by the notion that he has unrestricted licence to exploit Nature and its resources. Through agriculture and animal husbandry he learnt early in history that the land takes care only if he took care of it. Even so, his respect for forest and pasture was always subjected to his own greed. With the advent of the industrial age, exploitation took new shape. The problems created by the pollution of air and water, and by fear of the depletion of the mineral resources of the earth, have created a belated realization that we should be conservers, not destroyers, of this planet. For the first time, we have also become aware of the problems created by the geometric progression of [the] human population. Administrators and Governments are now conscious that it is only through the rational use of the earth's resources that they can ensure the future welfare of mankind. But the conservationists are still at the beginning of the battle. People must be re-educated to take a long-term view of the human environment.

The IUCN conclave, held in Asia for the first time, not only proved to be a milestone in contemporary India's ecological history, but also set the stage for Indira Gandhi's first speech on an environmental subject after she had become prime minister. This speech of 24 November drew encomiums. The prime minister started on an autobiographical note—something she was to do every time she addressed meetings of this sort:

> I have a special pleasure in coming [to] your Conference for, if I may strike a personal note, as an only child whose childhood was invaded

by the turbulence of a vast national upheaval, I found companionship and an inner peace in communion with Nature. I grew up with love for stones, no less than trees, and for animals of all kinds. I have always felt that closeness to Nature helps to make one a more integrated personality.

Long before the global discourse on climate change picked up steam, she went on to speak of how the 'wanton felling of trees has changed the landscape, affecting climate' and how 'deforestation is creating a major problem of soil erosion'. Indira Gandhi reminded the global audience that 'it is a sad commentary on our attitude towards nature that we still think of "exploiting" its resources'. This was, she said, 'an unpleasant word, for it implies taking an unjust advantage'.

Thanks to her father, Indira Gandhi had been a voracious reader. In this speech she gave a glimpse into the books she loved when she recalled Rachel Carson and her 1962 classic *Silent Spring*. She then gave a peep into what was to follow in the months ahead in terms of her government's actions:

> Some beautiful and interesting species have become extinct. At the rate at which secret poaching and shooting are taking place, the rhinoceros, the famous Bengal tiger and even the elephant might disappear unless we take vigilant and drastic steps to preserve them [...] We have a Wildlife Board which has placed a ban on the export of the skins of tigers and leopards. We do need foreign exchange, but not at the cost of the life and liberty of some of the most beautiful inhabitants of this continent.

The IUCN general assembly brought together some three hundred conservationists from across the world. It was of immense significance for India not only because the prime minister delivered an impassioned speech, but also because it decisively shed light on the ecological problems confronting the nation. George Schaller and Noel Simon set the tone with their overview of the endangered large mammals of South Asia. Two presentations were to galvanize Indira Gandhi into action after the assembly was over: one on the 'reasonably secure at the moment' Indian lion at Gir by Canadian ecologist Paul Joslin, and the other on the 'vanishing Indian tiger' by Kailash Sankhala himself—which surveyed the 'tiger situation throughout the sub-continent [...and arrived at] a tentative total of about

2500 tigers'. This was a shockingly tiny number and suggested a disastrous decline.

A number of sanctuaries had been surveyed by experts before the conference and their reports also were discussed: Dachigam in Kashmir for the Kashmir stag, Kanha in Madhya Pradesh for the tiger and the barasingha, Guindy Deer Park in Madras, Sariska for the tiger and Periyar in Kerala for the elephant. A report on the wetlands of Calcutta was also taken up.

The IUCN general assembly ended on 1 December with the adoption of over thirty resolutions, six of which related to India pointedly. Two of them on the lion and the tiger were to foreshadow some of Indira Gandhi's greatest ecological accomplishments in the years ahead. The four other India-specific resolutions were on school education in the country in the space of conservation; the effective management of the Periyar Sanctuary; the need to prohibit grazing in wildlife reserves; and the importance of establishing a bird sanctuary in the Calcutta Salt Lake Area. The resolution on conservation education in schools was the longest of the thirty resolutions adopted and ended with a recommendation that an Indian Committee of IUCN's Commission on Education be set up to oversee these efforts and the follow-up with individual states.

That Indira Gandhi took the IUCN seriously ensured that its resolutions had long-term impact. This was to be the beginning of India's conservation efforts with international assistance—some of the help being financial but the rest, almost wholly, scientific. Her presence signalled to the world that here was a prime minister who, though preoccupied with huge political and economic problems, was personally committed to conservation and was ready to walk the extra mile. It was also to begin a personal relationship between the IUCN and Indira Gandhi. Fourteen years later, the IUCN was to invite Indira Gandhi to be the chairman of its Commission on Education.

Two days after the IUCN session started, Indira Gandhi wrote to Karan Singh, drawing his attention to a survey done by the curator of the BNHS,

J.C. Daniel. The survey had suggested that only 1,531 tigers were left in the country, much less than Sankhala's estimate. She wanted to know what the states had been doing about regulating trade in the skins of big cats, saying that 'At Claridge's Hotel I saw what looked like a leopard skin for sale.' She wanted that the tiger should be declared a protected animal throughout the country, at the very least for the next five years. Then, she went on to reveal facts she had meticulously accumulated over time regarding India's imperilled wildlife:

> Our efforts to conserve wild life seem to be disturbingly disjointed. I find that the Delhi Birds and Wild Animals Protection Rules, published in the October 1969 issue of the Upper India Motorist allow a licensee to kill or capture three black buck per year. The black buck, as you know, is a protected animal throughout the country. An official advertisement issued by the Forest Department of Haryana permits the shooting of one peafowl per day, ignoring the fact that the peafowl and the peacock are both protected animals.
>
> There is also lack of coordination within the Central Government itself. Although the Ministry of Foreign Trade had agreed to ban the import of [various sizes of] cartridges, I understand that the National Rifle Association of India is importing such ammunition through the S.T.C. [State Trading Corporation].
>
> There is another important omission which I should like to bring to your notice. I understand that the proposed Kalagarh dam on the Ramganga makes no provision for fish ladders. In spite of scattered protests by various wild life enthusiasts it seems that this question has not been taken up officially with the Ministry of Irrigation and Power [...]
>
> I have also been told that elephant control licences in Assam, which are issued somewhat freely to resident foreigners in the tea plantations, are being abused [...]
>
> Such questions pose the question whether we have the right type of organization to handle the increasing menace to our wild life. It seems to me that the time has come to face the harsh reality that if we go on as we have been doing, our wild life is doomed. We require a distinct administrative entity, both at the centre and in the states, which would give undivided, whole-time and expert attention to the problems of

conservation [...] We must also urgently explore the possibility of establishing game forms to breed various species which are on the danger list.

She sent a copy of this letter to Jagjivan Ram expressing her deep disappointment that the states had not been taking the recommendations of the IBWL seriously at all and that the situation was getting out of hand. She wanted him to personally pursue with the chief ministers the matter of prohibiting grazing and forestry operations in sanctuaries and national parks. With its general assembly under way, she also suggested to him that India should become a permanent member of the IUCN 'in order to gain access to world-wide expertise' and that this should be announced during the on-going session itself.

26 November was to see the prime minister write a third letter on nature conservation, this time to Minister of Irrigation and Power Dr K.L. Rao. She said:

> It has been brought to my notice that the design of the Kalagarh dam on the Ramganga makes no provision for fish ladders. As you know, the Ramganga is one of the best mahseer rivers in India. In the absence of fish ladders, the breeding cycle of the mahseer will be endangered and the fish will gradually die. Could something be done even at this late stage?

In the mid-1980s and 1990s, building dams on the Narmada—particularly the gigantic Sardar Sarovar Dam in Gujarat—was to become a global environmental concern. The rehabilitation and resettlement of thousands of people, largely tribals, displaced overwhelmingly in Madhya Pradesh, continues to be of concern even now.

In September 1965, a master plan for the development of the Narmada river for irrigation and power had been made public. Madhya Pradesh objected to the master plan that was purely an engineering one on the grounds that while it bore the brunt of costs, the bulk of the benefits would be appropriated by Gujarat. The other two states aligned with one or the other—Maharashtra with Madhya Pradesh, and Rajasthan with Gujarat.

A political settlement had become virtually impossible with the stances taken by the two main parties to the dispute, namely Gujarat and Madhya Pradesh. Madhya Pradesh's chief minister, Shyama Charan Shukla, like his predecessors, insisted that the four states negotiate a settlement, but Gujarat pointed out that six years of negotiations had led nowhere.

After a lengthy discussion with her officials and with Dr K.L. Rao, Indira Gandhi decided sometime in March to refer the Narmada waters dispute to a judicial tribunal, invoking the provisions of the Interstate River Water Disputes Act, 1956. When on 6 March, Dr K.L. Rao wrote to her, asking for her permission to refer the dispute to a tribunal, Indira Gandhi was enraged and recorded her irritation at his letter:

> This is an extraordinary letter considering that I have been pressing the Minister to go ahead with the announcement of the Tribunal and it is he who has been prevaricating. What is the meaning of asking my permission?

Six days later, Dr Rao announced, in Parliament, the reference of the Narmada water dispute to a tribunal. The tribunal was finally set up on 6 October.

Notes

1. Ramesh (2016).
2. She was to make a second visit there in the last week of December 1976.
3. Alvin P. Adams, 'Flashy Aviation Executive Dies at 90', *New York Times*, 13 October 1996.
4. An opinion has held that the lion had been declared as a national animal by the IBWL at its very first meeting in Mysore in November–September 1952. This is not true. That meeting only drew attention to the lion as a national symbol and nothing else. Earlier in 1935, when the logo of the Reserve Bank of India was being designed, the original idea of having a lion was dropped and the tiger was used on the grounds that it was more representative of India.
5. Buckminister Fuller to Indira Gandhi, 4 January 1970, Stanford University Archives.

6. For example, in the Science Policy Foundation Lecture in London on 26 March 1982 and the Raúl Prebisch Lecture in Belgrade on 8 June 1983.

7. The prime mover for awarding the fellowships to Krishnan and Sankhala was actually Padmaja Naidu. Interestingly, although she held no official position, she was seated on the dais when the inaugural function of the IUCN general assembly took place in New Delhi on 24 November 1969.

1970

Two nature lovers: Indira Gandhi with Padmaja Naidu, Allahabad; November 1970.

After the Congress split in November 1969, Indira Gandhi's government had to depend on the left and some regional parties like the Dravida Munnetra Kazhagam (DMK) to survive in Parliament. It did so comfortably and perhaps the price for this support was that economic policy took a sharp leftward direction. This was indeed ironic since in mid-1966 the economy had been significantly decontrolled and strong signals sent to welcome foreign and private investment. But she was careful not to go the whole distance as was being demanded by her radical supporters within and outside the party. She resisted calls, for instance, for the nationalization of foreign trade and cancellation of concessions given to foreign investors.

A Bill was introduced in Parliament in September to abolish the privy purses and privileges that had been constitutionally guaranteed in return for the princes agreeing to join the Indian Union immediately following independence. Indira Gandhi took time to finally decide on the abolition—the initial impetus having come from her Home Minister Y.B. Chavan and others in 1967. But Haksar finally prevailed upon her. Indira Gandhi had close friends among the Maharajas, a number of whom were hunters-turned-conservationists. The son-in-law of the Maharani of Patiala was her close aide Natwar Singh and she enjoyed the company of the witty Maharaja of Dhrangadhra, a key negotiator on behalf of the Concord of Princes. She had appointed the son of the last Maharaja of Kashmir as the chairman of the Indian Board for Wildlife the previous year to replace the former Maharaja of Mysore and the Board itself had some prominent members of royal families. Billy Arjan Singh, for example, belonged to the Kapurthala family and R.S. Dharmakumar Sinhji to the Bhavnagar clan.

The Bill passed in the Lok Sabha but fell in the Rajya Sabha by the thinnest of margins. This was to have major political repercussions. The Supreme Court then overturned the legislation on bank nationalization and also held the presidential proclamation abolishing privy purses and privileges to be invalid. On the night of 27 December, an incensed Indira Gandhi broadcast to the nation that elections would be held in early 1971, a full year ahead of schedule.

A few months earlier, on 30 September, a decision had been taken by the Ministry of Industrial Development of which Dinesh Singh was minister that was to have fateful consequences for Indira Gandhi. A letter of intent was issued to Sanjay Gandhi for the manufacture of 50,000 small cars annually but with no foreign collaboration, no import of equipment, raw materials and components. The letter of intent would have to be converted into an actual licence within a period of six months during which a prototype was to be developed, tested and approved. Although it made no difference to the 1971 poll results, this decision in favour of her younger son would soon cause a gigantic furore and turn her personal and political world upside down. As things turned out, the licence was issued only on 25 July 1974 but there was to be no car.

∾

Shortly before the start of the year, Salim Ali had written to her on 13 December 1969, drawing attention to a crisis in the Keoladeo Ghana Bird Sanctuary in Bharatpur:

The delegates to the recent Conference of the International Council for Bird Preservation [ICBP] in Bharatpur (3 to 6 December) were shocked and nauseated when the Maharaja and palace-guests at his daughter's wedding, opened up a barrage with shot guns at the ducks and geese on the jheel even while we were in the midst of deliberations for their protection and conservation! [...]

All the fifty odd delegates to the ICBP Conference without exception, were loud in their praises of this unique waterfowl resort which they acclaimed to be one of the finest anywhere in the world. They were naturally horrified at the idea of birds being shot within a declared sanctuary, and were shocked and amazed that we should continue to tolerate this state of affairs.

I am appealing to you in the midst of your other pressing pre-occupations because I know your deep personal interest in birds, with the hope that you will get the matter explored immediately to see in what way the stoppage of 'princely' shooting in the Ghana Sanctuary can be effected since all our efforts to persuade the Maharaja have failed.

She responded to Salim Ali's cry of distress on 8 January. She wrote:

Your letter of 13th December, 1969 makes distressing reading. I can well understand your sense of embarrassment and horror. I did speak to the Maharaja of Bharatpur some time ago, and have also sent him messages from time to time but unfortunately it seems to have had no effect. He is rather a strange person.

It is difficult to abrogate the shooting privileges of one Maharaja alone. As you know, we are considering the question of the abolition of Privy Purses and Privileges.

The last paragraph in Indira Gandhi's reply needs some explanation. As Salim Ali had informed her in his letter, the Maharaja had got included in his 'instrument of accession' to the Indian Union in 1948, a special clause reserving for himself and his guests the sole right to shoot on the jheel and in the surrounding wildlife preserve. This was one 'privilege' the Maharaja enjoyed by law—it was one of the conditions that Sardar Patel and V.P. Menon had accepted so that the Maharaja of Bharatpur would dissolve his monarchy and join a newly independent, democratic India. As it turned out, all these privileges were finally abolished by Parliament in 1971, and the issue resolved itself.

◌

Sometime in December 1969, the prime minister had been approached by Chief of Naval Staff Admiral A.K. Chatterjee for her approval to set up a Boys Training Establishment (BTE) at Chilka Lake, Orissa—to guide youth in boat-sailing, motor-boat work, boat-pulling and practical seamanship. Before giving her consent, Indira Gandhi asked Moni Malhoutra to consult Salim Ali on whether birdlife would get affected if the Indian navy's proposal were to be approved.

The matter was approached delicately. While Salim Ali was not told about the navy's specific proposal, he was generally asked about Chilka Lake. In response, he indicated that from an ornithological point of view, the island known as Nalaban would make a first-class sanctuary for wintering water birds. When approached, the Orissa government—keen as it was to attract the training establishment to the state—offered, in addition to the shore site (which was for the BTE), one or two islands including Nalaban for use as camping sites.

Malhoutra jumped at the Orissa government's offer and wrote to the prime minister that 'we are in a position to kill two birds with one stone'— that is, get the site for the training establishment and also secure the most attractive birding island, both at no cost from the state government. It was a terrible choice of words and it did not escape her notice. She recorded on Malhoutra's note:

> An unfortunate phrase when the intention is to preserve! Admiral Chatterjee assured me that the navy would help in looking after the bird sanctuary and preserving its character.

On 6 January, Indira Gandhi sent this note to the defence minister:

> The proposal to locate the BTE at Chilka Lake is approved.
>
> However, I should like Naval Headquarters to ensure that the rich bird life in Chilka Lake is preserved. I find that the Orissa Government have offered to hand over one or two islands about ten to twelve miles

from the BTE proper. One of these is presumably Nalaban. I understand from the Bombay Natural History Society that it is this island which harbours the greatest and most varied concentration of migratory birds. Therefore I feel we should accept the Orissa Government's offer, and take over the Nalaban Island as part of the BTE.

It should be ensured that no motor boats are permitted within three miles of Nalaban and all shooting is strictly prohibited. No regular training programmes other than excursions should take place in Nalaban. In this way the island would become a first class natural sanctuary for birds.

This, however, was not the end of the navy's Chilka venture. It was to preoccupy the prime minister again two years later.

Peter Jackson came to India in 1953, acquiring worldwide fame on being the first to report Edmund Hillary and Tenzing Norgay's ascent of Mount Everest on 29 May 1953. He joined Reuters the year after, and stayed on in the country. After he left India in 1970, he came to be associated with the World Wildlife Fund (WWF).

On 29 March, Peter Jackson wrote to Indira Gandhi:

During the IUCN Conference I took a number of distinguished wild life experts and ornithologists to the jheels at Sultanpur in Gurgaon district, about 25 miles from Delhi. They were astonished at the wealth of wild life and decided on the spot that efforts should be made to have the jheels protected. [...]

All of us interested in the Sultanpur jheels feel that your interest would add immense impetus to the creation of this Nature Reserve of a kind which few, if any, capitals in the world boast within a short distance.

We know the heavy demands on your time, but, as you are a founder-member of the Delhi Bird Watching Society, we wondered if you would like to slip away for about three hours one morning to see the Sultanpur jheels [...]

Two days later Indira Gandhi noted on his letter:

I could. How long will the birds be there?

On 1 April, Moni Malhoutra, after speaking to Peter Jackson, informed Indira Gandhi that the flamingoes and pelicans would be around for a few more weeks though the ducks were already beginning to migrate. He suggested that the prime minister visit the Sultanpur jheel on Sunday, 5 April, to which she responded on the same day:

> US [Under Secretary] seems be innocent so far as security arrangements are concerned. I am very much afraid that the sanctuary may be ruined.

Subsequently, Indira Gandhi sent Moni Malhoutra to visit Sultanpur and brief her. The papers that Peter Jackson had dispatched were passed on to Chief Minister Bansi Lal of Haryana. Just a few months later, on 25 September, Bansi Lal wrote to Indira Gandhi that he had initiated steps to develop the jheel into a bird sanctuary and a tourist destination. Four days later, Indira Gandhi complimented the chief minister for the steps he had taken, adding:

> I hope one day to visit them [the jheels] myself, quietly and without fuss.

The sanctuary was notified on 2 April 1971. When the formal inauguration took place on 6 February 1972, Indira Gandhi sent a message:

> The development of the Sultanpur Jheel as a bird sanctuary will be widely welcomed by all lovers of wild life and conservationists. The potentiality of the Jheel, which attracts a large variety of birds, was first noticed during the IUCN Conference in Delhi. I congratulate the Government of Haryana for having acted so quickly to preserve and develop this great natural asset. The proximity of the sanctuary to our capital city will make it an obvious tourist attraction for all who are interested in our natural heritage. To the people of Delhi in particular it will afford easy escape from the monotony of urban life, and the joy of observing some of nature's most beautiful creatures in their own habitat.

It had taken only two years. Bansi Lal had acted with remarkable speed and it was this that would give him a special standing with the prime minister and her younger son.

∾

The Dachigam Sanctuary close to Srinagar was Indira Gandhi's favourite getaway. She visited it numerous times. After becoming prime minister, she began receiving reports about the steep fall in the population of hanguls (the Kashmir stag) in the sanctuary. On 11 February, she wrote to G.M. Sadiq, the chief minister of Jammu and Kashmir:

> Having stayed in Dachigam several times, I know what a great attraction it could become if the animals are well looked after allowed to multiply. I hope it will be possible to accept and stringently implement, the recommendations of the IUCN, especially in regard to poaching and illegal grazing [...]
>
> Few parts of the world have been so richly endowed by nature as Kashmir. We must therefore be specially careful not to squander irreplaceable assets. For a state whose economy depends a good deal on tourism, it would be doubly rewarding to make Dachigam a truly great sanctuary with an international reputation.

Indira Gandhi didn't stop with this letter; she kept pressing the issue with successive chief ministers of the state—until the early 1980s when she derived some satisfaction at the impact of her continued concern.

Moni Malhoutra took a holiday in early January and spent a couple of days at the Kanha National Park in Madhya Pradesh. On his return he sent a four-page report to Indira Gandhi describing what he had seen. He apologized for the long note saying that it was because 'I was genuinely excited by Kanha and suddenly realized what enormous tourist potential our wildlife holds if, even at this late hour, we take the measures which are necessary'. He praised the collector of Mandla district where Kanha was located handsomely for his 'wonderful' work. The collector was his IAS batch-mate, M.K. Ranjitsinh, who, Malhoutra informed the prime minister, had also taken 'a series of extremely beautiful and intimate films of Indian animals, especially the tiger'. He suggested that 'if PM can spare 45 minutes or so, I would like to ask Shri Ranjit Sinh to come to Delhi to show his films to PM. Could PM find the time?' He also told her that 'if PM has never been to Kanha I would strongly urge her to do so.'

Malhoutra sent his note to Indira Gandhi on 20 January. Within a few hours on the same day, she had sent it back to him agreeing to see the films and adding:

> But alas much as I would like to go to Kanha, I don't think I should. My experience of what the security men do before and during my stay in such places is heartbreaking.

But what Malhoutra had brought to her notice about Kanha stuck in her mind. On 11 February she wrote to Shyama Charan Shukla, the chief minister of Madhya Pradesh:

> I have heard high praise about the Kanha National Park. I understand that some of the IUCN delegates who recently visited it were very impressed. It should be a source of pride and satisfaction to Madhya Pradesh that it possesses what is probably the finest National Park in the country. I believe it is visited by a fair number of tourists already. In due course it could become one of India's major tourist attractions.
>
> It is to hasten this consummation that I am writing to you. I understand that the Government of Madhya Pradesh has, for some time, been considering a proposal to extend the southern boundaries of the Park by another 45 square miles which lie in Balaghat district. I am told the animals, especially the gaur, frequently stray into this area. I hope it will be possible to take an early decision so that the Park becomes a viable ecological unit with an assured future for its wildlife.

The chief minister replied within a few days saying that her instructions to extend the park would be executed soon. But within a few months he was to be at the receiving end of Indira Gandhi's ire.

In the first fortnight of 1970, Indira Gandhi received an unusual letter dated 4 January from a lady in Montreal named Loucia Stephens-Holmberg:

> Listening to the news on my TV set I heard with sadness about [there] being only 600 tigers left. [...] One cannot think of tigers and forget India [...] they are inseparable. I know, Madam, of all the great needs of your vast country and this might be a little down on your list but if you could

cast your attention on this matter for all of us, not just for India but the world would be better for it.

That this letter reached the prime minister was quite a wonder. It was a double wonder that the prime minister found time to reply herself on 1 February, rather than delegating such a task to one of her aides:

> I love animals and nature so can understand your feelings regarding the diminishing tigers in our country.
>
> We, the animal lovers and the Government, are deeply concerned regarding the encroachment on our wild life. Our Government organized a conference of conservation of wildlife a few months ago. We are now going to take some determined actions to prevent encroachment and also find ways to encourage wildlife to grow.
>
> The number of tigers has reduced mainly due to two factors— exploitation and apathy. Hunting gives pleasure to a few but poaching is the greater danger, for tiger-skins fetch high prices abroad. Most people just don't care for the animals or other wildlife. We are now taking steps to educate children and other citizens in this direction.

Perhaps Loucia Stephens-Holmberg's letter remained at the back of Indira Gandhi's mind; perhaps her commitment to the environment only grew firmer with each day.

Either way, by 1 July 1970, based on a directive from her, the IBWL recommended a complete moratorium for five years, with immediate effect, on the shooting of the tiger. This was a hugely significant shift in India's wildlife policy since the Board at its formation in 1952 had not even included the tiger in its list of fourteen species that were endangered and worthy of special protection—perhaps because of the heavy influence of ex-royals on the board in the 1950s and 1960s.

Indira Gandhi made it clear to Karan Singh that exceptions to the July 1970 moratorium on the shooting of the tiger would be allowed only when it was declared a man-eater. This was a powerful signal that she meant business and was prepared to take on the influential tourist-operator-cum-shikar lobby. The moratorium was to get converted into a ban two years later when the new wildlife protection law would be passed. In October

1974, following a directive from her, diplomatic immunity in cases of game-shooting was withdrawn.

That Indira Gandhi was serious about ensuring that these rules were foolproof is evident from a 1 September note she sent to the cabinet secretary B. Sivaraman who must have been quite bemused by the subject matter of the communication from the prime minister:

> Skins of tigers, panthers, etc. fetch very high prices abroad. The quantum of fine should obviously be greater than the price the seller is able to command in foreign markets. It should be at least Rs 10000 per skin or trophy exported.
>
> It is well known that despite the ban skins continue to be exported and the law is not being enforced. I am told there has not been a single prosecution or conviction so far. Cabinet Secretary should look into this aspect also.

The cabinet secretary was to get yet another directive from the prime minister two days later:

> Notwithstanding the ban on export of tiger and leopard skins, I find that a provision exists in our Export Control Regulations which permits tourists, subject to certain conditions, to take out of India, as part of their accompanied or unaccompanied baggage, skins of tigers, leopards and panthers shot by them with proper permission during their stay in India.
>
> The ban should be total. The special dispensation for tourists should be abolished.
>
> Wide publicity should be given to this change, both in India and abroad.
>
> The CBI should keep a special watch on the activities of Shikar Companies after this ban comes into force, so that no foreigner smuggles his trophies out.

The prime minister's notes had an immediate impact. The bureaucracy moved with rare alacrity and on 8 September a notification was issued banning the export of skins of tigers, leopards and panthers from India 'even by foreign tourists and hunters who have shot these animals after obtaining permission from the state government concerned, whether as accompanied or unaccompanied baggage'. The ban covered trophies as well.

While the bureaucracy toed the line set by the IBWL, it was really up to the states to implement the five-year moratorium on the shooting of tigers in whatever manner they wanted. Some states—of which Madhya Pradesh was the most important—were dragging their feet. It was, therefore, no surprise that Indira Gandhi shot off a letter on 3 September to Chief Minister Shyama Charan Shukla, who, incidentally, belonged to her own party—so much for her supposed clout! She said:

> Madhya Pradesh is one of the few States which had not yet responded to the Wild Life Board's appeal for a moratorium on tiger shooting [...] Madhya Pradesh has a special responsibility in the matter, because it is the most important of the tigers' few remaining strongholds in India.
>
> In the interest of conserving this famous and unique denizen of the Indian jungle, I request you to reconsider the matter and agree to implement the recommendation of the Indian Board for Wild Life. [...] Strict measures should be taken to prevent poaching in all its manifestations.
>
> I hope to visit Kanha one day [...]

It would take fourteen years for Indira Gandhi's hope of a visit to Kanha to be fulfilled.

∽

Indira Gandhi is showered encomiums for saving the tiger. What is generally not known—perhaps because it has not attracted international headlines—is that the lion conservation initiative predates that of the tiger.

Soon after the IUCN meeting of November–December 1969, conservationist Guy Mountfort wrote to Indira Gandhi on 27 January:

> Having had the honour of meeting you at the opening of the recent Assembly of the International Union for the Conservation of Nature in New Delhi, I am taking the liberty of sending you, on behalf of the Trustees of the World Wildlife Fund, a report on the Gir Wildlife

Sanctuary in Gujarat. This was prepared in consultation with leading Indian, British and American experts who examined the Sanctuary in December.

The IUCN General Assembly focused attention on the grave threats to the survival of the Asiatic Lion, the total world's population of which is now confined to the Gir [...]

In view of the determination to protect India's endangered wildlife, which was so stirringly expressed in your opening address to the IUCN Assembly, the trustees of the World Wildlife Fund earnestly hope that the recommendations in the report may merit your personal attention.

Indira Gandhi replied promptly on 8 February:

Thank you for sending me a copy of the report on the Gir Wildlife Sanctuary in Gujarat. We shall pursue your suggestions with the Government of Gujarat.

At her behest, an expert committee on national parks and wildlife sanctuaries visited Gir two months later. Finally, the Gir Lion Sanctuary Project for the protection and preservation of the species and its habitat was launched on 17 January 1972. Subsequently, because of her unflagging interest and persistent attempts at following up with the state leadership, Gir was to be declared a national park on 1 May 1975.

On 15 June, thanks to Haksar, Indira Gandhi got a thirty-year-old special assistant for science and technology—Ashok Parthasarathi. No prime minister before or after has appointed anyone with such a designation. Parthasarathi came with impeccable family connections—his grandfather was a minister in Nehru's cabinet, and his father was close to Indira Gandhi and Haksar and had held sensitive diplomatic posts. Ashok Parthasarathi himself had studied radio astronomy at Cambridge, and was to take a keen interest in issues such as pollution. That he understood and admired Indira Gandhi's ecological thinking came to be evident in his memoirs[1] where he recalled: 'Indiraji's concern for and commitment to the protection of the environment was a deep and abiding one. What is more it was a broad-

based and comprehensive concern [...].' She was, he wrote, committed to 'not only the maintenance but also the enhancement of environmental and ecological quality'.

By mid-June 1970, Indira Gandhi had created a Committee on the Human Environment under the chairmanship of Pitambar Pant. This committee was to coordinate India's preparations for the Stockholm Conference. To begin with, it had to prepare country reports for submission to the UN by around mid-1971. While the location was never in doubt—it was Stockholm all the way since the Swedes were the ones who had originally mooted the idea of the conference in 1967—the event itself was now firmed up for June 1972.

Vikram Sarabhai—who had been appointed chairman of the Atomic Energy Commission in May 1966 was keen to ensure that Indian scientists took the Stockholm Conference seriously. He went on to discuss this with Indira Gandhi and Haksar after attending a session of the Scientific Advisory Committee of the UN in late 1968, which had deliberated on the agenda for the Stockholm Conference. Subsequently, on 26 August he organized perhaps the first-ever seminar in India on 'Pollution and the Human Environment' in Bombay. In his remarks, he expressed the hope that in the UN Conference in 1972 'India would be able to make original contributions on the manner in which developing societies are tackling the problems of the pollution of the human environment.'

After the IUCN General Assembly in New Delhi the previous year, teachers, students and other professionals had come together and formed an Indian Society for Conservation of Nature or ISCON—not to be confused with ISKCON, the International Society for Krishna Consciousness! ISCON's objective was to promote and propagate conservation education in schools and colleges. Hari Dang, a well-known conservationist and the principal of the Air Force Central School, wrote to Indira Gandhi on 31 October 1970 on behalf of ISCON, asking her to be its patron. The letter was handed over to Sharada Prasad who wrote on it: 'PM does not normally wish to be patron of an organization.' He sent the letter to Moni Malhoutra to speak to Indira Gandhi about it.

Sixteen days later much to the pleasant surprise of her officials, she agreed, on her own, to Dang's request as a special case. During her entire prime ministerial tenure, which saw her receiving numerous requests, she agreed to be a patron of only two non-governmental organizations—the first was ISCON and three years later, the BNHS. This, above all else, was reflective of her life in nature.

Notes

1.   Parthasarathi (2007).

1971

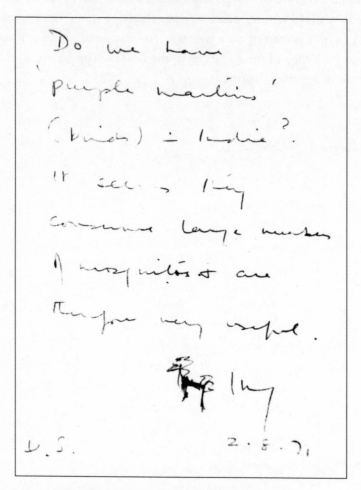

Indira Gandhi's note to Moni Malhoutra; August 1971.

This was to be Indira Gandhi's finest year. But it started with her expressing grave fears on her longevity. She wrote to Haksar on 2 February while in the midst of the election campaign, revealing the type of relationship they shared in those days:

> You know that I am neither morbid nor superstitious but I do think that one should be prepared. The thought of something happening to me has haunted

me—not so much now, as during the last tour—and I am genuinely worried about the children. I have nothing to leave them except very few shares which I am told are hardly worth anything. There is some little jewellery, which I had divided into two parts for the two prospective daughters-in law (this was done before Rajiv's marriage). Then there are some household goods, carpets, pictures, etc. It is for the boys to decide. I personally would like everything to be as evenly divided as possible, except that Rajiv has a job but Sanjay doesn't and is also involved in an expensive venture. He is so much like I was at his age—rough edges and all—that my heart aches for the suffering he may have to bear. The problem is where they will live and how [...] I can only hope and trust for the best. But I should like the boys to feel that they are not quite alone, that they do have someone to lean on.

Elections were held between 1 and 10 March. Nobody had campaigned like Indira Gandhi did. She was indefatigable and relentless, addressing over 400 meeting in about fifty-five days. The 1971 elections have gone down in history as the elections in which 'Indira was the issue'. This was the time in which she came up with her famous slogan 'Garibi Hatao'. This was a telling response to the one-point agenda of the opposition parties which was 'Indira Hatao'. The result was a stupendous victory for her and her party. It was described as an 'Indira wave'—actually it was a hurricane, not just a wave.

She was sworn in as prime minister a third time in five years on 17 March. She was unassailable but was very soon overwhelmed by the crisis on India's eastern border with Pakistan. This issue consumed the rest of the year. It was a massive humanitarian crisis with the influx of about ten million people from what was still officially East Pakistan to India following a brutal crackdown there by the Pakistani army. Indian political opinion demanded military action but she kept cool and firm, focusing on diplomacy instead. Somewhere along the line, she, Haksar and R.N. Kao the head of India's external intelligence agency took a far-reaching decision to train and arm local leaders and cadres fighting for an independent country of Bangladesh. And finally there was a war between India and Pakistan that erupted on the evening of 3 December, with India emerging victorious thirteen days later. March to December 1971 was to see Indira Gandhi at her magnificent best taking on the might of the USA, using the USSR cleverly to strengthen India's regional and global position, mobilizing international opinion in favour of India and providing inspired political leadership to the country's armed forces.

Her impassioned letter to President Nixon of 15 December is now enshrined in India's diplomatic history as are her meetings with him in the White House on 4 and 5 November. But in the midst of all the political confabulations she had found time to write to her friend Lucile Kyle on 3 October:

> [...] I can assure you that nobody here is 'Anti-American'. Nor do I think many of the young people who stand out against American policies are anti-American. We are only hurt that on many crucial occasions your Government shows scant concern for what is happening here and takes such a blatantly anti-Indian attitude. This attitude also seems to go against all that America has stood for. This may serve some domestic or other purpose. But we cannot help feeling that it is an extremely shortsighted view [...]

Even as international diplomacy on the Bangladesh issue gathered momentum, Indira Gandhi kept alive her keen interest in the environment. On 2 August, Moni Malhoutra was flabbergasted on receiving a most unusual slip of paper from the prime minister. Indira Gandhi had doodled a bird, and jotted down:

> Do we have Purple Martins (birds) in India? It seems they consume large numbers of mosquitos and are therefore very useful?

As it turned out, the prime minister had been misinformed. Purple Martins are found mainly in North America. It is generally believed that they feed on mosquitoes but science offers a different point of view—while some insects are a part of the birds' diet, mosquitoes are not, because of the heights at which they fly. It was a quick education in ornithology for Malhoutra and certainly an example of the prime minister's interests even while completely weighed down by crises.

This wasn't the only instance of her ecological commitment—on one occasion, even earlier in the year, she found time to ask Karan Singh how the ban on the shooting of tigers was being implemented in practice. When he told her that some states, most importantly Madhya Pradesh, were still dragging their feet, she was livid and shot off another letter to the chief minister of the state, Shyama Charan Shukla on 5 May:

> Dr. Karan Singh has shown me his correspondence with you regarding the 29 tiger shooting permits issued by your government this year.
>
> I am disturbed and unhappy that your Government should place a higher premium on the interests of shikar outfitters and foreign clients than the far worthier cause of preserving the tiger. This is great disservice to the cause of wildlife preservation, about which there is so much anxiety not only in India but throughout the world.
>
> Were the foreign clients informed by the shikar outfitters that they would not be allowed to take their trophies out? I should also like to know the number of tigers which have already been shot against these permits and how the skins have been disposed. I hope you will try to revoke the unutilized licenses.

The Madhya Pradesh chief minister, whose brother, V.C. Shukla, was a minister at the centre and would later become close to Sanjay Gandhi during the Emergency, replied a month later on 9 June. He told her:

> [...The] sudden ban on shooting of tigers had considerably disturbed the commitments of shikar outfitters with foreign clients. [The] Government decided to relax the ban fixing the maximum limit of permits at a figure not exceeding actual tigers shot during the last year. Hence a maximum of 29 permits were given this year as against 184 last year. Only 11 permits have actually been issued and only three tigers have been shot.

The prime minister was not satisfied and shot off another letter on 26 June in response to the chief minister's reply:

> I have your letter [dated] June 9 regarding the tiger shooting permits. I am afraid I am still left with the unhappy impression that the sudden relaxation of the ban was not justified. I hope no relaxation or exceptions will be made in the coming years, whatever the arguments advanced by the shikar outfitters.
>
> The ban on tiger shooting by itself is not enough. It must be followed by more stringent measures against poaching, habitat destruction and poisoning by insecticides. Attention should also be given to the mis-use of

crop protection licenses. The Govt of Tamil Nadu have recently taken an excellent step by withdrawing all crop protection licenses within a vicinity of 15 miles from wild life sanctuaries and parks. I hope your Government will also initiate measures along these lines so that the maximum benefit is drawn from the present moratorium.

1971 was a year in which she actually turned down invitations that she otherwise would have accepted. When Zafar Futehally, the secretary of WWF-India, asked her to speak at a ceremony in New Delhi to celebrate the organization's tenth anniversary, she replied on 25 June:

> I attach great importance to the work you are doing. Whether I come or not, you have my good wishes. We have some little headway with the State Governments, but the more important task of educating the public remains.

Not long after, on 12 July, Prince Bernhard of the Netherlands and the president of WWF-International, asked to her to come to Switzerland for the tenth anniversary function. She reiterated her earlier stance, only more emphatically, on 29 July:

> I am deeply interested in the Fund's activities in India. However, there doesn't seem to be any possibility of travelling abroad because of the very critical situation which confronts us.

As it turned out, 'the very critical situation' was an understatement, with Indira Gandhi having to deal with the rapidly escalating crisis with Pakistan.

An inter-governmental conference was scheduled to be held on 2 and 3 February at Ramsar, on the Caspian Sea in Iran. The aim was to arrive at an international convention to protect wetlands for which negotiations had been going on for eight years. In many ways, this was to be the first ever global treaty on any environmental issue.

The Government of India had been approached to send a delegation to the Ramsar meeting. On 18 May 1970, J.N. Dixit—later to be foreign secretary and national security adviser, but then a deputy secretary in the Ministry of External Affairs—had written to G.V.T. Matthews, director of the International Wildfowl Research Bureau which was coordinating the conference. The letter was quintessentially bureaucratic:

> Subject: International Conference on the Conservation of Wetlands and Waterfowl-Iran 1971
>
> I am directed to acknowledge receipt of your letter No GVTM/LVR dated May 4, 1970 on the subject mentioned above addressed to the Minister of Foreign Affairs Government of India which is receiving attention.

No doubt, Matthews would have smiled when he received this communication straight out of Sir Humphrey Appleby's book.[1] However, when matters remained at a standstill, Matthews, in sheer desperation, approached his good friend Salim Ali. In a 12 October 1970 letter, he urged Ali to goad the Government of India into taking a decision regarding participating in the Ramsar conference and communicating that decision to him since time was fast running out.

Salim Ali took up the matter with the officials in the Ministry of Food and Agriculture. Letters were exchanged and, to cut a long story short, official permission was granted only on 22 January for a two-man delegation to represent India at Ramsar. At the instance of the prime minister, one of the two was to be Salim Ali himself.

At Ramsar, countries signed off against the 'Convention on Wetlands of International Importance especially as Waterfowl Habitat'. The convention came into force in December 1975 but India finally ratified it only in February 1982—long after even Pakistan had in November 1976.

By mid-May, Indira Gandhi had approved India's official submissions to the UN Conference on the Human Environment to be held in Stockholm in June 1972. There were three reports—on environmental degradation, human settlements and natural resources. Today, such reports would appear commonplace. But this was mid-1971—India had little or no history when it came to engaging with such issues; no trained administrators; and few environmental scientists and other experts. If, despite these hurdles, the 1971 reports came to display a high degree of intellectual solidity, it was thanks to Pitambar Pant and his colleagues.

Indira Gandhi herself was not expected to attend the conference. Then things changed. Maurice Strong, the Canadian appointed to be the secretary general of the conference, knew that Brazil and India were perceived as being key representatives of developing countries (China was admitted to the UN only in October 1971). Well aware of the importance of bringing these two countries on board at an early stage, Strong landed up in New Delhi to make a personal appeal to the prime minister to attend the conference. The meeting took place in mid-June 1971 and Strong himself recalled it in his memoirs thus:

> It was immediately clear to me that she had a deep interest in and knowledge of the environment. I then raised a point I thought would get her attention. "If the developing countries sit out of the Conference" I suggested delicately, "it would leave the issue in the hands of the industrialised countries [...]
>
> "Why not come to the Stockholm Conference yourself, as you are the best possible person to articulate the concerns and interests of the developing world?" I asked. "I can promise you a special place on the program". She immediately accepted, much to the surprise, and in some quarters, consternation of her officials [...]

Moni Malhoutra, who was present when Indira Gandhi met Maurice Strong, put it less dramatically. According to him:

> Indira Gandhi had said clearly to Strong that she would like to come and would do her best to be there [at Stockholm]. The only caveat was that in June 1971, with the Bangladesh crisis gathering pace, she obviously could not give a cast iron assurance to an event a year away.

By September, the refugee crisis had reached cataclysmic proportions—with West Bengal bearing the brunt. Most of Indira Gandhi's time now was being consumed by sensitizing the world to it. Yet on 1 September, while in Calcutta to review the extremely serious situation, she found time to write a message for the American magazine *Architectural Forum* which was bringing out a special issue on Buckminster Fuller. She wrote:

> With Buckminster Fuller, architecture has gained new meaning. Like others of the profession he deals with living and working spaces, but he is a path-finder in his obsession with the architecture of the universe. His innovations in the use of materials and shapes follow from his endeavor to understand what science and man can do to each other.
>
> Every conversation with Buckminster Fuller is an exhilarating experience. He so clearly sees unity amidst specialization that he can dismiss the pervasive feeling that technology is a tool-room of destruction [...]

It goes without saying that Indira Gandhi considered urban design as an essential element of environmental planning. This is further evident in her response to an 18 December proposal from K.P. Singh, director of DLF, a private real estate company, who wished to build a 400-room luxury hotel in collaboration with Sheraton International, in the heart of Lutyens' Delhi, at 14–16 Aurangzeb Road, with all its broad roads and lush greenery. Indira Gandhi directed:

> [...] an over-all view should be taken of the planned re-development not only of Connaught Place Complex, but the remaining parts of Lutyens' New Delhi also [...] No multistoried buildings should be sanctioned in the Bungalow area of New Delhi without such an over-all view being first taken.

It was clear that she believed then that the DLF hotel plan would jeopardize, in the words of Moni Malhoutra, 'the whole future and character of Lutyens' New Delhi'. But she was to change her mind five years later. On 31 March 1976, the Tata-owned Indian Hotels Company Limited submitted a proposal to the NDMC for a five-star hotel on a four-acre plot just down the road from DLF's own site. Two days later, the NDMC accepted the proposal with unusual alacrity and then signed a formal agreement on 18 December 1976. The hotel opened in October 1978.

There is nothing in the written records to explain the reversal in Indira Gandhi's stance, although there have been speculations that Sanjay Gandhi had caused this change after meeting with the chief executive of Indian Hotels, Ajit Kerkar. All that can be definitely said is that by August 1975 itself, she had approved the lifting of the ban on high-rise structures in the NDMC area and in the rest of the city as well. One clue to her thinking could well be her observation on a file which her aide Salman Haidar had put up to her, raising some questions on the floor area ratio being allowed to be 4 in some cases as opposed to the normal 2.5. She noted on 29 August 1976:

> [...] the choice is between going skywards or occupying more agricultural land. The proposal [for enhanced floor area ratio] should be accepted.

On 10 September, even as the crisis on India's eastern borders was ballooning, Indira Gandhi met a small group of conservationists that included Karan Singh, Billy Arjan Singh, Kailash Sankhala, Zafar Futehally and Anne Wright. They were to play an important role in her life thereafter.

Moni Malhoutra had suggested their names—including M.K. Ranjitsinh's and Inspector General of Forests R.C. Soni's—although Indira Gandhi knew the invitees personally. In the meeting, the prime minister heard two views: one that had argued that India needed a new national law for wildlife protection and another one, articulated by Soni that held that existing laws enacted by state governments should be enforced more strictly.

Billy Arjan Singh launched a tirade against the prime minister and her officials; he said that wildlife, which was being slaughtered across the country, commanded no priority in Indira Gandhi's scheme of things. The prime minister 'flinched, became defensive, almost pensive'.[2] Anne Wright, in turn, spoke of how Calcutta had become the main centre of the illegal trade in furs and skins, and how sanctuary after sanctuary had fallen prey to poaching on account of the famine in the late 1960s.

Indira Gandhi did not say much at the meeting but what little she said had made it clear that the situation prevailing then was unacceptable and that some new initiative was required on the part of the central government.

Immediately after this meeting, Billy Arjan Singh wrote to Indira Gandhi on 15 September:

> All heads of state must relax and if ever you do wish to see some of the animals of India, I suggest you visit the Dudwa sanctuary which I hope will soon attain the status of a national park. I have the best swamp deer population of the Indo-Nepal subcontinent and regularly bait the resident tigers.

Indira Gandhi noted on his letter three days later:

> I should love to do so but I have already expressed my fears of the bull in a china shop actions of my security.

Two young people came into Indira Gandhi's official orbit during the year. The first was thirty-two-year-old M.K. Ranjitsinh. Hailing from the princely family of Wankaner, he was one of Malhoutra's IAS batchmates. He had served for a few years in Madhya Pradesh, and in May, came to New Delhi as a deputy secretary in the Ministry of Food and Agriculture dealing with farm mechanization. Malhoutra had asked him to the prime minister's meeting with conservationists on 10 September. The previous year Indira Gandhi had seen Ranjitsinh's thirty-minute film on Indian wildlife which included a most unusual scene of a tiger climbing a tree in Kanha. It was not too difficult for Malhoutra to convince Indira Gandhi that his friend was wasting his time dealing with farm mechanization and was just the right person to take forward her environmental agenda. Ranjitsinh was very soon appointed as the first deputy secretary looking after both forests *and* wildlife.

Then there was the thirty-one-year-old Ashok Khosla whose name came to be known in government circles thanks to Professor Roger Revelle, a well-known scientist at Harvard University. In March, Revelle wrote to Indira Gandhi, Vikram Sarabhai and a few others recommending Khosla as 'a young, bright Indian colleague who, having completed his PhD in physics at Harvard, wanted to come back to his country'. Sarabhai interviewed him and asked Khosla to join his staff. But with Sarabhai's death in December, that did not happen and thereafter Pitambar Pant pursued Khosla. Finally, in mid-1972, Khosla with Indira Gandhi's approval joined the newly created Department of Science and Technology. More than anyone else, it was he who established the foundations of environmental analysis and appraisal of irrigation, power, fertilizer, refinery and other development projects in a systematic manner.

Notes

1. One of the three stars of BBC's highly acclaimed serial *Yes Minister.*
2. Hart-Davis (2005) and Sahgal (2008).

1972

*Indira Gandhi addressing the UN Conference on the Human Environment,
Stockholm; June 1972.*

*The good times of 1971 continued for a while. In March, elections to state
assemblies were held as scheduled and the Congress, basking in the glory that
Indira Gandhi had engineered in Bangladesh, won 70 per cent of the seats. The
1967 debacle in six states was forgotten. She now had her own chief ministers in
every state, with her ally as chief minister in Tamil Nadu. After the elections were
over she devoted her time to winning peace with Pakistan. After considerable
suspense, the Simla Accord between the two countries was signed on 2 July.
The Accord has been both hailed and run down in each country. But what is
clear is that just as she had demonstrated unflinching courage in the months
of 1971, she demonstrated the highest statesmanship at Simla.*

*But unmistakable signs of trouble even before Simla were evident and
she sensed it strongly. On 29 April, Indira Gandhi wrote to Dorothy Norman
from Cochin:*

If at all there is a good God presiding over our destinies, I think He is excessively occupied in thinking up problems for India to solve! No sooner is one crisis over, than something else is looming over the horizon. Success brings its own responsibilities and also evokes jealousies. This year is going to be a testing of our nerves.

Her son's Maruti project had become a subject of much acrimony both in Parliament and outside. But she continued to defend it to the hilt. On 1 May, she wrote to Niren Ghosh, a Communist MP and an acerbic critic of Maruti's affairs:

> [...] So far as Sanjay Gandhi's project is concerned, he has bought all his machinery in India. No release of foreign exchange for machinery or components or technical assistance like drawings and designs has been asked for or granted. As regards your reference to reports current in the market, I can only say that there is no dearth of persons willing to indulge in mud slinging or of those who exploit such unverified reports for political propaganda. Incidentally, I received your letter after it was published in some newspapers.

On 22 October, while giving Lucile Kyle news of the family and of her travels to Darjeeling and Bhutan, she let slip:

> Here we have our usual crisis and troubles. I just do not know how we are going to get over them all.

By the middle of December, Haksar had decided to quit and Indira Gandhi did not make an effort to hold him back. But she did write quite an extraordinary letter to him on 25 December:

> My dear Haksar Saheb:
>
> I have hesitated to write or speak. Some things are too deep for words or it may be that I am not enough of a writer to find the right words [...] During a period which spanned so many crises you have stood like a rock [...] Your guidance has been invaluable [...] There can be no doubt that your retirement will greatly diminish the efficacy of the PM's Sectt and will be a great loss to me.

She was to utilize his services thereafter in a variety of ways, first in 1973 as a special envoy to Iran and then as special emissary for talks with Pakistan and

Bangladesh and thereafter, as deputy chairman of the Planning Commission from January 1975 onward. But he was no longer her day-to-day moral and ideological compass. Many years later, H.Y. Sharada Prasad was to write in an obituary of his one-time colleague that the reason why Indira Gandhi and Haksar, who were so close to each other for decades, drifted apart was because 'there was growing friction between sovereign and chamberlain over the doings of the prince'.[1]

∾

The armed forces had won a glorious victory for India in the war with Pakistan in December 1971. Indira Gandhi was now viewed with unparalleled respect and awe by the men in uniform. General Sam Manekshaw, the military hero of the war, was Indira Gandhi's personal friend. On 30 May he received an unexpected letter from her:

> All over the world there is a wave of concern for the conservation of the environment. We in India are no less involved in this movement. Since there has been a serious depletion of our wild life and forest wealth, we must now spare no effort to save what remains of our wild life.
>
> Reports of the indiscriminate killing of animals in different parts of the country, notably the Himalayas by army personnel are disturbing. Even the hangul, one of the most endangered of all animal species in the world has not been spared and there are instances of its having been shot near Dachigam. There are also reports of fish being killed by the use of explosives.
>
> The Armed Forces are the guardians of our national interest in peace as well as in war. Hence we need their help in preserving our fauna and flora, so essential not only for the beauty of our country but also for the well-being of our people.
>
> Please take personal interest and try to educate your officers and men that such destruction is harmful to the country's interest. Not only should they themselves not indulge in shooting, they should also help to prevent any poaching.
>
> Firm instructions should be issued about the strict observation of Game Laws by all officers and men. Commanding officers should be held responsible for their units, and infringements should be punished by Court Martial.

Similar letters were sent to other service chiefs as well as central para-military organizations like the Border Security Force (BSF). Each one of them, including the famed General Manekshaw, responded to her, immediately reassuring her that her instructions would be obeyed right away and there would be no question of condoning the infringement of any law. In about four months, the nation would get a tough new law for wildlife protection and a year hence Indira Gandhi was to repeat this exercise of writing to the service chiefs and others, re-emphasizing her ecological concerns.

On 15 March, Zafar Futehally, the secretary of WWF-India, wrote to Indira Gandhi:

> The World Wildlife Fund-International has decided to mount a massive fund raising campaign for conservation of the Indian Tiger [...] Basically the scheme involves the setting up of large reserves with a viable tiger population and then to protect these habitats as effectively as possible.
>
> [...] I am sure you yourself will welcome this initiative but quite rightly Guy Mountfort feels that in this important matter he should have your blessings before any formal decisions are taken. [...] Mountfort intends to come out to India on the 16th of April, and I wonder whether you would agree to meet him for a few minutes either on the 16th or 17th.

Prince Bernhard of the Netherlands as chairman of WWF-International followed this up with his own letter dated 23 March:

> At the time of the meeting of the International Union for the Conservation of Nature in New Delhi in 1969, you were good enough to express your support for the efforts of the World Wildlife Fund in trying to save the Tiger from extinction [...]
>
> The World Wildlife Fund is therefore preparing a major international campaign to raise the equivalent of one million dollars to save the Tiger in the three countries where sufficient numbers remain to offer a reasonable chance of success [...]
>
> I have asked one of our Trustees, Mr. Guy Mountfort, who is now directing this project, to seek an audience with you in order to outline

this proposal in more detail [...] He will be in Delhi in mid-April and I shall be grateful if you find it possible to grant him an audience.

Indira Gandhi did indeed grant Guy Mountfort an 'audience' as the prince had requested and gave her 'blessings' to him as Futehally had beseeched earlier.

18 April was a busy day for the prime minister. Parliament was in session. Preparations for bilateral talks with Pakistan were on. The prime minister of Nepal was visiting. Yet, she took out an hour to meet Mountfort, Futehally and Charles de Haes. Mountfort has published an account of this historic meeting in his memoirs and in a couple of other books but I prefer to use his unpublished memo of 30 April which he sent to his fellow trustees.

> Prime Minister Gandhi is a remarkable woman, with a genuine interest in both wildlife and conservation [...]
>
> Her manner in discussion alternates between feminine charm and impressively masculine decisiveness [...] She was determined, she said, that everything possible should be done to save the tiger. We had been told that if we could secure her personal interest in Operation Tiger, success would be assured. After hearing the details, she indicated her full approval. When we raised the question of a coordinating committee, she said she would form a special "task force" which she would require to report to her personally. I obtained her permission to announce this at my press conference the same evening. To everyone's astonishment the task force was formed the next morning and it met the following day.

Guy Mountfort did announce the formation of this task force in his press conference on the evening of 18 April, and the executive committee of the IBWL met on 19 April to finalize details of the proposed task force for 'Operation Tiger'. Zafar Futehally who had attended this meeting reported the next day to his colleagues at WWF-International in Switzerland:

> I am glad to say that Karan Singh was very enthusiastic about "Operation Tiger". He had a meeting with the Prime Minister after our India International Centre meeting and obviously the PM injected some of her own enthusiasm in him.

On 7 September, Karan Singh sent Indira Gandhi the final report of the Project Tiger Task Force. She had personally included Anne Wright and Duleep Matthai, the conservationist, in this task force. It had taken about four months of intensive work to produce this very first institutional design for saving the tiger and securing its habitat in the process. Nine days later after having read the report in its entirety, the prime minister replied to Karan Singh:

> The financial estimates are much higher than I had expected. In the present situation, there is need for the utmost economy. Each item of expenditure should, therefore, be carefully scrutinized [...]
>
> I hope the Joint Directors will work and live within the Reserves, rather than at the District Headquarters. Their immediate and whole-time presence inside the areas of their jurisdiction will be an important factor in the Project's success. I hope they, as well as their subordinate staff, will be carefully selected and properly motivated [...]
>
> It will be necessary [to involve] each of the concerned State Governments in the processing of the Report, because the Project cannot succeed without their willing and whole-hearted cooperation. They must be handled with the utmost tact [...]
>
> When Guy Mountfort and Charles de Haes met me, they mentioned a figure of one million dollars only as a tentative target. However, they did say that this figure could be revised upwards depending on the estimates of the Project Report. While I agree that Project Tiger should essentially be an Indian venture, we should not hesitate to secure as much international assistance as possible [...] I am emphasizing this point in anticipation of likely criticism within the country against the allocation of so much of our own scare resources to this project [...]
>
> I find the enlarged Reserves which have been projected will almost all contain large numbers of human beings and domestic cattle. This will add to the problems of management. [...] Even if the villages cannot be outside the Reserves, they may well have to be regrouped so that there are large uninterrupted areas of wilderness in each Reserve, apart from the sanctum sanctorum. An attempt may also have to be made where alternative grazing arrangements are not feasible to introduce stall-feeding of cattle [...]

I agree that the Task Force should now be replaced by a Steering
Committee.

It is abundantly clear that the prime minister was taking extraordinary
interest in the design of Project Tiger, getting into its nitty-gritties. That
Project Tiger was to be formally launched on 1 April 1973—less than a
year after the Indira Gandhi–Guy Mountfort meeting—and that it was a
success is owed hugely to the personal interest the prime minister evinced
at every step. Of course, the WWF helped but it is not often realized
that it contributed just around 13 per cent of the project cost in its first
phase of six years. The project was financed overwhelmingly by Indira
Gandhi's government and she was acutely conscious that considerable
money—almost six crore over a six-year period—was being spent for tiger
protection—in an era when resources were extremely scarce and competing
demands were many.

On 18 November, Indira Gandhi decided to support the
recommendation of the IBWL to have the tiger declared as the national
animal. Dr Karan Singh had on 9 July 1969 chaired the IBWL meeting
that decided to have the lion as a national animal. Now, about three-and-
a-half years later, the same Dr Karan Singh explained that the main reason
for changing over from the lion to the tiger was that tigers were found
in many parts of the country—in about sixteen states—while lions were
confined to only one state. The fact that the protection of the tiger had now
assumed international importance must also have steered the changeover.

Following the directions he had received after the 10 September 1971
meeting, Ranjitsinh had drafted the Indian Wildlife Conservation and
Management Bill, 1972 by mid-February, and it was to be taken up by the
cabinet by mid-March. But there was a constitutional hurdle to be overcome
since 'wildlife protection and conservation' was a subject allocated to the
states under the Indian Constitution. However, the same Constitution
also provided a way out—a resolution by legislatures of two or more states
authorizing Parliament to pass such legislation.

On 12 April, Indira Gandhi herself wrote to all chief ministers to get their support for the national law as required under the Constitution:

> I have written to you in the past about wildlife conservation and management. Although there is now greater consciousness about this problem than a few years ago, we have not been able to significantly arrest the continuing decline of our fauna, including many endangered species. Poaching is on the increase and we continue to receive reports of a lucrative trade in the furs and pelts of even those animals, like the tiger, whose shooting is in law prohibited throughout the country.
>
> My colleague, the Agriculture Minister has already written to you about the difficulties of controlling trade and taxidermy in the absence of a uniform Central law applicable to the entire country. Experts are unanimous that only an integrated and countrywide policy of wildlife conservation and management can arrest the present precipitous decline.
>
> It is for these reasons that we now seek your cooperation to enact Central legislation on wildlife conservation and management. [...]
>
> This is not a political issue. It concerns the survival of our famous natural heritage. Past experience reveals the limitations of the regional approach [...] The Centre and the States must now act in concert on the basis of common legislation which should be strictly enforced.

The letter had an immediate impact. By the end of July, legislatures in eleven states had passed resolutions asking Parliament to pass a law for the protection of wildlife. The way was now clear for Parliament to legislate. On 21 August, the Lok Sabha passed the Wildlife (Protection) Bill, 1972 after a three-hour debate. The Rajya Sabha gave its approval five days later after a much shorter deliberation of about an hour. It was notified on 9 September and thereafter it was made applicable in various states on different dates as determined by their respective legislatures. Most of the states were to come on board by the end of 1973.

When Indira Gandhi wrote the letter to the chief ministers, she sent them a copy of the Indian Wildlife Conservation and Management Bill, 1972. But ultimately Parliament passed the Wildlife (Protection) Bill, 1972. Something had happened between April and July 1972 to change the name of the Bill. That *something* was this: even though Ranjitsinh himself preferred 'Conservation and Management', Indira Gandhi wanted 'Protection'. Her argument was that 'Protection' was simple, direct and easily understood. 'When you protect you can't kill'—this was a remark she made to Moni Malhoutra. In her view, 'Conservation and Management' was liable to misinterpretation and did not convey forcefully the objective of the new law.

The law was to be a turning point in the history of wildlife protection in India and put in place an elaborate system and network of protected areas including national parks and sanctuaries. Without this law, to put it bluntly, there would have been very little wildlife left to protect and conserve.

On 12 April, Indira Gandhi launched the National Committee for Environmental Planning and Coordination (NCEPC)—a committee that was to play a crucial role over the next eight years. The Committee on the Human Environment she had set up in the Planning Commission to prepare India for the 1972 Stockholm Conference now became part of the NCEPC that was chaired by Pitambar Pant.[2] The prime minister started her inaugural address thus:

> As one who has been deeply interested in this subject since long before I had ever heard of the word ecology, I am naturally glad that people have woken up to the dangers which threaten the world as we know it. I know that in this audience I am speaking to the converted and many of the things which I say may be obvious to you but I feel they have to be said for a larger audience also because there is not sufficient appreciation of this in the country as a whole.

For the first time, she would speak publicly on the broader issue of environment and growth; so far, she had focused predominantly on wildlife:

> [...] The environmental problems of the industrialised countries are the result of earlier exploitation as well as of present affluence while those of the developing countries are primarily determined by the manner in which machines are used or abused. In the poorer societies these problems are essentially those of inadequate development and of continuing poverty,

unsafe drinking water, malnutrition, poor sanitation, inadequate housing
and disease. [...]

We should move away from the single dimension model which
equates growth of GNP with development. [...] Our attention cannot
be diverted from the main question before us which is to bring basic
amenities within the reach of our people and to give them better living
conditions without alienating them from nature and their environment.
[...] Concern with economic and social development need not be a choice
between poverty and pollution.

Indira Gandhi's firm stance was, to some degree, in response to an early
March report prepared by a team of academics at Massachusetts Institute
of Technology (MIT), released at the Smithsonian Institution in
Washington. Titled 'The Limits to Growth' and based on computer models,
it hit international headlines—not least because it appeared just three
months before the Stockholm Conference. The report virtually predicted
doom for the world given the inexorable rise in population, the build-up
of pollution and the increasing depletion of natural resources like oil.
The tenor was distinctly Malthusian while the tools of analysis were very
sophisticated.

Indira Gandhi asked Pitambar Pant to study 'The Limits to Growth'.
On 19 April, T.N. Srinivasan, one of India's most distinguished economists
who had been working with Pant, prepared a devastating critique which
was just two pages long. This critique had already been articulated in her
speech launching the NCEPC a week earlier and it was to be an important
part of her Stockholm address as well. Srinivasan raised two questions and
he contended that answers to them were not to be found in 'The Limits
to Growth'. The questions were:

(a) What is a reasonable norm for 'desirable level of living [that the report
talked about]?'

(b) Given that the levels of living in a small section of the world
population are very high and that of the overwhelming section very low,
relative to this desirable level, what are the policies that will reduce these
disparities across nations and across groups within a nation in a reasonable
period so that we can think of stabilizing at that level?

Pant sent this on to the prime minister with his observations; saying that the authors of 'The Limits to Growth' seemed to be completely ignorant of 'a perfectly valid implication' that could be drawn from their own computer models that 'poorer countries must develop their economies as rapidly as possible to reach the global equilibrium while the richer countries should immediately slow down their economies to reach the same point'. This was to be the leitmotif of not just her Stockholm speech two months later but of other speeches she would give in global forums. It is a theme that continues to be argued by India even today.

Besides working relentlessly to protect wildlife, Indira Gandhi kept alive her passion for birds. On 12 May, Salim Ali—who had been regularly sending the prime minister each volume of the richly illustrated *Handbook of Birds of India and Pakistan*—sent his fifth volume, which evoked this response from her five days later:

> I am delighted to have your latest Handbook of Birds. Unfortunately, it is no longer possible for me to go on bird watching expeditions. I seem to be as great a curiosity as any bird to many watchers, including the security people! However, in my garden in Delhi and on tours I keep a sharp look out and it is surprising how many birds I do manage to spot sometimes even from an open jeep.

Indira Gandhi, as a birdwatcher, was aware of the importance of wetlands. The Bharatpur Bird Sanctuary, about which Salim Ali kept writing to her, was just one habitat that was under considerable stress. At her behest, the NCEPC now took up the issue of wetlands, and Pitambar Pant wrote to Salim Ali on 10 July:

> You will recall that in February last year an International Conference on Conservation of Wetlands and Waterfowl Resources was held in Ramsar, Iran in which you participated on behalf of the Government of India [...] It may be expected the Government of India will soon be approached to sign the Convention.
>
> [...] It has occurred to me that it may be worthwhile to constitute under the auspices of the National Committee on Environmental

Planning and Coordination, an expert group with you as Chairman, to examine the various issues related to this convention, and to develop an action programme for the conservation of wetland ecosystems.

This was to begin India's systematic efforts to identify wetlands as well as measures to protect them.

Towards the end of 1972, Salim Ali raised another issue that would bring the BNHS into public limelight and invite an inquiry by a Parliamentary Committee. On 6 October, Ali wrote:

[…] Let me give you a summary of the background. The Bombay Natural History Society had been trying since the twenties to initiate a long-term programme of bird migration study by ringing birds, which is now the recognized universal technique in order to obtain authentic factual data. […] I may mention that of the 2100 odd species and sub-species of birds found in the Indian subcontinent almost 300 are migratory, of the movements and dispersal of which practically nothing is known […] It was not until 1960 that the next opportunity came, rather fortuitously for the Society to resume its bird migration study. At that time the World Health Organisation had become seriously concerned about a 'mysterious' anthropoid-borne virus which seemed to have suddenly erupted in the Kyasanur forest area in Mysore […] This virus appeared to be closely related to a group of viruses whose natural focus was known to lie in Western Siberia […] the problem of how the virus bridged the intervening gap of 3000 km called for investigation.

Salim Ali then went to say that, at first, the World Health Organization (WHO) funded the investigation which was carried out in collaboration with Russian virologists. But after two or three years, WHO funding stopped and the responsibility was passed on to the US Army Medical Research Department which was already engaged in similar studies in Southeast Asia. When the US Army decided to discontinue its research in this area, it transferred the funding responsibility to the Smithsonian Institution which funded the BNHS beginning 1968–69. He continued:

The grant of Rs 1,44,440 ($19,000) for the current year (July 1972 to June 1973) which was duly approved by the Screening Committee of the

UGC is the one now held up by the Ministry of Finance. In the absence of these funds, all our bird migration studies will have to be suspended and unless the situation can be eased without delay we may be obliged to wind up the project.

Salim Ali ended the letter by admitting that 'this is a rather lengthy and disjointed "summary" of the position'. But he need not have worried. Even before his letter had arrived, on 28 September itself, Indira Gandhi had been briefed about his woes by Moni Malhoutra and Indira Gandhi instructed him two days later:

Shri Salim Ali should certainly be helped for his project.

Salim Ali's funding was now assured till the end of March 1974. In 1974, a fresh controversy would erupt but the prime minister was to be unfazed.

Indira Gandhi's desire to secure the well-being of birds would also dictate her response to Orissa Chief Minister Biswanath Das, when he requested her to lay the foundation stone for the navy's Boys Training Establishment at Chilka. While she had approved of the project two years earlier, with certain conditions to be fulfilled by the navy, she now perceived fresh complications. On 4 May she wrote:

I would have liked to come. But the National Committee on Environmental Planning and Coordination (NCEPC) has asked some fundamental questions about the location of the [Boys' Training] Establishment at Chilka. I believe the Committee considers Paradeep a better location. The Ministry of Defence is therefore examining the matter further.

As it happened, Defence Minister Jagjivan Ram was less than enthusiastic about moving the BTE from Chilka to Paradeep. Consequently, Indira Gandhi wrote to him on 19 July:

It is true that I had approved the earlier proposal to locate the [Boys' Training] Establishment on the Chilka Lake. However, since work on the project has not yet begun, and further facts have been brought to light by the National Committee for Environmental Planning and Coordination, my earlier decision need not be regarded as sacrosanct. Chilka's unique and internationally important ecosystem embraces much more than the bird life of the area, although even the bird life is sure to be greatly disturbed by the large-scale construction activities which the project will necessitate. In due course of time, the Establishment will also generate economic activity and attract further clusters of population thus threatening all that Chilka is today. Hence the question arises whether we should run this risk when equally good sites are available for the Establishment.

Annexure II of the note accompanying your letter itself raises doubts about the wisdom of the proposed location. Although the relative weightage of the different criteria has not been indicated, I find that Paradeep scores over Chilka, being classified as highly suitable on five counts out of ten as against four for Chilka. Further, it has the inestimable advantage of providing facilities for boat work than Chilka's shallow waters. Again, while Chilka is unsuitable from the point of view of access to the sea, Paradeep is highly suitable. [...]

I suggest, therefore, that the Boys' Training Establishment be located at Paradeep instead of Chilka. I have spoken to the Chief Minister of Orissa, who has no objection to the change [...]

That she had done a complete U-turn in two years was entirely Pitambar Pant's doing. Given his equation with Indira Gandhi, what he said carried a great deal of significance for her. In this instance, he believed that the BTE project at Chilka was a recipe for ecological disaster.

The Chilka story was not over. It would revive a year later and Indira Gandhi would do yet another U-turn to come back to her original decision of 1970!

Mira Behn, born Madeline Slade in England, was one of Mahatma Gandhi's closest disciples. In the 1950s, she had settled down in Vienna, but remained in touch with Indira Gandhi. In December 1966, she wrote to her about Robert Bolt's screenplay for a film on Gandhi. On 26 May 1972, she wrote another of her 'My dear Indira' letters:

You will remember our conversation in Vienna [in 1971] regarding the Pollution problem. I am following developments with keen interest, and shall be grateful if you will remind your secretary to send me relevant literature on the subject. I hope India is going to be well represented at the Stockholm Conference.

She need not have worried one bit; fighting pollution was very much on Indira Gandhi's agenda. Even before receiving Mira Behn's letter, on 17 May, the prime minister had written to her Industry Minister Moinul Haq Choudhury:

One of the major problems engaging the attention of most countries is that of the pollution of air, water and soil resulting from the operation of industrial plants. In our country [...] all available evidence indicates that we already face qualitatively significant problems. Also our limited resources will be totally inadequate to deal with this problem if we neglect it now and allow it to grow. Hence the urgent necessity to take preventive measures now.

The Water Pollution Bill has already been passed. I do not know what is delaying the Bill regarding air pollution. This should be expedited. In the meantime, some measures can be taken immediately in order to minimize the pollution caused by the new projects—perhaps under the provisions of the Industrial Development and Regulation Act for the private sector and by executive orders for the public sector. For instance, would it not be possible to stipulate in the industrial licenses given to enterprising companies that the entrepreneur must satisfy an agency designated by Government that the plant proposed to be installed has adequate provisions for preventing pollution?

Please have the whole matter examined in your Ministry so that a specific set of executive measures can be worked out in a month's time.

The prime minister seems to have been misinformed by her aides regarding the law to prevent and control water pollution—that was to be passed by Parliament only two years later. The law against air pollution that Indira Gandhi wanted expedited became a reality only in 1981.

What can't be gainsaid though is that this letter shows Indira Gandhi's commitment to combating pollution. Since this was the very peak of the licensing era that was to be abolished lock, stock and barrel in July

1991,[3] there was some willingness to make industrial licensing more environmentally friendly and place a premium on projects with superior pollution control technologies.

By September C. Subramaniam had taken over as minister of industrial development and he sent a long response to the prime minister's letter to his predecessor detailing how her instructions were going to be implemented. On his letter of 14 September, she wrote four days later:

> 'Executive orders against pollution and formation of state [pollution control] boards. We should advise State Governments on these two points.'

Indira Gandhi had already given a clue to what she might say at Stockholm at the launch of the NCEPC. Preparations for her formal speech, which was to be delivered on 14 June, started sometime in late April. The NCEPC sent her drafts, as did her own officials. Sharada Prasad, Indira Gandhi's sounding board, must have taken all of them into account. Interestingly, in the Haksar archives, I discovered a draft speech that P.N. Haksar had sent Indira Gandhi and Sharada Prasad on 9 June with the note: 'I place below a somewhat enlarged and revised draft of a speech to be made at the UN Conference on Environment at Stockholm.'

This must have been his reworking of the basic draft incorporating whatever Pant, Malhoutra, Khosla and others had to offer. It is impossible to figure out what Haksar added—this was an era well before 'track changes'—but that he would have made hugely substantive contributions is almost certain. I checked the final speech as delivered against the Haksar draft. They are 75 per cent identical. If they differ, it's because major new themes had been added—for instance, a whole paragraph on war and peace (hugely relevant in the context of what was happening then in Vietnam) and the stockpiling of nuclear weapons. Most crucially, the line in Indira Gandhi's speech that has made it immortal was missing in the draft in the Haksar archives. She obviously added this between 9 and 13 June when the speech had to go for printing:

> Are not poverty and need the greatest polluters?

Notice, she is asking a question. But the world read it differently. In fact, that line has gone down in history as:

Poverty is the greatest polluter.

Another version has it as

Poverty is the worst form of pollution.

Maurice Strong—the secretary general of the conference, who was on the podium when Indira Gandhi spoke—wrote in his memoirs in 2001: 'Also at the opening session Prime Minister Gandhi made what was one of the most influential speeches of the entire conference, with its theme that "poverty is the greatest polluter of all".' Martin Holdgate, an eminent scientist who was part of the British delegation, wrote in 2013 that 'the pollution of poverty [was] a concept developed to telling effect by Indira Gandhi in the most memorable of the speeches at the Conference'.

Clearly, what she is widely accepted as having said and what appears in her printed speech are not identical. She may well have changed the speech as she was speaking—she had been known to do that. But Malhoutra who was with her then was certain she made no change in the written text.

While the encomiums for her speech were to come much later, at that point of time, what she said was barely covered by the US media. The head of the US delegation, Russell Train, made no reference to it in his report back to Washington. A few days later, on 26 June, while Indira Gandhi's speech found mention in a piece by Robert Bendliner in the *New York Times*, there was, surprisingly, no reference to the catchy 'poverty-pollution' line:

> Mrs Gandhi put the case for the world's poor with eloquence "…how can we speak to those who live in villages and in slums about keeping the oceans, the rivers and the air clean, when their own lives are contaminated at the source?" […]
>
> Mrs Gandhi went on to plead that a higher standard of living for the impoverished people of the earth be achieved without alienating from their heritage, "without despoiling nature of its beauty, freshness and purity so essential to our lives". And she sought to assure those same people that a regard for ecology would not work against their interests but, on the contrary, would enrich their lives.

The Indian media had some coverage of Stockholm but, again, the phrase which was to become the prime minister's calling card for posterity was conspicuously absent. Here is what *The Hindu*, often called India's newspaper-on-record, had to say about her speech.

Cooperative Approach to Environment: PM's Call

Stockholm, June 14:

The Prime Minister Mrs. Indira Gandhi today warned the UN conference on human environment against an ecological crisis adding to the burdens of the weaker nations by the introduction of new considerations in political and trade policies of the rich countries. [...]

After referring to various aspects of the problems of human environment Mrs. Gandhi said they were all inter-linked and that there was no alternative to a cooperative approach on a global scale to the entire spectrum of these questions.

Dealing with the problem of population growth, Mrs. Gandhi said it was an over-simplification to blame all the world's problems on over-population. Countries with a small fraction of the world's population consumed the bulk of natural resources [...]

Another leading daily, *Hindustan Times*, had the following dispatch on its front page as a box item:

Atharva Veda quoted

Stockholm, June 14

Prime Minister Indira Gandhi today quoted a hymn from the Atharva Veda to emphasise India's age-old concern over ecological balance.

Mrs. Gandhi, who was addressing the UN Conference on Human Environment said: Modern man must re-establish an unbroken link with nature and with life. He must again learn to evoke the energy of growing things and to recognize, as did the ancients in India centuries ago, that one takes from the earth and the atmosphere only so much as one puts back into them.

She then quoted the hymn which runs as follows:

What of thee I dig out,
Let that quickly grow over,
Let me not hit thy vitals.
Or thy heart.

The Times of India had the most detailed report of the 14 June speech the next day. Under the front-page headline—'Poor Nations Merit Attention: Indira'—and another in the inside pages—'India's basic principles outlined by Indira'—it carried extracts of the speech extensively. It also stated that the prime minister got a standing ovation at the end of her lecture with only the Chinese delegate in the hall sitting passively and with Pakistani delegates joining the applause after some initial hesitation. While the line that has made this speech illustrious wasn't mentioned even in passing, some compensation seems to have been made in an editorial on 16 June:

> [...] Mrs Gandhi pointed out in her address to the conference that the colonial powers had raised themselves to their present levels of prosperity—and pollution—by exploiting the third world as well as the underprivileged among their own people. Poverty, she insisted was the greatest source of pollution [...]

The Swedish media gave Indira Gandhi phenomenal coverage—but for a different reason. In his speech the Swedish prime minister had accused the USA of an 'ecocide' in Vietnam. On her part, Indira Gandhi said:

> The most urgent and basic question is that of peace. Nothing is so pointless as modern warfare. Nothing destroys so instantly, so completely as the diabolic weapons which not only kill but maim and deform the living and the yet to be born; which poison the land, leaving long trails of ugliness, barrenness and hopeless desolation. What ecological projects can survive a war?

Indira Gandhi became a sensation in Stockholm for this particular paragraph—which, incidentally, got added by her between 9 and 13 June. In the Haksar archives, there is a telex message from the Indian embassy giving the English translation of an article by Anne Norlin that had appeared on 18 June in *Aftenbladet*:

> Indira Gandhi, the 54-year-old Prime Minister of India took Stockholm by storm. Everywhere she went, Swedes took up long and spontaneous applause. She took the time to sign autographs and shake hands. It is just ten years since Nikita Khrushchev was here. He was guarded by

hundreds of policemen. U.S. President Richard Nixon would not dare make an intermediate stop at Arlanda.

Indira Gandhi—the world's most powerful woman and ruler of the world's most populous nation and six months ago one of the parties to a merciless war—could walk about in Stockholm nearly unprotected.

Indira Gandhi is the victor of the Environment Conference. Her speech at Folkets House Wednesday brought the House down. [...]

It is difficult to pinpoint an exact moment or occasion when her Stockholm speech came to acquire its iconic status. While it certainly created ripples— when any reference to Stockholm was made in the international community in the 1970s and 1980s, her speech would invariably get mentioned—its impact remained restricted to a limited circle for quite some time. It was most probably in the run-up to the famed Rio Earth Summit of 1992 that it was rediscovered with a bang, as it were. That it continues to resonate is proved by the fact that Karl Mathiesen wrote an article in *The Guardian* on 6 May 2014 with the title 'Climate Change and Poverty: Why Indira Gandhi's Speech Matters'. The Pakistani economist Tariq Banuri told me in September 2009 that her speech ranks with Rachel Carson's book of 1962, Paul Ehrlich's book of 1968, and *The Limits to Growth* study of 1972 as one of the four crucial milestones in the global environmental discourse.

India's delegation at Stockholm was itself high-powered, undoubtedly the most high-powered of all among the 113 countries attending. Three cabinet ministers accompanied the prime minister—Karan Singh; C. Subramaniam, the minister of planning and science and technology; and I.K. Gujral, the minister of works and housing. This demonstrated how seriously Indira Gandhi took the Stockholm Conference and the issue of the environment.

The Stockholm Conference adopted a declaration on 16 June, the fourth paragraph of which was derived almost entirely from Indira Gandhi's speech. It read:

In the developing countries most of the environmental problems are caused by under-development. Millions continue to live far below the minimum levels required for a decent human existence, deprived of adequate food and clothing, shelter and education, health and sanitation. Therefore, the developing countries must direct their efforts to development, bearing in mind their priorities and the need to safeguard and improve the environment. For the same purpose, the industrialized countries should make efforts to reduce the gap between themselves and the developing countries. In the industrialized countries, environmental problems are generally related to industrialization and technological development.

The declaration also identified twenty-six principles for environmental management and planning both at the national and international level. The fourth principle was put forward by Karan Singh after a discussion with Indira Gandhi. It was incorporated *in toto* in the declaration, and read:

Man has a special responsibility to safeguard and wisely manage the heritage of wildlife and its habitat, which are now gravely imperiled by a combination of adverse factors. Nature conservation, including wildlife, must therefore receive importance in planning for economic development.

People attribute a range of meanings to Indira Gandhi's Stockholm speech. One Nobel Laureate was sufficiently moved to write to her on 30 June. Norman Borlaug was no stranger to India. He had a long association with the nation's agricultural scientists and had played a crucial role in triggering India's Green Revolution. The issues he raised in his letter continue to resonate even today:

I want to congratulate you for the strong position you took at Stockholm defending the rights of developing countries of the world to use science and technology to improve the standard of living of their people.

It is frightening to see the influence and power that has been acquired by a small group of well-organised eco-maniacs in a number of affluent nations [...] The case of DDT illustrates the point very well. Two weeks ago, in the USA its use was banned [...] The decision will have adverse indirect effects [...]

I urge you as leader of India and also effective spokesman for the developing nations to continue to demand the right to use these and other chemicals and technology which are needed to increase production, to alleviate human suffering and misery and bring a higher standard of living to all people [...] I assure you that in this battle against the eco-maniacs you have my whole-hearted support and I am confident I speak also for thousands of scientists who have been muffled by the hysterical campaign of the environmentalists.

This was not the first time Borlaug had written to her—having shared, from time to time, his views on Indian agricultural research in some detail. He had come to India most recently in March 1971 when, with the prime minister's approval, he had been treated as a 'state guest'—considered a rare honour and privilege.

Indira Gandhi's response on 9 September was more measured and poured considerable cold water on the scientist's sweeping generalizations. She conveyed to him in no uncertain terms that she did not accept his characterization of the protesters as 'eco-maniacs'. Her letter is worth quoting at length because it shows her concerns for both an improvement in living standards as well as conservation.

> It is naturally important for all of us who live in the developing countries that concern for ecology and conservation should aim at improving the lives of the people. We do acknowledge the beneficial impact of fertilisers, insecticides and weed-killers on our agricultural and public health programmes. The Green Revolution, taking place in many parts of the Indian countryside, depends in no small measure on the increased use of chemical fertilisers and timely plant protection measures for its success. Malaria, once a scourge in large tracts of India, has been greatly controlled by the use of D.D.T. However, in recent years there has also been evidence of certain adverse side effects and long-term disadvantages of the indiscriminate use of some of these chemicals.
>
> We are interested in the world debate on the use of persistent pesticides like D.D.T [...] Our policy decisions on the use of these compounds should be based on well-established scientific facts keeping in view the needs of the economy and taking into account the economic gains as also the social costs.
>
> We are deeply concerned at the erosion of natural resources and the encroachment on natural beauty that is taking place at such a tremendous

rate all over the world. However, accentuated economic growth cannot
lose sight of ecological considerations [...]

I hope the scientific community, of which you are a leader, will
develop integrated methods combining biological and agronomic controls
with the judicious use of chemicals to raise crop yields and fight insect
and pest menaces with minimum damage to nature's balance. The aim
must surely be to act and maintain a higher environmental quality along
with decent material standards of living.

Without meaning to, the legendary scientist's letter reeked of arrogance. The
prime minister's reply gently but surely reminded him that there were more
things in the world than were dreamt of in his philosophy. Coming from a
leader who had done much to make the Green Revolution a reality—and
addressing a scientist who had rendered yeoman service to make such
advance possible—the letter had a touch of irony as well.

To be fair, Borlaug had huge admiration for Indira Gandhi and she,
in turn, had enormous respect for him. He would continue to write to her
regularly—for instance on 25 April 1977 when she was no longer prime
minister and he praised her handsomely for her leadership in making the
Green Revolution possible; and in April 1980 when he welcomed her
becoming prime minister again.

One of the outcomes of the Stockholm Conference was the decision to
establish a new institution—the United Nations Environment Programme
(UNEP). For a few months, the choice of location was debated—it was
to be either New Delhi or Nairobi. There was not much enthusiasm in
India but the Kenyans were very keen because this was to be the first UN
agency located in the developing world outside North America and Europe.
The contest, if at all there was one, continued until early November 1972
when India gracefully withdrew in favour of Kenya, citing its fraternal
links with that country.

Two Indians must have made that decision in favour of Kenya. One
was Haksar who had studied with Jomo Kenyatta, the first president of
Kenya, at the London School of Economics in the late 1930s and had a

pretty dim view of the UN system itself. The other was Indira Gandhi who had been to Kenya twice, and was a close friend of Kenyatta. Kenyatta had himself been an admirer of Nehru.

There may also well have been a realization in India that Kenya had lobbied more skilfully. Besides, India's own relations with the USA were not particularly warm with Nixon and Kissinger itching to teach the country a lesson.

There is yet another reason attributed for India's withdrawal. Lars-Goran Engfeldt, the Swedish diplomat, later wrote that President Kenyatta threatened to expel all Indians from Kenya unless Indira Gandhi withdrew the Indian offer. I find this very hard to believe and in the absence of any documentary evidence it has to be considered as speculation.

Two days after speaking in Stockholm, Indira Gandhi was back in India. The Simla Summit, between her and the prime minister of Pakistan Zulfikar Ali Bhutto, began on 28 June. The bilateral agreement was signed on 2 July. Indira Gandhi then decided to stay back and take a holiday for a few days in Simla—from where she wrote to the chief minister of Bihar, Kedar Pande on 5 July, just a day before leaving for the capital:

> I enclose a copy of a letter I have received from Shri Umesh Prasad Verma, MLA regarding [the] preservation of wildlife in Bihar. You already know of my interest and concern. The Bihar Assembly has not yet passed a Resolution in favour of a Central legislation on this subject about which I wrote to you on April 12, 1972. I hope you will get it expedited. I am disturbed what Shri Verma says regarding the release of forest land. Please look into this personally and stop it.

She was referring to a letter she had received from one of her party colleagues who also happened to be a member of the state wildlife board. He had complained to her that the state government was trying to denotify large tracts of forest land in the Kaimur plateau. Her letter stopped the denotification.

The letter from Simla was not the only time Indira Gandhi tried protecting forest cover and trees.

Just before leaving for Stockholm in early June, Malhoutra had been in touch with the NDMC regarding expanding the tree plantation programme in the nation's capital. M.W.K. Yusufzai, its president, replied on 31 May, and on his letter, Indira Gandhi remarked:

> Why not have a programme of tree planting on new roads—Gul Mohar on both sides one road, Jacaranda on another and so on. The trees chosen should be sturdy and not messy. Flowering trees are best.

This dispatch might have been propelled by a letter she had earlier received on 17 April from Dr B.P. Pal—a world-famous authority on roses; and one of India's most distinguished agricultural scientists whose role in establishing the foundations for the Green Revolution has not been fully appreciated:

> [the] unique character of this Garden-City and its surroundings is being transformed as a result of concrete paving and if the present rate of construction is kept up the trees from New Delhi and its surrounding areas will have no place to breathe or spread their roots.

He also informed Indira Gandhi that many of the trees on several roads in New Delhi would complete their life span over the next seven years, and that he wished to launch a programme involving various residents' associations across different areas to save trees.

Five days later, the prime minister replied to Dr Pal, saying:

> It is an excellent idea to have a group dedicated to saving trees. This is a cause which I cherish and I wish your efforts success [...] If you need my help, do let me know.

Her subsequent instructions to aides and other officials were to result in a frenzy of tree-planting activity. The vice chairman of the Development Authority, Jagmohan, who was going to be a major figure during the Emergency period three years later, took up the cause in right earnest. The prime minister was informed on her return from Simla that all the agencies in Delhi would combine and plant 'two lakh plants of over one and a half feet height'.

143

Despite Indira Gandhi's best efforts to keep the green lungs of Delhi alive, there were times when she had to make hard choices. Sometimes, these provoked complaints—as, on one occasion, on 12 October. She received an irate letter from Mridula Sarabhai—the sister of Vikram Sarabhai and a political activist close to Sheikh Abdullah. While she had been very critical of Nehru's handling of the Kashmiri leader in the 1950s, there remained a deep personal bond between her and Nehru's daughter. Mridula Sarabhai wrote:

> I hope to be excused for taking your time for a matter which may look a trifle but actually it is not so. I do so because you are a lover of nature and trees and I think you believe that as far as possible, trees should be saved and planning should be such that it does not unnecessarily destroy them.
>
> Leading newspapers [...] have expressed concern at the unwarranted and merciless destruction of trees that is going on [in the city of Delhi...] Trees are felled under various pretexts. Currently it is said that these trees are being cut down to widen roads for the Asian Exhibition. The Exhibition will last for a few weeks. Then what? For how many years will Delhi suffer without trees? [...]

Indira Gandhi's response was super-fast. She replied the very next day:

> I am indeed concerned at the cutting down of trees. However, roads have to be widened, not just for the Fair [Exhibition] but because of the health and safety of citizens. I have repeatedly instructed all concerned to avoid the cutting of trees, unless absolutely necessary. Now that you have reminded me, I shall write to them again.

Environmentalists worry about a single objective. Political leaders have to balance competing demands and choose, if not the most desirable, then at least the least undesirable option from among them. In this case, it turns out that Indira Gandhi had approved the cutting of trees in order to widen the road leading to the Delhi airport. She had felt, in her own words, 'I had no choice but to agree'. But Mridula Sarabhai's irritation made her rethink the wisdom of what she had done. She could not undo it but at best could limit the damage.

A year later she was to again take up this subject with Radha Raman, the chief executive councillor of Delhi. She wrote to him on 30 December 1973:

> [...] Trees give parts of Delhi special beauty. But there are many areas without them. I have for long been urging the importance of greater tree plantation and although the Municipal authorities and the DDA have been taking considerable interest, the survival rate of new trees is poor. If each householder could be asked to look after just one sapling near his house, water it and protect it, the city will wear a different look in a few years. Citizens should not be fed only with general talk but motivated to take up specific tasks, no matter how small.

A number of Members of Parliament (MPs) interested in nature conservation would write to the prime minister from time to time. She would take these letters seriously and use them to question the chief ministers on what was happening in their states.

Dr Karni Singh was one such MP representing Bikaner in Rajasthan. He wrote to Indira Gandhi on 4 December, telling her that he had recently visited Udaipur and had been 'shocked to see that the lovely hills which were once full of tigers and wild animals are now barren rocks because of cutting of beautiful trees of this forest area continuously'. Four days later she expressed her distress to Dr Karni Singh on the information he had given and told him that she would be asking the chief minister of Rajasthan, Barkatullah Khan to take a personal interest and address his concerns.

Nothing much happened for a few months till, on 22 March 1973, the prime minister got a letter—a cry of pain, really—from a middle-level forest official in Jhalawar, Rajasthan complaining that the hills surrounding the historical town of Bundi, which were once full of forest cover, were now almost naked. That this letter reached the prime minister and that she took immediate note of it was remarkable.

On 6 April 1973, she wrote to Barkatullah Khan again, reminding him that he had not yet responded to her concerns regarding what Dr Karni Singh had said and now a similar issue in Bundi had been brought to her notice:

Of all our states, Rajasthan most of all needs to look after its existing forests. I am told that four whole forest divisions which existed in 1947 have totally disappeared. [...] I hope you will take personal interest in this matter, because of the crucial importance off adequate forest-cover to Rajasthan's long-term economic development.

B.B. Vohra was an IAS officer who belonged to the very first batch that had been recruited through competitive exams in 1948. In 1967 he came to the Government of India as joint secretary in the Ministry of Agriculture. Passionate about land and water issues, he wrote a long paper titled 'A Charter for Land' in September 1972 that was to receive much acclaim. Yet, acutely aware that his writing was having no policy impact whatsoever, he brought his work to Moni Malhoutra's attention who, in turn, alerted Indira Gandhi to it. This paper resonated with her. She read it carefully and sent it around to the Planning Commission and the Ministry of Agriculture for them to follow-up. On 29 December 1973, she would record her comments on an internal note on Vohra's recommendations:

> Based on our experience of soil erosion, droughts and floods and their increasing liability, a large part of which has to be borne by the Centre, it argues in favour of a creation of a Central Land Authority or a Land Use Commission. I am in broad sympathy with its approach and feel that we can no longer afford to neglect our most important natural resource. This is not simply an environmental problem but one which is basic to the future of our country. The stark question before us [is] whether our soil will be productive enough to sustain a population of one billion by the end of this century at higher standards of living than now prevail. We must have long-term plans to meet this contingency.
>
> Please request B. Sivaraman to assemble a small team in consultation with the Agriculture Ministry which could go into this matter further and report within the next two months, how such a Commission could be set up, the discipline it would represent, the manner in which it would function and the degree of financial autonomy which it would require.

It is sad but true that her observations still remain relevant and the fact that land is a state subject under the Constitution has prevented any meaningful action by the centre as she and Vohra had wanted.

◆

In the 1970s, human settlements and the environment were seen as two sides of the same coin. In fact, the first UN Conference on the Human Environment at Stockholm in June 1972 was followed by the first UN Conference on Human Settlements at Vancouver during May-June 1976. One of the three reports India had submitted to the Stockholm Conference was titled 'Some Aspects of Human Settlement in India'.

On 17 September, Indira Gandhi wrote three letters. In the first, to deputy chairman of the Planning Commission, D.P. Dhar, she expressed her astonishment that Bombay was yet to have a metropolitan authority. She was worried that the Backbay Reclamation Scheme, that was being pushed through by the state government, was wholly incompatible with the Twin City project (the project to set up New Bombay).

Her second letter was to V.P. Naik, the chief minister of Maharashtra, which went thus:

> I am concerned to hear reports that the Twin City Project, which was launched with such fanfare, is now almost at a standstill [...]
>
> I am also concerned that the Bombay Metropolitan Region does not yet have a unified Metropolitan Authority, which could plan and direct a rational allocation of resources [...] The Backbay Reclamation Scheme [...] is wholly inconsistent with, and indeed threatens to make nonsense of the Twin City Project.
>
> [...] My own concern arises not only from considerations of the quality of our urban environment, but a more immediate fear that a fine city with great traditions should not, for want of foresight or adequate determination, drift into a Calcutta-type of situation. [...]
>
> The large concentration of commerce and industry in the Greater Bombay-New Bombay region gives the entire country a stake in its future. We simply cannot afford mass social discontent arising out of urban chaos.

The third letter she wrote was to Governor of Maharashtra Ali Yavar Jung, drawing his attention with personal notes to 'disturbing reports about the handling of urban problems in Bombay' and to the 'many unsavoury allegations being made'.

Most concerned by what the prime minister wrote, the chief minister sent an elaborate four-page defence of his policies and actions. He claimed that contrary to her apprehensions:

> [...] the development of the commercial area in the Backbay area will not in any way affect the development activities of CIDCO [City and Industrial Development Corporation] which will mainly concentrate on the setting up of new industries and expansion of existing industries in the Twin City.

He went on to reassure her that: 'We do not, therefore, apprehend the development of the Backbay area will compete with or adversely affect the prospects of developments in the Twin City.'

But Indira Gandhi was not to be rebuffed easily. She failed to get the Backbay Reclamation Project reviewed but the Bombay Metropolitan Regional Development Authority came into being on 26 January 1975.

Her interest in New Bombay was to continue. On 10 June 1973, impressed by an article on New Bombay written by the noted planner-architect Shirish Patel in *The Hindustan Times*, and by another article by Ajit Bhattacharjea on the same subject in *The Times of India*, she wrote to minister of urban development in Maharashtra, Rafiq Zakaria, drawing his attention to these reports and saying: 'I hope you will continue to pursue these ideas, so that the Twin City becomes an example to the rest of India.'

Manohar Singh Gill, later to be chief election commissioner and MP, had been deputy commissioner of Lahaul and Spiti—when they were a part of an undivided Punjab—in the early 1960s. He wrote a book on his experiences there and asked his friend K.K. Sharma of *The Statesman* in Chandigarh whether it would be possible to get the prime minister to write the foreword since his writing dealt with mountains and nature—subjects she was so fond of.

Gill had no contact whatsoever with the prime minister and neither did Sharma. But Sharma presumably met Sharada Prasad and left the manuscript with him. There was no expectation that Indira Gandhi would actually write a foreword to a book[4] by somebody she didn't know or hadn't even heard of. But on 17 July, Indira Gandhi—much to the author's amazement—did, in fact, write the foreword. It was short but replete with personal reminiscences that offered a peek into her personality. She wrote:

> [...] As one who loves the mountains, I have deep concern for the mountain people. In order to survive, they must have great faith and fortitude. They are sturdy and hard-working, yet full of laughter and gaiety.
>
> Shri Manohar Singh Gill's book has awakened old memories of my own crossing of the Rohtang with my father many years ago. I am sorry that lack of time prevented us from proceeding to Lahaul and Spiti and since then I have nursed a desire to go to this lovely part of our country. Shri Gill captures something of the majestic beauty of this area [...]

Her wish to get to Lahaul and Spiti was to be fulfilled just two months later. She would go back a second time—just about three months before she was to be shot dead.

Notes

1. Prasad (2003).
2. Pitambar Pant demitted office as member of the Planning Commission on 2 December 1971. It had been speculated that Indira Gandhi was unhappy with him for his opposition to the nationalization of banks and other initiatives. He was also a very sick man by then. In any case, by mid-February 1972, his appointment as chairman of NCEPC had been announced. This would not have happened had she not been fond of him and had she not respected his intellectual abilities.
3. Ramesh (2015b).
4. Gill (1972).

1973

Indira Gandhi at the Butchart Gardens, Victoria, Canada; May 1973.

1973 was to be a horrible year for Indira Gandhi. The monsoon failed miserably and shortly thereafter oil prices trebled. The combination was deadly and sent inflation to over 20 per cent for the first time in India's history. Haksar was no longer by her side daily. She also lost another close colleague and friend from the Haksar circle, Mohan Kumaramangalam in a plane crash in May.

Indira Gandhi's own assessment of 1973 is in two letters of hers to Dorothy Norman. The first was on 24 April and she wrote:

> *This year we in India seem to have more than our share of difficulties. They are partly inherent in the process of growth but aggravated by the war and the burden of ten million refugees followed by terrible drought which has caused shortage of food and drinking water and of power which has affected our industries also. So the Opposition is having a field day.*

The second letter, written on 3 June, is comparatively longer and more poignant. It reveals Indira Gandhi in a depressed state of mind, something unusual for her considering her public persona. She confessed:

> *I have been very moody these days […] I am feeling imprisoned by the security people […] but also and perhaps more so because of the realization that I have come to an end, that there's no further growing in this direction […] Is it because the situation is so maddeningly frustratingly difficult—because one cannot see a solution—simply because the steps to be taken depend not on a limited group with whom one has rapport and can therefore guide, but on numbers who cannot think beyond their own advantage and find glee in things going wrong […] It is exasperating to see people enmeshed in pettiness and greed and meanness.*

Her spirits appeared to have revived in June when she went to Canada and spent time visiting the famous Butchart Gardens near Victoria. She also flew across the border literally for a few minutes to see her good friend Lucille Kyle at Lake Placid.

Even though the year was turbulent, her courage had not deserted her. The newly appointed chief economic adviser in the Ministry of Finance had suggested the toughest anti-inflation package possible. He was convinced that it was desirable but was not sure if it was feasible. Indira Gandhi told him to worry about the economics while she handled the politics. The man in question was Dr Manmohan Singh, later to become the prime minister himself in May 2004.

On 1 April, Project Tiger was formally launched at the Corbett National Park. While Indira Gandhi was against large meetings in forest areas, she allowed Karan Singh to go ahead with his plans. She also sent a message placing Project Tiger in a larger context:

> The Project is a comment on our long neglect of our environment as well as our new-found, but most welcome concern for saving one of nature's most magnificent endowments for posterity.
>
> But the tiger cannot be preserved in isolation. It is at the apex of a large and complex biotope. Its habitat, threatened by human intrusion,

commercial forestry, and cattle grazing must first be made inviolate. Forestry practices, designed to squeeze the last rupee out of our jungles, must be radically reoriented at least within our National Parks and Sanctuaries and preeminently in the Tiger Reserves. The narrow outlook of the accountant must give way to a wider vision of the recreational, educational, and ecological value of totally undisturbed areas of wilderness [...]

The prime minister personally handpicked Kailash Sankhala as the first director of Project Tiger—this despite the fact that he was not popular at all in the forest bureaucracy and many were irked by his working style and actions. If Indira Gandhi persisted with him it was because she knew he was passionate about conservation and also incidentally, enjoyed the full backing of Padmaja Naidu.

On 23 April, she wrote the foreword to Sankhala's *Tigerland*—a book based on his Nehru fellowship project. The foreword drew from her own personal experiences over the years and was memorable both for its content and how it was conveyed:[1]

An inborn love of animals and the wild was encouraged by my parents and enhanced by Kipling's jungle stories and later by Jim Corbett's entrancing description of tigers in the Kumaon Hills [...]

Once driving through a thickly wooded area in Karnataka, I was told by my hostess that although there was a large variety of wild life, the season and time of the day precluded our meeting any. Hardly had she ended her sentence when right in front of us I espied a tiger—the largest I have seen—stepping on to the road. Hearing the car, he paused to look us up and down. So did we. After a while he crossed over but squatted behind a bush by the roadside. We drove as softly as possible and stayed alongside to see more of him. I was lost in admiration of his grace and the controlled strength of the muscles rippling under his splendid coat. I would gladly have remained there but the others were impatient of the delay and consequent disruption of the already tight schedule.

My next acquaintance with a tiger was even closer. We had three cubs and one of them we called 'Bhim' became exceedingly ill. I sat up nights to give him the prescribed treatment. On the third day, he lifted his head and from then we were good friends. [...]

Not long after my father was presented a beautiful tiger skin and, for want of a better place, I kept it in our State sitting room. But every time I saw it, I felt a pang at the thought of this proud king of the jungle being so humbled, and within a week I gave it to an American visitor.

By mid-May 1973, there was a mini-crisis confronting Project Tiger. Moni Malhoutra discovered that Rs 20 lakh raised by WWF was about to be spent for purchasing an aircraft for use by the Project Tiger officials—it emerged that this was Karan Singh's idea. Indira Gandhi was livid and shot off a letter to her ministerial colleague on 25 May:

> I understand that the money which the World Wildlife Fund has raised so far for Project Tiger is being used to purchase a small aeroplane.
>
> Have we got our priorities wrong? I should have thought it is more important to get the Project going on the ground than to spend so much money on an aircraft which will yield no direct benefit to the parks and their animals […] An aeroplane would be a luxury which we can ill-afford.

This was not the end of the story. Karan Singh, who obviously didn't get the message that the prime minister was sending, tried to justify his stance. This forced her to write to him a second time on 28 June:

> You wrote to me on May 28 and June 22 regarding purchase of aircraft for Project Tiger. I have thought deeply over the matter and have considered the reasons you have urged but I still feel this proposal should not be pursued at this stage. I hope you will inform the World Wildlife Fund accordingly.

That closed the matter once and for all.

Later in the year, on 29 October, Air India organized a 'Night of the Tiger' in London to raise funds for Project Tiger. It was chaired by Lord Mountbatten and managed to raise a decent 5500 pounds in just a few hours. The highlight was the message from the prime minister who invoked one of the most famous poems by William Blake:

> "What immortal hand or eye could frame thy fearful symmetry?" Thus wrote Blake of the tiger. To us who have had occasion to have closer acquaintance with this magnificent beast, the tiger is not a symbol of fear but of grace and strength. He is king of the Indian jungle.

Wanton hunting, commercial poaching and the pressure of human and cattle populations on the great forests of India have reduced the tiger to its present perilous position. We are determined to reverse this trend in spite of the many competing claims on our resources. The tiger can no longer roam the length and breadth of India as it did even 25 years ago but our effort is to preserve it for posterity in eight of our national parks. The world, not India alone, would be the poorer if this splendid creature were to become extinct.

There was a slight error in her message. She mentioned eight national parks for the protection of the tiger population. The fact was that there were nine. The ninth was the Sunderbans. On 24 January, Indira Gandhi had paid a flying visit to this ecosystem straddling both India and Bangladesh, with the largest mangrove forest in the world. The prime minister took a steamer cruise along the creeks and rivers that define the Sunderbans, and ventured close to the Lothian and Prentice Islands—both habitats of the tiger. While she did not get to spot the national animal, her trip led to the inclusion of the Sunderbans as the ninth of the tiger reserves that would form Project Tiger—the Project Tiger task force having recommended eight.

By the end of the year 1973, Indira Gandhi, in a rather unusual way, came to the aid of WWF-India—which had played an important role in Project Tiger, and which remained a valuable source of information for the prime minister on ground realities plaguing wildlife protection. Anne Wright, WWF-India's founder-trustee—for whom Indira Gandhi had a soft corner—had asked the prime minister for a message for a film premiere to raise funds for her organization, and the prime minister readily obliged on 19 December:

The World Wildlife Fund has been a major factor in mobilizing people throughout the world for the cause of conservation. I am glad that it is enlarging its activities in India. Although public opinion in our country is still not fully alive to this problem, consciousness is slowly spreading and more and more people are becoming involved. As one who is deeply committed to the preservation of our unique fauna, I hope the people of India will come forward in increasing numbers to participate in and generously support programmes for the conservation of our dwindling wildlife.

∽

Billy Arjan Singh belonged to the princely family of Kapurthala in Punjab. He had a long association with Indira Gandhi—one of his cousins had been a fellow patient of tuberculosis along with her mother in the early 1930s in Switzerland; his paternal aunt was health minister in Nehru's first cabinet; and his mother's Lucknow house had been rented to Indira Gandhi and her husband in the late 1940s.

Billy Arjan Singh had settled down in Kheri in the Terai region of Uttar Pradesh. He had attended the meeting of conservationists called by Indira Gandhi in September 1971, and had given her a long talk on wildlife protection. They had communicated with each other often since then, and she liked him even though she knew he had the remarkable ability of rubbing officialdom the wrong way. On 16 July she wrote to him:

> I am delighted to have your book "Tiger Haven". I have been deeply concerned about saving our tiger. Any imaginative plan to preserve wildlife has my unreserved support. Our main problem is to create the right public consensus. I hope your book will help in this.

Singh had reared a male leopard cub he called Prince and released it into Dudhwa—his beloved sanctuary. He was now looking for a female cub he could rear and release so that Prince's biological desires would be fulfilled. In September he wrote to Indira Gandhi who had, just then, been presented with two leopard cubs from Bihar. While these were to be sent to the Delhi Zoo, Indira Gandhi—recalling her maverick friend's quest—presented the cubs to him instead. Singh named them Harriet and Juliette after two young English women he had just met. Subsequently, he was to chronicle the fates of Prince, Harriet and Juliette.

31 December was the last day for Moni Malhoutra as the prime minister's aide, after seven years in her secretariat. One the very last letters he dictated and dispatched was to Billy Arjan Singh:

> Before handing over charge today, I would like to give you one piece of good news. The Prime Minister has written to the Chief Minister [of Uttar

Pradesh] requesting him to give the whole North Kheri Forest Division the statutory status of a national park with the present Dudhwa sanctuary forming its sanctum sanctorum, free of commercial exploitation. In recognition of the work which you have been doing, she has also asked the Chief Minister to give you every encouragement.

Could you wish for a better New Year's gift?

Indira Gandhi's letter to the chief minister of Uttar Pradesh, H.N. Bahuguna, on the same day was warm in praise of Billy Arjan Singh. The unusually long letter speaks for itself:

> I do not know whether you are familiar with the Dudhwa sanctuary in the North Kheri Forest Division. It owes much to the dogged determination and single handed efforts of a man called Arjan Singh, whose book Tiger Haven I have recently read. His efforts to rehabilitate panthers bred in captivity back into the wild have attracted international attention.
>
> Dudhwa has the potential of being the finest wildlife reserve in the whole of North India if it is properly cared for. If developed, it will offer attractions surpassing those of the Corbett National Park, portions of which are now going to be submerged by the Ramganga Reservoir. I am told that the North Kheri Forest Division still retains 10–15 tigers, a viable nucleus for further growth. It has also the largest herd of swamp deer (1500) in the entire subcontinent as well as a variety of animals, including [the] marsh-crocodile. The State should safeguard this precious asset which apart from its recreational and educative value can earn substantial revenue from tourists.
>
> Unfortunately the nature of commercial forestry operations presently under way in that area makes this unlikely unless you take a personal interest and give a new lead. The whole of the North Kheri Forest Division (c. 220 square miles) should be given the statutory status of a national park.
>
> The present Dudhwa Sanctuary (32 square miles) should be the sanctum sanctorum of the national park where no commercial forestry should be allowed. Controlled exploitation of major forestry timber may be permitted in the remaining two-thirds of the park and a buffer zone created where cattle grazing and extraction of dead wood by concessionists can go on. There should be an absolute ban on the auction of minor

forest produce which does enormous damage to wildlife habitat. A non-shooting buffer of about 5 miles should be established right round the park so that animals straying outside do not get killed.

A small number of people may be affected by these decisions. If so, I am sure a satisfactory solution could be found for their problems, as has been done in some of our reserves like Kanha and Gir.

I hope you will give every encouragement to Shri Arjan Singh. He has ploughed a lonely furrow for many years. It is easy to come by arm-chair conservationists but rare indeed to find a man with the dedication and perseverance to act in support of a cause he loves.

A few weeks later Billy Arjan Singh, moved by this letter, wrote to Indira Gandhi requesting her to be a patron of the Tiger Haven Wildlife Trust. She, however, very politely declined. It took three years, even at the height of Indira Gandhi's powers, for the Dudhwa National Park to actually come into being on 1 February 1977.

∾

On 3 December, Indira Gandhi had sent a slip of paper to Karan Singh, as was her custom, which read:

Isn't the black buck a prohibited animal? I have heard many are being shot indiscriminately even quite close to Delhi, for example, in Dadri and other places. Will you please check and advise what steps we could take to maintain greater vigilance and prevent the destruction of this beautiful animal.

Then, later in the month, on 27 December, Indira Gandhi wrote to the chief ministers:

[...] I think that the time has now come to introduce more specialized management for our parks and sanctuaries [...] Throughout the world wildlife management is becoming increasingly specialized. Our conservation efforts cannot yield the desired results without a similar effort on our part [...]

Despite the enactment of the Wildlife (Protection) Act, 1972, enforcement at the field level leaves much to be desired. [...] I continue to receive reports of even endangered animals listed in Schedule I of the Act being killed illegally. The tiger and leopard have received considerable publicity in this connection. The black buck merits similar vigilance. It would be desirable to set up black buck sanctuaries wherever sizeable herds of this rare and beautiful animal remain.

Indira Gandhi is associated with tigers. Her role in highlighting the importance of blackbucks is not widely known. Tal Chappar in Rajasthan had already been declared a blackbuck sanctuary in 1971, but following this letter from the prime minister, other states also started recognizing the importance of protecting the animal. For instance, Karnataka notified the Ranebennur Blackbuck Sanctuary in 1974, and Gujarat went one step further and notified the Velavadar Blackbuck National Park in 1976. Moreover, her letter also helped initiate separate wildlife wings and departments in various states.

It appears ridiculous that an all-powerful prime minister would plead with one of her colleagues for Rs 1.5 crore for wildlife protection. But this is exactly what happened on 12 November, when Indira Gandhi got to know that the Planning Commission had cut the allocation for a particular scheme for wildlife conservation from Rs 2.5 crore to Rs 1 crore. She dashed off a letter to D.P. Dhar, or 'DP' as she called him—one of her closest advisers, a part of the Haksar circle, and a vital figure in 1971 during the Bangladesh crisis—and gave him an elaborate epistolary lecture:

> Our fauna is already dangerously depleted. It is an asset to be cherished and conserved. In recent years, I have had to intervene more than once with the States in this matter. It is essential for the Centre to give a lead [...]
>
> Inevitably planning concerns itself primarily with our future. But it should take as liberal a view as possible of the need to conserve our past heritage. Many of our monuments require special repairs, restoration and better protection. Excavations, especially of historical sites on the periphery of growing urban concentrations like Mathura must be undertaken before they are swallowed up by town developers [...]

We have set up very few museums since independence, and they are given ridiculously small sums for adding to their collections [...] Museums must be provided adequate funds [...] and steps should be taken to establish more museums [...] Unless this is done, our country will continue to be denuded of its artistic heritage.

Our fauna, monuments and art treasures contribute distinctively to the quality of the nation's life. They are a source of pride to us all. I hope the Fifth Plan allocations will give due consideration to these intangible but important factors.

D.P. Dhar had no option but to agree to the prime minister's request for a Rs 1.5 crore increase in the allocation for wildlife conservation. A few weeks later, on 7 December, he was again told a few home truths about forest policy by Indira Gandhi:

[...] forests and sanctuaries are gradually being eroded. While industrial forestry must naturally be given first priority, we must ensure that certain areas are preserved in their pristine condition in the interest of our wild life without plantation of exotics. In such areas, forestry operations should be restricted only to those measures which are needed for the sustenance of our animals, rather than earning of revenue. If the States can set aside even two or three percent of their total forest area for this purpose in carefully selected regions, it would be a great gain.

This is the closest Indira Gandhi would ever come to advocating a policy of keeping specified areas inviolate—although she did not use that word. Many years later her idea would get reflected within tiger reserves—each of which now has a delineated 'core' area which is sacrosanct and a larger 'buffer' area.

Laws passed by Parliament do not automatically apply to Jammu and Kashmir—where the state legislature is empowered to pass its own laws. Thus, the Wildlife (Protection) Act, 1972 could not by itself be enforced there.

Indira Gandhi had been, from time to time, getting reports from Kashmir on the sale of the skin and fur of animals on the banned list. On

16 December, she told Kashmir's Chief Minister Syed Mir Qasim that the 'fauna not only of Kashmir but also of the entire country will continue to be subject to the caprice and greed of tourists and traders'. She added that by not adopting the 1972 Act, the state had created a 'premium on the illegal killing of endangered species, including those whose habitat is Kashmir'. She went on showing her knowledge of and concern for the state:

> I do appreciate that a considerable number of Kashmiris are engaged in the fur and skin trade. But there seems to be a misplaced apprehension among them that the adoption by Kashmir of the Central law will deprive them of their livelihood. This is not the case.
>
> It is true that items like the tiger, panther and snow leopard have the greatest snob value and command the highest price. Fortunately, however, they constitute a small fraction of the total turnover of the local trade, both in value and volume. For items of bulk sale like gloves, furcaps, fur-lined leather, suede jackets, local animals like the weasel, musk rat, hare, marmot, otter, stoat, pinemartin, flying squirrel and fox are used. These will continue to be available to them even if J&K adopts the Central law, with this difference only that the trapping will be controlled through licenses issued by the Forest Department in order to ensure that these species do not become extinct by excess catching [...]
>
> The furriers also use domesticated animals like sheep, goats and rabbits. No permits are necessary for these or for jackals [...]
>
> [...] Kashmir's adoption of the Central law will be a notable victory for the wider cause of conservation.

The chief minister belonged to Indira Gandhi's own party and had she been dictatorial, as is often portrayed, she could have forced the issue. Yet, even while being politically supreme, she did not exert undue pressure. It would, thus, take five years for the state to pass a law that was similar to the national law in structure and intent.

It is generally believed that Indira Gandhi always got what she wanted; what she ordained and ordered, happened. Nothing could be farther from reality as this exchange with successive Rajasthan chief ministers—her hand-picked men—demonstrates. At the height of her political glory, in July 1971, she had selected Barkatullah Khan as the state's chief minister. She wrote to him on 14 May:

> In 1968, Sukhadiaji offered to give the Ghana Bird Sanctuary, Bharatpur on lease to the Central Government for conversion into a National Park. I understand that you are no longer in favour of this proposal.
>
> [...] I am glad to learn that you are willing to convert Ghana into a National Park, albeit under state auspices. [...]
>
> I have written to you several times about the forest problems of Rajasthan. I am glad you are giving them your personal attention. Sanctuaries like Bharatpur and Sariska naturally deserve priority [...] The Central Government will gladly give appropriate technical and financial assistance provided there is a corresponding determination to take well-conceived and firm action on the ground. If for some reason, the state finds itself unable to stop grazing and exploitation, you might like to reconsider the idea of Central management for a limited period of ten years.

The chief minister replied on 31 July saying that he had no absolute desire to retain control with the state government and that he would be glad to consider leasing out these sanctuaries 'if control by the Central Government by itself will result in better management and protection'. He offered to have his officials discuss this matter further with the Government of India but it was clear what his position was. He did not want the central government to manage the sanctuaries.

By August, Harideo Joshi had replaced Barkatullah Khan as chief minister. On 14 December, the new chief minister wrote to the prime minister stating clearly:

> [...] there does not appear to be valid ground for supposing that Central management would be an answer to the problem of over-grazing and exploitation. The Central Government would itself not possess the machinery to deal with the exploiters but would seek the assistance of the State Government officials.

The prime minister would not give up—at least not yet. Ten days later she replied to the chief minister:

As I made clear to Barkatullah Sahib, the idea of a lease to the Centre was suggested not as a matter of principle but only for improved management. I say this because more than a year ago the Wild Life Wing in the Ministry of Agriculture indicated the measures which needed to be undertaken in Bharatpur and Sariska. Unfortunately, they have not been implemented by the State authorities.

She then went on to discuss the problems afflicting Bharatpur and Sariska with the kind of perceptiveness that would have astonished the chief minister and his officials. She concluded by reminding him that 'the management of wild life parks and sanctuaries is a specialized subject requiring the full-time energies of capable and dedicated personnel', and that both Bharatpur and Sariska lacked such personnel. But her pleas were ignored.

Rukmini Devi Arundale, a noted dancer and cultural figure, was nominated as a member of the Upper House of Parliament in 1952 by Jawaharlal Nehru. She was also a passionate animal lover and was largely responsible for Parliament passing the Prevention of Cruelty to Animals Act in 1960. On 11 January, she wrote to Karan Singh:

> I am also sending herewith a press cutting and trust you would do whatever is necessary to ensure that Mudumalai game sanctuary and adjoining places are not allowed to be inundated by the proposed Moyar hydro-electric project. You may recall that enough damage to wildlife and forests was caused by the Kabini project in Mysore.

Rukmini Devi was drawing the attention of the IBWL to the plans of the Tamil Nadu government to build a 150 megawatt hydroelectric project; four dams were to be constructed on the Moyar river which separated the Mudumalai Sanctuary in Tamil Nadu from the Bandipur Sanctuary in Mysore, Karnataka. One of these dams—Theppakadu—was to fall in the heart of the Mudumalai Sanctuary.

It was a fact that both sanctuaries were rich in elephant herds, spotted deer and sambar. Mudumalai was, in addition, the principal habitat of the

Nilgiri gaur (bison). Not surprisingly, environmentalists were perturbed by the developments. A few days after Rukmini Devi, M. Krishnan, the well-known naturalist, also wrote to Karan Singh expressing his fears about the impact of the hydroelectric project. The prime minister was alerted, and she asked the NCEPC to examine the project proposal.

In May, the NCEPC sent a two-member team—which included Kirit Parekh, who was later to become a member of the Planning Commission and an authority on energy planning—to visit both the sanctuaries and get the views of both the state governments. The team concluded that the project would cause considerable disturbance to the wildlife population, submerge rich forest areas and the benefit likely to flow from it would simply not be commensurate to the damage it would certainly inflict. Indira Gandhi supported scrapping of the project.

But the Tamil Nadu chief minister, M. Karunanidhi had a different view. On 9 December, the prime minister finally sent Moni Malhoutra a handwritten note:

> I have given the article re Mudhumalai Sanctuary (in Junior Statesman)
> to Shri Karunanidhi. Can Min of Irrigation & Power help Tamil Nadu
> to find another site for their hydel power plant?

She followed this up with a letter on 1 January 1974 to the Tamil Nadu chief minister, informing him that the NCEPC report 'confirms that the Project will destroy one of the finest wildlife areas in our country because the Theppakadu reservoir will submerge that portion of the sanctuary which contains the greater part of its total bamboo vegetation and luxuriant low grass'. She expressed full support for increasing the state's electricity generating capacity but noted that the proposed project's addition to irrigation and power generation was not 'particularly large'. The chief minister made one more effort to defend his pet project but Indira Gandhi was unmoved. Bandipur and Mudumalai were saved.

Indira Gandhi also managed to save a beautiful deer sanctuary in Tamil Nadu. In 1958, 555 acres were set aside from the sprawling Raj Bhawan complex in Madras for a deer park. But by 1973, only 330 acres of that remained since the state government had merrily been allocating land there to different institutions.

On 24 November, Fatehsinghrao Gaekwad, who was president of WWF-India's Indian affiliate and a Congress MP, wrote to the chief minister of Tamil Nadu urging him to secure the remaining 330 acres as a permanent deer sanctuary—this would, in his words, also act as a 'lung to the fair city of Madras'. He sent a copy of the letter to the prime minister, pleading for her intervention. She replied to him on 4 December:

> I do agree that it [Guindy Deer Park] should be preserved without further whittling down its area. I have spoken to the Governor on more than one occasion, but the Chief Minister has his own views. However, I shall write again.

True to her word, she wrote to Governor K.K. Shah on the same day along with a copy of Gaekwad's letter. She stated:

> [...] You probably remember that I have mentioned this matter to you earlier. I am sure you could help in securing a favourable response from the Chief Minister.

The governor responded ten days later saying that he had spoken to the chief minister and that there was no intention of any further encroachment on the land of the deer sanctuary. The issue was settled momentarily—but three years later, it was to resurface.

Indira Gandhi believed that the built environment had to be in harmony with the natural world. A good example of this is the care she took looking over the designs of forest lodges. She had received complaints of 'ugly' structures being built at Bharatpur, Corbett and Gir—so, on 11 December, she wrote to the new Minister of Tourism and Civil Aviation Raj Bahadur:

> I had long ago urged that nothing should be built in our jungles which is not in harmony with the surroundings. I see little evidence of this in the new buildings we are making. They are disconcertingly urban in their orientation. Surely we are capable of greater imagination and creativity.

I know it is not easy to go on sending people to Africa but there is a fine example of a wildlife lodge nearer home, Tiger Tops in Nepal. In inspiration, it is half way between the African concept and the old two-storey Rana Shooting Camps and is built entirely of local materials. The rooms are dispersed in a number of thatched buildings which rest on sal stilts. Despite its sylvan appearance, it is extremely comfortable from within and offers a whole new experience to tourists. I think we might send some of our architects to study it carefully and re-design our own lodges afresh.

The precise location of lodges is also important. Each of them will have a fair complement of permanent staff living in adjacent buildings, presumably with their families. Their presence inside the sanctuaries as well as the flow of visitors to and from their quarters may cause undesirable problems. I suggest, therefore, that the location of these lodges should be settled in consultation not only with the local authorities but also with the Wildlife Wing in the Department of Agriculture.

That Indira Gandhi was finicky about such matters was evident; she could not tolerate manmade structures that interfered with the natural order of things.

A year earlier, Indira Gandhi had expressed her commitment to nurturing Bombay—India's financial hub. At the behest of her friend Begum Ali Yavar Jung, the wife of the governor of Maharashtra, Indira Gandhi had written to all chief ministers on 14 July 1972 on the subject of cleanliness—in the country in general and in cities in particular. She wrote again on 24 December confessing that 'there is not much evidence as yet of any broad-based people's movement for basic civic consciousness'. In this letter, she referred to the Begum's attempts at keeping Bombay clean and encouraged the chief ministers to launch Clean Cities Week in mid-January 'throughout the principal cities of your State, in order to give the movement some momentum'. She also wanted them to involve voluntary organizations in a big way.

This letter had an amusing sequel. Syed Mir Qasim, the chief minister of Jammu and Kashmir, replied that it would not be possible to organize the Clean Cities Week in the Kashmir Valley and Ladakh in mid-January given that it would be winter there. But he promised to do so over the summer or early autumn. On his response of 18 January 1974, the prime minister remarked self-deprecatingly three days later:

> It was stupid of me not to mention this in my letter.

❧

Indira Gandhi had also taken keen interest in the development of the nation's capital. Already, she and Padmaja Naidu had helped design the Nehru Park in the city's diplomatic enclave. Indira Gandhi had also been a member of a committee that had created the sprawling Buddha Jayanti Park along the southern edge of the Delhi Ridge to mark the 2500th anniversary of the Buddha's enlightenment, celebrated in 1956; she had also been a member of the group that had planned the Delhi Zoo that opened in November 1959.

Sometime in mid-1973, Indira Gandhi suggested that the time had come to set up a separate body to preserve and develop the aesthetic quality of urban and environmental design in the nation's capital—this would then serve as a model for other cities. Thus it was that in December legislation was introduced in Parliament to establish a Delhi Urban Art Commission (DUAC). The law was passed in the Lok Sabha without a debate on 21 December, and three days later in the Upper House after about an hour of discussion. It became effective from 1 May 1974.

Very soon after, Indira Gandhi personally selected Bhagwan Sahay to serve as the commission's first chairman. The choice wasn't surprising—given that, as chief commissioner of Delhi in the 1950s, Sahay had worked with Nehru to draft the first master plan of the city. He was also a painter and sculptor who was well known to her. The noted architect Achyut Kanvinde and the eminent theatre personality Ebrahim Alkazi were to be the commission's members, again hand-picked by her.

In a letter to the chief minister of Maharashtra on 5 July 1974, Indira Gandhi was to recommend the DUAC's structure—which had 'the mandate of applying enlightened aesthetic judgement on construction plans in Delhi'—for the city of Bombay as well.

❧

Indira Gandhi would write to Karan Singh in his capacity as the chairman of the IBWL every other day. But she did not forget that he was also the minister of tourism and civil aviation. On 17 February, she dispatched this letter to him:

> I understand that the Department of Tourism and its counterparts in the States do not always pay sufficient attention to the wishes of the Archaeological Survey in the matter of siting of hotels and rest houses for tourists. Some years ago, the Survey was apparently bulldozed into permitting the construction of a restaurant within the outer enclosure of the Taj. A tourist bungalow and restaurant has come up within 50 yards of the Hazara Rama Temple at Hampi. Similar tourist facilities have been created opposite the Kailasa Temple at Ellora and Ajanta Caves. To make matters worse, none of the structures are of any great architectural distinction.
>
> I am sure you will share my concern at such insensitivity. [...] The Survey should invariably be consulted beforehand. Please take this up with the State Governments also. Are there any plans to put up a new hotel at Konarak? [...]

The same day, she also sent a long letter to Finance Minister Y.B. Chavan making a strong case for increased financial allocations for the preservation of monuments:

> From my own travels as well as from what I hear from Indian and foreign tourists, I am becoming concerned about the preservation of our protected monuments. These are not merely of sentimental or historical value but a sound investment for the future.
>
> During my visit to Lahaul and Spiti last year, I was distressed to find the Tabo Monastery in a state of disrepair. [...] One of the places at Deegh is in imminent danger of collapse.
>
> I understand that the Survey was given only Rs 34 lakhs for special repairs in the current financial year. It has asked for Rs 70 lakhs in the next financial year for this purpose. I know how difficult it is to balance the budget but I hope you can give further consideration to this matter and try and accommodate their request in full. Our monuments are too important and precious for us to take any risks with them [...]

Apart from the structural safety of the monuments themselves, I am sure you will agree that it is equally important for their environs to be well kept. There is therefore need for additional horticultural staff. The Survey also wishes to acquire a belt of land around the monuments to prevent new building activity from engulfing them, as has already happened in many places including Delhi. This is important and adequate financial provision should be made for this purpose every year [...]

We need more site museums and the existing ones need to be developed further. [...]

Also I am told that the Survey's officers and specialists are unable to travel as frequently as they should [...] for want of adequate funds.

[...] It is better to err of the side of generosity with an organization which is the chief custodian of our ancient heritage.

With no less an advocate than the prime minister herself, the finance minister went along, even though the country's overall finances were in a perilous condition.

After this letter to the finance minister, on 23 December Indira Gandhi put together what must surely be amongst her longest notes—four-and-a-half pages on legal-size paper—on any subject during her prime ministership. It was addressed to the minister of education and culture, Professor S. Nurul Hasan and she summed up her case thus:

As you know, I have deeply concerned about the Archaeological Survey and the National Museum and have been writing to you about these matters. The information I have been receiving is not happy. The Survey seems to be going downhill and its problems are not receiving the kind of attention they deserve.

When I took Castro sight-seeing a couple of months or so ago, I myself noticed an air of neglect in the Red Fort. A recent visitor tells me that at the Taj, the sandstone paving along the water courses has been repaired in a most inept fashion. [...]

Funds are limited but I do feel that even [with] what is available much more could be done [...]

She then went on to describe what she saw as the operating problems at the ASI as well as the National Museum. The kind of detail she went into showed that she had deep interest in the subject; had multiple sources of information, mostly non-official; and had a keen sense of what ailed these two organizations, largely collected during her numerous trips.

∾

After paying the customary floral tributes at Rajghat on Mahatma Gandhi's birth anniversary on 2 October, Indira Gandhi went to Mathura, approximately 100 kilometres from the capital, to lay the foundation stone of an oil refinery—India's first in many years and certainly the largest ever by the standards of the day. The location of this refinery was to lead to huge controversy over the next few years—and right up to the 1990s.[2]

The refinery's history could be traced back to the late-1960s. A site selection committee had been appointed by the Indian Oil Corporation (IOC). Indira Gandhi's government decided that the refinery would be in the northwest of India where the demand for petroleum products was growing rapidly.

A number of chief ministers then lobbied with the prime minister canvassing the case for their respective states. The chief minister of Uttar Pradesh was the first off the block with his letter of 8 April 1971. The chief minister of Rajasthan followed with his plea on 15 July 1971, and then the chief minister of Haryana on 30 July 1971. The chief minister of Karnataka—disregarding the decision to restrict the refinery to the northwest—also jumped into the fray, making a strong pitch on 8 January 1973 for his state.

The prime minister personally replied to the first three chief ministers on 2 September 1971, blandly acknowledging their correspondence with: '[…] the points urged in your letter will be borne in mind while taking a decision'. As for the Karnataka chief minister, his aide received a letter of acknowledgement from the prime minister's aide.

The site selection committee examined locations in Haryana, Madhya Pradesh, Uttar Pradesh and Rajasthan. Strangely, Delhi had also been considered as a possible site—as also Agra, which is baffling. Mathura was finally selected because it had superior connectivity—it was on a national highway and also on a broad gauge railway line. Besides, land was expected to be made available easily.

However, there was also the fact that the Taj Mahal was about 40 kilometres from Mathura, and the Bharatpur Bird Sanctuary was at roughly 60 kilometres. Indira Gandhi wasn't oblivious to the impact that a refinery could have on them. An internal note prepared by the IOC sometime towards the end of 1974 suggests as much:

> Subsequent to the decision on setting up the refinery at Mathura, some doubts have been raised in certain quarters about the risk to the Taj Mahal from the gaseous effluents from the Mathura refinery. In fact, the Prime Minister has been very much concerned about the effect of the refinery on the Taj Mahal. The then Minister of P&C [Petroleum and Chemicals], Shri D.K. Barooah took a meeting on 13th September 1973, when senior officers of the Ministry of P&C, representatives of the National Committee on Environmental Planning and Coordination, Planning Commission, Bhabha Atomic Research Centre and other experts were present. On the basis of his discussions he had given an undertaking to ensure that the atmospheric pollution from the Refinery is within limits and monuments will not be affected. It was also decided at that same meeting that a study in depth should be undertaken about the problems of pollution by effluents whether liquid or gaseous and adequate measures to be taken to eliminate them.

Moreover, records available at the ASI show that the organization was concerned about the impact of the pollution caused by the Mathura Refinery as early as July 1973. These, the internal notes reveal, were evidently because of press reports that had been appearing. Such reports continued and on 20 September there was a long 'letter to the editor' in *The Times of India* by the well-known environmentalist Dr P.J. Deoras, highlighting the adverse impact of the Mathura refinery on both the Taj Mahal and the Bharatpur Bird Sanctuary. It's hard to believe that Indira Gandhi missed reading such concerns. Yet, Indira Gandhi laid the foundation stone. Why she didn't put her foot down is inexplicable.

Pollution worries did not subside after the foundation stone was laid. There were soon reports even in the international media. Indira Gandhi—always sensitive to such coverage and conscious of the reputation she held after Stockholm of being a champion for the environment—now directed her officials to ensure that the IOC did no harm to the Taj Mahal, even as it went ahead with the refinery. At her insistence, belated no doubt, a committee was set up on 16 July 1974, under the chairmanship of one of India's most distinguished technologists, Dr S. Varadarajan, who was then the chairman of the Indian Petrochemicals Corporation (IPCL). Her officials, speaking on her behalf, told the committee that, whatever the cost, pollution control had to receive the highest priority and the best technical expertise in the world had to be sought. A record of a key review meeting in the Ministry of Petroleum on 27 October 1975 had this to say:

> V. Ramachandran of Prime Minister's Secretariat expressed concern over any remote possibility of any detrimental effect on monuments on account of Mathura Refinery. He reiterated that it was essential to take all steps to ensure that the monuments were preserved. He also suggested that he may be informed of the steps being taken and any problem or impediments that may crop up in the speedy implementation of the studies as may be required to be conducted in order to establish beyond doubt the steps necessary so as to ensure that the Mathura refinery will not affect the monument.

Having committed a mistake, Indira Gandhi was committed to ensuring that there would be no adverse fall-out. As it turned out, the Varadarajan Committee submitted its report in December 1977 by which time Indira Gandhi had left office. Before finalizing the report, Varadarajan had consulted Salim Ali, the Nature Conservancy Council in the UK and the Royal Society for the Preservation of Birds.

On its part, the IOC got expertise and assistance from Italy where, as the records quoted above noted, '[…] there are numerous monuments using marble and other stones and in some parts of that country the atmospheric pollution problem is severe'. Indira Gandhi's resolve to protect the area had added something like 4 per cent to the project cost. It also extended the time for commissioning. While Barooah announced in Mathura that the refinery would be commissioned by 1978, it finally got operational five years later—the delay entirely because of the concerns surrounding its pollution impacts on the Taj Mahal and the Bharatpur Bird Sanctuary.

The question thus remains—why did Indira Gandhi knowingly accept a location fraught with risks?[3] The same question could well be asked of the BTE at Chilka, too.

After Indira Gandhi overturned her own decision to establish the navy's BTE by Chilka Lake—stating that further environmental audits were needed—the NCEPC got into the act with gusto; a four-member team comprising Moni Malhoutra, Ashok Khosla, C.K. Varshney and Chief of Naval Staff Admiral S.M. Nanda spent 2–4 February 1973 at Paradeep and Chilka. The four-page report was written and signed by Khosla and Varshney. While Malhoutra accepted it orally, Admiral Nanda was most unhappy. The report read:

> Taking into account the unique nature of this lake, it is our considered view that all possible efforts should be made for finding a suitable site for the Boys Training Establishment other than Chilka, and Chilka lake should be left undisturbed.

Yet the report also offered an escape window, which Indira Gandhi was to use:

> In case it is decided to locate the BTE at Chilka, the selection of the site for BTE will have to be carefully examined from the environmental angle to satisfy at least that (a) natural beauty of the area is not spoiled; (b) the lake is not polluted; and (c) there is least disturbance to birds. It may be necessary to insist on certain minimum conditions for safeguarding these results.

The report of Khosla and Varshney dated 24 February also contained an assessment of the environmental impact; a recommendation of nine specific guidelines that ought to be imposed on the navy if the site were to be cleared; and four steps to be taken by the state government—including making Chilka a sanctuary, and some portions a national park.

While Admiral Nanda remained resolute that the training establishment had to be at Chilka, Pitambar Pant in his letter to him on 24 February once again asked that other sites be considered and analysed, especially since they had been rejected without any study and analysis. Tragically, Pant, who was just fifty-four, died two days after sending this letter. His untimely demise altered the situation.

This was evident, when on 9 April, the defence minister wrote to the prime minister asking for her final decision in view of the NCEPC's report and the navy's acceptance of the ecological safeguards recommended at Chilka.[4] Before replying to him, the prime minister wrote to the governor of Orissa, B.D. Jatti, informing him that in the event of Chilka being selected, the state government also would have to implement certain conditions.[5] It is only after the governor had written accepting these terms, and after exhaustive discussions with her officials, that the prime minister responded to the defence minister on 12 June:

> The two experts from the National Committee for Environmental Planning and Coordination who accompanied Admiral Nanda to Chilka have suggested a slight modification of the safeguards [accepted by the navy]. I agree with the revised safeguards. A copy is enclosed.
>
> Subject to these safeguards being enforced, I agree that we now finally announce the location of the Boys' Training Establishment at Chilka.

The safeguards included restricting the built-up area to a section of Chilka; forbidding outdoor firing or shooting; confining training and recreational activities to specified areas; preventing the discharge of untreated sewage into the lake; keeping critical wildlife habitats completely out of bounds; banning the use of helicopters; using motor boats only in times of emergency; establishing a scientific station for the study of local ecology; prohibiting the shooting of birds, and so on.[6]

This was yet another U-turn by the prime minister but she and the NCEPC had made their ecological point forcefully. The navy got what it wanted, as did the NCEPC—though my belief is that both she and the NCEPC would have been happier had the navy not been so adamant.

Indira Gandhi laid the long-delayed foundation stone of the BTE on 16 October. But the worry that nagged her—that Chilka's ecological well-being could get compromised—would just not go away. On 30 December, she wrote to all the service chiefs once again reiterating the points in her letter of 30 May 1972, adding a special line for Admiral Kohli:

I have even heard Naval Units going to Chilka for reconnaissance work in connection with the BTE have been shooting the birds, even though the area is in a sanctuary.

On 29 February 1980 when she was informed by her officials that the navy was setting up a thirty-bed hospital at Chilka, she was to query:

By the way, what is the situation in Chilka so far as the ecology and birds are concerned?

Given the prime minister's love for birds, it wasn't wholly surprising that Zafar Futehally,[7] in his capacity as the honorary secretary of the BNHS, wrote to her on 13 July with this request:

At our Executive Committee meeting today, it was decided to request you to honour us by becoming the Patron of our Society. We are making this request because of your great interest in natural history and conservation and because your patronage will be a great fillip to all of us connected with this institution.

Formerly, the Viceroys used to be Patrons, and Rajagopalachari was in that tradition—as Governor General. I shall look forward to your reply.

Incidentally, I hear that you are going to be in Bombay in early November and wonder whether you would agree to pay a visit to Hornbill House at that time and give us a talk on any aspect of conservation or natural history that you think appropriate.

Moni Malhoutra replied to Futehally on 10 August:

The Prime Minister has asked me to thank you for your letter dated 13th July, 1973 requesting her to be Patron of the Bombay Natural History Society. She will be glad to do so.

It is not possible to make any commitment as yet about a visit to Hornbill House. But the Prime Minister will certainly try to find time to visit the Society during one of her visits to Bombay, not so much to give a talk, but to meet the members of the Society informally and learn a little more about the Society's activities.

Seventeen months later, Indira Gandhi was to visit Hornbill House but that story comes a little later. That she had agreed to be patron of the

BNHS at a time when it was coming under attack in the media for its alleged association with the CIA because of Dillon Ripley's collaboration with Salim Ali is remarkable—all the more so since Indira Gandhi herself often spoke of the CIA having its tentacles in India.

During the height of the Cold War, it was inconceivable to imagine the American ambassador in New Delhi writing to the prime minister's secretary to support a joint India–USSR initiative. Yet that is what happened when on 25 November, Daniel Moynihan wrote to Haksar's successor P.N. Dhar, conveying a message from Dillon Ripley who was then convalescing in Calcutta. The message, which Moynihan supported, was this: 'Salim Ali and I most earnestly request Your Excellency [to] at least raise [the] possibility of initiating talks on a Bird Migration Treaty with Chairman Brezhnev this week […]' Three days later Indira Gandhi wrote to Salim Ali:

> My Secretary, Professor Dhar, has received a letter from the American Ambassador. I enclose a copy.
>
> As you know, this is a subject which interests me greatly. By coincidence, Mr. Brezhnev and I spoke about it at the President's lunch before I had seen or knew anything about Mr. Moynihan's letter. After seeing the letter, the subject has been mentioned to members of the Russian party. However, before taking further steps, it is necessary to have more information about what exactly you have in mind […]

On 6 December, Salim Ali sent her a detailed letter explaining why such an accord on the protection of migratory birds was needed and how India would stand to gain. He drew her attention to similar agreements between the USA and Canada, between Japan and the USA and most recently between Japan and the USSR. Indira Gandhi recorded on his letter four days later—the first and only time she expressed irritation at Salim Ali:

> I welcome such a treaty. My objection was to Salim Ali approaching us through the US embassy.

Thereafter, the bureaucracies in India and the USSR started discussions and by mid-1974 Salim Ali had given his approval to a draft of the convention that the Indian officials had prepared. After that, matters remained at a standstill—until eleven years later, a few days before Indira Gandhi's assassination.

∾

After Captain M.S. Kohli, it was the turn of Major H.P.S. Ahluwalia to have a foreword to his book penned by Indira Gandhi. Major Ahluwalia had been a member of Kohli's team when he had led India's first successful expedition to Mount Everest in May 1965. Sadly, soon after reaching the world's highest point, Major Ahluwalia became permanently disabled in the 1965 India–Pakistan war.

On 12 March, in her foreword to Ahluwalia's *Higher Than Everest*,[8] she paid a rich tribute to him for his 'grit and perseverance'—acknowledging his courage while conquering mountains, as also while facing a 'long and dreary treatment and convalescence'. She also wrote of her own inner life:

> Although I was born on one of the flattest plains of the world, I have always regarded myself as a child of the mountains. Not merely because that is where my ancestors belonged, but because I feel more at home there and they seem to fulfill an emotional need [...]
>
> [...] What do I see in the mountain—beauty of landscape, purity of air, solitude or the greater challenge to one's endurance and resourcefulness? Perhaps all these and something more. [...] The heights give another perspective—man is but an insignificant speck, dwarfed by the giant forces of nature. [...]
>
> [...] I love all mountains. What fun it is to run up and down the hills. How soothing to the eye is the cool green of the higher, forest-clothed ones, heady with scents of pine and myriad other trees and plants, where one must make one's own path. No less attractive are the many and changing hues of the barren rocks, so stark and strong looking. And, of course, there are the majestic snow-covered peaks glistening gold and silver in the sunshine, coyly veiled with wisps of cloud. I never cease to be astonished at the sight of wild flowers in the high mountains, their tiny colourful heads peering out of unlikely nooks and crevices, tenaciously defying the most inhospitable elements.

Notes

1. On 1 September 1974 she was to write the foreword again for another of Sankhala's books—this time in French called *Tigre*. She praised Sankhala, spoke of Project Tiger, acknowledged the contributions of the World Wildlife Fund and also wrote that 'the belated global concern for endangered species of fauna and flora is not merely because of their beauty and the delight that they afford to our senses—although to my mind that is not a negligible point—but is due to the serious ecological consequences and the imbalance in nature with which the world is threatened'. Ecological imbalance is an expression that occurs frequently in her writings and speeches. It obviously meant a lot to her.

2. The best account of this is D'Monte (1985).

3. C.K. Varshney who was in the NCEPC then and was involved in the pollution studies still feels Gwalior in Madhya Pradesh would have been the best site from an environmental point of view. But Indira Gandhi was obviously committed to Uttar Pradesh.

4. These included: (i) declaration of Chilka as a sanctuary with areas of particular wildlife interest within the sanctuary to be declared a national park; (ii) an overall plan for the appropriate and compatible use of the whole lake; and (iii) a buffer zone surrounding the BTE and free from private construction to be set aside.

5. Orissa was then under President's Rule.

6. A year later she was to have a similar experience, this time in connection with the location of an air defence system for the nation's capital. The system consisted of a tower and associated facilities. The proposal of the Ministry of Defence was to locate the entire system on the Delhi Ridge. Being aware of its ecological value, Indira Gandhi was to ensure that only the tower was put up on the Ridge and all other facilities were transferred elsewhere. This involved additional expenditure but she justified it on environmental grounds. Parthasarathi (2007) has details.

7. Four decades later in his memoirs *The Song of the Magpie Robin*, Futehally was to write: 'Without ever having admired her political style, I have to admit that she supported and encouraged all conservation projects. On one occasion in 1978 I received an urgent message from a conservation contact that a large number of magnificent ancient trees in Assam were on the point of being cut down for a Congress pandal. Just one call to Mrs Gandhi saved

the trees […] While Mrs Gandhi had real interest in nature conservation, she also seemed to have genuine regard and affection for Salim [Ali] and I, as his deputy, sometimes benefitted from this.' Futehally (2014).

8. Ahluwalia (1973).

1974

Indira Gandhi with Salim Ali at her residence; September 1974.

If 1973 was bad, 1974 was to get even worse for Indira Gandhi. Inflation continued to be in very high double digits and industrial stagnation loomed large. Mass movements in which students were in the forefront were launched and gathered momentum first in Gujarat and soon thereafter in Bihar. There were many local issues but two common themes of the agitationists were the spiralling prices of essential commodities and the perceived venality and incompetence of her party leadership in these states. They acquired national significance because of the leadership provided by Jayaprakash Narayan.

For a brief moment there was exultation in the country as on 18 May India conducted what Indira Gandhi insisted was a 'peaceful nuclear experiment' but what the world considered a nuclear test. Such a major event could not have taken place without preparations that would undoubtedly have gone on for around two years or so. She wrote a detailed four-page letter to Olaf Palme giving the background to and the rationale for the 'peaceful nuclear experiment'. She reiterated her commitment to the use of nuclear energy only for peaceful purposes and her commitment to the total elimination of all nuclear weapons. She assured her Swedish counterpart that 'our peaceful experiment […] has neither military implications nor political objectives' and informed him that after the 'experiment' she had immediately written to Prime Minister Bhutto 'assuring him in categorical terms that our experiment was not meant for making nuclear arms'.

The nuclear test drama was being enacted when the nation had been crippled by a huge strike by the railways which were its lifeline in so many ways. The strike began on 8 May and lasted twenty days. It was put down in what has been described as 'a brutal manner', but did she have any choice when the strike itself had been taken over by the most strident of her political opponents and when the political discourse had been so vitiated by them to make any calm or composed negotiations impossible?

On 15 September, Indira Gandhi wrote to Lucile Kyle about the marriage of Sanjay Gandhi that was to take place a fortnight later, gave her news of the family and then added in her own hand:

> Centuries of Indian heritage are working on me and I long to retire gracefully
> to some quiet place. I have never believed in rebirth but am coming close to
> it now for I feel I must have committed some grievous wrong in some past
> birth to be sentenced to such hard labour in this one!

Perhaps, the 'quiet place' Indira Gandhi dreamt of was Himachal Pradesh—for, the mountains of Manali, Mashobra and Simla had been her haunts in the past.

On 25 June, the prime minister wrote to Y.S. Parmar, the first chief minister of the state, articulating views that later became commonplace in the early twentieth-century debate on climate change.

I learn from the Ministry of Agriculture that there is a great deal of deforestation in Himachal Pradesh. It is naturally a matter of grave concern and the cutting down of trees is adversely affecting our climate and rainfall and often leads to floods and landslides. I hope you take a personal interest in the matter. I am sure that you know that in Switzerland and in some other countries there is a law that a tree must be planted before one is cut down.

Indira Gandhi had taken personal interest in ensuring that Himachal Pradesh became a full-fledged state on 25 January 1971. Because of the special respect with which she was held by the chief minister, her letter was to trigger serious action there. Two years later, she would have occasion to praise the state for these actions.

Moni Malhoutra, Indira Gandhi's key aide for environmental matters, had left after an unusually long seven-year tenure. His replacement was a foreign service officer named Salman Haidar. He may well have been identified as Malhoutra's successor by Haksar under whom he had served in the High Commission in London in the 1960s. Like Malhoutra, Haidar supervised many areas in the Prime Minister's Office (PMO)—including 'ecology', as Indira Gandhi liked to call it. It helped that he was a nature-lover himself and known to Salim Ali.

On 2 July, Salim Ali wrote to Indira Gandhi:

> I regret having to trouble you but as the point in question may involve reversal of a policy already in operation I am compelled to write to you.
>
> I understand from one of our knowledgeable members that vast tracts of forests in the Andamans and Nicobar group of islands are being cleared for resettling refugees. While it is necessary to find land for these unhappy people it should not be at the cost of destroying the environment which will in the long-run defeat the purpose for which the clearings were made to find a home for the homeless.

A perturbed Indira Gandhi got Salman Haidar to follow-up and report the factual details to her. Many protracted inter-ministerial meetings and correspondence followed. Finally, based on what she was informed, on

11 March 1975, the prime minister sent a note to the minister of agriculture and irrigation, as well as to the minister of supply and rehabilitation with clear instructions:

> I am told that the rehabilitation and commercial plantation projects in the Andaman and Nicobar Islands are having unexpected environmental effects. These programmes need clearance of substantial areas of virgin forest. When we drew up the plans we were perhaps not fully aware that removing the forest cover may be so damaging as to threaten to reduce the islands to a wasteland. It is said that already it has been necessary to abandon some of the land brought under cultivation owing to its sharp deterioration.
>
> A thorough review of the feasibility of the projects must be made with particular reference to the effect of deforestation on these islands. There would be little point in going to the trouble and expense of clearing the forest if we are not assured of a favourable long-term outcome. The Departments of Rehabilitation and Agriculture should establish a joint team to go into the issues. If necessary the assistance of experts from abroad should be sought. The International Union for the Conservation of Nature is making a special study of tropical rain forests and may be in a position to provide expertise.
>
> Pending such a review, forestry operations in the Andaman and Nicobar Islands intended to clear land for fresh settlers or for commercial plantations should be halted.

Indira Gandhi's intervention triggered by Salim Ali's letter were to lead to two studies on the ecological preservation of these strategic islands—one by a group of Indian officials, and another by a IUCN expert D.N. McVean who met the prime minister on 12 March 1976 and, three months later, submitted his report titled 'Land Use in the Andaman and Nicobar Islands'. The report was comprehensive in scope and meticulous in detail. It ended by acknowledging 'the Prime Minister of India Mrs. Indira Gandhi for her closely informed interest in the study'. Little did the prime minister know at that point that in the last years of her life the subject would engage her attention once more.

Salim Ali faced virulent criticism from various quarters for his 'Bird Migration Study'. He was accused of having links with the CIA through his partnership with Dillon Ripley, and it was insinuated that the Bird Migration Study itself was a part of a biological warfare strategy of the US army. Questions were asked by MPs—mostly belonging to the Communist parties—and Indira Gandhi's government was forced to set up two inquiry committees to look into the allegations.[1]

The committees exonerated Salim Ali and found nothing 'anti-national' in the project but that did not prevent Parliament's most important committee—the Public Accounts Committee—from launching its own investigation. It submitted its report in April 1975 and put both Salim Ali and the BNHS in the dock. On his part, Salim Ali did not take things lying down; he went on the offensive saying that MPs were badly informed and were making wholly false allegations. He even wrote a longish letter to the editor in *The Times of India* on 6 August in which he repeated many of the points of defence he had made to Indira Gandhi.

As for Indira Gandhi, she remained unperturbed throughout the brouhaha. On 16 November, she released the tenth and final volume of the Salim Ali–Dillon Ripley handbook at her residence. It was as though she were telling Salim Ali's critics—'You shout what you want, but as far as I am concerned he is perfectly okay and continues to enjoy my friendship'. Ripley himself was to write to Indira Gandhi on 22 November:

> It was with the greatest delight that I heard from Salim Ali of the launching of Volume 10 of our Handbooks of the Birds of India at the Oxford University Press on November 16th by your good self. What an honour for your bird friends of many years...
>
> I was saddened during the past summer to notice comments in the Indian Press that seemed antagonistic to the work of the Bombay Natural History Society, which is one of the finest of its kind in the whole world [...]
>
> To study birds and to be conscious of their presence in the world is one of the refined joys of living. I could only wish that somehow you yourself, Prime Minister, could escape for a moment or two from the heavy cares of office and join us in the field!

News of Indira Gandhi's support of the BNHS had travelled far. On 18 December, Charles 'Mac' Mathias, a Republican senator in the US from the state of Maryland, and also a keen naturalist, wrote to Indira Gandhi:

> Several years ago, when I visited India, you were kind enough to arrange for me to meet Selim [*sic*] Ali in Bombay. As a result of that meeting, I spent an extremely pleasant and interesting day with him in the country learning about the wild life of India.
>
> At that time, due to the suspension of all grant programs between India and the United States, the Bombay Natural History Society was unable to receive very modest assistance that had been previously available. Since there is now a prospect for a resumption of grant programs, I would hope that the Bombay Natural History Society might be able to continue its work and would like to volunteer any assistance that I can lend to bring this about.

Very early in the new year, on 2 January 1975, Indira Gandhi was to reply to the senator:

> I have your letter of December 18, regarding the Bombay Natural History Society.
>
> It is good of you to volunteer your assistance for the further activities of the Society. Just a few days ago, I visited the Society's premises in Bombay and had a glimpse of the excellent work it has done. We have every intention of assisting the Society in its future activities.

As she had told the senator, on 28 December, Indira Gandhi spent roughly forty-five minutes at the BNHS where she was received by Salim Ali and others. It was her first-ever visit, and she was going after becoming the patron of the society.

There were no speeches and she spent her time looking at rare books and specimens, three of which attracted her special attention as a birdwatcher—Tickell's flowerpecker which is the smallest bird in India; the monal pheasant, said to be the most beautiful bird found in the Himalayas; and the fulvous griffon vulture, one of the largest birds of prey.

Indira Gandhi was to return to the BNHS nine years later on the occasion of its centenary.

✦

On 8 March, the ex-Nawab of Malerkotla had informed Indira Gandhi about a case of poaching in the Pipli Reserve Forest in Rampur, Uttar Pradesh leading to the death of a tiger.

Indira Gandhi dispatched Kailash Sankhala to investigate and he confirmed that the tiger had indeed been deliberately killed. But he came back with an ever more disturbing discovery—Pipli was no longer a viable habitat for the tiger since the space under natural forest cover had shrunk and covered a bare 10 per cent of the original reserve wooded area. His suggestion was that some of the tigers in the place—the population estimate being around ten—could be trapped and transported to other jungles or zoological parks.

After mulling over Sankhala's suggestions, Indira Gandhi noted on 12 June:

> I do not know whether we have the requisite expertise in trapping tigers without hurting them in any way. We must do whatever is necessary to save our tigers. If it is feasible and necessary to move them to safer areas, a plan should be made accordingly.

A week later she again observed:

> The plan should now be drawn up along with a note as to which people have to be convinced and what has to be done by us. Costs and other consequences must also be worked out.

As it turned out Sankhala's translocation plan did not materialize—it was an idea ahead of its time, and would only be attempted, under different circumstances, on a couple of occasions in the first decade of the new millennium. I was privileged to play a small part in the translocation initiatives (to Sariska) as the minister concerned.

✦

On the morning of 17 September, Salman Haidar found a note from the prime minister waiting for him on his desk, along with a clipping from *The Times of India* with the caption: 'Seized Leopard Skins To Be Auctioned'. Since the article spoke about the auctioning of uncured leopard and tiger skins dispatched from Satna in Madhya Pradesh to a party in Delhi, Indira Gandhi wanted to know how the auction could be held when there was a ban on animal skins.

Salman Haidar made enquiries and brought to her attention that there was an established racket in the poaching of wild animals in Madhya Pradesh. He suggested that she write to the state's chief minister, P.C. Sethi, to which she responded by hand on 18 September:

> I doubt if the CM can do much. At one time the Shukla brothers were involved in arranging shoots and it was hinted that there was a trade in skins too.

It was a damning indictment of two of her own colleagues. But Indira Gandhi finally did see merit in Haidar's suggestion, and wrote to Sethi the next day:

> You may have seen reports in the press about an illegal and singularly unpleasant trade in animal skins centred on Satna in Madhya Pradesh. Substantial numbers of skins seem to have been finding their way from Satna to New Delhi where they are processed and sold. [...]
>
> Such acts of deliberate violation of the law against shooting wild animals should not go unpunished. [...] Please do all that is possible to catch the guilty party in this case. I hope you will give the matter your personal attention.

Indira Gandhi would be accused of many things by her political opponents. But she was never attacked for failing to protect wildlife. However, there was one occasion when even that commitment was seemingly called into question. It had hardly caused any ripples but she was stung to the quick and confronted the issue boldly. On 2 April she wrote somewhat agitatedly to the vice president of India and the chairman of the Rajya Sabha, G.S. Pathak:

While speaking in the House on the Economic Offences (Inapplicability of Limitation) Bill, 1974 on 20th March, Shri Mathew Kurian [a CPM, Communist Party of India (Marxist) MP] alleged that a senior officer of the Central Board of Excise and Customs was involved in the export worth Rs 8,00,000 of leopard skin which was a banned item. He further alleged that "this happened with the direct understanding of some high officials of the Prime Minister's Secretariat".

My own deep concern for the preservation of wildlife is well known not only in our country but in the whole world. My personal initiative has prompted Government to take various steps to tighten the law, prohibit exports, enhance penalties and urge more effective implementation of the ban on exports. The officials in my Secretariat have been alert in pursuing these matters. I have had the matter looked into and insofar as my Secretariat is concerned, the allegation is totally false.

The allegation against the senior officer of the Finance Ministry is being looked into by that Ministry. I thought I should write to you to bring the above on record.

Sometime in September the prime minister called Salman Haidar and told him that she had information that diplomats stationed in Delhi had been violating 'our game laws with impunity'. On 25 September, Haidar confirmed that the information she had was indeed accurate and 'businessmen, ex-Maharajas and other such agents normally accompany them and make the arrangements'. He proposed that diplomatic immunity be waived and the import of ammunition for shotguns and rifles by diplomats be banned. While endorsing Haidar's plan, she wrote:

> Whatever action is taken should be done after letting the Diplomatic Corps know that we take a serious view of the violation of our game laws.

On 8 November, a sternly worded circular went to all diplomatic missions. But this was not to be the end of the story. A year later, on 14 September 1975, Indira Gandhi sent this directive to her top officers:

> Some time ago, I had written a note drawing your attention to the poaching in our sanctuaries indulged in by members of the Diplomatic

Corps. I learn that this is continuing. Strong action must be taken and all heads of Missions should be warned. Otherwise they will not be permitted to go to our sanctuaries.

Please see that this matter is dealt with on an urgent basis in whatever way you think proper.

Just a few days later, on 20 September 1975, another strong circular from the Ministry of External Affairs reached all diplomatic missions in New Delhi. On 23 November 1975, on being shown a copy of it, she was to note:

Please keep close watch. What are the penalties proposed if a diplomat is caught shooting, poaching or (just as important) exporting antiques? This latter is a huge racket. One other pt [point] which needs consideration is the liquor which they are allowed. Why can't the bottles be marked with the name of the country, so that we can identify them when given to Indian officials, etc.?

By now Indira Gandhi's passion for wildlife had become well known. On 11 June, one of her bitterest political opponents, Madhu Limaye, had written to her about Gir and Bharatpur and the problems being faced in managing these sanctuaries. She replied to him nine days later:

[…] I am glad that you are taking interest in wildlife preservation. This has long been a particular interest of mine.

I agree that both Gir and Bharatpur need attention. In each the basic problem arises from the large-scale influx of domestic cattle. In Gir, there is also the problem of human settlement […]

We are constantly in touch with the State Governments regarding these two sanctuaries and are ready to provide suitable assistance from the Centre.

The irrepressible Madhu Limaye wrote to her again on 23 July on the prevailing conditions at Bharatpur based on his recent visit there. It was a three-page letter that ended with this sentence: 'In view of your publicly stated interest in the preservation of wild life I have ventured to write to you this letter'. The socialist MP assumed that the prime minister knew nothing about what was happening in Bharatpur. It was no wonder therefore, that the next day she wrote on his letter:

> He cannot even give me credit for liking birds! However, some of his suggestions are good!

∾

If Bharatpur held great interest for Indira Gandhi, it was not just because it was a famous bird sanctuary but also because it held a historic fort. On New Year's Day she wrote to the chief minister of Rajasthan, Harideo Joshi, when she got to know from the eccentric ex-Maharaja that the state irrigation department was executing a drainage and flood control scheme in Bharatpur that would endanger the walls of the old mud fort:

> The safety and welfare of the inhabitants of Bharatpur naturally deserve first priority. But this is not incompatible with adherence to basic archaeological principles so far as the Mud Fort is concerned. In olden days, when the Fort was well cared for and protected from erosion, it was an effective bulwark against floods. To repair the damages wrought by time and the elements is worthwhile: but this should not be done in a manner which transforms or jazzes up a famous landmark beyond recognition. […] Such contouring or filling up as is necessary should certainly be done without making the walls an object of modern conveniences like a motorable road, or planting of exotics like the eucalyptus. Local shrubs and grass would look much better and afford better protection against erosion.

The ex-Maharaja would be a source of heartache for Indira Gandhi as far as the bird sanctuary was concerned. But on the issue of the mud fort, she had intervened as he had wanted her to and got the state government moving. A year later, she got her officials to pursue with the state government the cleaning of the moat around the fort which, she had been told, had become very polluted.

∾

While Indira Gandhi came with the deep-rooted belief that nature and culture were the warp and weft of India's historical heritage, in August she was confronted with a very sensitive issue that would call into question how firm that belief really was.

It all began on 28 May, when Devraj Urs, the chief minister of Karnataka, wrote to her asking for the revival of worship at the Sixteen Pillar Mosque in Bidar Fort. Turning down the request, on the grounds that the mosque had already fallen into disuse in 1951, she went on to give the chief minister a mini-lecture on 28 August on her convictions:

> Leaving aside the immediate issue, I feel the general question of the protection for monuments should be examined in its broader perspective. An attempt should be made to educate people about historical values and the need for preserving ancient monuments [...]
>
> Where past generations have laboured to create monuments of enduring aesthetic worth, it is our duty to look after them. They are part of our national heritage and they should not be regarded as primarily the property of one community or the other. [...] The Sixteen Pillar Mosque is of such historic and architectural value that in the interest of conserving our heritage *we should preserve it as a monument of all rather than a place of worship serving only a few* [italics mine].

The issue of heritage conservation reasserted itself towards the end of 1974, when Indira Gandhi—who was to spend just 28 December in Bombay—extended her visit by a day and visited the nearby Elephanta Caves. This is what she had to say about it to Chief Minister V.P. Naik of Maharashtra on 29 December before leaving for New Delhi:

> The trip to Elephanta was very pleasant but I was shocked to see how dirty the surroundings are. Empty coconut shells, paper, tins and all kinds of things were strewn around. The toilets were also very dirty with broken seats and the flush not working. When I spoke about this to the person who was with us, he thought he should have cleaned up for my visit. It is not at all important how things look when I go. What is important is what impression our visitors—especially foreign—take with them. I am strongly of the view that if it is not possible to keep such places clean, it is better to close them down to tourist traffic.

She also sent a letter on 1 January 1975 to Raj Bahadur, the minister of tourism and civil aviation:

The enclosed letter to Shri V.P. Naik speaks for itself. Although the monument is under the Director of Archaeology, it is certainly the business of those in charge of Tourism to look at them and their surroundings from the tourist point of view. I think you should get reports from the main places of tourist attraction as to the specific state of the approach, toilets, and the general level of cleanliness, even when there are no important visitors.

Indira Gandhi's prodding led to a decision to preserve the island as a natural sanctuary. In other words, its ecological balance would be maintained, without any drastic change to its physiognomy—this ran contrary to the state government's former plans of elaborate landscaping, the introduction of exotic species of trees, and the establishment of recreational facilities. Eventually, in 1985, Elephanta became a protected island with a buffer zone, which included 'a prohibited area' stretching one kilometre from the shore.

The Mudumalai issue—perhaps the first irrigation-cum-power project to be subject to environmental scrutiny—had bothered the prime minister a great deal. Her experiences in 1973 convinced her that a proper system of ecological audit needed to be put in place.

On New Year's day, therefore, a long, three-page letter followed to Minister of Irrigation and Power K.C. Pant—who had worked closely with Indira Gandhi to defuse tensions in Andhra Pradesh in the early 1970s,[2] and whose new ministerial assignment was a recognition of the confidence that the prime minister had in him.

She first appraised Pant of her conversations with the Tamil Nadu chief minister and of the NCEPC report. Then she spoke of the survey being conducted for the construction of a dam in the Betla Sanctuary in the Palamau National Park in Bihar, in addition to another dam that was already in progress. Her concern, which she expressed strongly, was that this would be the death knell for the national park which had been identified as one of the first set of nine tiger reserves to be protected in the country. After emphasizing the fact that the Ramganga reservoir would submerge parts of the Corbett National Park in Uttar Pradesh, she urged Pant to 'take a personal interest in these matters and keep me informed'. Her parting shot to the minister trained as an engineer was:

> There is need to evolve guidelines regarding hydro-electric and irrigation projects that prima facie conflict with the ecology of areas of natural and wildlife interest. Could something be done to sensitise our engineers and technical experts who undertake locational investigations?

1974 saw Indira Gandhi aligning herself even more decisively with technology to control pollution. On 3 January, she spoke at a research institute in Nagpur—set up in 1956 as the Central Public Health Engineering Research Institute, and about to get a new name after the prime minister's lecture. Invoking her speech in Stockholm, Indira Gandhi commented:

> So far as India is concerned there are two types of pollution. There is the old pollution, which is the effect of poverty, which brings dirt, insanitary living habits, disease and so on. And the other type of pollution is that which is now being caused by factories and other such projects. Now, both are equally dangerous [...]
>
> There must be a major national campaign to create a consciousness of the dangers of pollution of any kind, whether it is due to poverty or whether it is due to industrialisation. We have also to include in this campaign a feeling for Nature and to conserve what is worthwhile whether it is the trees, which are very vital to the existence of mankind and I would even say though not directly linked, our architectural and other heritage.
>
> So, I do hope that scientists and technologists in this institution as well as other establishments all over the country will take the lead in educating the public and in advising the Government on what it can do in this matter [...] This Institute is doing much valuable work but its present name is a bit limiting. I think [...] there should be a change of name. The name suggested is that it should now be called "The National Environmental Engineering Research Institute".

Clearly, Indira Gandhi was firm in her belief that the key to conservation lay in the development and application of new science and technology.

ॐ

A couple of months after her Nagpur speech, on 23 March, the Water (Prevention and Control of) Pollution Act, 1974 came into force. It had taken five years to pass this law.

Even before the Stockholm Conference, the Bill had been introduced in Parliament on 22 December 1969. The fall-out of the June 1972 conference, of which Indira Gandhi was one of the stars, and the prime minister's own commitment to the issue, certainly gave the Bill's consideration momentum.

Even so, it took extremely long for the law to become a reality—the delay caused mainly by the fact that there was a wrangle about whether the central government could have such a national law since according to the Constitution the states were responsible for dealing with water pollution. One state in particular, Maharashtra, passed its own law to deal with water pollution and resisted Indira Gandhi's initiative.

If there was a lag, it was also because Indira Gandhi strongly chose not to impose her authority—as she had done in the case of the wildlife protection law two years earlier and as she was to do with the forest conservation law six years later.

Once the Water (Prevention and Control of) Pollution Act, 1974 came into force, the Central Pollution Control Board (CPCB) was established along with similar pollution control boards in states. These institutions continue to be essential instruments for the enforcement of the country's environmental management plans and the quality standards promulgated from time to time.

ॐ

On 5 July, the prime minister wrote to the chief minister of Maharashtra; this was after her meeting with him and his cabinet colleagues to discuss future development plans for Bombay. She reiterated her commitment to having a 'Bombay Metropolitan Development Agency', repeated her serious reservations about the Backbay Reclamation Project and re-emphasized her unstinted support for the New Bombay project:

> The problem of environment and ecology is in urgent need of greater attention. At the meeting I had pointed out that Maharashtra had not yet passed a Resolution to make the Central Act on Water Pollution applicable to the State. The existing State law is not stringent enough. Please take quick action in this regard.
>
> Apart from pollution control, positive efforts must be made to preserve what can be preserved of the remaining green spaces and recreational areas in the city. This is essential for the health and welfare of citizens.

Notwithstanding her own beliefs, sometimes, Indira Gandhi deferred to the views of her officials. The expansion of the fertilizer factory in Chembur, Bombay, especially is a case in point—more so, when her stance is compared to that of the Maharashtra chief minister she had been berating.

On 9 July, the chief minister wrote to her that the expansion being proposed by the Fertilizer Corporation of India (FCI) in Trombay would have adverse environmental consequences. In his letter, he quoted the prime minister's own belief that:

> [...It is] important to have and to strictly enforce rules against the pollution of air and water by industrial projects, whether public or private, with a view to ensuring that the need for economic development which is urgent and inescapable does not become an excuse for neglecting our national environment [...]

The letter could be considered somewhat cheeky because here was a chief minister who was paying the prime minister back in her own coin! He went on to say:

> [...] you have suggested that the cure for an environmental problem is always much more expensive than its prevention [...] I feel that a solution of the problem of the expansion of the F.C.I. Trombay may lie in this observation made by you [...] I am sure it would not be too

difficult to find such [an alternative] location not too far away from the existing factory [...]

The chief minister's letter triggered a quick study by the NCEPC on the pollution impacts of erecting the new plant and taking control measures in the old plant. It concluded that while emissions of sulphuric acid mist would come down drastically, sulphur dioxide emissions would go up; particulates would reduce marginally. The recommendation was that the 'pollution generated should be accepted as a necessary social cost' with, of course, the maximum precautions being taken.

Then there was the clincher—that the installation of additional capacities to existing plants would take less time than the establishment of new plants and hence save precious foreign exchange. The fact that financing arrangements had already been made with the World Bank was also brought to the prime minister's attention.

Indira Gandhi replied to the chief minister on 7 August:

> I have your letter of 3rd July regarding relocation of the expanded Trombay fertilizer unit. You know how strongly I myself feel about pollution. Here, there is the familiar conflict between economic compulsion and environmental purity. My own inclination is always for the latter but in today's critical situation, can we by-pass the former?
>
> After re-examination, the Fertiliser Corporation of India and the Ministry of Petroleum and Chemicals have concluded that, for technical reasons, any proposal to relocate the proposed Trombay IV and V units will compel complete reconsideration of the project [...] Also the loan arrangements already made with the World Bank for Trombay IV and V will have to be renegotiated. [...]

The chief minister had incurred Indira Gandhi's wrath for persisting with the Backbay Reclamation Project. He may also have been indulging in some political grandstanding on the Trombay issue, trying to hoist the prime minister on her own pollution petard. But I have to say that history vindicates him. When I was growing up, Chembur came to be referred to as 'gas-chembur'; and years later, as environment and forests minister, when I asked IIT Delhi to identify the most critically polluting industrial clusters in the country, Chembur was placed in the top ten.

But the chief minister's first letter of 9 July had one positive impact. In a cabinet meeting shortly thereafter, Indira Gandhi 'stressed the need for tightening arrangements against environmental pollution'. The minutes recorded on 24 July by Cabinet Secretary B.D. Pande mentioned two specific suggestions she had made:

(i) It should be made a condition for the grant of an industrial license that provision will be made for the installation of anti-pollution devices in setting up any plant and machinery pursuant to the approval it carries; and

(ii) Research and development should be undertaken to introduce new devices and make the available devices more effective.

Notes

1. Lewis (2003) has discussed this at length.
2. I have described this in Ramesh (2016).

1975

Indira Gandhi taking a walk in the hills, Himachal Pradesh, 1975.

The year started ominously for Indira Gandhi. On 2 January, a ministerial colleague and main fundraiser for her party, L.N. Mishra, was killed in a bomb blast. The anti-corruption movements in both Gujarat and Bihar proceeded apace with students in the forefront. In the midst of turmoil, she demonstrated her sharp political skills and characteristic resolve to mastermind the merger of Sikkim with the Indian Union in mid-April.

On the morning of 12 June, her close confidante D.P. Dhar died of a heart attack. That very day a single judge bench of the Allahabad High Court upheld an election petition filed against her four years earlier by the man she had trounced in the 1971 elections, Raj Narain. She was held guilty of corrupt practices although the widespread consensus even among those opposed to her was that her sins were of a technical nature. Twelve days later, a single judge bench of the Supreme Court granted her relief and she did not have to resign. But within twenty-four hours of the Supreme Court order, her nemesis Jayaprakash Narayan urged the army and the police to disregard the orders of what he called an 'illegal government'. That was provocation enough for Indira Gandhi to impose the dreaded Emergency from the early morning of 26 June invoking Article 352(1) of the Constitution. Although the Emergency had been declared twice before in 1962 and 1971 following external aggression, this was the first time it was being proclaimed to meet a threat to 'internal security'. Her aide P.N. Dhar had tried to bring about an accord between her and Jayaprakash Narayan. He was to write about his efforts a quarter of a century later in which he apportioned blame equally between Indira Gandhi and Jayaprakash Narayan for the Emergency. Her other close aide Sharada Prasad who also had close connections with Narayan wrote about the Emergency contemporaneously to Natwar Singh on 20 July:

> As for friends of India their instinct and yours and mine is right that this country and this person can never be despotic—and the entire operation was necessary to save our political structure. Secularism is the base of Indian democracy. The cardinal mistake of JP and company was to hand over the controls to RSS and no man in his senses can ever say that an RSS-led Opposition Front can preserve a system based upon religious tolerance and equality.

On the morning of India's twenty-eighth Independence Day she got news of the killing of her Bangladeshi counterpart, Sheikh Mujibur Rahman, and his family members. This may well have dashed any hopes of the Emergency being lifted early. But Indira Gandhi herself had not lost her sense of humour because on 19 September she was to write to Dorothy Norman:

> If you can bear to accept a gift from the 'Great Dictator' here is something which I had kept for you some years ago—it is from Bhutan. […] While I write, the Chief Minister of Kerala is watching me patiently. So,

On 25 November, she told Lucile Kyle about what was happening in her life:

> The Indian way of honouring a person on his birthday is to make as much noise as possible and make the day as tiring and burdensome as possible! Hence, I always try to be away from Delhi on that day […] I spent two days in Sikkim and two in Darjeeling […] For me the mountains and the view of the eternal snows are a revitalizing experience.

On 3 April, Indira Gandhi received a somewhat unusual letter from Prince Abdorezza Pahlavi, president of Iran's High Council of Environment and a well-known naturalist. He asked for representative specimens of the Indian swamp deer and the Indian hog deer to add to the National Museum of Natural History at Tehran. Indira Gandhi replied on 14 May:

> [...] We will be happy to give you facilities to collect specimens of the Indian Hog Deer. This animal is not uncommon in India and there is no bar to its collection for scientific purposes.
>
> The Swamp Deer, however, is one of the rarest animals in India and is under extremely strict protection. We do not allow collection of specimens even for our zoos. The Delhi Zoo has a few Swamp Deer, and these are perhaps the only such animals in captivity in India. Until our conservation measures have led to a significant increase in their numbers, we are not able to authorize the collection of any Swamp Deer, even for scientific purposes. I am sure you will understand our need for caution.
>
> If your Department of Environment desires, however, we can try and arrange for an animal that has died from natural causes, either in the wild or in the zoo, to be prepared for a complete mount and sent to Tehran.

Incidentally, three years earlier, Indira Gandhi had authorized Ranjitsinh to negotiate with the Iranians to get some of the nation's cheetahs since they had become extinct in India. (The cheetah was and still is the only mammal to have become extinct in India—an irony given that the word 'cheetah' is derived from Sanskrit). But those negotiations led nowhere. My efforts with Iran as minister in 2010 also did not yield results because by then the animal had become endangered there.

By mid-August 1975, Ranjitsinh had decided to leave for UNEP—his signature achievement clearly being the Wildlife (Protection) Act, 1972. He was succeeded by another passionate environmentalist–administrator N.D. 'Nalni' Jayal. Salim Ali may well have had a hand in Nalni Jayal's appointment in the ministry of environment, for his archives are full of letters between 'Salim Chacha' and 'Nalni', the two having known each other since Jayal had been in school in Dehra Dun.

❧

Mid-1975 marked a little over two years since Project Tiger had been launched. Karan Singh wrote to the prime minister giving a progress report. To this, she replied on 4 July:

> [...] I wonder if the proposal to expand Project Tiger is not premature. The tiger must have scope to prosper in some selected areas, without being forced to compete for primacy with humans. The re-location of villages from tiger sanctuaries is essential. I realize this is a delicate and long-drawn out operation, but unless it is tackled, the whole Project will ultimately fail [...]
>
> I am glad to see that emphasis is to be placed on research. If we are to look after the species properly, we must know more about its habits and way of life [...] The proposed research programme would be better located in the Forest Research Institute in Dehra Dun [which] would also have the advantage of helping to orient entire batches of IFS trainees.

While such letters have made many believe that Indira Gandhi only cared for tigers and mega-fauna, the assumption is flawed. The prime minister was worried about the fate of all species. A good example of this is a letter she wrote on 25 March to Chief Minister of Manipur R.K. Dorendra Singh:

> [...] I am greatly alarmed to learn that the population of the Manipur Brown-Antlered Deer in its natural habitat is down to as little as fourteen. Obviously this species is only a hair's breadth away from extinction. Its fortunes continue to decline although the Keibul Lamjao sanctuary at the south-eastern corner of Log Tak Lake has been established for its preservation.
>
> This beautiful animal is found nowhere in the world but Manipur. It is today the most threatened animal in India and one of the half-dozen most endangered species in the world. If it is to have any chance of survival, the management of the Keibul Lamjao sanctuary has to be greatly tightened up. Grazing and fishing must be stopped and cultivated land taken over. Entry to the sanctuary must be controlled and the protective staff augmented [...]
>
> You should consider the possibility of elevating the sanctuary to the status of a National Park. [...] I am asking our wildlife people to send detailed proposals for the management of the sanctuary, which I hope will receive your personal attention.

Not confident that the chief minister would take her plea seriously, she sent a similar letter to the governor, the redoubtable administrator L.P. Singh, asking him to take special interest in the matter. Her letters did have an impact. On 15 November, the chief minister reported to her that the sanctuary had indeed been notified as a national park—just as she had desired. The fact, however, is that the notification would take place only two years later.

The fate of the 'sangai'—as the deer is commonly known—continued to bother the prime minister. Five years later, on 6 August 1980, she would write to the chief minister again, asserting that 'although the National Park was constituted in 1977 specially for the protection of the rare brown-antlered deer', it continued to be under grave threat. 'The whole ecosystem in that area required proper management,' she added, and exhorted Dorendra Singh to 'do something concrete in this matter immediately'.

Another example of Indira Gandhi's concern for all species emerged exactly two years after the inauguration of Project Tiger, when Project Crocodile was launched on 1 April.

For a couple of years there had been alarming reports that crocodiles were fast becoming endangered in India. All three species—the gharial, estuarine crocodiles and the mugger—were under threat but the gharial was in a particularly vulnerable position.

A decisive turning point was in May 1974, when Robert Bustard—a Scot who had studied physics, switched to biology and then had made a name for himself in Australia as one of the leading authorities on crocodiles—came to India as a FAO/UNDP (Food and Agriculture Organization/United Nations Development Programme) consultant. Forty years later, Bustard recalled to me the chronology of events, admittedly with some embellishment:

> I was fully committed in Australia at the time and FAO recommended two other crocodile experts. Mrs Gandhi was determined to have me and waited till I was available. [...] I visited India in early 1974. At that time India had an outstanding Inspector General of Forests in

K.C. Lahiri [...] I wrote a report [...] stating that the gharial could be saved in the wild, that the estuarine crocodile was facing extinction and required speedy action and that the mugger was seriously depleted [...] Mrs. Gandhi said she would accept the report if I would return to India to supervise the work.

Bustard could not refuse the prime minister's personal request. He conducted a series of field surveys, and his report was made available six months later. It was to be the basis for the crocodile conservation programme. Bustard's work positively impacted not only crocodiles but also sea turtles (which were to engage Indira Gandhi's attention in 1982 and 1983), and the Bhitarkanika Wildlife Sanctuary in Orissa. This sanctuary had been notified on 22 April, but it was soon under serious threat, with thousands of refugees from Bangladesh intending to cut down the mangroves, bund the area to desalinate it and then grow paddy. The sanctuary staff was overwhelmed and it was on Bustard's intimation that Indira Gandhi deployed the CRPF to protect it.

Bustard was to spend eight years in India guiding the crocodile conservation programme; training students such as C.S. Kar, Sudhakar Kar, B.C. Choudhury and L.A.K. Singh—some of whom went on to become leading conservationists, particularly in Orissa; and rescuing the gharial from a point of extreme crisis. While Project Tiger is undoubtedly the most glamourous of India's conservation programmes, Project Crocodile's impact is no less significant.

Indira Gandhi remained concerned about the homes of the animals she loved. On 17 January, she wrote to Jagjivan Ram:

> I am told that now there are hardly any animals in the Kaziranga, Manas or Periyar sanctuaries, with the result that tourists going there to see wildlife return disappointed [...]
>
> This needs closer examination. These places have been designated as National Parks because they are areas of natural concentration of wildlife. Either there is large-scale poaching or human encroachment, or else the

necessary facilities for transportation and viewing within the sanctuaries are not available.

The technique of management of wildlife sanctuaries has become highly specialized. I feel there is some advantage in taking a fresh look at this question and making every effort to improve on our existing performance. If necessary, we should ask knowledgeable foreign experts to give us the benefit of their experience [...]

There is another matter relating to Manas sanctuary. I learn that parts of it have been given for a Government seed farm [...] It is a pity that the farm has been located at this particular place. Please re-examine plans that may exist for expanding the farm and for cutting down any more of the forest in the area.

This letter did lead to greater care being taken in these three sanctuaries—two in Assam and one in Kerala—although Jagjivan Ram did contest the prime minister's contention that Kaziranga was in poor shape. What is especially significant in this letter is her reiteration of the need for specialization in wildlife management. For someone who had a reputation of looking suspiciously at things foreign, Indira Gandhi was remarkably open to getting foreign experts in this area! She demonstrated this time and again.

The prime minister's willingness to engage with naturalists, Indian or foreign, was evident when Steven Green and Karen Minkowski—two young scholars specializing in primates who wished to work in Tamil Nadu—were granted visas. If this episode needs to be highlighted it is also because it was extremely difficult, if not impossible, for American academics to get visas for field research in India—whatever be the subject—in the 1970s.

Here is what Green, now an emeritus professor at the University of Miami, recalled to me:

Indira Gandhi did indeed have a direct role in helping to pave the way for our research permits and the related long-term visas (we were the first Americans to be so granted after the India–Pakistan war) and, then, later in helping to have the Kalakkad Reserve area gain protected status.

But for both these essential activities we went through an intermediary
[…] Salman Haidar […] Our introduction to and working with Haidar
was via the Bombay Natural History Society's renowned ornithologist
Salim Ali […]

In March, Green and Minkowski were joined by John Oates. Their research
was confined to the Kalakkadu Reserve Forest in the southernmost portions
of the Western Ghats. This area was noteworthy not just for its evergreen
shola forests but also for being home to the largest surviving population
of the lion-tailed macaques estimated by Green and Minkowski at around
195 in 1975.

While Oates continued his field work, Green left India in April—but
before leaving, he sent a report on his research to Salman Haidar. Haidar
forwarded the report to the prime minister on 21 October. After reading
it, she queried:

Is he still in India? If in Delhi I should like to meet him.

Clearly impressed with Green's analysis, on 4 November, the prime
minister wrote to B.D. Nag Chaudhary, vice chancellor of JNU and also
the chairman of the NCEPC:

I enclose a copy of a report regarding the lion-tailed monkey of South
India […] It tells us how close the animal is to extinction and how we
can set about saving it […]

Surely, this is the kind of activity that should be undertaken by our
own scholars. I am not aware of similar field work by our universities.
It is high time we started.

On the same day she educated her senior colleague, Jagjivan Ram:

The attached report of the lion-tailed monkey of South India is alarming.
This beautiful animal, found only in India, is rapidly approaching
extinction. Large-scale habitat destruction and indiscriminate hunting
have reduced its numbers to a dangerously low level.

The report also throws light on the decay of our forest wealth. As
plantations take over from virgin forest and as forests continue to be over-
exploited for revenues, far-reaching and potentially disastrous changes in
the eco-system are taking place.

Urgent actions are needed to remedy this. The report pinpoints the Ashambu Hills as a crucial area to be preserved untouched […]

Please get in touch with the Chief Ministers of Tamil Nadu and Kerala and ask them to draw up concrete proposals […] This matter cannot be delayed.

The next day, Indira Gandhi got Haidar to write to Green who was now at New York's Rockefeller University:

It has been a long time but finally we have been able to do something on the strength of your report on the lion-tailed monkeys. The report itself was excellent. We could not have asked for a clearer statement of the problem and a more complete indication of how precisely it should be tackled.

The Prime Minister has seen your report and passed instructions that attempts should be made immediately to set up a sanctuary of the kind described by you in the Ashambu Hills. This will involve getting the two State Governments together in a joint project […]

Your report also gives an indication of how academic activity can be of direct relevance in the conservation effort. We are trying to encourage such activity in our own universities […Your] report deserves wide circulation and I would like to ensure that it reaches all those who will be interested.

This was not all. When Indira Gandhi came to learn that John Oates was having major problems getting clearances from the Ministry of Education for primatology studies, she asked Salman Haidar to attend to the matter. On 1 December, Haidar informed Oates that all clearances for his field work had been issued and that the prime minister was keen that he stayed in touch.

In the meantime, the issue of setting up a sanctuary was more complicated than the prime minister had imagined. The area had been leased out for exploitation to a private company, Bombay Burmah Trading Corporation, and a crucial corridor of forest land connecting two larger patches had already been scheduled for felling by the private company. Fortunately, Indira Gandhi was scheduled to be in Chennai on 14 and 15 February 1976. Since the state was then under the President's Rule, she used this opportunity to speak directly to the governor and his adviser,

P.K. Dave. Less than three weeks later the Kalakkadu Reserve Forest was notified as a sanctuary for the lion-tailed macaque, and a ban on felling was also introduced in the company's lease document.

ॐ

Indira Gandhi had written to the chief minister of Uttar Pradesh in 1973, on behalf of Billy Arjan Singh and the Dudhwa Sanctuary. The chief minister had vowed to expand the sanctuary, convert it into a national park and put a curb on commercial forestry. Evidently, Billy Arjan Singh complained to the prime minister that none of these promises had been kept—for on 8 April 1975, she reprimanded the chief minister:

> [...] Nothing more has been heard about expanding the Sanctuary and introducing the necessary legislation to convert it into a national park. Instead the UP Government has decided that the selective felling of trees will be undertaken throughout the Sanctuary, even in areas where the heaviest concentration of animals is found [...] I understand, also, that the normal commercial practice of auctioning minor forest produce continues as before [...]
>
> These decisions are in drastic contradiction to what was originally proposed. Far from showing progress, Dudwa's future is today less secure than when I last wrote to you.
>
> There is need for urgent re-examination of the plans for Dudwa. As a first step, I feel you should appoint Arjan Singh as a Honorary Wildlife Warden. This year he was decorated with [the] Padma Sri [...]
>
> Thereafter, detailed plans should be drawn up for the consolidation and expansion of Dudwa Sanctuary along the lines I have already suggested. The existing sanctuary should be the 'sanctum sanctorum' for a larger park. Within the 'sanctum sanctorum' no forestry operations whatsoever should be permitted [...]
>
> Dudwa is potentially the finest sanctuary of the Terai region [...]

The chief minister got her message loud and clear. While he immediately went on the defensive and promised not to let her down this time around, it was too late—she forced him to resign seven months later. There were far weightier political reasons behind her move to get him to quit—but

Indira Gandhi's unhappiness with him over the neglect of Dudhwa, despite her urgent petitioning, may well have contributed a bit to her ire at him.

∾

Indira Gandhi had sparred with Rajasthan Chief Minister Harideo Joshi a couple of months earlier on the issue of the central government's takeover on lease of the Bharatpur Bird Sanctuary and the Sariska Tiger Reserve. Simply put, Joshi had politely snubbed the prime minister and retained state government control.

Indira Gandhi, not one to be taken lightly, dispatched a fresh letter on 6 March. She spoke of the sharply deteriorating conditions at the bird sanctuary because of unregulated over-grazing and the unauthorized felling of trees. She suggested building a perimeter wall or a simple barbed wire fence as a remedial measure. She wanted the chief minister to send her a proposal for protecting the sanctuary and added that the proposal had to take into account the legitimate needs of the villagers in the vicinity. This was a fresh development—while, so far, Indira Gandhi had listened to conservationists, now she expressed equal concern for the fodder and fuelwood requirements of those living around the sanctuary. She recognized that 'without their cooperation, no physical barrier will prove adequate'.

A few months later, Indira Gandhi had made up her mind that the barbed wire fence would not suffice—vulnerable as it would be to cutting—and that a wall was the only solution. On 14 December, she informed Jagjivan Ram about her views on the matter—that 'in the long run, a perimeter wall will ensure the survival of the sanctuary and its development as a park for the benefit of the people from a large area around Bharatpur'. She wanted him to discuss a detailed management plan with the state government 'to ensure continuity and good order in the running of the sanctuary', and concluded by saying: 'I should like work on the wall to start as soon as possible.'

Again, as an example of how she did not always have her way, Jagjivan Ram wrote to her on 23 December that—presumably because it is less expensive and funds were difficult to come by—the option of a barbed wire fence had to be exercised. The matter rested there for a while and would get resolved only after the prime minister herself visited Bharatpur for the first time in February 1976.

ॐ

On 14 April, Salim Ali wrote to the prime minister informing her that the Maharashtra government had revived a proposal to build a highway that would cut through the Borivali National Park, Bombay. The highway would naturally lead to a wide area of trees being cleared. He told her that his efforts to persuade the state authorities to abandon the project had proved infructuous and she was now the 'only hope'.

Salim Ali's 'only hope' took up the matter with Maharashtra Chief Minister S.B. Chavan eight days later. She told him that she understood the need for such a project in a city like Bombay. At the same time she underscored the need for preserving the open spaces in the city which were already heavily congested, and for respecting 'wildlife and nature conservation and this means preservation of parks and sanctuaries'. In her view, it was imperative for the chief minister to suspend the existing highway project and find an alternative alignment for the link highway.

The chief minister replied to her on 30 April with the news that her directive had been complied with right away. The Borivali National Park—which, in later years, would hit the headlines for its leopard population—was thus saved.

ॐ

The Calcutta Zoological Gardens celebrated its centenary anniversary on 24 September. There was a demand that the prime minister visit the zoo to mark the occasion but conscious that it would not be possible, she sent a message on 12 September:

> As a child I loved zoos. Later it made me sad that creatures which had roamed so freely and proudly in the jungle should be forced to pace up and down narrow cages. In India, children and adults too sometimes harass and harm animals in zoos and outside. The modern zoological garden has greater regard for animals and attempts to put them in surroundings as similar as possible to their natural habitat. [...]

Animal species which were formerly plentiful are now rare or under threat of extinction. This is not merely because of the growing population but due largely to carelessness and rapacity which cloud the larger vision. The conservation of flora and fauna is neither a whim or a luxury. It is essential for mankind's survival [...] Zoos must help teach people to know animals and to love them; to reverse the trend towards destruction and to give a fair chance to our wildlife.

As Indira Gandhi's reputation for being a champion of wildlife conservation spread globally, a noted German filmmaker Karl-Heinz Kramer approached her for a message to be broadcast on German and European television alongside films on Indian sanctuaries. He met her and on 5 March, she sent him this message:

I have always been fascinated by the beauty and infinite variety of the wild. Preservation of this priceless heritage should be the concern of every human being. For, the extinction of any species upsets the ecological balance and threatens the human race. I hope this film will convey a sense of wonder and delight in the ways of animals and birds to our people and help them in the movement of conservation.

This message, like a number of others, had her favourite term 'ecological balance'. Even earlier, on 26 February, the phrase had cropped up during her speech in Parliament. Generally, when the prime minister replied to important debates in Parliament, she had a prepared text, which she would not read from, but certainly consult along the way. Yet, when she had to comment on issues related to nature conservation or wildlife protection, she would speak without notes or slips of paper in front of her. She said:

In our treasures I would include not only monuments and architectural treasures but also the art of the region, the wildlife of the region and the forests of the region. Honourable Members are very anxious to have paper mills and industries, and I am for them too. Please do not think I am cancelling any licence to a paper mill. But we must not denude our mountainside and our countryside of their forests. This is having an adverse affect on our rainfall and climate. Unfortunately you do not see the results of such vandalism immediately; when you do realize, it is too late. [...] The same goes for wildlife [...] the elimination of any species has a bad effect on the general *ecological balance* [italics mine] and thereby also affects the human species.

A similar message was conveyed on 1 April when industrialist S.P. Godrej, who shared a passion for nature with Indira Gandhi, asked her for a message for a WWF-India event:

Man often forgets that he is part of this earth, so full of beauty and wonder, and that his survival depends on the maintenance of nature's balance. Thus the utilization of natural resources must go hand in hand with conservation. The reckless manner in which resources have been consumed and wasted has created alarming problems.

India is not yet highly industrialised, so the petering out of minerals is not the most immediate danger. But the increasing needs of our population are fast encroaching upon forests and pasture areas. Our forests must be preserved because of a variety of benefits as well as their crucial influence on climate. They are the chief habitat for our wildlife, which deserves protection as much as any other resource. A widespread campaign is necessary to bring home to our people the need to conserve the land, its mineral and plant resources and its animal life.

I am glad that the World Wildlife Fund is vigourously propagating the message of conservation in our country.

Indira Gandhi was a silviculturist first. This was evident on 29 August—a little over two months after the Emergency had been imposed—when she spoke to the chief secretaries of all states on the challenges confronting the country; the opportunities for good governance that presented themselves; her expectations from the administration on the implementation of economic policies and social programmes; and most significantly, her concerns regarding the environment:

[...] Some way must be found that the minimum forest requirements are not interfered with. I don't think there is any State which has the full area which should be under forest. Trees are cut down mercilessly [...]

More trees should be planted; there should be greater afforestation […]
We put up industries without bothering about air or water pollution
with the result that people become ill […]

So alert was Indira Gandhi about forest cover that she sent out anguished
letters each time she learnt of a breach. On 8 July, she sent a quickly
scribbled note to Salman Haidar:

Someone who has recently returned from Manali (H.P.) tells me that
trees are being cut recklessly.

Fifteen days later, a letter to the chief minister of the state, Y.S. Parmar,
followed:

You know how I am deeply concerned that our forests should be preserved
and developed. With proper management, we can extract a great deal of
wealth from our forests and yet conserve them. Himachal is one of the
key areas and merits special attention.

I am greatly distressed to learn that the forest around Manali is being
cut down recklessly. Manali's character and charm as a hill resort owe
much to the splendid forest cover in the area. This must be preserved.
Please look into the plans for forestry operations in the vicinity and try
to ensure that they are kept in control.

I should like to be kept informed.

A second letter from the prime minister followed two months later
on 14 September and on the same day, a similar letter was sent to
H.N. Bahuguna, the chief minister of Uttar Pradesh—the other state in
which forest contractors purportedly held sway:

I have already written to you regarding the cutting of trees in Himachal
Pradesh. I learn that this continues unabated and that your laws or
rules in this respect are defective. I am told that contractors are allowed
to cut a large number of trees in a particular area over so many years.
Naturally, this will result in denudation of that part of the forest. Trees
should be cut not from one area but in-between, and planting should
be done simultaneously.

Please let me have your rules under which such contracts are given
as soon as possible.

One consequence of these letters, dispatched in quick succession, was that the chief minister of Himachal Pradesh soon took over the forests portfolio himself!

On 15 May, Indira Gandhi wrote to Sarat Chandra Sinha, the chief minister of Assam, on a similar issue:

> I learn that the Diju forest in Nowgong District is being cut down by contractors, who are making a handsome profit. There may be plans for replanting, but meanwhile the forest is being denuded and the wildlife in the area is in danger. There is a threat of irreversible damage.
>
> This is disturbing news and I should like to have a fuller report. I need hardly stress the need for careful regulation of forest wealth. Assam, with its splendid and extensive forest ranges, including some of the finest in the country, needs to be specially watchful.
>
> I would also like to bring to your attention a matter that has been causing some anxiety. You would be aware that Assam is one of the few States which have not till now acceded to the Wildlife (Protection) Act, 1972. [...But] I feel that the Central legislation should be accepted by your State even if only partial implementation can be managed at this stage. Assam is a key State for wildlife protection [...]

On 25 July, the chief minister replied that the information she held regarding the devastation of forests was incorrect and that the annual rate of clear felling was just 1 to 1.5 per cent. This worked out to no more than 25 hectares per year—so in his view the situation was not as alarming as the prime minister had been given to understand. But on the other issue of the Wildlife (Protection) Act, 1972, he promised expeditious action, claiming that the delay had been caused by the uncertainty of the receipt of funds from the centre. As it turned out, Assam was to adopt the law only on 27 January 1977, showing that even as she was portrayed as being authoritarian on occasion, chief ministers could get by, by doing what they wanted—even on matters about which the prime minister felt passionately.

Indira Gandhi was as concerned with the preservation of India's historical heritage as she was in protecting nature; nature and culture were, in her view, interlinked. A couple of her letters in early January stand testimony to this.

Indira Gandhi wrote to Harideo Joshi, the chief minister of Rajasthan, on 5 January regarding Jaisalmer. She had written to his predecessor once-removed, Mohanlal Sukhadia on the same subject seven years earlier:

> After visiting the site of our nuclear explosion,[1] I went into Jaisalmer to have a quick look at the beautiful and famous Havelis. I was distressed to see how far this historic city has fallen into decline. The old Havelis which embody the traditional architectural skills of Rajasthan, are being used for herds of goats and cattle. New constructions are being put up without regard to the preservation of the special character of the city. At this rate, it is only a matter of time before our rich heritage in Jaisalmer is irretrievably lost.
>
> We must make a determined effort to preserve and revitalize Jaisalmer [...]
>
> We must also develop a longer view regarding the future of Jaisalmer. The School of Planning and Architecture of Delhi has been commendably active in studying Jaisalmer as an urban and artistic phenomenon. [...] I suggest that the Head of the School, Shri Jhabvala might be asked to undertake a town planning study of Jaisalmer [...]
>
> Pending the finalization of a broader plan for the city, you should consider banning further construction activity. Jaisalmer should be spared the haphazard urban building activity that has disfigured so many of our cities.

Incidentally, her long-time personal physician Dr K.P. Mathur has given a hilarious account of her trip to the historic havelis of Jaisalmer in his memoirs.[2] Evidently the visit was top-secret and planned at the very last minute after she had been to Pokharan.

> It was early in the morning and there were very few people on the streets. As we were winding through the streets of Jaisalmer, some people recognized PM in the car and news spread that she was in town. The people were surprised and when we reached the havelis in question and

the officer started to explain things and answered her queries, a small crowd consisting mostly of ladies had collected. A small girl came out of the crowd and questioned PM in a challenging tone, "You are Indira Gandhi?" PM nodded in assent. This was repeated once more and then the girl, as if she had made a great discovery, exclaimed: "I have recognized you; you are Indira Gandhi!" PM burst out laughing and, to further satisfy the girl's curiosity, suggested to her, "*Choo kar dekh* (touch and see)."… everyone had a good laugh at PM's sense of humour.

The other telling example of Indira Gandhi's nature-culture stance is seen in a long letter of 15 January to Professor S. Nurul Hasan, the minister of education and culture:

I remain anxious about the functioning of the Archaeological Survey of India. In the last few years, the Survey has taken on a good deal of additional responsibility, principally to exercise control on the holdings and movement of antiquities. It has also had to keep in view the needs of tourism at some of our major monuments. This expansion of its original functions has necessitated a change of orientation which has not always been achieved, with the result that demands are being raised for structural changes in the Survey itself.

The enforcement function is of paramount importance. What new staff have been appointed and put in position for the implementation of the Antiquities Bill? What progress has been achieved in recording holdings of antiquities in private hands? Has there been any meaningful progress in protecting far-flung architectural sites and bringing loose sculpture into sheltered storage? These matters are urgent and require careful and sustained attention.

There is also the question of tourism and therefore of the Survey. Our ancient monuments are among the major attractions for tourists to our country. It is obvious that the Survey and the Department of Tourism must work in close concert to ensure that tourists are provided with all necessary facilities. It is my impression that coordination between the two is inadequate. You should try [to] work out in consultation with the Department of Tourism, a list of monuments of primary tourist interest and then set up a Cell in the Survey to devote special attention to tourist requirements at these sites. While giving every protection to

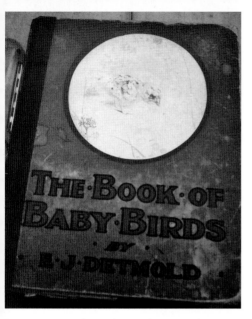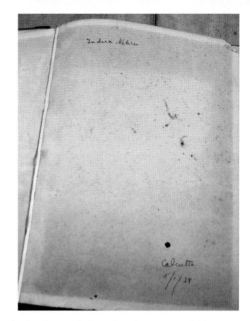

An inscription by Indira Nehru in Calcutta in *The Book of Baby Birds* found in her personal library.

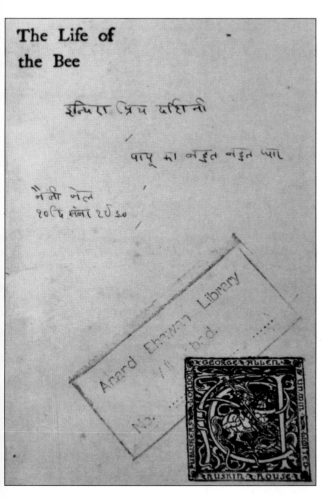

A book gifted by Jawaharlal Nehru to Indira Priyadarshini with his inscription in Hindi, Naini Jail; 10 December 1930.

Jawaharlal Nehru and Indira Gandhi watching lions in Gir, Gujarat; November 1955.

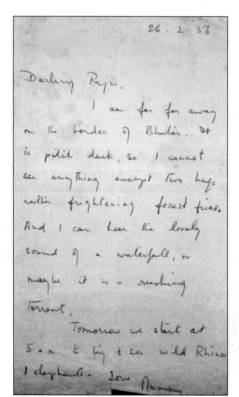

Indira Gandhi's letter to Rajiv Gandhi from Manas Sanctuary, Assam; 26 February 1956.

Indira Gandhi in Himachal Pradesh; winter 1956.

Jawaharlal Nehru with Himalayan pandas, Teen Murti House; 1957.

Indira Gandhi on a yak on trip to Bhutan; 1958.

I have come here for rest and quiet again with my daughter. The garden continues to be attractive and well looked after. It is a pleasure to stay here.

Jawaharlal Nehru
25th May 1964

Familiarity bred of countless visits has not dimmed my joy in this garden. Each time 'my heart leaps up,' as Wordsworth would say, to behold the wonder of this setting — the delicate loveliness of the flowering trees against the imposing background of the Mussoorie hills. I must confess, however, that the attraction of the garden lies in its setting & its magnificent trees. The pot plants are good but the layout of the flower beds leaves much room for improvement.

Indira Gandhi

Entries of Jawaharlal Nehru and Indira Gandhi in the visitor's book,
Dehra Dun; May 1964.

Indira Gandhi at the Nehru Institute of Mountaineering, Uttarkashi; June 1966.

प्रधान मन्त्री भारत

PRIME MINISTER,
INDIA.

Raj Bhawan,
Jaipur.

February 10, 1966

Dear Major Kumar,

Thank you for your message of congratulation.

I do not know how much can be done in these few months when people seem to be more concerned with the coming general elections, but I shall certainly try. I hope the spirit of the Himalayas will help us. With good wishes,

Yours sincerely,

Indira Gandhi

(Indira Gandhi)

Major N. Kumar,
Indian Everest Expedition,
55, Kotah House,
New Delhi.

Indira Gandhi's letter to Major Kumar; February 1966.

Indira Gandhi's address to the Tenth General Assembly of the IUCN, New Delhi;
November 1969.

12.   There are one or two wider questions which
arise. We have made a provision of Rs.50 lakhs for
wild life tourism. This will be spent on the creation
of tourist facilities in our Parks and sanctuaries.
Could not GOI put aside an equal sum for the welfare
of the animals in the Parks? This could be used to
train specialised staff; to grow scattered patches
of crops to prevent animals from straying outside
in search of food; to build fences or dig trenches
to keep cattle out; to provide more water holes and
salt licks; and to establish special veterinary units
etc. None of our Parks has a development plan with
emphasis on wild life rather than creature comforts
for human beings. With a little bit of money such
a scheme could be initiated, and easily fitted in to
the larger programme of rural works.

13.   PM is the last hope for our vanishing animals.
If she does not succeed, no one else can.

Yes to 'A' & 'B'. But alas
much as I would love to
go to Kanha, I don't think I
should. My experience of what the security
men do before & during my stay in
such places is heartbreaking.

DS

M. Malhoutra
(M. Malhoutra)
20.1.70

20-1-70

Indira Gandhi's observations on Moni Malhoutra's note
on Kanha; January 1970.

Indira Gandhi with Buckminster Fuller in the *Architectural Forum*; September 1971.

Indira Gandhi at the inauguration of the National Committee on Environmental Planning and Coordination (NCEPC) with C. Subramaniam (left) and Pitambar Pant (right); April 1972.

Indira Gandhi's note to Moni Malhoutra; May 1972.

Indira Gandhi with four chief ministers—(left to right) V.P. Naik, chief minister of Maharashtra; Ghanshyam Oza, chief minister of Gujarat; Barkatullah Khan, chief minister of Rajasthan; and P.C. Sethi, chief minister of Madhya Pradesh—signing an agreement on projects along the Narmada; August 1972.

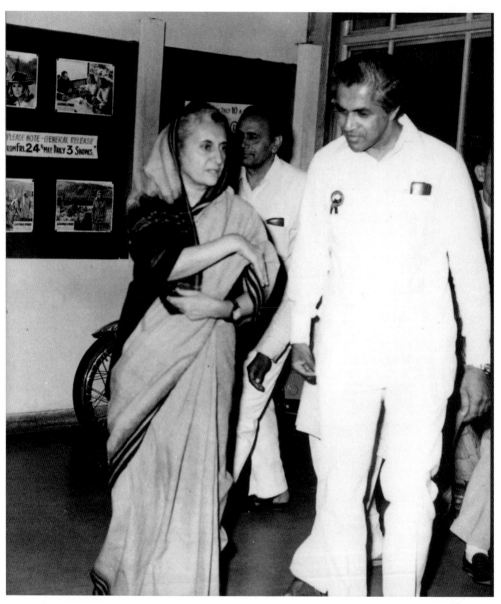

Indira Gandhi with Duleep Matthai at a special screening of *Living Free*, circa April/May1972.

Indira Gandhi flanked by P.N. Haksar (left) and P.N. Dhar (right) at Haksar's farewell; January 1973.

Indira Gandhi's note to Moni
Malhoutra on Mudumalai Sanctuary;
January 1973.

Indira Gandhi with Major H.P.S. Ahluwalia; May 1973.

Indira Gandhi laying the foundation stone of the Mathura oil refinery;
October 1973.

Indira Gandhi laying the foundation stone of the Indian Navy's Boys Training
Establishment, Chilka, Orissa; October 1973.

Indira Gandhi at BNHS, Bombay; September 1974.

Indira Gandhi's note on Manali to Salman Haidar; July 1975.

Indira Gandhi's observations on a note sent to her on Sesbania Grandiflora; March 1976.

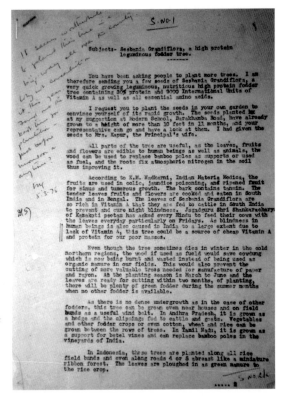

Some time ago it was brought to P.M's attention that Sesbania Grandiflora, a high protein leguminous fodder tree, could profitably be grown on a large scale. PM had thought that this might be useful and had asked whether the best time for planting would be before the monsoon or any other time.

IG Forests has now told us that a number of field investigations have already been carried out at the Forest Research Institute about Sesbania grandiflora. The species is useful for paper manufacture and for various other purposes, though it does not have much value as fuel wood. In rural areas this provides a useful hedge plant; it is used for browsing and its flowers are used as a vegetable.

Instructions are being issued to Forest Departments to raise the plant under the Farm Forestry Programmes during the ensuing monsoon. The best time for planting seems to be just before the rains.

Submitted for information.

S. Haidar.
(S. Haidar)
9.4.1976

*I looked it up
P.M. myself last evening in my little book*

14.4.76

Indira Gandhi's observations on Salman Haidar's note on
Sesbania Grandiflora; April 1976.

Indira Gandhi in a national park in Zambia; October 1976.

Indira Gandhi with Billy Arjan Singh (centre); June 1978.

Indira Gandhi with Anne Wright; late 1980.

Indira Gandhi's note in the visitor's book, Gir National Park; January 1981.

Indira Gandhi with Peter Scott and Diane Pierce after the presentation of a painting of
Siberian cranes; February 1981.

Indira Gandhi feeding kangaroo during a retreat organized by the Commonwealth Summit, Melbourne, Australia; May 1981.

SALIM ALI
46 Pali-Hill, Bandra
Bombay-400 050

21 June 1981

Mrs Indira Gandhi
Prime Minister of India
New Delhi

7377–PM-81
dt. 24-6-81.

Dear Mrs. Gandhi

    I am forwarding herewith a letter addressed to you by my friend and fellow-ornithologist Dr S.Dillon Ripley, co-author of our <u>Handbook of the Birds of India and Pakistan</u>. Together, in early 1979, we had started a field study of the birds of the Namdapha area of Tirap district (Arunachal Pradesh)- a pristine rain forest as yet totally 'uncivil-ised' by man - which is earmarked for a Biosphere Reserve. It has seldom been visited by a naturalist,and we know exceedingly little about its wildlife. For this reason the area has remained perhaps the least documented in our Hand-book.

    Both Dr Ripley and I are most anxious to rectify this deficiency before it becomes too late (for me at any rate!), and I therefore hope it will be possible for your Govern-ment to consider favourably our request for permission to resume field work in the Namdapha area in the coming winter season, particularly since Arunachal Pradesh is fortunately not involved in the inanities of Assam and some other states of the N→E region!

With warm greetings

Yours sincerely
Salim Ali

I should very much like to oblige Shri Salim Ali for whom I have high regard. So far as I know Dr Ripley is reliable. But please look into the matter.

If 26.6.

Indira Gandhi's observations on Salim Ali's letter; June 1981.

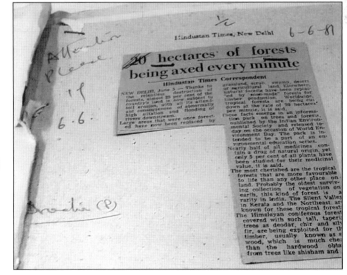

Indira Gandhi's noting on a news clipping on deforestation; June 1981.

Indira Gandhi planting tree at her old school in Bex, Switzerland; October 1981.

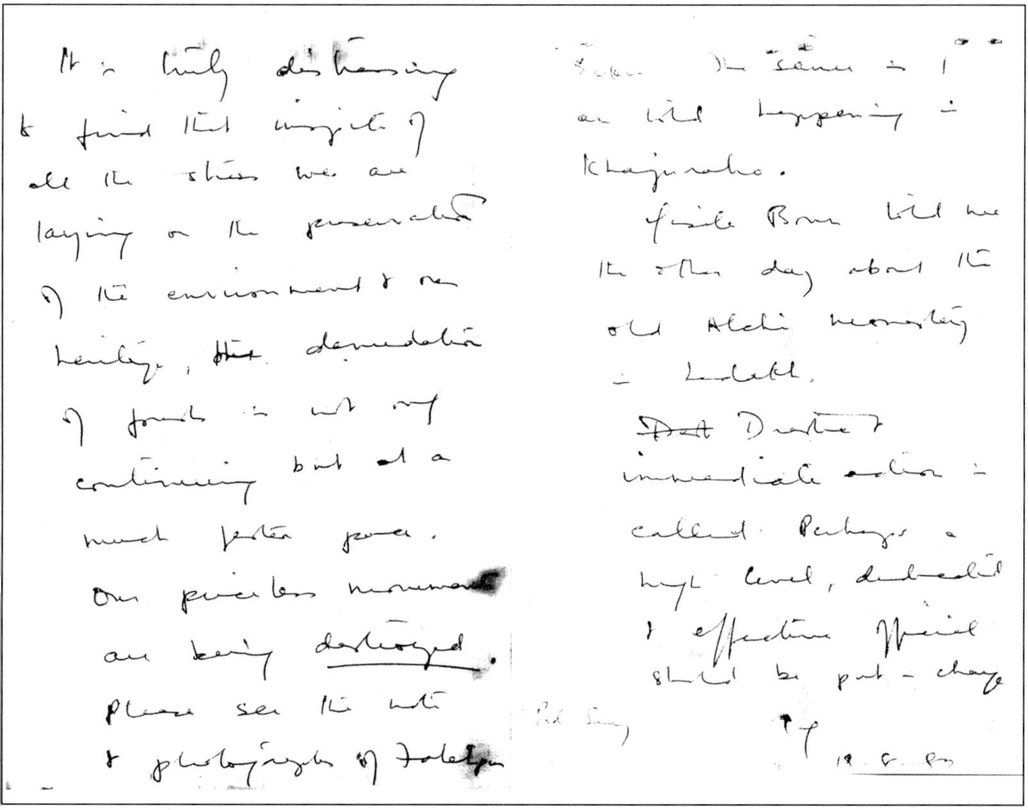
It is truly distressing to find that inspite of all the stress we are laying on the preservation of the environment & our heritage, ~~this~~ degradation of forests is not only continuing but at a much faster pace. Our priceless monuments are being destroyed. Please see the note & photographs of Fatehpur Sikri. The same is I am told happening in Khajuraho.

Gisele Bose told me the other day about the old Alchi monastery in Ladakh.

~~Dest~~ Drastic & immediate action is called. Perhaps a high level, dedicated & effective official should be put in charge.

IG 18.8.82

Indira Gandhi's note to P.C. Alexander; August 1982.

ON AUGUST 4, 1982, HER
EXCELLENCY MRS. INDIRA
GANDHI, PRIME MINISTER
OF INDIA, PRESENTED MARI,
A YOUNG FEMALE ELEPHANT,
FROM THE CHILDREN OF INDIA
TO THE CHILDREN OF HAWAII

A plaque at the Honolulu Zoo in honour of Indira Gandhi's visit; August 1982.

Indira Gandhi presented with the Order of the Golden Ark by Prince Bernhard of the Netherlands, New Delhi; August 1982.

In the circumstances, Home Ministry feel the permission
should be declined politely. However, if it is decided to
clear the visit, an alternative could be that a senior offi
from the Department of Environment is instructed to accompa
Dr. Ripley.

Secretary, Environment, in his note on the matter,
points out that he had written to Dr. Ripley on 23rd Novemb
requesting him to send the report about the survey and stuc
already completed for the area covered also indicating wha
remains to be done. This was considered necessary as Dr.Rip
has visited Arunachal Pradesh twice in the company of Dr.
Salim Ali, but no report has been received about the work
accomplished and what remains to be done. Instead of reply:
to the Secretary, Environment, Dr. Ripley has chosen to wr:
to P.M. on 26th January,1983, without giving any report of
the type required. Secretary, Environment, also referred t
the fact that Dr. Ripley did fire at an animal from a vehi
at dusk time. This was violation of the provisions of the
Wildlife(Protection)Act of 1972, but presumably the Union
Territory administration did not go beyond lodging the pro
because the visit of the team has the clearance and suppor
of the Government of India. Keeping all the factors in vie
Secretary, Environment, has expressed that the Department
of Environment cannot possibly give clearance for another
visit of Arunachal Pradesh by Dr. Ripley unless his report
is received and studied and until such a visit has the ful
concurrence and support of the U.T.Administration and Mini
of Home Affairs. (Secretary, Environment, is looking at th
possibilities of taking up the work done by Dr. Ripley on
own with the help of BNHS, ZSI and eminent orinthologists
the country).

Indira Gandhi's observations on a note on Salim Ali and Dillon Ripley's expedition
to Arunachal Pradesh; April 1983.

Indira Gandhi's favourite place of stay in Dachigam National Park, Jammu and Kashmir.

I am delighted to have this brief respite in one of our best known & best kept national parks. I hope such efforts will enthuse others to take a greater interest in conservation.

Indira Gandhi

17-1-1984

Indira Gandhi's observations in the visitor's book at Kanha National Park;
January 1984.

A baby elephant has been promised to the Imparo PD for the children of Imparo. Please locate one quickly.

I P

P.S. —

I thought we could have a MOTI — which could suit a male or female & also easy pronounceable

Indira Gandhi's note to Samar Singh; May 1984.

Indira Gandhi enjoying a moment of quiet by a beach probably in
Lakshadweep; 1976.

Shakti Sthal, Indira Gandhi's samadhi.

the monuments themselves, we should not be unduly conservative in developing their environs so as to attract more visitors, especially from abroad.

℘

In mid-May, the Union cabinet gave its final approval to the Kudremukh project. Like the Mathura refinery, this would become somewhat of a blot on Indira Gandhi's environmental record.

Under normal circumstances, the prime minister may not have approved of the project. But the alacrity with which she responded reminds us that those were highly abnormal years—when India suffered from an acute shortage of foreign exchange and was doing all that it could to build up its economic relationship with oil-exporting countries, among them Iran.

Indira Gandhi herself had visited Iran between 28 April and 2 May 1974. On the last day of her trip, the foreign ministers of both countries had signed a memorandum of understanding (MoU) in which pride of place was given to the Kudremukh project—a venture to develop low-grade iron ore mines in the Western Ghats area of southern Karnataka.

The numbers seemed attractive. The project—which was to be commissioned by 1980 and have a life of twenty years—would see the production of around 7.5 million tonnes of iron ore concentrate per year that would be picked up by Iran for its steel plants. Iran was to extend low-cost (at an interest rate of about 2.5 per cent per year) credit for financing the total cost of the project which was around US$630 million. It was to make an immediate down payment of US$100 million and an advance payment of US$250 million. The Indian side estimated that even during the repayment of the loan, there would be substantial *net* foreign exchange earnings to the country to the tune of about US$100 million per year. This may seem like a small amount today when India's foreign exchange reserves exceed US$350 billion, but back then, it was not a sum to be sneezed at, given that reserves stood at just about US$2 billion.

During the entire period of negotiations, the term 'environmental impact' was not mentioned. All that was kept in view was that the project had to begin immediately—after all, the Iranians could not be expected to wait, and India had scarce foreign exchange.

215

Regardless, all plans came unstuck even before the Iranian Revolution of February 1979. By October 1978, Iran suspended loan disbursements because it was unhappy with the terms of the contract and feared that it could end up paying for the ore concentrate a higher price than it had bargained for. Till then, only about US$250 million of the promised US$630 million came from Iran. Ironically, therefore, India ended up bearing an additional burden of US$375 million.

The Iranians may have withdrawn, but the project, having started, continued and commissioning took place in August 1980. New markets had to be quickly found and indeed were. However, very soon the environmental impact in an ecologically fragile area became evident. Since the iron content in the ore was just about 30 per cent, 70 per cent waste mud had to be dumped. Besides, the construction of roads and slurry pipelines destroyed rich forest areas. It was only thanks to a conservation NGO in Karnataka that the Supreme Court, in October 2002, ordered all mining activity to cease by 31 December 2005. By then, much damage had already been done.

At the height of her political power, on 22 July 1972, Indira Gandhi had called four chief ministers, all from her party, from the states of Gujarat, Madhya Pradesh, Rajasthan and Maharashtra, to try and arrive at a political settlement to the dispute over sharing of the water of the Narmada river. But the chief minister of Madhya Pradesh, P.C. Sethi, stood his ground firmly and the only point of consensus was that 'the various viewpoints with regard to the height of the Navagam Dam [in Gujarat] would be gone into and a suitable height may also be fixed by the Prime Minister of India'. The ball had now landed fairly and squarely in Indira Gandhi's court. But no easy compromise that would satisfy both Gujarat and Madhya Pradesh could be found.

On 12 July 1974, the prime minister had again called the four chief ministers. By this time, Gujarat had come under President's Rule and was therefore, represented by the adviser to the governor, who happened to be none else than Indira Gandhi's mountaineering friend H.C. Sarin. But this meeting, too, proved unproductive and all that could be achieved was an agreement that 'the height of the Navagam Dam [was] to be fixed by the Tribunal after taking into consideration various contentions and submissions of the parties hereto'.

Obviously, there were limits to Indira Gandhi's power. There were also limits beyond which she was reluctant to use her authority—especially when issues proved to be politically contentious. Besides, the prime minister had come to realize that the safest route would be to refer the matter back to the judicial tribunal which had been set up in October 1969. Fortunately, she got the parties concerned to agree that the tribunal would decide how the costs and benefits of the Navagam Dam could be shared among the four states.

In 1975, the prime minister made a final effort to resolve the Narmada issue, but this time she did not intervene directly. She asked Minister of Agriculture and Irrigation Jagjivan Ram to liaise with the three chief ministers and the Gujarat governor's adviser on 8 March and see whether a compromise was possible. That very day, she was informed by her aide V. Ramachandran that while no agreement could be reached because of the firm stand of the chief minister of Madhya Pradesh, Gujarat and Madhya Pradesh had agreed that four smaller projects in each state—and eight in all—could go ahead. This, she was told, was 'another small step forward'.

The tribunal, on its part, worked painstakingly and submitted its report on 16 August 1978 but its recommendations were soon challenged by the states concerned. The tribunal then examined these challenges and handed its final report about four months later. It was the award of the tribunal that formed the basis of the construction of dams on the Narmada in Madhya Pradesh and Gujarat. Before any new controversy could arise, Indira Gandhi got the Narmada Control Authority up and running from 23 December 1980 to implement the tribunal's decisions.

But this did not provide any respite. The decision to go ahead with the dams proved hugely contentious and led to the emergence of one of India's most well-known ecological movements—the Narmada Bachao Andolan. While most of the major agitations would unfold after Indira Gandhi's death, by the early 1980s, it had become amply clear that large forest areas in Madhya Pradesh would be submerged and thousands of families in both

Madhya Pradesh and Gujarat would get displaced on account of the dams.[3] Sardar Sarovar, the name given to the Navagam dam complex to honour Sardar Vallabhbhai Patel, was to get a final environmental clearance on 13 April 1987 at a meeting presided over by the then prime minister Rajiv Gandhi—ironically on the same day that he was to speak at a function on conservation organized by Salim Ali.

Notes

1. On 22 December 1974, she had visited Pokhran, the site of India's 'peaceful nuclear experiment' of 18 May 1974.
2. Mathur (2016).
3. There is a vast body of literature on the Narmada issue. Khagram (2004) is a well-researched, scholarly account.

1976

Indira Gandhi's note to Rajiv Gandhi; September 1976.

The Emergency became firmly entrenched in 1976. This was also the year in which Sanjay Gandhi, his ambitions to be the Henry Ford of India having failed, emerged from the background to become a very visible political figure. He enunciated an unexceptionable five-point national programme to promote literacy, abolition of dowry, eradication of casteism, tree planting and family planning. Chief ministers genuflected to him as did ministers. Those who were even mildly critical of him like Defence Minister Swaran Singh who had *served in every cabinet since 1952 were dropped or sent off to political exile like I.K. Gujral who had been once part of his mother's inner circle. Sterilizations, often forced, became the crucial anchor of India's population planning drive. However, after three consecutive bad years, the economy started looking up and the public investment programme, always a key catalyst for economic growth, began to see signs of revival.*

In September, Indira Gandhi wrote what must surely be her longest letter extending to eight pages. It was to Olaf Palme again and I suspect it went to her counterparts elsewhere as well. It was an elaborate defence of the Emergency and a detailed account of what it had achieved in fifteen months in terms of economic growth and social reform. She took pride in the fact that 1975–76 had seen the economy growing by 6–6.5 per cent, that inflation after shooting up to 23 per cent in 1973–74 and 30 per cent in 1974–75, had now reduced very substantially, that production of foodgrains, coal, power and fertilizers had touched an all-time high, bonded labour had been abolished, land ceiling laws and rights of tenants were being strictly enforced and 6.8 million house sites distributed to the landless poor. She also spoke of different political parties and their mindsets, some feudal, some purely agitational and some communal and chauvinistic. She urged Palme as a social democrat to be more appreciative and understanding of the problems she faced, challenges she confronted and the initiatives she had taken which had been lauded even by the World Bank.

In October she went on a three-nation trip to Africa, a continent she was returning to after a long interval. When she was in Zambia, she asked to visit one of that country's best-known nature landmarks, the South Luangwa National Park. It was a delight for her to see so many different animals moving about freely in a large area, something unimaginable in her own country although some of her conservationist friends would often praise the African model of game reserves to her.

❧

April would be the mid-way mark of Project Tiger. Guy Mountfort, the man who had played a huge role in making it happen, had written to the prime minister on 18 December 1975, suggesting that this 'anniversary' would present an excellent opportunity for an international review of what the project had accomplished, so that the directions for future growth could be clearly established.

Indira Gandhi marked the letter to Karan Singh; his response to the suggestion was far from positive. The prime minister, somewhat dismayed by his reaction, wrote to him on 20 January:

> Why should we prevent WWF and IUCN from sending a mid-term appraisal group? It sounds a good idea to have the benefit of outside opinion, especially in what is for us the new field of wildlife conservation. [...] Please tell them we shall be glad to receive the team.
>
> The names suggested by Guy Mountfort are high-level experts and we should have no hesitation in accepting them. As far as the Indian representative is concerned, it would be useful to get Ranjit Sinh, who is familiar with Project Tiger. Please ask UNEP if they can spare him. If he is not available, we should ask S.P. Shahi, the retired Chief Conservator of Forests from Bihar. The Indian representative should be designated "coordinator" rather than leader.
>
> [...] It is important for the appraisal team be given every facility to visit all our sanctuaries and to have access to all relevant information.

Karan Singh, it emerged, was opposed to the word 'mid-term appraisal', but Indira Gandhi saw no harm in it at all. Finally, as a compromise, the word 'appraisal' was replaced by 'study'.

A three-member team comprising Colin Holloway, Paul Leyhausen and Ranjitsinh visited twelve tiger sanctuaries in March and April and submitted a detailed report in November. The expansion of Project Tiger owed much to the analysis and recommendations contained in this report.

12 February was a typically cold Delhi evening. After a cabinet meeting, Indira Gandhi saw a film on gorillas by the noted filmmaker Dieter Plage, and enjoyed it immensely. Plage mentioned to her that after seeing the film, President Mobutu of Zaire had declared a very vast area as protected territory for gorillas. Ashish Chandola, who was present as Plage's colleague, recalls her response: 'That is the kind of thing we cannot do in our country.' She also wondered why such films could not be made in India to which

Plage replied that he had been waiting to get permission to film tigers. He secured the go-ahead he sought within a few days.

During her conversation with Plage, the prime minister remembered a request that her friend Billy Arjan Singh had made to her—that he wanted a tiger cub which he would rear and then introduce into Dudhwa. She asked Plage whether he could help and the matter was left at that.

Four months later, Billy Arjan Singh heard from Plage and he was soon on his way to Twycross Zoo near London to get the tiger cub he wanted. The cub left Twycross on its long journey to Dudhwa on 31 August. A Siberian tiger, it came to be known as Tara and was to mother four families after being let loose in Dudhwa. Billy Arjan Singh recounted this entire episode in *Tara: A Tigress*, and went on to write:

> I am deeply indebted to Mrs. Indira Gandhi, who granted me permission to attempt a Tiger Reintroduction Project; without her moral support it would surely have foundered in the rapids of bureaucratic and political obstruction.

Dieter Plage had another important contribution to make. A few months after his meeting with Indira Gandhi, he had a conversation with Salman Haidar. Based on that chat, Haidar sent a note on 11 June to Indira Gandhi:

> Goetz-Dieter Plage told me that European spear fishermen were devastating coral reefs of the Andaman and Nicobar Islands. The Italians were the worst offenders. They had already shot out all the sizeable fish in the reefs of Madagascar, Eritrea and elsewhere. The Mediterranean, of course, has been utterly ruined. Plaige claimed that spear fishing ruins the ecology of a reef because the target is usually the big groupers. Once these fish are shot out, starfish move in and they ruin the reef as they feed on the coral.

Haidar recommended a ban on spear fishing, to which the prime minister responded the next day in her hand:

> Yes. Urgent action is indicated.

The chief commissioner of the Andaman and Nicobar Islands, S.M. Krishnatry was informed about the prime minister's orders by telegram. Some days later, he complied with Haidar's request, and added:

[...] the Andamanese and Onge also use harpoon spears in their own indigenous form to catch fish or turtle for their meat from the sea. I am not interfering with that however as I feel sure you do not intend me to disallow that.

Indira Gandhi reassured him that he done the right thing.

Project Lion got initiated a year before Project Tiger, in January 1972. In mid-April, Salman Haidar brought to Indira Gandhi's attention an article on Gir by a Yale University academic Stephen Berwick[1] that had appeared in the journal *American Scientist*. The article was based on the author's doctoral dissertation. She directed her aide to immediately follow-up with the state government and those directly concerned with the management of the Gir National Park on the article's recommendations.

What had captured the prime minister's interest was the methodology adopted by the academic and the meticulous manner in which he had carried out his field investigations. She sent the director of the University Grants Commission this note on 30 April:

> I attach an article on the Gir sanctuary by an American professor. This comes out of detailed enquiry over a period of time encompassing the entire ecosystem of Gir. Useful practical suggestions have emerged. Can we not adopt a similar approach in studying other sanctuaries? This could be part of the university wildlife programme now under formulation. Please see what can be done.

It would take at least another decade-and-a-half before the analytical scrutiny of different ecosystems that Indira Gandhi wanted became a part of Indian academic discourse.

The ambitious crocodile conservation programme that had been launched on 1 April the previous year experienced several teething problems—and the gharial continued being under threat. Noted comedy actor and author Spike Milligan—who, incidentally had been born in Ahmednagar and worked out of London—wrote to Indira Gandhi on 6 January about this species:

> I approach you as Head of the State of India on behalf of a rapidly diminishing creature in your country, the gharial. [...]
>
> Remembering my childhood in India as a magical one, I remember this creature very well and am appealing to you [...] to take dramatic steps to help this creature. Only you carrying out a crash programme will have any effect.

The prime minister marked the letter to Salman Haidar who sent her a note on 12 January:

> He [Spike Milligan] seems to be a passionate wildlife conservationist— he had earlier written to PM about the incident in which 2000 birds aboard an Air India flight died when the plane was detained for repairs in Kuwait.[2]

Spike Milligan's letter was one occasion when Indira Gandhi was a step ahead of a conservationist asking her to do something. Three days later, in response to the man whose hilarious books I had read as a teenager, she said:

> Wildlife conservation has long been one of my particular interests, well before it became a widespread movement. I am glad you share this concern.

She offered him details about the crocodile conservation programme which had been launched the previous year in Orissa with the help of Dr Bustard. She stated that this programme continued to educate and motivate the fishing and tribal communities who lived near the rivers and at whose hands crocodiles had suffered grievously. She made it a point to stress that the conservation initiative was for all three types of crocodiles, including Mulligan's favourite—the gharial—and that she hoped the results, in the future, would be positive—which indeed they were.

On 25 April, she took up the issue of crocodile protection with renewed vigour, when she wrote to Nandini Satpathy, the chief minister of Orissa:

> There is an UN-aided Crocodile and Sea Turtle Conservation Programme in your state. Being as yet largely unspoilt, Orissa can be a pace-setter

for wildlife conservation. However, I am told that the Project is meeting with mixed results. On the technical side it is doing well but the State Government does not seem to have provided all the support it promised.

Action is required on many fronts. To begin with, the Gharial sanctuary in Satkosia Gorge must be firmly protected. I am told that nylon gill netting, destructive both to fisheries and to the Gharial, is still permitted in the sanctuary. You should stop this. Poaching also must be stamped out [...]

She then went on to encourage the posting of the 'right kind' of officers and wished for sufficient administrative support to make the conservation programme successful. To demonstrate how deeply worried she was, she told the chief minister that she was asking Jayal to visit Bhubaneshwar 'in the next few days' and requested her to assist him. The chief minister was galvanized into quick action by the prime minister's letter. She personally went to the place Indira Gandhi had complained about and had the Satkosia Gorge Sanctuary notified on 19 May, one day after her visit.

After visiting the famous Pallava monuments at Mamallapuram with her family the previous evening, Indira Gandhi opened a memorial to K. Kamaraj in Madras on the evening of 14 February. He had played a decisive role in her becoming prime minister in January 1966 and again in March 1967. While Kamaraj and Indira Gandhi had drifted apart subsequently, the Nehru link ensured that the natural affection and respect they had for each other survived, and by 1973, a rapprochement had taken place.

On the evening of 15 February, the prime minister addressed a public meeting that is widely considered to be the most mammoth in Indian political history and that heralded the formal return of Kamaraj's followers into the Congress led by her.

During the few hours she had to herself that morning, she spent around ninety minutes at Kalakshetra, the cultural complex, founded by Rukmini Devi. Then she visited, for about forty minutes, the Madras Snake Park which had been started by the well-known herpetologist Romulus Whitaker. Whitaker recalled his encounter with the prime minister to me:[3]

I met her [Indira Gandhi] only once when she visited the Madras Snake Park [in February 1976]. I was kind of amazed that she'd take an interest in snakes but she admired the python we brought out for her to touch.

While at the Snake Park, Harry Miller, an active conservationist of the city, spoke to her of the Guindy Deer Sanctuary next door. She had intervened in December 1973 to ensure that it was not whittled down but now Miller told her that there was again talk by the state government of allotting land in the sanctuary to institutions. The only permanent solution, in Miller's view, was to declare the deer reserve as a national park.

Indira Gandhi asked Miller to send her a note—which he did three days later. We can assume that she informed Salman Haidar about it. On 26 May, the adviser to the governor of Tamil Nadu, P.K. Dave, wrote to Haidar:

You wrote to me [...] on February 26 [...] about the Guindy Park. We have since declared the Guindy Park minus the area the Governor considers essential for Raj Bhavan requirements, as a National Park [...]
     In your letter you have also written about the fear of conservationists that the Snake Park lease will not be renewed. This is incorrect [...]

And indeed, as it turned out, the Snake Park remained secure.

1976 should also be remembered for the pygmy hog episode that Gerald Durrell wrote about in his autobiography *The Ark's Anniversary*.[4] Durrell, a best-selling author of books on nature and the founder of a conservation centre in the Jersey Islands, was born in Jamshedpur but moved back to the UK when he was three years old. He had been concerned with the imminent extinction of the pygmy hog, the smallest species of pig in Assam.

On 6 March, Durrell approached world-famous conservationist Sir Peter Scott with the lament that 'my pygmy hog file is considerably bigger than the pygmy hog itself'. Durrell had been trying for seven years to set up a captive breeding colony, and Scott conveyed the author-conservation's commitment to protecting the species in a letter to Indira Gandhi on 15 March:

The Survival Service Commission of the International Union for the Conservation of Nature, of which I am the Chairman, concerns itself with the survival of endangered species and is therefore greatly interested in the pygmy hog. As these unusual animals are now being successfully bred in India, we believe it would be of great biological and conservation value if a further breeding colony could be established in Europe. The Jersey Wildlife Preservation Trust was formed by Gerald Durrell [...] I am satisfied that it would be a most suitable place for such a project.

The Trust has suggested to the Chief Conservator of Forests in Assam and to the Assam Valley Wildlife Scheme that perhaps it might be allowed to obtain a breeding nucleus of two or three pairs from those bred in tea estates for transfer to Jersey, and it seems that the idea has met with their full approval, except that the parties concerned have felt that it would be essential to get confirmation for such an important decision from yourself.

Scott went on to add that Durrell also would also be writing a book and articles on how India's pygmy hog conservation efforts were worthy of global appreciation. He assured her that the IUCN, too, would give its 'blessing' to this initiative. Indira Gandhi replied with uncharacteristic delay two months later on 25 May:

In your letter of 15th March you have asked for two of three pairs of Pygmy Hogs from Assam for the Jersey Wildlife Preservation Trust.

This animal had reached the very edge of extinction, but because of our strict protection, it is now making good recovery and we are able to spare some for breeding. I hope they will do well in Jersey.

Unfortunately, the prime minister's hopes were dashed. As Durrell writes, he could get only a pair, which was taken to the Zurich Zoo. They bred and soon produced a litter of five piglets—four males and one female. The female piglet died in childbirth.

The Jersey project ended right there. But India's conservation programme didn't and over a hundred pygmy hogs have since been bred near Guwahati and released into the Manas National Park.

∞

The Wildlife Institute of India in Dehra Dun acquired a fine reputation internationally, in the 1990s and thereafter. However, what is not generally known, is that the idea to establish such an institution had been floated first by Indira Gandhi on 16 December 1976. In a note to her ministerial colleagues dealing with forests and wildlife, she said:

> It is unfortunate that for several years the Forest Research Institute in Dehra Dun seems to have failed to run any courses on wildlife. There is no good reason for this failure which, moreover weakens our case in pressing the States. [...]
>
> At the FRI [Forest Research Institute], wildlife training will have its place in giving proper orientation to trainees, but it must necessarily take lower priority than forest management. There may be a case for another centre devoted exclusively to wildlife, intended for those officers who show aptitude for wildlife management.

Indira Gandhi had always been concerned with the attitude of the forest bureaucracy towards wildlife, and had written to the chief ministers on 23 December 1973 emphasizing the need for specialization in the management of animals. She ended the year by reiterating this stance in another communication to them three days later:

> [...] I cannot avoid the feeling that Forest Departments continue to treat wildlife as a peripheral and unimportant matter. If such an attitude of indifference persists, attempts at conservation will not succeed. [...]
>
> I should like you to ensure that departmental apathy and resistance to the effective functioning of wildlife wings are overcome. Please keep me informed of progress.

༄

When the country woke up to read the newspapers on the morning of its twenty-sixth Republic Day on 26 January, it got to know that Salim Ali had been awarded the Padma Vibhushan, the highest civilian honour (barring the Bharat Ratna which is given but rarely).[5] He had received the Padma Bhushan eighteen years earlier. The Public Accounts Committee of Parliament had submitted a report in April 1975 which had been severely critical of the BNHS and Salim Ali, all but calling them CIA stooges. None of this had mattered to Indira Gandhi though, and the Padma Vibhushan was the ultimate public seal of approval she could give Salim Ali, other than her friendship and access which would continue till her death.

Just a few days later, on the evening of 7 February, Indira Gandhi finally went to Bharatpur along with her entire family—her two sons, their wives and two grandchildren. Salim Ali had already reached the venue a few days earlier.

Before she left for Bharatpur, Indira Gandhi was informed that a camping site was going to be constructed right in the middle of the bird sanctuary, that too, by the Tourism Department of her own government. She was irritated to say the least and made her opinion known clearly to Minister of Tourism and Civil Aviation Raj Bahadur who, ironically, represented Bharatpur in Parliament. On 21 January, she sent him a note:

> I am told that the Tourism Department has begun work on a camping site right in the middle of the Ghana Bird Sanctuary in Bharatpur. This is most unfortunate [...] Please ensure that an alternative location for the tourist camping site is found outside the sanctuary. If any construction or levelling work on the camping site has already begun, the affected area should be restored to its original condition.

After reaching Bharatpur, at the crack of dawn, Indira Gandhi and her family boarded their vehicle, accompanied by Salim Ali and V.S. Saxena (an authority on Bharatpur). They went around the sanctuary lake by boat for about an hour, came back for breakfast and then went out again, returning a little before mid-day.

The journalist, Harsh Vardhan, got a first-hand account of her birdwatching expedition from Saxena, and wrote about it in *Amar Ujala* the next day. At my request, he went through his papers and found the notes he had jotted down as Saxena spoke:

> Indira Gandhi observed about sixty bird species at Keoladeo Bird Park. She spotted most of them and used her own binoculars. She admitted similar birds having been observed by her in Kashmir, in particular the Dabchick, tiny swimmer which dives in water to extract feed. The

question of availability of water surfaced up and VSS [V.S. Saxena] informed that this year [1975–76] it was abundant though last season it was inadequate.

Cranes came in for admiration on the boat drive—nearly 75 Siberian Cranes in the park then. Salim Ali explained about their ecology and outlined that these tall, all-white birds with a long red beak, was spread up to Bihar during early decades of the 20th century but their number had drastically declined. Reason, she asked. He said—loss of wetlands which were being drained or silted up.

While leaving the forest lodge for a public meeting at Bharatpur, the prime minister wrote in the Visitor's Book:

> A delightful and peaceful experience made all the more enjoyable and interesting by having Dr. Salim Ali with us. I hope something will be done to close the lateral road, which brings buses and noise into the middle of the Sanctuary.

The very next day, on 9 February, she wrote to Natwar Singh, her former aide and India's high commissioner in Zambia:

> We all enjoyed the trip especially as Salim Ali was there and accompanied us to the sanctuary. Fortunately I had insisted no one else should go with me.
>
> Regarding the wall—the first step is to build along the areas adjacent to villages. After that we think about its extension.

The wall she referred to was clarified in a spate of letters the following week. In a letter to her minister of agriculture, she highlighted that a permanent wall barrier along the perimeter of the sanctuary had to be erected to prevent the ingress of cattle from the surrounding villages. Next, in a letter to the chief minister of Rajasthan, she added that the construction of the protective wall had to commence immediately and that funds would somehow have to be found for it.

Nalni Jayal was then asked to go to Bharatpur, which he did on 12 and 13 July, and prepared a detailed report on what needed to be done to protect the area. The nation's first hydro-biological research station was started at the sanctuary by BNHS and WWF-India along with the state forest department. Thanks to Indira Gandhi's tenacity, by November 1977 reports[6] started appearing on how the wall had meant more winged visitors to the sanctuary.

The prime minister had met Joseph Linduska, the vice president for science of the National Audubon Society, and Salim Ali's friend, on 19 February, and discussed with him management possibilities for Bharatpur. He was clearly surprised at her level of interest in wildlife and especially birds. He said as much in a letter to her on 11 August and sent her some books that he hoped would be 'a welcome diversion from your onerous duties'. She replied on 30 August:

> How good of you to send me the books on birds. They are beautiful and I am delighted to have them [...] We are not very experienced in the managing of sanctuaries and have to do a great deal to inculcate love for birds and wildlife amongst our people.

The idea of having a national bird, so as to focus public attention on a species needing the greatest protection, seems to have sprung from the May 1960 world conference of the International Council for Bird Preservation, held in Tokyo. The IBWL in its February 1961 meeting favoured the peacock. However, Salim Ali had dismissed the IBWL's suggestion in March 1961 in the *Newsletter for Birdwatchers*:

> I submit that the selection of the Peacock by the Indian Board for Wildlife is totally misconceived and meaningless. It was not at all obligatory for India [...] to adopt a national bird but if it is conceded that doing so may further the ends for which the step was recommended, then it is obvious that the Great Indian Bustard is a species that merits this distinction. This bustard is a large and spectacular bird, indigenous to India, whose numbers, in spite of the legislative ban on its killing, are dwindling at an alarming rate due to poaching by vandalistic gunners and also encroachment upon its natural habitat. It needs an urgent nation-wide effort to save the bird from its impending doom.

Salim Ali's views on the choice of a national bird were ignored and after a two-year debate, the IBWL at its December 1963 meeting finally decided that for compelling historical, mythological, religious and cultural reasons, the peacock would be the national bird. Meanwhile the bustard, already endangered,[7] faced near-extinction, till the bird came to Indira Gandhi's attention in June.

The prime minister went to Haldighati near Udaipur, Rajasthan on 21 June to celebrate the 400th anniversary of the famous battle in which Rajput hero Rana Pratap had valiantly fought Mughal Emperor Akbar. While flying to Udaipur that morning she appears to have read a prominent news item in the *Hindustan Times* on the threat confronting the Great Indian Bustard. The paper had even placed a photo of the bird on the front page.

Harsh Vardhan, who was also a member of the Rajasthan Wild Life Board, met Indira Gandhi in Haldighati. He presented to her the articles he had written when she pointedly asked him, 'What is happening to the Great Indian Bustard in Rajasthan?' She then told him to send her a note.[8] But by the time the note reached her and she could do anything about the bird's fate, elections were called which led to her exit.

Indira Gandhi's love for birds persisted through the political ups and downs that followed. When Rajiv Gandhi—then a pilot in Indian Airlines, and also a very keen camera enthusiast—came back from his flying duties on the night of 1 September, he found a handwritten note from his mother waiting for him

> You missed a beautiful picture. This morning in Akbar Road, two parakeets posed for quite a long time on the side of a tree trunk. There were also a couple of lovely woodpeckers but flittering about restlessly.

Salim Ali wrote to Nalni Jayal on 10 March, bringing to his notice a reported proposal of the recently formed Kerala State Forest Corporation to clear-fell 65,000 hectares of forest in the Western Ghats in south Kerala. Salim Ali had been informed of these developments by a Trivandrum-based whistleblower, N. Sudhir, who was an employee of the forest department. What happened thereafter illustrates vividly how Indira Gandhi moved in such matters.

Jayal replied to Salim Ali seventeen days later:

Immediately on receipt of your letter, we took steps to obtain factual information on the foregoing report. Meanwhile, however, the Prime Minister acted swiftly after seeing the copy of the letter you had endorsed to Salman Haidar. She wrote firmly to the Chief Minister of Kerala asking him to halt the clear-felling operation and refer the matter to an independent authority, viz., the Inspector General of Forests before embarking further on the project. The first step has thus been promptly taken [...]

Salim Ali had begun his letter to Jayal by saying: 'This is your first test!' Thanks to the prime minister, he passed with flying colours almost immediately. A letter from her to the chief minister of Kerala, C. Achuta Menon, on 18 March had made all the difference:

It has been brought to my attention that the State Government has embarked upon a project for clear felling 65,000 hectares of virgin evergreen forest on the Western Ghats in Southern Kerala. The intention seems to be to plant instead some hybrid eucalyptus, in the hope that these will yield more immediate profit. I am appalled by this information. Kerala has already suffered badly through ill-considered removal of its original forest cover. The disastrous floods and landslide last year were largely due this cause [...]

Proposals of this nature should invariably be assessed by a competent independent authority before implementation [...] Meanwhile, please have the clear felling operation halted. I hope not much damage has been done till now.

Zafar Futehally—who had played a key role in bringing the Tenth General Assembly of the IUCN to New Delhi in November–December 1969—had already been awarded a Padma Shri in January 1971 after M. Krishnan, the previous year. Subsequently, he had been closely involved with the launch of Project Tiger. WWF-India owed much to his efforts.

On 2 February, Futehally wrote to Ashok Khosla who was then in his final few weeks with the NCEPC:

In Delhi you referred to the letter which the Prime Minister is sending out to the Chief Ministers of the southern states and wanted me to think about the people who could constitute a team for making an overall plan for the Western Ghats. I shall write to you about this in a week's time.

The prime minister had been concerned about the Western Ghats—not least because her conservationist-friends, including Salim Ali and Zafar Futehally, had been telling her about the threats confronting the area. Apart from all else, they said, the southern states had been planning major power irrigation and railway projects in this ecologically sensitive area.

In his memoirs, Futehally wrote about his meeting with Indira Gandhi (most probably in December 1975 or January 1976) in which he told her about the need to have public hearings before reaching a decision on a particular project in the Western Ghats. Indira Gandhi listened to him and, according to Futehally, said: 'If we have a public hearing we will have to listen to them.'

But the conversation with Futehally must have registered, since soon afterwards she wrote to the chief ministers about 'following proper conservation measures in the fragile sections of the Western Ghats'. She also appointed a nineteen-member task force with Futehally as chairman to look at the question of ecological planning in the region.

Unfortunately, nothing much came of this exercise since, as Futehally himself confessed, 'the report was not incisive enough and consisted of too many generalisations on conservation issues'. Worse, it also opened a path for the Silent Valley Hydroelectric Project to be taken up by the Kerala government. This was to become a cause célèbre a few years later.

In early March, Indira Gandhi was handed over a two-page unsigned note, clearly by someone she knew well but whose identity, unfortunately, cannot be established. It was on the *Sesbania grandiflora*, a very quick growing leguminous, high-protein tree, found in various parts of India like Tamil

Nadu and West Bengal, and known by a range of names, including 'agasti' in Sanskrit.

The writer of the note waxed eloquent on the virtues of this tree, saying that all its parts offered health benefits to humans and animals alike. He also sent the prime minister a few seeds and informed her that after he had bequeathed a similar gift to Modern School in the capital, there had been luxuriant growth within ten to eleven months.

Indira Gandhi observed on the note on 5 March:

> It seems worthwhile to plant this tree in a big way all over the country. Why not concentrate on it this year? Find out the best time for plantation—just before monsoon or any time?

On 9 April Salman Haidar reported to her that forest experts had opined that the species was indeed valuable and was eminently suitable as a hedge plant in homesteads as well. Five days later the prime minister remarked on Haidar's note:

> I looked it up myself last evening in my tree book.

Evidently, the book was the 1966 classic *Common Trees* authored by Dr H. Santapau.[9] Soon after, instructions were issued to the state forest departments to raise this plant during the subsequent monsoons.

Indira Gandhi arranged a meeting of the chief secretaries of states on 7 May. Much like the previous year, she delivered a long lecture on her expectations from these administrators. It was almost like a school headmistress speaking to her wards—the subjects ranging from the redressal of public grievances, to sensitivity to the needs of farmers, scheduled castes and scheduled tribes. Towards the end, she said:

> I don't want to outline various things to which you should devote attention [...] But because the monsoon will soon be with us, the question of afforestation has assumed a great urgency, especially in the hill areas, the areas from which water comes down. With the relentless and ruthless cutting down of trees, a great deal of silt is coming down with the rain

water and melting snows. The result is that river beds have grown so high that even if there is much less water there are far more widespread floods and then the flood waters remain much longer instead of going back to the river bed. So, the plan for the plantation of trees must be made which can be carried out before the monsoon, especially in these areas. In planting trees, we have to give some thought and not just plant any tree. Where there is a problem of landslides and so on, there you must plant whatever grows faster than whatever holds the land quickest, even though it may not be such a useful tree or giving so much resources.

The audience must have been dumbfounded—was this the prime minister speaking, or a botanist or hydrologist intent on taking a class?

After obliging Anne Wright and S.P. Godrej with messages for WWF-India fundraisers and events, it was the turn of Fatehsinghrao Gaekwad, the president of WWF-India and her party's MP. On 27 May, in response to his request, she sent him a message—but this time instead of wildlife she focused on forests.

India's rich flora and fauna are under severe threat. The denudation of forests has wide ranging harmful consequences. The climate is affected, landslides take place, river beds get silted, hence humans suffer, while many species of wildlife and valuable plants become extinct. These are matters for grave concern.

The main reason for the cutting down of trees is the money they bring. The growth of the population and expansion of land needed for industrialization are also responsible.

But apart from timber, many trees have food value and provide non-edible oil and other important substances, which are now being wasted. Information on all these aspects must be collected and disseminated. People living in and around forests should be enabled to make a living of forest produce without having to destroy the forest. Along the edge of the desert, it is especially necessary to plant such bushes or trees which need hardly any water and can hold up the soil. If done in a systematic way, the desert can be pushed back.

To an extent, [the] Government can and is trying to solve these problems and check the decline in our forest areas. But this is not a matter for [the] Government alone. Effective protective and other measures must rest on enlightened public opinion. Every attempt must be made, especially in our schools and colleges, to educate young people [about] the urgency of conserving the environment.

The World Wildlife Fund has already made a beginning in involving people in the conservation effort. I wish them success in their new venture of starting a series of nature clubs for young people.

This was 1976 and here was a prime minister talking of issues that are part of the political discourse now—climate change and how it is impacted by deforestation; the spread of deserts or desertification and the need to arrest it; and, livelihood security for those families that depend on forest produce. This is what makes these little-known messages quite remarkable.

Indira Gandhi was always concerned about the diversion of forest land for non-forestry purposes, however socially justified such a diversion may have been. This clash of objectives came up quite frequently when forest land was used by state governments to resettle people displaced by irrigation projects.

On 18 May, the prime minister wrote to S.B. Chavan, the chief minister of Maharashtra:

I understand that the Maharashtra Government has ordered the transfer of about 17000 acres of virgin forest land in Chandrapur and Yeotmal districts and in the Dhulia Reserved Forest to rehabilitate displaced persons who have been affected by various projects. Can this not be avoided? Displaced persons have to be looked after, but if this is to be at the expense of our dwindling forest reserves, the harm may outweigh the benefit.

Please see if some alternative resettlement scheme is possible. The removal of as much as 17000 acres of virgin forest can have dangerous consequences and should not be allowed.

The chief minister took her views seriously and found alternative land for resettlement. While a few hundred acres of forest land had necessarily to be diverted, the scale was not as large as was originally proposed.

The issue of the diversion of forest land resurfaced—this time in Uttar Pradesh. A year earlier, Indira Gandhi had written a stiff letter to the chief minister of the state about the extensive deforestation that was taking place. After N.D. Tiwari took over from H.N. Bahuguna as Uttar Pradesh's chief minister, Indira Gandhi wrote to him on 17 July, using, for the first time, the word 'forest estate':

> I am most distressed to learn that, notwithstanding all efforts to the contrary, encroachment on U.P.'s forest estate continues unabated [...]
>
> This whittling away of the forest estate cannot be permitted. It is a shortsighted view to permit agriculturists to take over forest area. It is well-known that without adequate forest cover, agriculture itself will become untenable over large tracts. There must also be extreme caution in allocating any part of the forest for purposes such as university campuses or other development projects. It should be possible to find alternative solutions that do not involve the despoiling of forests.
>
> Please take personal interest in this matter. Is it at all possible to modify these decisions at this stage? Also please ensure the adoption of a firmer policy of conservation in the future. This is imperative in the larger and long-term interest of the state.

If this problem had arisen it was because large contiguous areas of land were available only with the forest department, and when land was needed for resettlement—states instinctively looked at forest areas. Indira Gandhi was right to raise the issue, even though the political economy of that time offered little room for manoeuvre. Her letter had an impact and instructions were issued by the chief minister to ensure the barest minimum diversion of forest land for non-forestry purposes.

However, given the demographic pressures and developmental imperatives confronting the state, these instructions could not have been expected to have any appreciable outcome. Four years later, the prime minister brought in a tough new central law on forest conservation to deal with such situations.

But before this, in 1976, Indira Gandhi got the Constitution amended and brought 'forests' into the concurrent list—thus paving the way for the centre to legislate four years later in an area in which the states too had jurisdiction.

The Emergency is known for an elaborate 42nd Amendment to the Constitution. The noted scholar Granville Austin has described in detail in his book *Working a Democratic Constitution* how and why the 42nd Amendment came about.[10]

Indira Gandhi first set up a committee of senior party leaders—known as the Swaran Singh Committee after its chairman—on 26 February, to suggest various amendments. This committee's report was discussed in a 28 May meeting of the Congress Working Committee (CWC)—the highest policy-making body of the party—and by a larger party forum, the All India Congress Committee (AICC), the next day. The AICC made only two important changes—that agriculture remain on the state legislative list and not be placed in the concurrent list as recommended by the Swaran Singh Committee;[11] and that there be a separate section in the Constitution for 'certain fundamental duties and obligations which every citizen owes to the nation'.[12]

Thereafter the bill was introduced in the Lok Sabha on 1 September, taken up for discussion in both houses of Parliament, and became a law on 18 December.

The sequence of events is critical to this story. The Swaran Singh Committee said nothing about changing the existing constitutional arrangements for forests, environment and wildlife. The CWC said nothing. The AICC said nothing. The changes obviously came between the end of the AICC meeting on 29 May and the day the Constitution Amendment Bill was tabled in the Lok Sabha.

This means it was the cabinet that added these provisions, and there can be only one conclusion—that the prime minister was personally responsible. With her intervention, the 42nd Amendment added the following sections to Entry 17 in the concurrent list titled Prevention of Cruelty to Animals:

17A Forests

17B Protection of Wild Animals and Birds

If Indira Gandhi had intervened, it was because of her experiences in the recent past. In August 1972, she had got a national wildlife protection law passed. This had not been easy, for the subject of wildlife protection was within the domain of state governments, and she had to pressurize different states to pass the enabling resolution. The 42nd Amendment, however, proposed a much more convenient solution. Incidentally, 'population control and family planning' also came into the concurrent list through the 42nd Amendment.

Indira Gandhi was convinced that the central government had to take on a more direct 'hands on' role both in forestry management and wildlife protection. All her friends in the conservation community, particularly Salim Ali and Billy Arjan Singh, had been telling her so repeatedly. The Emergency seemed to offer her the moment she had been waiting for, and she grabbed the opportunity.

After Indira Gandhi had been ousted in March 1977, substantial parts of the 42nd Amendment were to be repealed in 1978 by the 43rd and 44th Amendment—with the Congress' support. But Entries 17A and 17B in the concurrent list survived and were left untouched by these Amendments. Indira Gandhi, the political leader, may have lost ground, but Indira Gandhi, the naturalist, had won.

On 22 November, the Congress had its convention at Guwahati. Indira Gandhi gave her customary presidential speech. She defended the achievements of the Emergency and offered a vivid picture of how disciplined Indian democracy had become—all for the good of the people. Then, suddenly, she took off in another direction:

> It [tree plantation] has been a national programme right from the very beginning and we also are giving it all importance. Like it, there are other programmes as well. All those present here know that whether it is a drought or flood the cause lies in our having denuded our forests. Till very recently, we thought that forests could yield revenue through sale of timber or at the most manufacture of paper. But forest farming, which is a way for forest development, can yield much more money,

besides opening vast employment opportunities. We are also paying due attention to this aspect. This programme is bound to progress very rapidly. I am happy that Himachal Pradesh has taken it up in a big way. Our hill areas, specially, specially should pay due attention towards this programme. Besides there are other states like Orissa and parts of Bihar and Uttar Pradesh where we can provide employment to very poor people through this.[13]

This was a new concept she proposed—forest farming. It was basically a programme to bring barren and uncultivable lands under tree cover. In later years, this would come to be called 'wastelands development' and become a major governmental initiative.

The Himachal Pradesh chief minister was, of course, ecstatic. Two years earlier, she had berated him for allowing deforestation in the state; now he was being singled out for praise. He wrote a profuse letter of thanks and reassured her that he would vigorously implement her plans for conservation.

Indira Gandhi's frequently expressed concern was that architects and builders in India do not pay adequate attention to their natural surroundings. She accepted that government departments were the worst culprits in this regard as her criticism of forest lodges showed. Now she trained her guns on an agency controlled by her own government, by way of a note to the minister of works and housing on 28 August:

> All too often, the first step taken by the CPWD [Central Public Works Department] when putting up a new building is to cut down all the trees. This shows lack of imagination and disregard for environmental values. It is perfectly possible to design around the trees, without cutting a single one. One such development is Trombay, where huge buildings have come up without any trees being cut—Homi Bhabha was most particular. Why is it beyond people in public works departments to do likewise?
>
> A firm directive should be given to all architects and designers in the CPWD and State PWDs to avoid the felling of trees in the course of fresh building activity. Where tree cutting is absolutely unavoidable,

as for example in the widening of roads, then adequate new plantings should be made to compensate for the loss simultaneously.

Please issue instructions and let all concerned know that a serious view will be taken of any lapse.

Homi Bhabha, the scientist, had been very close to Nehru. If Indira Gandhi also held him in high regard, it was because he was a great aesthete, with deep interest in music, painting, sculpture and nature.

Indira Gandhi spent the last three days of the year in Lakshadweep. It clearly was a holiday-cum-work excursion to a place she had visited seven years earlier. Unlike that trip which was hurried, this one was more evenly paced.

While she had her usual quota of public meetings as well as political workers' conventions, she took out time to discuss the idea of a marine national park which at that time was quite a novelty in the country. What transpired during her deliberations with local officials was revealed a few days later in a letter that the administrator of Lakshadweep, M.C. Verma, wrote to Dr A. Ramachandran, secretary, Department of Science and Technology, on 11 January 1977:

> I should be visiting Delhi in the first week of February when I should be able to brief you on the Prime Minister's visit to many islands and our discussions with her on an informal basis about many projects including a National Marine Park. As you know, she could find time to visit one of the most beautiful lagoons in our group viz., Bangaram which could have been equally recommended for National Marine Park [...] However, since Bangaram lagoon is being used for bait fishing and for other recreation purposes of other foreign tourists I had always recommended Suhelipar to be a better site for [a] National Marine Park.

The trip had evidently left a deep imprint on the prime minister. *The Times of India* reported that 'the myriad colours of the sea, the coral beaches, the transparent lagoons [...] drew out the best in her'.[14]

Notes

1. Nineteen years later, Berwick was to co-edit a book with V.B. Saharia called *The Development of International Principles and Practices of Wildlife Research and Management: Asian and American Approaches* (Oxford University Press; 1995). The preface ended thus: 'Long ago Francis Bacon observed that the prerogative of Gods was the hiding of facts and the privilege of kings was to discover them. Discovery is a noble game, central to improving the human condition. No participant had a clearer understanding of the significance of this endeavour than the woman who commended the efforts described herein. We dedicate this effort to the memory of Indira Gandhi.'

2. On 30 September 1975, 2,120 birds (mainly parakeets and mynahs) took off in the hold of an Air India flight to London. The plane developed a technical snag at Kuwait airport and remained at the tarmac for thirty-one hours. On arrival at the hostel of the Royal Society for the Prevention of Cruelty to Animals (RSPCA) at Heathrow airport on 1 October 1975, only 89 birds were found alive with over 2,000 having died as a result of the heat and lack of ventilation during the period the plane was stranded at Kuwait airport. Unfortunately, I have not been able to trace the Indira Gandhi–Spike Milligan correspondence on this tragedy.

3. Email communication on 24 July 2016.

4. Durrell (2007).

5. The previous year Reuben David, an Indian of Jewish descent and a very popular conservationist of Ahmedabad, who had created the zoo in that city and other nature landmarks, was awarded the Padma Shri. Indira Gandhi made it a point to congratulate him personally at the award ceremony in March 1975.

6. Promilla Kalhan, 'Ghana Gets More Birds This Year', *Hindustan Times*, 11 November 1977.

7. On 8 July 1969, the day the reconstituted IBWL was meeting, Zafar Futehally wrote an article in *The Times of India* in which he said: 'Conservationists have never lacked support from high quarters. Some years ago on a report of a Great Indian Bustard, a protected bird of Gujarat, the Chairman of the Bird Wing of the IBWL appealed to the then Prime Minister Mr. Jawaharlal Nehru to do something about it. Though burdened with a hundred problems, he found enough time to attend to this matter and order swift action.'

8. Harsh Vardhan confessed to me that article in the *Hindustan Times* which she appeared to have read was written by the paper's Jaipur correspondent R.C. Mathur at his instigation because he knew that it would catch the prime minister's attention!
9. Santapau (1966). The other tree book she had was M.S. Randhawa (1957)
10. Austin (1999).
11. The Committee had also recommended that education be brought on to the concurrent list which was endorsed by the CWC and the AICC.
12. In a letter dated 17 June 1994 to Granville Austin, the eminent jurist V.R. Krishna Iyer wrote: 'The Environment provisions and the Fundamental Duties provision [in the 42nd Amendment] are good and significant and must have proceeded from the Prime Minister herself who, after the Stockholm conference, was convinced of the need for preventing damage to environment and ecology'. Actually, this conviction preceded Stockholm.
13. This speech was originally delivered in Hindi.
14. 1 January 1977.

V. Out of Office

(1977–79)

Indira Gandhi resigned as prime minister on 22 March 1977, following a huge rout in the elections that she had called to the surprise of many.

The next thirty-three months were just as eventful as her prime ministerial years. Even as huge demands were made on her resilience and fortitude, she confronted every challenge head-on. Adversity had steeled her. In these months, too, her fondness for nature was evident.

1977

Indira Gandhi's note to Pupul Jayakar; April 1977.

On the night of 18 January, Indira Gandhi delivered a veritable bombshell. In a nation-wide broadcast, she announced that elections to Parliament would be held a little less than two months later. It was a stunning development which nobody had expected. Till today, there is no authoritative explanation of why she did what she did. It is possible that she expected to win, which would vindicate her completely for the 'gains' of the Emergency. It is also possible that she wanted to re-establish her democratic credentials internationally, more so since Zulfikar Ali Bhutto had, on 7 January, announced that elections would be held in early March in Pakistan.[1]

Two days later, a proud mother wrote to Lucile Kyle about a news item on a poll conducted by the magazine Illustrated Weekly of India *for 'Indian of the Year'. Indira Gandhi told her friend that Sanjay had got over 60 per cent of the votes and went on to give more information on why he had been the most admired choice of the readers of the magazine.*

Elections were held on 16, 17, 18 and 20 March. On the night of 20 March, the first results were announced—both Indira Gandhi and her younger son had suffered ignominious defeats. By the next day, it was all over. Her party had received a drubbing. It still had over 34 per cent of the popular vote and won handsomely in the south and in the northeast and did respectably in the west. But that was small consolation for the decimation in the north where opposition unity and memories of forced sterilizations spelled ruin for her. The very next day on 21 March, Indira Gandhi's final decision as prime minister was to announce the lifting of the Emergency and of the freedoms that had been severely curtailed as part of the clamp-down. On the morning of 22 March, she and her government resigned.

By 3 April when she wrote next to Lucile Kyle, her world had been turned upside down. She bemoaned to her American friend that:

> *My own circumstances have changed so dramatically and drastically. It is not due to recent events but to a long sustained campaign of vilification in which forces abroad have had a big hand. They want to destroy me completely and I think they will pursue me wherever I go [...] The saddest part is that those whom I have helped so much should desert without a backward glance [...] What can I do? [...] I am anxious not for myself but for my little ones and the country's future.*

She was thinking of giving up politics, as a note she wrote to her friend Pupul Jayakar revealed. The latter was going to meet the new prime minister to offer her own resignation from the position created for her by Indira Gandhi. With this in mind, Indira Gandhi wrote some time in early or mid-April:

> *I do not know if it would be wise for you to talk to Morarjeebhai [Morarji Desai] about me. Probably better not on your first visit.*
>
> *But [if] he initiates the subject or if you could convey to others so that it reaches him—that the stories appearing in the press about me or Sanjay or the rest of the family are incorrect.*
>
> *I am gradually disengaging myself from politics as it was not possible to do so immediately. I am not in the running for any post [...] I truly have no desire to remain in any sort of politics.*

But this defeatist mood did not last long. By August the political Indira Gandhi was back in the public eye.

∾

By the night of 20 March, the news had come that Indira Gandhi had been defeated by the very same person she had trounced six years earlier. However, during the day one last letter, was sent and this was to Chief Minister of Assam Sarat Chandra Sinha who got a quick lesson on the value of natural forests:

> It has been brought to my notice that all the remaining primary forests in Assam are scheduled for clear-felling so that they can be replaced by mono-cultures of commercially profitable species. I do not know if these reports are correct, and I hope they are not, for the proposal could have disastrous effects. Assam would suffer as would areas in West Bengal and also in Bangladesh.
>
> It is no longer possible to regard forests primarily as a revenue-yielding resource. The long-term benefit to climate and water management is equally important. Monocultures do not have the same capacity to hold and regulate water supply as do primary forests which have evolved over ages.
>
> Before any more primary forest is cut, the Assam Government should re-examine its working plans in order to ensure that environmental benefits are not overlooked.

As if this was not enough, this very day she sent a note to her colleague, the minister of petroleum, based on the information she had received earlier from Paul Leyhausen, who had been to the Sunderbans the previous year as part of the WWF-IUCN mid-term appraisal team of Project Tiger:

> I understand that oil prospecting in the Sunderbans may pose environmental dangers. There is a risk of oil seepage into the tidal basin, and that the oil will be spread extensively by the tides, leading to severe damage. [...]
>
> The Sunderbans are already one of the constituent wildlife reserves under Project Tiger, so the interest of wildlife should be taken into

account. Those in charge of drilling should be asked to keep in touch with the forest officers so as to select the most suitable sites [...]

The need for speedy exploitation should not blind us to environmental considerations which would have long-term harmful effect[s] on the area.

Despite the fact that she would be resigning less than forty-eight hours later, Indira Gandhi could not help worrying over the forests in Assam and the protection of the Sunderbans Tiger Reserve. Maybe this was her way of diverting her mind from what was in store for the party and her. Or maybe this was just indicative of the fact that, win or lose, Indira Gandhi's commitment to the environment would not wane.

She conveyed as much, after her defeat, in the note to Pupul Jayakar:

[...] I am gradually disengaging myself from politics [...] I am not in running for any post [...] My special interests have always been children, welfare, environment, wild life, etc. I shall try and take up some such work.

A couple of weeks after the election results were announced, on 8 April, Indira Gandhi received a letter from her birdwatching friend, Horace Alexander—a note that reminded her that, during this time of upheaval, her love for nature could be a source of strength and solace:

You will not be surprised to hear that we have been thinking of you daily during these past few weeks. Our feelings about the election results have been mixed. It is wonderful that you had the elections, and wonderful that the people of India have voted with [what] can only be called independent judgment; and we were naturally sad at the result of your own election.

However, I hope you will find plenty of compensations and that you can enjoy a time quite away from politics [...] Perhaps you can spend some time enjoying birds , up in the Himalayas or in Kashmir. And then there are always books [...]

We shall try to keep up with the news from India, and perhaps in five years from now, you will be in office again with the biggest majority ever. Such is democracy.

Horace Alexander was a man of many parts but this letter shows his powers of clairvoyance. His prognostication about her return to power came true but much sooner than he had anticipated.

∾

Indira Gandhi's defeat seemed to make little difference in the international environmental community. The Second International Conference on Environmental Futures, held in Reykjavik, Iceland, between 5 and 11 June, invited Indira Gandhi as a part of a select group of scientists, economists and administrators. The conference was being organized by the Switzerland-based Foundation for Environmental Conservation, whose founder was the British conservation biologist Nicholas Polunin who had, some years earlier, launched the well-known journal *Environmental Conservation*.

In response to the invite, Indira Gandhi, sent a cable message:

> Deeply regret unable to attend Conference. Good wishes for success. It is wrongly propagated that there is a conflict between progress and protection of the environment. Progress cannot be equated with immediate profit but with development activities which raise the standard of living, relieve drudgery, bring beauty to life. Progress and healthy survival are dependent on our ability to conserve the environment and preserve the balance of nature. Urbanisation must be controlled. This implies better coordination with and improvement of rural conditions.

Indira Gandhi was only one of three political leaders to have a presence—even if it was by way of a cable message—at the Conference. The other two were the prime minister of Iceland who opened the event, and the president of the Swiss Federation.

∾

Another community that seemed unaffected by the vagaries of Indira Gandhi's political career was the mountaineering cohort. She had both their respect and gratitude.

On 31 May, an Indian team led by Colonel Narinder Kumar scaled the world's third highest peak, considered amongst the most difficult—

Kanchenjunga in Sikkim. If Indira Gandhi was the patron of the expedition, it was for good reason.

Colonel Kumar had been the principal of the Himalayan Mountaineering Institute in Darjeeling in the late 1960s and had long wanted to climb the Kanchenjunga. But he had been dissuaded by the Chogyal of Sikkim and his wife on the grounds that the Kanchenjunga was sacred to the local people, and its sanctity could not be defiled by a mountaineering expedition, however well-intentioned.

Indira Gandhi had been fond of the Chogyal because of his special relationship with her father. But that did not prevent her orchestrating his overthrow in April 1975. A direct result of this was that Colonel Kumar could start planning his Kanchenjunga ascent. When he reached the peak, in deference to the ex-Chogyal's sentiments, the Indian tricolour was placed a few hundred feet below the summit.

Colonel Kumar, not surprisingly, admired Indira Gandhi. When he congratulated her on becoming prime minister the first time in January 1966, she responded on 10 February in her own hand: 'I hope the spirit of the Himalayas will help me.' Later, in February 1971, when he again congratulated her for securing a massive mandate in the elections, she had replied a little later, on 5 April:

> I am not a mountaineer but you would have noticed that in my speeches
> I often compare India's path to progress to mountain climbing, where
> the higher you go the narrower the steeper the path and the greater the
> challenge.

These words seemed especially relevant in 1977.

❧

Gertrude Emerson Sen, an American, had married an Indian botanist named Boshi Sen in 1932. The couple had settled down in Almora where he had started a research laboratory. They were to get close to Nehru and his daughter, and Indira Gandhi came to refer to Mrs Sen as Aunt Gertrude. They exchanged books and articles, and corresponded regularly; fourteen letters from Nehru's daughter to Aunt Gertrude, written between 1968 and 1981, have survived.[2]

The letters cover a wide variety of subjects, but are also very personal. On 10 September, when the full might of the Indian state was against Indira Gandhi for the 'excesses' of the Emergency, India's former prime minister wrote:

Dear Aunt Gertrude:

How sweet of you to write [...]

You know how much I love the mountains and how I should like to come up to Almora but I do not know if I shall be able to do so [...]

We are well and have learnt to live with people of the Intelligence Bureau at our elbows! Heavens knows what they are trying to discover. [...] Anyone remotely connected with me is being harassed. All those whom I have especially helped are the ones who are crying hoarse against me! Such is life.

Indira Gandhi visited Almora in January 1982 and spent a few hours with her beloved 'aunt'. The latter was to pass away ten months later.

Notes

1. In her biography of the philosopher J. Krishnamurti, Mary Lutyens writes that a 'long private talk' he had with Indira Gandhi in the winter of 1976 may have led to the decision to hold a general election in 1977 and that Krishnamurti himself thought so.
2. Mehra (2007).

1978

Indira Gandhi's letter to Salim Ali; January 1978.

The year began with another split in the Congress party on 2 January—its second in nine years. In 1969 the split happened because Indira Gandhi had been expelled by the party bosses. There were personality clashes no doubt but there was also a strong ideological angle with Indira Gandhi staking out a more progressive position. In 1978, however, there really were no ideological issues other than her own leadership and that of Sanjay Gandhi. In fact, the party she headed after the break-up was called Congress (I).

On 15 April, she wrote to Lucile Kyle saying that it was always good to hear from her and:

> As for India, you must be getting the usual distorted news. The entire Government machinery in the Centre and in States where there is a Janata Party Government is pitted against us. People say they are afraid of me. Can you imagine? Such a meek and mild person as I am!

Cracks were beginning to appear in the ruling combine. There were many points of fissure but for the most part personality clashes showed the government in poor light. By the middle of the year, Home Minister Charan Singh had resigned ostensibly because he believed that his policy was bringing Indira Gandhi to book quickly and jailing her for the excesses of the Emergency was not being supported by the prime minister. But by the end of the year he was persuaded to return, this time as finance minister though.

Whatever may have been Charan Singh's lament, the ruling coalition was determined to wreak vengeance on her. She was arrested on charges of corruption on 11 October. But that move turned out to be farcical since she was released from custody after just twenty-four hours. A few weeks later she contested and convincingly won a by-election from Chikmagalur—incidentally, the town of my birth. Coming after strong victories in the assembly elections in Karnataka and Andhra Pradesh and a by-election victory in Uttar Pradesh, this indubitably signalled her political revival. It also set the stage for her second arrest.

On 19 December, she was expelled from the Lok Sabha and jailed for a week. This was because the Lok Sabha's Committee on Privileges had held her guilty of 'obstruction, intimidation, harassment and institution of false cases against certain officials who were collecting information for the answer to a certain question in the Fifth Lok Sabha on Maruti Ltd' and had left the nature of her punishment to 'the wisdom of the House [Lok Sabha]'. Ironically, the man who had first wanted action initiated against her was the same Madhu Limaye who had been writing to her on issues related to the Gir and Bharatpur sanctuaries and who, in her own words, had given 'good suggestions'. After she had been expelled and was headed to jail, she was asked by the press for a message and she replied:

There used to be a popular song when I was studying in England which I wish to sing:

Wish me luck as you wave me goodbye
Without a tear in your eye;
Give me a smile I can keep all the while
When I am away.

∿

The year began for Indira Gandhi with a handwritten note to Salim Ali—who must have had as tough a time deciphering it as I did! She had scribbled on 17 January:

Thank you so much for sending the beautiful Nature calendar. I have it on my table and it will be a source of cheer in these difficult days.

With every good wish for 1978.

PS. All my life I have wanted to go to the Valley of Flowers, so two of the pictures made [me] long for it over again.

Six months later, as Indira Gandhi found herself in the eye of a storm, she heard from another environmentalist, Billy Arjan Singh. Here was a man who kept in touch with her, even at a time when she was perceived as 'damaged goods'. When he informed her that he was to be honoured with a Dutch award, she replied on 23 June:

How good of you to want me to be present at the ceremony at the Dutch Embassy. I am pleased that you are being so honoured. May I say you richly deserve it.

PS: I shall try and come but cannot be sure. I have written to the Ambassador. I have to appear before the Privileges Committee of Parliament that day.

Four days later she again wrote to Billy Arjan Singh:

I have heard from the Dutch Ambassador that your function has been postponed to the 13th of July. I shall certainly come.

Interestingly, the Order of the Golden Ark—a special honour instituted by Prince Bernhard of the Netherlands to recognize achievements in conservation—awarded to Billy Arjan Singh, was to be conferred on Indira Gandhi four years later.

ॐ

Indira Gandhi had first seen a tiger in the wild on 19 October 1955 on her way to Jog Falls in Karnataka and 1978 offered her a second sighting in pretty much the same area—but this one was purely accidental.

Elections were being held in February to the state assembly in Karnataka—one of the few states where the Congress was in power—and Indira Gandhi campaigned for the party there with Chief Minister Devraj Urs. After a rally in Sagar in Shimoga district, when she was driving to her guest house late at night, her convoy was suddenly confronted with a tiger in the middle of the road! Indira Gandhi requested her driver to switch off the headlights. The tiger stood for just about a minute or so, then vanished into the jungle.

A few months later, Indira Gandhi visited Nagarhole, Karnataka. On 28 May, she wrote to her grandchildren:

> Dadi is far from you and from Delhi [...] We spent a night at a game sanctuary in Nagarhole. As it was dark we could not see much. Still, we spotted lots of deer and sambhar and bisons. At night the deer were barking [...]

In a letter to Billy Arjan Singh a couple of days later—in response to his letter of 16 May[1]—she relived her experiences:

> I visited the Nagarhole sanctuary in Karnataka the other day. We saw various types of deer and bison. Unfortunately, the time was evening and it was getting dark and we had to leave in the morning.

Indira Gandhi's visit to Nagarhole was part of a seven-day trip to Karnataka, a good part of which she spent writing a foreword to *Eternal India*—a coffee-table book[2] of photographs on India, shot by a Frenchman. As a part of this foreword, she marvelled at the diversity of India and its fundamental unity. Then, she expanded on one of her favourite subjects:

> We have two types of pollution. The dirt of poverty and under-development and the fumes and grimes of industry. Which is worse?

257

Population and pollution have to be viewed within a total view of political, economic and social situations. [...]

The inherent conflict is not between conservation and development but between environment and the reckless exploitation of man and earth in the name of efficiency or profit [...] We have to prove to the disinherited majority of the world that ecology and conservation will not work against their interest, but will bring an improvement in their lives [...] The environmental problems of developing countries are not the side-effects of excessive industrialization but reflect the inadequacy of development [...]

Our ancients were deeply concerned with ecology and advised that one should take from the earth and the atmosphere only as much as one put back into them. Such an ecological man was Tagore.

To be sure, she had made some of these points six years earlier at Stockholm, but the reference to Rabindranath Tagore as an 'ecological man' was new. It is a reminder of, how profoundly she had been impacted by her stint in Santiniketan.

Notes

1. In this letter he stated that he wanted to show her two films made by East Anglia Television: *The Leopard Who Changed His Spots* (about Prince) and *Tiger, Tiger* (about Tara).
2. Indira Gandhi (1980).

1979

*Indira Gandhi with Sunderlal Bahuguna (extreme left) and other
anti-Tehri Dam activists, Tehri; September 1979.*

*1979 was a year of many political twists and turns and saw Indira Gandhi
slowly but definitely regaining the upper hand. The ruling coalition was
increasingly been torn apart from its own contradictions. The prime minister
invited attacks from his own colleagues on account of the dealings of his son and
also because of his inability to carry people along. The issue of some ministers
and many MPs continuing to be members of the Rashtriya Swayamsevak Sangh
(RSS), raised hackles—with Madhu Limaye being in the vanguard of the
opposition to this 'dual membership'. The moral conscience of the coalition—
Jayaprakash Narayan—retired to Patna ostensibly unhappy with the man who
he had helped become prime minister in succession to Indira Gandhi.*

*By the middle of the year, she was again in a pensive frame of mind and
wrote to 'Aunt Gertrude' on 13 June:*

[...] One of the burdens of getting on in years is that there are fewer people with whom one can share thoughts. Present-day politics have become more and more a matter of money and maneuvering. Having neither money nor power, not that I either conceived of or used power in that way, I feel terribly isolated in my gang, if I may put it that way. The Janata Party had created conditions in which anybody else except the ordinary tourist has to be quite intrepid to attempt to visit me.

But just a month later Indira Gandhi found her ally to bring down the Morarji Desai government in its finance minister, Charan Singh. He harboured prime ministerial ambitions himself and she opened channels to him. It was actually quite bizarre since, as long as he was home minister till early June 1978, Charan Singh's one-point agenda was to jail Indira Gandhi without bothering too much about legal processes. In mid-July, Morarji Desai finally quit when his government lost the vote of no-confidence and Charan Singh took over as prime minister on 28 July with Indira Gandhi's support. But less than a month later she withdrew support to him because some of her party's demands had not been met. He went down in history as the only prime minister never having had to face Parliament. Charan Singh remained a caretaker prime minister and national elections were called for in early January 1980.

February saw 'The International Symposium on Tiger' in New Delhi. It was a big show, sponsored by the Government of India, which had received Indira Gandhi's support before she had resigned in March 1977.

When the symposium took place, Indira Gandhi was a persona non grata. The only acknowledgement of her role came from R.S. Dharmakumar Sinhji who wrote an article titled 'The Tiger "Lionised"'—ironically, in *Swarajya*, associated with C. Rajagopalachari, the Congress's bitter political opponent since the mid-1950s.

Despite being ignored by the symposium organizers, Indira Gandhi retained her sense of fun. This was evident in her 14 March letter to Salim Ali which was delightfully chatty:

One day I found a typescript of your Azad Memorial Lecture on my table. I do not know who sent it but I was delighted to read it. The story of Maulana Saheb's friendship with the sparrows reminded me of my father's experience with the creatures in his barracks in various jails. An aunt of mine, now advanced in her 80s, has suddenly blossomed as a trade union leader. But she was the wife of an ICS officer and most of her life was spent in the districts. In Mainpuri or some such place, she got very annoyed with a sparrow who used to enter her room to peck at the looking glass. So she had it arrested and caged for a week or so as a punishment! I cannot now remember whether or not this cured the sparrow.[1]

Here too we have a problem. Early mornings Sanjay has been scattering grains of *bajra* for the birds. Gradually more species were turning up. Our favourites were a growing family of partridges. However, since the last two months crows have decided to come, not to feed but to prevent the other birds. They rush at the smaller birds and clutch at the tails of the parrots and partridges. The result is that only the most intrepid birds now show up. The partridges who, as you know are over-cautious and have good reason to be, have deserted us and the number of other species has also decreased.

Apart from Salim Ali, Billy Arjan Singh continued standing by Indira Gandhi like a rock. As always, he greeted her on her birthday and invited her to visit him—to which she replied on 23 November:

Tiger Haven is very tempting but I do not know when I can come.

Earlier, on 12 October, she had written to him:

No, I have not forgotten wildlife. But what can I do right now?

Everything would dramatically change in just about three months.

This was also the year in which Indira Gandhi began to get involved with Silent Valley—an evergreen forest in the Palakkad district of Kerala, in which a hydroelectric project was being planned. Her struggle to save it was the crowning achievement of her life as a conservationist. On 2 October, she wrote to Salim Ali:

I have just received your letter of the 27th September. I share your concern about the Silent Valley and have been following the press campaign in favour of its preservation. I shall try my best to project your view to our party people but when the interests of conservation conflict with those of economic development, I am afraid it is not easy to persuade people to forego what they consider to be political and economic gain.

I should have been delighted to meet you but I am leaving Delhi tonight and will be back only on the 7th of October. If there is any special message you would like to convey to me could you please have it sent to one of my sons, Rajiv or Sanjay, who also love animals dearly and are deeply interested in conservation? At the moment, Rajiv is out on a flight but I am leaving a message with Sanjay.

I wonder if it will be possible for the International Union for the Conservation of Nature and Natural Resources to find people who could help us in suggesting alternative schemes to help North Kerala.

A few days later on 14 October, Indira Gandhi wrote to Salim Ali again:

When you saw me last you spoke of our including a passage on ecology in our manifesto. Some words have been put in but before we finalise the draft, it might be better for you to suggest the wording yourself. I cannot promise to accept it in its entirety but shall try to do my best. Could I please have this as soon as possible?

Salim Ali sent her a full page of formulations on 26 October, but what appeared in the manifesto released on 1 December bore virtually no resemblance to what he had suggested. There was a section titled 'Ecology', drafted largely by P.V. Narasimha Rao[2] and Pranab Mukherjee, with Indira Gandhi providing her own ideas and thoughts.

The Congress-I feels deep concern at the indiscriminate and reckless felling of trees and the depletion of our forests and wild life, which upsets the ecological balance with recurring misery to the people and disastrous consequences for the country's future. Projects which bring economic benefits must be so planned so as to preserve and enhance our natural wealth, our flora and fauna.

The response to the economic and social necessity for ecological planning, the Congress-I will take effective steps—including setting up in the Government a specialized machinery with adequate powers—to ensure the prudent use of our land and marine resources by formulating clear policies in this regard for strict implementation.

If any idea mooted by Salim Ali survived, it was the one he had discussed with another conservationist, Duleep Matthai—they wished to create a separate Department of Environment. While Indira Gandhi did not enunciate this idea explicitly in the manifesto, she did give a clear indication of what was to come later in 1980 by mentioning a 'specialized machinery with adequate powers' in the manifesto. Incidentally, while she was very fond of the word 'ecology', this was the first and last time it was used in a Congress manifesto. From 1984 onwards, it was replaced by 'environment'.

Notes

1. Indira Gandhi was referring to Raj Dulari Nehru, wife of Jawaharlal Nehru's cousin Shridhara Nehru.

2. There is a hilarious story narrated to me by Ralph Buultjens, a Sri Lanka-born political scientist at New York University who had known Indira Gandhi well. Apparently in the summer of 1978 or 1979, Indira Gandhi, Narasimha Rao and Buultjens travelled by car from Bangalore to Mysore. Indira Gandhi kept pointing to the trees on the way and reeling off their names. When they stopped somewhere, Indira Gandhi mingled with the crowd, while Narasimha Rao turned to Buultjens and said: 'She should have been a botany teacher, not a politician.' But he swore Buultjens to secrecy. Many years later when Narasimha Rao had himself become prime minister, Buultjens reminded him of this episode. Narasimha Rao laughed heartily and thanked him for not betraying his confidence. My own guess is that she would have enjoyed the crack at her expense. Unfortunately, my efforts at establishing such a trip did ever take place proved futile but Buultjens was in no doubt that this incident occurred.

VI. The Naturalist Prime Minister–II
(1980–1984)

F.No. MF PL/1462

Subject: Name/Badge - Hospital at Chilka.
....

Government have recently approved setting up
of a 30 bedded hospital at Chilka, in Orissa. The
Internal Nomenclature Committee has recommended 3
names (TULSI, AMRIT and NIVARINI) as the name of the
hospital to be considered in their priority. The
Chief of the Naval Staff has recommended that the
hospital be named as NIVARINI. Badge design is placed
at Encl. 24-A.

2.   The name of the hospital as suggested above and
the design of the badge at encl. 24-A may be approved.

(V.S. Tripathi)
S.A. TO R.M.
27-2-1980

Secy. to P/M.

27/2/198

P.M.

M.

Indira Gandhi's noting on Chilka; February 1980.

Indira Gandhi returned as prime minister on 14 January. She had been thrown
out in March 1977 in a spectacular fashion. But she was back in an equally
dramatic manner with a near two-third majority. The very people who had
taught her a lesson gave her new lease of life. She had campaigned relentlessly
and had won across the country. It was almost as if the people had forgiven
her for the Emergency.

But the euphoria did not last long. In less than six months on 23 June, her younger son and widely considered to be the political heir apparent, was killed when his small plane crashed very near to where he lived. Sanjay Gandhi's death was a shattering personal blow to the prime minister. On 7 July, she opened up to her intimate family friend A.C.N. Nambiar who then lived in Zurich:

> *Oh Nanu what can I write? Other deaths in the family have followed grave illness. But Sanjay was so vitally, so vibrantly healthy, of such a resplendent personality [...] To me he gave the sort of support that comes not from a son but from an elder brother.*

Eleven days later, India successfully put its own satellite into orbit through its own launch vehicle lifted off from the country itself. India's space capability was now established and would grow leaps and bounds—her putting Satish Dhawan in charge of the programme in early 1972 on Haksar's advice and the excellent personal rapport she developed with him had played a key role in this achievement.

Two features of the 1980 Indira Gandhi are worth recalling. First, she had always taken the oath of office in the name of the Constitution. But this time around, she took the pledge in the name of God. Second, she roped in L.K. Jha, who had been her secretary from January 1966 to May 1967, to advise her directly on reforms in economic administration. Over the next four-and-a-half years, a cautious liberalization of the domestic economy would take place beginning with the cement industry in February 1982.[1] She also made use of her cousin B.K. Nehru's trip to New York to open a channel of communication with president-elect Ronald Reagan.[2]

The last letter that Indira Gandhi and Dorothy Norman had exchanged was in December 1976. The relationship resumed with the latter's letter of condolences on Sanjay Gandhi's death. Indira Gandhi replied on 3 August and followed it up with another letter on 14 September:

> *[...] You know me well enough to appreciate that I am neither authoritarian nor cold. But I am not effusive, and perhaps this is misunderstood [...] We now face a terribly difficult situation economically and politically [...] There is utter indiscipline and many agitations all over the place.*

The agitations she was referring to were in Punjab and Assam and were to consume much of her time and energy in the years ahead.

ॐ

In 1980, Indira Gandhi was to be confronted with three big 'dam' issues—Silent Valley, Tehri and Lalpur. Each of them was hugely contentious with strong proponents and opponents.

On 12 January, Indira Gandhi was in Kerala campaigning for the state assembly elections. At a news conference in Trivandrum, after she had offered prayers at the Sree Padmanabhaswamy Temple,[3] she was asked about the Silent Valley issue that had been dominating the headlines for the past few months. She replied:

> [...] All were concerned deeply over Kerala's economic development and availability of power. Everything should be done to help improve the situation, especially to create greater employment opportunities and infrastructure. At the same time, the world is getting more and more conscious that all such developments should keep in view ecosystem or ecology because destroying or disturbing it will have long-term adverse effects. Today world opinion is quite agitated about the Silent Valley. I am also told that for the amount spent the return is not going to be much. It is worthwhile to see whether we can get some benefits without destroying these forests.

This was a hugely courageous answer to a loaded question just before the state elections—especially given that the project, which promised 240 megawatt of cheap, hydel electricity, apart from irrigation to around 10,000 hectares, was supported by the left parties, the Congress's main opposition in Kerala, and by local Congress leaders themselves.

Two days after winning the national elections, Indira Gandhi wrote to Governor of Kerala Jothi Venkatachallam;[4] and handed over her letter personally when they met on 17 January in Trivandrum:

> There has been some previous correspondence on the execution of the Silent Valley Hydro Electric Project. Now I see Press reports that the Kerala State Electricity Board is going ahead with the project on the ground that the Stay Orders of the Kerala High Court have been vacated.

This is not a legal matter but a question of the protection of the environment and the conservation of one of the only remaining tropical rain and forest areas in the world. Eminent people all over the world have expressed concern over the project.

In my view further execution of the project should be stopped until it can be discussed with whichever government comes in power in Kerala.

As it turned out, Indira Gandhi's party lost the state elections, and the Left Democratic Front (LDF) came to power with E.K. Nayanar as chief minister. When the director-general of the IUCN, David Munro, wrote to her on 25 January, petitioning the protection of the Silent Valley forest,[5] she replied on 8 February:

I share your concern for the conservation of Kerala's Silent Valley.

Even before the elections [state] I had requested the Governor to keep the matter pending. Now there is a Marxist Government in Kerala which is anxious to go ahead with the project and unless we can quickly identify some other way for them to get power, I am afraid we may not be able to save the Valley.

Indira Gandhi started working on Nayanar. She wrote to him on 6 March:

I wrote to the Governor of Kerala on the 16th February about the Silent Valley Hydro Electric Project, pointing out that what was involved was the protection of the environment and the conservation of one of the only remaining tropical rain forest areas in the entire world [...] Since then I have received a preliminary report on the 'Botany of Silent Valley' by a team of the Botanical Survey of India which points out that the Silent Valley is an untapped gene pool and has a number of medicinal plants of great value to our medical scientists. I had suggested further execution of the project should be stopped until the matter would be discussed with the new Government in Kerala.

We have not heard anything further from the Government of Kerala but there was a report in the Press that the State Government may be taking into consideration opinions for and against the Silent Valley Project before taking a decision in consultation with the Centre. If this is so, I must compliment you on taking a very reasonable view of the matter. I suggest that there should be a preliminary discussion at official level between your officers and the concerned Ministries of the Government of India. We can discuss the matter further after that.

There was silence at the other end but the prime minister persisted. Two months later, on 5 May, Indira Gandhi again wrote to the chief minister:

I have not heard from you in reply to my letter of the 6th of March regarding the Silent Valley Project. I am glad to hear from Dr. Swaminathan that he, Prof. Menon and some senior officers had detailed discussions with you, your colleagues and officers about the preservation of the Forest. I understand you agree that further damage to this priceless natural asset by unauthorized persons should be prevented and that action should be taken to establish a Silent Valley National Park under Section 35(1) of the Wildlife (Protection) Act of 1972, with Central assistance, by combining the Kundas, Attapadi, New Amarambalam and Silent Valley Reserve Forests (a total area of 38,952 ha.) into a National Park, and stopping all encroachments and tree felling.

The question of going ahead with the Hydro-electric project can be examined as soon as data from studies currently in progress in the area become available. I am informed that the data collected by the scientific teams now in the Silent Valley area will be available for analysis in another month. This could be analysed by a joint Government of India–State Government Committee, so that decisions which are in the best interests of all concerned can be taken soon.

The chief minister finally replied on 20 May that the law passed by the state legislature in 1979 was adequate to protect Silent Valley and that he was willing to consider additional safeguards later. But he pressed for the early clearance of the project. Indira Gandhi noted on his letter on the same day:

We must immediately provide an alternative scheme.

Besides becoming impatient with all the press reports on the Silent Valley issue, Indira Gandhi was getting overwhelmed by letters from overseas as well as from Indian environmentalists like Salim Ali urging her to prevent an ecological catastrophe. Finally, in one letter from Salim Ali on 2 June, she noted:

There has been much talk. Now ACTION is required urgently.

The action she wanted was the identification of an alternative project to meet Kerala's power needs since she had actually made up her mind that the Silent Valley project could just not be approved. On 17 July, she conveyed her feeling to E.K. Nayanar a third time:

> I have your letter of the 20th May about the Silent Valley Hydro-Electric Project. I appreciate the reasons for your anxiety to take up the project and your concern with the need to develop power potential in your State. But I am sure you will agree that if this problem of creation of power potential quickly can be taken care of without damaging the environment, we should do our best to proceed in that direction. Teams composed of scientists from the Botanical Survey of India, Birbal Sahani Institute of Paleobotany, National Bureau of Plant Genetic Resources and Centre of Advanced Study of Botany, University Botany Laboratory, Madras have submitted their preliminary reports the first level analysis of which leads to the conclusion that from the point of view of ecology and importance of biosphere reserves, it would not be desirable to approve the Silent Valley Hydro-Electric Project. However, I understand that alternative projects for building up power potential are possible and can be taken up immediately if your Government agrees. I suggest we discuss this at the earliest. Meanwhile, I am sure you will agree that the work connected with the development of the Silent Valley National Park should start without further delay.
>
> I hope you will let me know the date of your next visit to Delhi when we can discuss this matter.

The chief minister decided to take the prime minister up on her offer. He, along with the state's electricity minister and others, met the prime minister and her colleagues on 7 August. The chairman of the Kerala Electricity Board, C.K. Kochukoshy, who was a part of that meeting, wrote in his memoirs much later:[6]

> We discussed the issue for a long time and it was surprising that the Prime Minister was able to devote so much attention to this project [...] She said a committee of scientists and some other officers should make a special study and submit a report within three months. Our suggestion that the committee should be under the chairmanship of M.G.K. Menon

was accepted. We returned to Trivandrum convinced that the project had been salvaged for the time being.

M.G.K. Menon was then the secretary of the Department of Science and Technology and would soon become the first secretary of the Department of Environment. He had been a protégé of Homi Bhabha and had had a sterling scientific career at the Tata Institute of Fundamental Research before moving to Delhi as a science-administrator in 1970. Indira Gandhi had appointed him to a series of key positions.

The M.G.K. Menon Committee was appointed to 'determine whether the Silent Valley Project could be taken up without significant ecological harm'. It had three officials from the Kerala government, three academics from Madras, Trichur and Calcutta, the director of the Indian Agricultural Research Institute and Dr Madhav Gadgil—brought to Indira Gandhi's notice by Salim Ali. It was asked to 'report in a period of about 3 months'. It had its first meeting on 26 November, in which the chairman said that 'the committee is assigned the specific term of reference to examine whether the Silent Valley Hydel Power Project could be taken up without significant ecological harm'. But the wheels moved slowly, and the committee took slightly over two years to complete its analysis. It submitted a final report to Indira Gandhi only in mid-December 1982.

The 1,000-megawatt Tehri Dam project—which involved the construction of a 260.5 metre-high dam on the Bhagirathi river—had been proposed by the Uttar Pradesh government, and had been approved way back in 1972. But work started only in 1977. A direct consequence of the project was that the ancient town of Tehri and about ninety-six villages would be submerged either totally or partially, affecting about 14,500 families. This immediately triggered protests.

An appeal had been presented to the Petitions Committee of the Lok Sabha on 14 August 1978 by anti-dam campaigners—chief amongst them being the venerated Gandhian Sunderlal Bahuguna. The Petitions Committee met the protesters in February 1979, but before it could finalize its report, its term expired and it was dissolved. While the committee was clearly veering around to agreeing with the petitioners, with its disbanding, the state government announced a decision to go ahead with the plans for a dam.

H.N. Bahuguna—a former chief minister of Uttar Pradesh, who had been by Indira Gandhi's side, then deserted her, then returned once more to be made secretary general of the Congress in late 1979—wrote to the prime minister on 1 February:

> As you are aware, a great deal of controversy has been raised over the building of the Tehri Dam over the past few years. Ecologists and geologists have raised a number of objections [...] During my recent tour of the area, I was told by the people that they had raised this question with you when you had gone on a tour to that area sometime in September 1979.
>
> [...] May I request you to kindly ask the Ministry concerned to have the issue examined by them departmentally also in consultation with geologists and other experts on ecology.

The prime minister's reply on 5 February was brief but left no doubt about where she stood:

> On my visit to Tehri, my attention was drawn to these points. In the past, we were not as careful as we might have been. It is time to try and rectify our approach. I am having the matter gone into again.

A day later, her father's close colleague K.D. Malaviya, who had also been a mentor of sorts to her husband, wrote to her saying that the decision to construct the Tehri Dam was 'questionable'; that such work in the Himalayan region was totally undesirable; and the situation in Uttar Pradesh had, in any case, changed since the construction of the Bhakra Nangal Dam. Indira Gandhi's reply to him was similar to the one she had sent Bahuguna—that the matter had been raised during her visit to Tehri and that she was having the pros and cons of the project examined again.

Actually, the Department of Science and Technology—at the behest of Indira Gandhi's predecessor Charan Singh, who had met the protesters—had constituted an expert group to look into the environmental impact of the Tehri Dam on 12 December 1979. But after Indira Gandhi came into office, the expert group assumed fresh significance and got a new chairman in mid-February in Sunil Roy, a retired diplomat and a well-known environmentalist. It presented its interim report on 31 May. The report was guarded in its conclusion. Nowhere did it take a stance that the project had to be scrapped or that it ought to be continued. Instead, it called for more studies and, since work had already commenced on a modest scale, for corrective measures to be taken in the catchment area. After the submission of the interim report, Indira Gandhi was clearly in a quandary.

On 30 August, Sunderlal Bahuguna[7] sent her a handwritten letter from the Sivanand Ashram in Tehri-Garhwal:

> Dr. Richard St. Barbe Baker the Grand Old Man of Trees was full of admiration for you [and] for your idea on environment protection after your meeting with him on 26th. He is now here and will be in Mussoorie and Dehra Dun during the next 3 days.
>
> I hope you remember his anxiety about a very high dam over Bhagirathi at Tehri which Sarala Behn had also referred in her letter. You had kindly taken keen interest and assured to look into the matter [...]

Barbe Baker—a Canadian who had embraced the Baha'i faith and was known the world over as the 'tree man'—in turn wrote to Indira Gandhi on 5 September:

> Yesterday, I went with the Conservator of Forests into the Chipko area, Adrani, Tehri Garhwal, being introduced by Sunderlal Bahuguna. We were met with an advance contingent of the villagers with drums and singers [singing] "the crusade has begun in the Himalayan forests [...] come on, sisters, hug the trees full of life and save them and plant more and more fruit and nut trees" [...]
>
> The people of the hills are fully aware of your wisdom and support and are anxiously awaiting the application of moratorium on green fellings and the planting of mixed forests including nut, fruit and fodder bearing trees with the people's active participation in forestry management.
>
> May I be allowed to thank you for the special interest you have taken in organizing my programme.

The prime minister replied five days later that 'the felling of trees has become a major problem for us'. Regarding Tehri, she told Barbe Baker that

> There is an opinion for and against the Tehri Dam. We are having the entire question looked into.
>
> I hope you had a pleasant stay in India.

Indira Gandhi succeeded in stalling any further work in the Tehri Dam area. There were studies and more studies, and letters exchanged between the newly formed Department of Environment and the Ministry of Irrigation regarding her concerns. But a categorical 'yes' or 'no' was not forthcoming. Discussions on the project were to resume in 1987 but not before the environmental impact of the project had come to occupy centre-stage in all discussions.

On 9 March, Indira Gandhi received a memorandum from people protesting against the Lalpur Dam on the Heran river in Gujarat. She gave the protesters a patient hearing. One of the main complaints was that while the tribal areas were going to be submerged, the benefits of the project would accrue to relatively well-to-do farmers.

Indira Gandhi directed her officials to address this imbalance urgently. She also observed in a note put up to her on large irrigation projects that

> issues of conflict between those who benefit from such project[s] and those who lose as a result of submergence of land are bound to arise and suggestions for addressing this asymmetry are seldom implemented

and that

> we need to go more thoroughly into such schemes to ensure protection to the weakest sections even before final sanction of such projects.

The Lalpur Dam would engage Indira Gandhi's attention over the next two years. Eventually, she would be forced to take a call that would disappoint those agitating against its construction.

Irrespective of the decisions she eventually took, what cannot be denied is that Indira Gandhi had firm views on big dams in her last ten years. These came to be revealed most emphatically in a memo dated 13 March. The Prime Minister's Office (PMO) wrote to the Department of Science and Technology, with the following observations from the prime minister herself:

> There are several proposals which were agreed to earlier but would need to be looked at again. Amongst them are Silent Valley, the Dam in Tehri Garhwal and the Dam in Lalpur, Gujarat. It seems that larger areas of very fertile land are being submerged without any commensurate gains. There may be other such cases also. It is true that these decisions have been taken over a period of time. But there is great local distress and a feeling that contractors and other such groups will be the main gainers. Hence, it is necessary to have another look in depth.

Salim Ali was both indefatigable and incorrigible. He would write long letters to Indira Gandhi over the next four-and-a-half years—the shortest one being an express telegram he sent on 9 January when the elections results had been declared. The telegram, which undoubtedly would have made Indira Gandhi smile, read thus:

Shabash (.) Am delighted.

Salim Ali would go on to congratulate Indira Gandhi on 15 January for her statement on Silent Valley in Kerala. The very same day—while apologizing for 'bombarding you with complaints, which seem to increase day by day'—he dashed off another letter to the prime minister. He was extremely disturbed 'about the location of the Thal Fertiliser Plant within Bombay Metropolitan Region and in the Green Belt surrounding Bombay'.

India's first and biggest gas-based fertilizer plant had been a bone of contention ever since plans for it were announced in 1977. The plant was to be in somewhere in a coastal area near Bombay—on that there was no dispute. The controversy was revolved around its exact location. Initially, in mid-1977, Rewas/Mandwa was selected. Environmentalists and local politicians objected to it. On the basis of an expert committee's recommendations, the site was shifted to Tarapore in April 1978.

While the environmentalists were happy, all political hell broke loose with powerful Maharashtra leaders like Vasantdada Patil and Sharad Pawar firmly rejecting Tarapur. The expert committee was then asked to reassess its recommendation, which it did and again opted for Tarapur a second time around. This further inflamed passions, leading to intense lobbying in the nation's capital. Finally, on 28 July 1978, H.N. Bahuguna, the minister of chemicals and fertilizers, had announced Thal-Vaishet—5 kilometres north of Alibag on the coast and 21 kilometres south of Bombay—as the location.

Indira Gandhi had not been involved in the controversy in any way since she had been out of power all through. But with her return Salim Ali must have thought he now had an ally. Strangely, that was not to be. Perhaps because a year's work had already been done at the project site, the prime minister was reluctant to get involved and reopen the issue. She referred Salim Ali's letter of 15 January to the ministry concerned, which defended its choice of Thal-Vaishet to Salim Ali.

Salim Ali remained adamant, and again wrote to the prime minister, pleading for her personal attention and re-emphasizing the fact that the location was environmentally damaging. Indira Gandhi kept quiet and the next thing that happened was that her government presented a 'White Paper on Thal-Vaishet Fertilizer Project' in the Rajya Sabha on 9 July. It justified the site selected and said that all proper procedures had been followed, appropriate clearances obtained and the necessary safeguards put in place.

For the four years and ten months that she was prime minister the second time around, Indira Gandhi was to be bombarded with letters every other day from an organization called the Bombay Environment Action Group (BEAG)—one of the earliest environmental NGOs, spearheaded by Shyam Chainani, educated at MIT and working in the Tata Group. While he hadn't met the prime minister, he had the support of Salim Ali and perhaps that gave him instant credibility with her. Chainani was a prolific letter writer, and a tireless campaigner for the issues he took up. Indira Gandhi didn't reply to him directly but invariably acted on his letters and issued directives. Her aides, too, kept in touch with him.

Since the mid-1970s, Chainani and others in the BEAG had been battling for the preservation of the two islands of Nhava and Sheva near Bombay. In the late 1970s, during Indira Gandhi's time itself, a decision had been taken to allow the Oil and Natural Gas Corporation (ONGC) to build an oil terminal at Nhava and also to develop a new port at Sheva; the plan was to decongest Bombay's port which was bursting at its seams.

As soon as Indira Gandhi returned as prime minister, she instructed one of her senior aides R. Rajamani to collect the details on what had been planned at Nhava.

R. Rajamani was an IAS officer of the Andhra Pradesh cadre who had been inducted into the PMO by Morarji Desai in 1978. But it was only under Indira Gandhi that Rajamani rediscovered his deep-rooted passion for environmental causes—much like Moni Malhoutra and Salman Haidar earlier. Before his death, Rajamani was to recall his association with Indira Gandhi, particularly on issues related to the conservation of nature.[8]

> [...] as we came out of an inspection bungalow we were camping at, she pointed out to me a small plant with pink and white flowers and asked if I knew what it was. Not hiding my ignorance I said I do not know the name but in my part of the country it was known as the *smashan* flower, being found only in crematoria and burial grounds. She smiled and educated me that it was the plant *vinca rosea* (since renamed *catharanthus rosea*) which bore the common name of Periwinkle. She added for good measure that the chemical extract of the flower was being used for treatment of a type of cancer.

Rajamani wrote to the petroleum secretary on 2 February, just nineteen days after Indira Gandhi had taken over a second time:

> PM has observed that she would like to have all the details of the exact location proposed in the entire ONGC project. She would also like to know whether complaints have been received that the location proposed would lead to environmental damage or pollution. The Ministry of Tourism and Civil Aviation have informed us that they are of the view that it would be desirable to shift the ONGC installations elsewhere in the Bombay harbour. PM would like to have a note very early dealing with all these points.

C.P.N. Singh was then minister of state for defence and had been part of the Sanjay Gandhi brigade. She asked him to visit Bombay and give her a report on all the projects that were agitating the BEAG—the ONGC terminal at Nhava, the Sheva port, and the expansion of the Sassoon fish harbour at Colaba in South Bombay. Singh visited Bombay and the project sites on 8 and 9 April, and submitted his report to the prime minister soon after. Three months later, she asked Rajamani to issue a directive to the ministries concerned. This was done on 4 July:

> Prime Minister has ordered that in respect of the first issue of Sassoon Dock, Agriculture Ministry may be requested to find an alternative site for the augmentation of facilities above the existing level which can be handled without affecting the environment. [...] The land already reclaimed could be considered for conversion into a botanical garden [...]
>
> With regard to the second issue of setting up offshore facilities at Mazagon Dock in the Nhava Sheva Island and ONGC's supply base, the Prime Minister has ordered that Ministry of Petroleum may be asked to go ahead with the project limiting it to the level now contemplated and that they may be informed that no further expansion of the activity of any Central Agency should be allowed on this Island (meaning Nhava). Further, they should constitute a Committee [...] to ensure that the safeguards for planting of trees, etc. are observed.
>
> Prime Minister has also concurred about the need to preserve Elephanta Island and that trees should not be allowed to be cut there and its development should be part of the regional plan [...]
>
> Minister of State for Defence has also made a reference to the pollution caused in the Bombay area by the thermal power station of the Tatas which was approved without obtaining the clearance of the Central Agency in regard to environment. This may kindly be verified and a note sent separately to the Prime Minister on this.

The prime minister's directives set alarm bells ringing in different ministries; she was forced to call a meeting very soon thereafter on 4 August. The previous day, her officials had contacted Salim Ali and Shyam Chainani for briefs. After hearing everyone, Indira Gandhi issued another set of directives on the same day reiterating what she had decided, and adding a couple of new decisions. The 4 August directives in short were:

a. No further expansion on Nhava Island other than the supply base of ONGC and Mazagon Dock's offshore facilities. The village, picnic spots, Nautical Institute, Museum, etc. to be left untouched and environmental safeguards rigourously monitored.

b. Environmental safeguards to be incorporated into the feasibility report for the new port at Sheva which should provide for the release of land and dock areas in existing Bombay Port area for parks, etc. Areas around the new port to be planned as a green belt.

c. No augmentation of existing facilities at Sassoon dock and an alternative site to be found.

d. The Thal-Vaishet fertilizer plant to go ahead but location of township to be reviewed from an environmental angle.

That the prime minister took the campaign of Shyam Chainani seriously is borne out by the fact that she sent Rajamani to inspect Nhava and Elephanta as well. She was clearly concerned not just about the natural environment of Nhava but equally about what Elephanta represented in terms of India's cultural heritage. After his visit, Rajamani reiterated the prime minister's directives to the ministries concerned on 10 August 1982.

On the morning of 19 February, Indira Gandhi saw an article in the *Hindustan Times* titled 'A Coral Isle Dies', which referred to the destructive impact of the mining of lime on marine life in the Pirotan Island in the Gulf of Kutch. As had now become routine, she asked her officials to gather more information on the situation.

A report was yet to be received, when she got a letter from Governor of Gujarat Sharada Mukherjee.[9] The governor's letter, dated 24 May, came with two observations that alarmed the prime minister:

> The famous coral reefs of the Pirotan Islands off the coast of Jamnagar are being jeopardized by the grant of a fresh lease in the neighbouring islands in 1978 for a period of twenty years to Digvijay Cement Company Ltd. for the dredging of calcareous sand which is used in place of limestone for cement production.
>
> The Nal Sarovar (Ahmedabad District) which has been a natural bird sanctuary, has been so cruelly misused since was handed over to

the Tourism Department that it is claimed that fewer birds are visiting the area now.

Indira Gandhi was furious and directed her officials to intervene right away. This started an eight-month tug-of-war between her officials and the state administration. One of her officials, N.S. Sreeraman, wrote to the chief secretary of Gujarat on 7 June, essentially repeating the information sent by the governor, and asking what action was being proposed on the two issues by the state administration. The state had gone to the polls, and a new chief minister had been sworn on the day the letter had been dispatched. Keenly aware of the prime minister's interest in the environment, the new chief minister Madhavsinh Solanki very soon got the Gulf of Kutch Marine Sanctuary notified on 12 August.

But this was not to be the end of this story.

Six years earlier, in response to a letter from Salim Ali, Indira Gandhi had taken a series of decisions to preserve the ecological balance in the Andaman and Nicobar Islands. In early April, the MP representing the islands, Manoranjan Bhakta, wrote to the prime minister that plans were afoot to develop large areas presently under forest cover.

Indira Gandhi asked her officials to assess the situation. The result was that the Ministry of Home Affairs decided to send a study team to visit and analyse the ecosystem of the Andaman and Nicobar Islands and submit recommendations 'regarding the future strategy to be adopted in respect of development and exploitation of forest wealth and if possible also of Marine resources around these Islands'. When this was brought to the prime minister's attention, she noted on 30 April:

> Should they not associate some non-officials? Recently when Salim Ali went to the Andamans, the arrangements were so inadequate that he had to come away I am told.

She was also unhappy that the study was to take a full year and wanted interim reports to be submitted so that decisions could get taken soon. As it turned out, the multi-disciplinary team prepared a report within six months and this was to provide the essential framework for all environmental policies in the Islands. In the years to come—in March 1981 and again in February 1984—Indira Gandhi would herself have occasion to speak about this during her visits to this archipelago.

~

It would be fair to assume that the prime minister noticed a clear trajectory in her experiences with large development projects—like power plants, irrigation projects, fertilizer factories, mining and refineries. They would be designed; then environmental objections would be raised; then, there would be a controversy over the additional costs to be incurred. To change the narrative, on 10 June, Rajamani, recorded a note at her behest:

> P.M. had suggested that the cost of anti-pollution measures or measures for safeguarding environment should be treated as an integral cost of all projects now being formulated. This was suggested with a view to ensure these measures are anticipated and provided for in project costs even at the beginning. The Deptt. of Expenditure, Ministry of Finance, have issued instructions to all the Ministries accordingly.

It appears obvious now but at that time the stance was a novel one. It had taken a nature-sensitive prime minister to think aloud. While controversies would not disappear, at least financial considerations were no longer to be used to deny due place to environmental considerations as a part of project planning.

A month later, Indira Gandhi expressed her concerns regarding the level of air pollution in the nation's capital on account of Indraprastha. This resulted in the formal installation of new anti-pollution devices like electrostatic precipitators over the next eighteen months. While at that time, this granted considerable relief to the city, as events were to show in later years, this was not enough.

~

Indira Gandhi had established an excellent rapport with the IUCN, which had helped considerably during the launch of Project Lion in early 1972 and had played a crucial role in mobilizing international funding for the launch of Project Tiger in April 1973. She had been in fairly regular touch with Peter Scott and Peter Jackson. She had also acquired an international reputation for being seriously committed to conservation.

It was no surprise, therefore, that the IUCN chose Delhi as one of the key centres to launch its first-ever World Conservation Strategy (WCS)—in the preparation of which Ashok Khosla played an important role. The WCS was perhaps the first to put down the term 'sustainable development' in print. Indira Gandhi, in turn, startled the audience with her candidness during her 6 March speech:

> I have been critical of the methods adopted by industrialised countries not because we are wiser but because we, who call ourselves developing, tend to imitate the developed countries and have not yet evolved a non-exploitative strategy for development. The need of the poor for a livelihood, the greed of middlemen for quick profit, the demands of industry and the shortsightedness of the administration have created ecological problems. It is sad that even scientists, because of their collection activities, have contributed to the disappearance of several species of orchids and other plants in our Himalayan foothills. The manner in which we are encroaching upon our forests and mountains […] is alarming […] As a result there have been soil erosion, floods and the silting of reservoirs and rivers. Large tracts of land have become saline or alkaline […]

She ended her speech by recalling 'Vande Mataram', India's national song by Bankim Chandra Chattopadhyay, first written in the 1870s. This song, that had inspired the freedom movement, was remembered by her as one that 'describes our land as one endowed with water and fruit, rich with the greenness of growing plants'. The national song has now acquired political overtones but I wonder how many who fight over it appreciate its ecological underpinnings.[10]

One of the observations made by Indira Gandhi in her speech concerned the Indian neem tree—'once so popular and put to hundred uses in sickness and in health'. She bemoaned its neglect in India, and spoke of how it was being used to bring greenery to desert areas in Nigeria. Immediately after the speech, instructions were sent to all state forest officials that intensive neem tree planting programmes should be launched at appropriate sites.

This IUCN meeting must have left quite an impact on her mind because she was to write about it to Aunt Gertrude on 11 May:

> [...] For whom do we struggle? At a recent meeting on conservation, the point was continuously being made that the preservation of all the diverse species was essential to the survival of man. I could not help asking myself and I said so publicly that is the human race as it is developing itself worth survival?

Soon after her IUCN speech, Indira Gandhi convened an informal meeting with conservationists on 2 April. R.S. Dharmakumar Sinhji, Billy Arjan Singh, Zafar Futehally, Sunderlal Bahuguna, Madhav Gadgil and Dr B.P. Pal were there, among others. There was a freewheeling discussion on wildlife and forests. The prime minister shared her anguish over ecological devastation, specifically mentioning the Valley of Flowers in Garhwal district of Uttar Pradesh as an example. She also expressed her doubts over how far conservation programmes could really succeed in the country unless the fuel needs of people—for cooking and lighting—were met through sources other than firewood. It was a concern she would keep highlighting in the months to come. On their part, the environmentalists told her in no uncertain terms that the time had come to establish a new national agency to handle conservation problems. Predictably, the functioning of forest and wildlife departments in states came under attack.

After the meeting, Indira Gandhi wrote a long letter to all chief ministers on 20 April:

> The preservation of our environment is our collective concern. [...] Since our Government took office, and even before, we have been getting numerous reports and complaints about the denudation of our forests and depredations on our wildlife. Felling of trees, indiscriminate shooting

of animals, poaching, smuggling of precious wood and animal skins, and similar destructive activity have gone on unchecked for some time now. The time has come when we can no longer look upon all this with equanimity or try to rationalize it by treating it as part of the inexorable process of development.

Underscoring the point that 'the maintenance of the ecological balance should be as much part of the development process as the working of our national resources', she spoke of the pressing need for 'conservation and renewal'. She ended up calling for 'specific and immediate action by the State Governments to check the activities of forest contractors and poachers [...] and to extend the area under forests and vegetative cover'. She gave the chief ministers a sharp nine-point action plan and asked them 'to devote some time every week to review the development in this field personally or through one of your senior colleagues'.

She wrote again to the chief ministers on 2 May on wildlife matters, and on 21 September on the subject of tree plantations:

> I understand that a beginning has been made in Madhya Pradesh, where, in one district children, have been involved in a Social Forestry programme. Under this programme, the idea is to make every child in the district plant a fruit-bearing tree and make the child responsible for looking after it. A name-plate is affixed on the tree exhibiting the name of the child. It will be the property of the child for which he or she will be given a "patta" (ownership).
>
> [...] If each child, particularly in the rural areas, could be encouraged to plant one tree and look after it until it reaches a maturity, we shall have a massive tree plantation programme and also a new generation of people who are oriented to the growing and rearing of trees. The planting [of] fruit, fodder and fuel wood trees under this programme would to some extent meet the requirements of the rural community for fuel and nutrition [...] I do hope you will take personal interest in this and start such programmes to induct children into tree plantations [...] The totality of effort should lead to an increase in effective forest cover by at least 10% of country's area in this decade.

Unfortunately, even after nearly four decades, we are yet to maintain the forest cover in the country to the level recommended by Indira Gandhi towards the end of her letter.

ॐ

Arvind Netam was a respected tribal leader representing Bastar in the Lok Sabha. He was to have a migratory political career many years later, but in the 1970s and early 1980s he was an 'Indira-loyalist'.

In a long letter of woe on 3 October, Netam brought to Indira Gandhi's attention the fact that the Madhya Pradesh government had embarked on a project to convert 'the most beautiful and luxuriant sal forest into tropical pines'. He complained bitterly against the policies and the practices of the state's forest department which, he said, were 'against the ethos of the tribal life'. In his view, the 'replacement of the even green sal by eucalyptus and teak which may have a utility for a distant market' would adversely affect the indigenous population's means of livelihood.

After asking her officials to examine Netam's letter, Indira Gandhi wrote to Chief Minister Arjun Singh of Madhya Pradesh on 25 October:

> I understand this is one of the projects taken up by your Forest Development Corporation with the help of the World Bank. I am not sure whether the adverse effects this will have on tribals have been gone into. I do not know whether it is in the interest of the country to replace sal trees by tropical pines like eucalyptus. I suggest that this matter be gone into deeply and urgently.

The chief minister viewed himself as a follower of Indira Gandhi. But that did not prevent him from sending her a six-page defiant reply on 11 November: '[...] the letter of Shri Arvind Netam may be a result of misconceptions about, or inadequate appreciations of what is intended in the project'. He then took a political stance:

> I would like to point out that some opposition parties are also fishing in troubled waters and are aligning themselves with various vested interests to score a political point against the State Government, even though the project is one which is likely to change the face of Bastar district and make it a more prosperous area.

He concluded that 'the project will provide large-scale employment for the tribals and also help inculcate in them new technical and forestry skills'. In effect, the chief minister presented an argument on behalf of the paper industry, which was evidently behind the move with the support of the World Bank.

The issue got further ammunition when an Arjun Singh-baiter and a minister in Indira Gandhi's cabinet, V.C. Shukla, wrote to the prime minister on 8 December expressing his grave concerns about the determination of the state government to 'cut down very large areas of ever green sal trees and to replace them with tropical pine'. He drew her attention to the way 'forests are being destroyed in Chhattisgarh area' and in his Lok Sabha constituency itself.

The very next day Indira Gandhi wrote a stiff letter to Arjun Singh:

> I wrote to you in October regarding the cutting down of ever-green sal trees in Bastar district and replacing them with tropical pines. I find from your letter of the 12th November that the project is being proceeded with in spite of the objection to the proposed plantation and disturbance to the tribal culture. Whatever project has been sanctioned must be reassessed. The value of the sal tree in economic and other terms far excels that of the pine. I have also received many complaints about disturbing the forests in Jagdalpur area, and more specifically in Mainpur. These complaints cannot be dismissed out of hand. They should be examined in depth and meanwhile no action be taken to cut down the trees.

This was not to be the end of the story. The chief minister's reply in the New Year was to trigger a whole sequence of events of great significance to forest policy.

Swami Chidananda, president of the Divine Life Society, wrote to the prime minister on 17 March:

> [...] a very dear and very highly esteemed friend of mine, Sri Sunderlal Bahugunaji comes with this letter seeking audience with you. He comes to represent the case of our Himalayas, that are being ecologically devastated, as your esteemed self must surely be well aware.

He went on to speak specially of the hardships faced by women in the hill areas and wanted Indira's Gandhi's personal intervention to ameliorate their lot. The prime minister knew the holy man well but Sunderlal Bahuguna did not need anybody's recommendation to meet her.

The prime minister replied to Swami Chidananda on 8 April, after a meeting with Bahuguna at the conclave of conservationists she had called six days earlier:

> The Himalayas have been our greatest asset and protection. But we have forgotten the lesson which our ancients proclaimed, that Dharma will protect us only if we protect it. This is true of Nature too.
>
> I have long been perturbed by the reckless exploitation of Himalayan forest wealth. The movement organized by Shri Sunderlal Bahuguna, with the cooperation of women of the hill regions, has evoked the admiration of people far and wide. On behalf of the Government, I should like to assure you that we are determined to put an end to the best of our ability the misuse of our forest wealth. If we fail to do this, we shall imperil the nation's very life.
>
> I have had some discussions recently with persons active in this field of work. Shri Sunderlal Bahuguna participated in the meeting and made some valuable suggestions. We plan to follow these up.
>
> Any Government programme can succeed only if it becomes a peoples' programme. Spiritual leaders can do a great deal to awaken the consciousness of people to their duties, to the nation and to themselves.

The principle that the prime minister enunciated in the letter—nature protects those who protect her—is at the entrance of the Ministry of Environment, Forests and Climate Change in New Delhi—appropriately called 'Indira Paryavaran Bhawan'.

By September that year—given that the delicate Himalayan ecosystem was still under threat—Sunderlal Bahuguna sent a petition to Indira Gandhi 'to save the fragile Himalayan environment from further destruction, commercial felling of forests above 1000 metres altitude must be banned'. Indira Gandhi was sympathetic and did two things post-haste—she sent him a message, and also got her office to pursue the matter with the Uttar Pradesh government.

The message sent on 19 September highlighted what she had been saying for some time—that forests have great ecological value and that deforestation in the name of progress and development has led to both drought and floods. She recalled how 250 years ago, a king, in what was now Rajasthan, had ordered the felling of trees in forests and how more than three hundred men and women belonging to the Bishnoi community had sacrificed their lives while resisting this order. This was, she pointed out, an inspirational example and it is with this same sentiment that recently women and others in Uttar Pradesh had launched an agitation. As in her letter to the chief ministers, she called for a country-movement to protect trees and for a campaign with the slogan 'a tree for every child'.

Her instructions were clear. That is why, soon after, in March 1981, the state government imposed a temporary ban on tree-felling, and the following month set up an experts' committee headed by Kailas Nath Kaul to examine the issue in greater detail.

The committee was to submit its report in March 1982. However, since Indira Gandhi wanted some eminent 'forest ecologists' like Madhav Gadgil also to comment on the matter—and such consultations took about a year—it was only on 3 June 1983 that the Government of India, through its Agriculture Secretary S.P. Mukherji communicated its views to the state government. The most important part of the directive was:

> [...] there should be moratorium on commercial fellings in the UP Himalayas right down to the Siwalik foothills, irrespective of considerations of altitude or gradient. This moratorium should apply to all forests [...] and may extend [...] for a period of 15 years.

A caveat was added at the very end:

> The Prime Minister has observed that many Members of Parliament are worried about the hardship to which poor people are put because of shortage of wood. She has further observed that the suggestion for extending the complete ban on felling of trees to all hill areas of UP should be reviewed to the extent that availability of firewood for the local population is ensured by permitting very selective felling of dead and dying trees and those in slopes of less than 30 degrees.

This was the kind of tightrope walking Indira Gandhi had to do at every step—she listened to her ecological conscience, while also recognizing socio-economic realities.

∾

The Chipko movement of the 1970s in the hill districts of Uttar Pradesh was a watershed in the nation's environmental history. In May, Indira Gandhi gave an interview to Anil Agarwal who had then returned to India and was in the process of launching the Centre for Science and Environment that was to later become a premier advocacy organization. The interview appeared in the form of an extended conversation in the British science magazine *Nature*. He wrote:

> In the Himalayan region of the State of Uttar Pradesh, local villagers have launched a unique movement against the state government's auctions of vast tracts of forests. For several years they have prevented felling by hugging the trees—hence the movement's name Chipko Andolan. To what extent does Mrs. Gandhi appreciate such a popular movement? "Well, frankly, I don't know all the aims of the movement," she replied diplomatically. "But if it is that trees should not be cut, I'm all with it [...] The cutting of trees has immediately brought havoc because it has increased our drought, it has increased our floods. And it has made vast areas much more difficult to live in."

The interview was wide-ranging and covered issues of solar energy, nuclear energy, science and technology, north–south relations and also the environment. It also offered a tiny window to Indira Gandhi's inner life. In her words:

> I happen to deeply love the earth and I have from childhood been concerned about the cutting of trees. I sympathise with Bernard Shaw when people asked him why don't you keep flowers and he said that I love children but I don't chop off their heads and keep them in my drawing room. So that's the sort of outlook I have always had. The aesthetic point of view is very much there. Most urban life is an uglification. To me personally, this is the most serious aspect. Now we find that progress

itself and the use of science and technology is creating its own pollution, which is very much worse [...]

The interview may not have had much of an audience in India but it evoked a response from Indira Gandhi's old friend, Barbara Ward or Lady Jackson.[11] On 10 May, Lady Jackson wrote:

> May I thank you warmly for your kindness in making place in your very busy schedule for Mr. Anil Agarwal. He was most gratified that you could spare the time to see him and came away impressed with your interest in and dedication to India's environmental integrity. He particularly told me of your insistence on reforestation—from big schemes to village plantations—and I am sure your example will interest and stimulate other leaders and governments.

Soon after the *Nature* interview, Indira Gandhi would refer to the Chipko movement again—this time during an unusual debate in the Lok Sabha on 11 August. It was perhaps for the first time that issues related to the environment were taken up exclusively. The prime mover was a new MP from Gujarat, Digvijay Sinh who was also a well-known conservationist. He was to impress Indira Gandhi sufficiently for her to induct him, a few months later, into the council of ministers as deputy minister in the newly formed Department of Environment. Her old colleague Karan Singh also spoke.

Indira Gandhi was not a great parliamentarian like her father or some of her opponents. She considered speaking in Parliament a duty to be discharged. But on this occasion, she was different. She spoke with passion and conviction, with no notes, no text in front of her except for the points she had jotted down. She said: 'I should like to pay a tribute to those, especially in UP who have prevented contractors from cutting down their trees and have mounted a movement [...] the Chipko Movement.' She admitted that 'certain projects have resulted in deforestation which, in time, has caused siltation of rivers, floods and other such effects which have caused and are causing year after year tremendous damage to people'. She talked about subjecting 'each development project to environmental and socio-economic evaluation' and agreed with Karan Singh regarding the need to spread environmental awareness and education. It was not a long intervention—possibly twenty minutes at best—but she was speaking from the heart.

∾

Echoes from the Wild was a magazine privately circulated among young nature enthusiasts in New Delhi, some of whom went on to become well-known names—Mahesh Rangarajan, the historian, and Ashish Kothari, the activist, being two of them. These young men had met Indira Gandhi for hardly about two minutes in her 'Janta Durbar' on 17 February and—even as being told to 'keep up the good work'—handed over a copy of the December 1979 issue. The editorial in this issue had said that the regulations in place for protection of the Delhi Ridge area were being flouted with impunity—and that trees were being felled without the permission of the lieutenant governor.

Indira Gandhi obviously read the editorial because her secretary, C.R. Krishnaswamy Rao Sahib wrote to Lieutenant Governor Jagmohan on 21 March that the prime minister wanted serious notice taken of it and also wished to see 'urgent action taken to preserve the environment of the City including its ridge, and green belts'. He marked a copy to his colleagues in the Ministry of Agriculture and Ministry of Works and Housing, adding: 'Prime Minister is anxious that urgent action should be taken to ensure that in both old and new areas urban development takes note of the need to preserve ecology.'

Mahesh Rangarajan—who was in school when she took this stand—went on to use the anecdote in his books and articles to illustrate Indira Gandhi's concern for the environment.

∾

Indira Gandhi's concern for a new approach to forest administration found expression in her address to the eighteenth meeting of the Central Board of Forestry on 25 August. She admitted that, as against the desirable goal of having one-third of India's geographical area under forest cover, the actual achievement was just about 23 per cent. Worse, out of this only around

10 per cent could be considered good quality forest cover. Thus, India faced the twin problems of both depletion and degradation. While Indira Gandhi had made similar impassioned speeches in the past, never before had she given actual numbers to support her arguments.

A theme she highlighted, and that was to develop over the next four years, concerned people's participation in the management of forests. Salim Ali had told her that the FDCs—forest development corporations—set up with great hope had transformed into 'forest destruction corporations'! She echoed this sentiment and urged foresters to think of themselves as custodians of the forests.

Being custodians is one thing, but arrogating to themselves all knowledge and wisdom on matters related to forests is another. It is the latter tendency she warned against and reminded the audience that while they held professional expertise, there are others, particularly tribals and voluntary agencies working amongst them, who had considerable wisdom that needed to be harnessed constructively.

Conscious of the tough new law for forest conservation that she was about to announce, she spoke of how it is not enough to pass decrees, and that it was far more important to rouse public consciousness, particularly in the younger generation, for the protection and regeneration of trees.

She injected a little humour into these serious proceedings by giving an example of a law whose letter was very much alive even if its spirit had died. This law had been enacted way back in 1873 in the Madras Presidency to protect wild elephants. In October 1953 a separate state of Andhra had been created out of what was then Madras, and in 1956 a new enlarged state of Andhra Pradesh was created. The law, she pointed out, 'was preserved while the elephants disappeared' in Andhra!

Later, when she came back to her office after the speech, she sent Sharada Prasad a note:

> Someone complained in the Forestry Conference that the elephant story
> did not apply to Andhra Pradesh. Please check.

Sharada Prasad checked with his colleague Rajamani who sent the prime minister an explanatory note promptly:

[...] The Act was designed to protect wild elephants which were found in all areas of the Madras province that included parts of what is now Andhra Pradesh. Slowly elephants started vanishing from the Andhra area only, while even today they survive in Kerala, Karnataka and Tamil Nadu. The continuance of the Act by Andhra Pradesh for a number of years after its formation [...] was not altogether fanciful as there were chances of elephant habitat in area like Srikakulam district where even now elephants stray from Orissa occasionally [...] It is likely that P.M.'s remarks in good humour may make Govt. of Andhra Pradesh to consider whether there are chances of having an elephant sanctuary.

The prime minister was mollified but the anecdote tells us much about Indira Gandhi—someone could go to her and tell her that her joke may have been factually incorrect, and she would, true to character, come back and crosscheck with her officials.

Both Madhav Gadgil and Ramachandra Guha who have written extensively on India's ecological history believe that Indira Gandhi was an 'authoritarian' ecologist much like, in their view, Salim Ali as well. This appears to me to be a colossal exaggeration but there was indeed one occasion when she was peremptory in her approach to policy-making. This was in connection with what came to be the Forest (Conservation) Act, 1980. It is perfectly possible, however, that her approach to this matter was influenced by her experiences with legislation for curbing water pollution that had taken four years to get finally enacted in 1974; and the one to deal with air pollution that was first mooted in 1973 and took eight years to become a law in 1981.

In mid-March, Indira Gandhi had convened a meeting of conservationists. All the prominent names in the field of conservation were there, as was Samar Singh—an IAS officer who was working as secretary (forests) in Madhya Pradesh. It was also known that he would soon be dealing with forests and wildlife at the centre. He revealed to me that almost everyone at the meeting bemoaned the condition of India's forests—in their view, states were not taking forest protection and regeneration seriously. Indira Gandhi, true to style, did not say a word. She listened intently.

After Samar Singh took over from Nalni Jayal in June, he was called by Rao Birendra Singh, the minister of agriculture, and told that the prime minister wanted a new central law for forest conservation. It was not an idea that had been thrown up in the meeting with conservationists. It is conceivable that, having brought forests on to the concurrent list in the Constitution in 1976, Indira Gandhi felt it was time for a bold move by the centre in this area, much as what had already been done for wildlife protection eight years earlier. Samar Singh set to work and proposed a draft law which was less than one page long—unprecedented in India's legal and political history, especially considering the importance of the subject:

> Notwithstanding anything contained in any other law for the time being in force in a State, no State Government or any other authority shall make, except with the prior approval of the Central Government, any order directing—
>
> (i) that any reserved forest (within the meaning of the expression "reserved forest" in any law for the time being in force in that State) or any portion, thereof, shall cease to be reserved;
> (ii) that any forest land or any portion thereof may be used for non-forest purposes.
>
> Explanation—For the purpose of this section "non-forest purpose" means breaking up or clearing of any forest land or portion thereof for any purpose other than reafforestation.

Its brevity was amazing. But what happened thereafter was even more astounding. Indira Gandhi—unsure that a consensus would emerge on a national law for the preservation of forests, and fairly pessimistic about states taking forest protection seriously—took recourse to Article 123(1) of the Constitution. She got an ordinance issued on 25 October, with the substance I have just mentioned in its body. This was hailed by Salim Ali, Billy Arjan Singh and all other environmentalists. Forest officials also joined in the applause.

Parliament debated the ordinance in November, and Indira Gandhi came under attack from a number of MPs for having taken this unusual route to law-making. Nonetheless, the ordinance was notified as an Act on 27 December—perhaps making it a law that took the shortest time to become a reality. The basic architecture of this Act remains to this day and is generally acknowledged to have very drastically cut down the rate of diversion of forest land for non-forest purposes. When I became environment minister, for instance, I discovered that during 1950–80 some 4 million hectares had been diverted, but in the next three decades, this had spiralled down to about 1 million hectares.

Just nine days after she took over as prime minister for a second time, Indira Gandhi got a paragraph on ecology included in the customary president's annual address to both Houses of Parliament.[12] On 23 January, President Sanjeeva Reddy told the MPs that 'there is need to set a specialized machinery with adequate powers to incorporate in all development measures to maintain ecological balance'.

Soon after, on 28 February, Indira Gandhi constituted a committee—comprising both officials and outside experts like M. Krishnan, Zafar Futehally, Billy Arjan Singh and Madhav Gadgil—to prepare a report that would 'recommend legislative measures and administrative machinery for ensuring environmental protection'. The chairman of the committee was to be the deputy chairman of the Planning Commission, and in April, when a leading political figure N.D. Tiwari was appointed to this post, he became chairman of the committee—which, consequently, came to be known as the Tiwari Committee.

By 15 September, which is fast work by committee standards, a report had been prepared. It was formally presented to the prime minister two days later. There were many recommendations but the most significant was the one regarding the creation of a new Department of Environment under the direct charge of the prime minister.

Indira Gandhi herself became India's first minister of environment on 17 November and was to remain so till her death. As for the department itself, the first three secretaries she personally hand-picked were all scientists—physicist M.G.K. Menon; marine biologist S.Z. Qasim; and botanist T.N. Khoshoo. After Khoshoo's retirement in early 1985, no scientist has occupied that position.

Apart from the fact that she was comfortable with scientists, my own feeling is that Indira Gandhi saw environmental issues largely through the prism of science and technology—in other words, she was convinced that ecological problems could be addressed through cleaner technologies, for which research and development were essential. She may well have changed her views had she lived longer and acknowledged the narrowness of this 'tech-fix' perspective.

The functions of the Department of Environment were to radically change after the passage of the Environment (Protection) Act, 1986 which was a legislative response to the horrific Bhopal gas catastrophe of December 1984. When Indira Gandhi had been alive—despite conservationists like Salim Ali demanding a government body that would have the power to approve of or reject projects after an analysis of their environmental impact—Indira Gandhi chose to retain the Department of Environment, not as a regulatory body, but as an advisory, policy agency with, of course, a strong scientific base. However, if she had lived longer, she may well have changed her mind.

The Tiwari Committee's report was written mostly by Jayal. After a tenure extended for over a year at the intervention of Salim Ali, on 5 June, he had been transferred to the Department of Science and Technology to work as part of this committee. He was to join the new Department of Environment when it was formed in November and stayed there till May 1983. He contributed much because of the prime minister's backing. It was in the early 1980s, for instance, that a couple of scientific institutions for providing research and training facilities in environmental conservation were established, as also national parks in the Himalayan range extending from Ladakh to Arunachal Pradesh. The two in which Indira Gandhi took a keen personal interest were the Valley of Flowers National Park which was notified on 6 September 1982, both in what is now Uttarakhand.

As pointed out earlier, Jayal was replaced as joint secretary (Forests and Life) by Samar Singh, an IAS officer who, like Ranjitsinh, had worked in Madhya Pradesh and made a name for himself in the forestry area, He was actually Ranjitsinh's cousin and belonged to the erstwhile princely family of Dungarpur in Rajasthan. He was later to write about his experience of working with Indira Gandhi, giving a number of examples of her deep interest in and concern for forests and wildlife.[13]

∾

Over the past few years, the entire discourse on energy policy has revolved around renewable energy and on how to move the world away from fossil fuels like oil and coal. Indira Gandhi was a very early bird on this debate.

After returning to power in January 1980, she had been telling the officials that India needs to do something dramatic in the field of energy. No doubt, the second oil shock following the Iranian Revolution of February 1979 was fresh in her mind, as was the first oil shock of 1973. Her belief was that just as India had pledged to food self-sufficiency in the 1970s and had succeeded, a similar objective of energy self-sufficiency needed to be pursued in the 1980s.

On 29 October, one of the officials in her office sent the cabinet secretary this note:

> Prime Minister would like the Secretaries Committee on Energy Policy to work out details for constituting an Alternate Energy Commission under the Department of Science and Technology to concentrate on solar, wind, tidal energy etc. and also biogas.[14]

On 18 November, the top officials of the Government of India met, with the cabinet secretary in the chair. The record of that meeting said:

> Initiating the discussion, Cabinet Secretary said that the Prime Minister was of the view that the country should pledge itself to energy self-sufficiency in the 80s. High prices of oil and diminishing availability of other fossil sources had made the task of developing energy from renewable sources and exploitation of non-conventional sources particularly urgent. Research and Development efforts in the field of alternative energy sources like solar, wind, biomass and biogas had to be intensified and steps taken to see that these got translated from the laboratory to a wider field.

Clearly, Indira Gandhi wished to create an institutional structure akin to what existed for atomic energy and space, so that the new energy sources got the importance they deserved.

ॐ

Karan Singh had been chairman of the IBWL from 1969 to 1977. Even while he had moved from the Ministry of Tourism to Health and Family Welfare in 1974, Indira Gandhi had kept him on at the IBWL.

However, he fell out with her and left her side in January 1978 when the party split. He went to the extent of contesting against her candidate in the 1980 Lok Sabha elections. So, when Indira Gandhi returned as prime minister in January, conservationists worried over the fate of the IBWL.

This is when Anne Wright came up with a bold idea. She was a well-known name in conservation circles. She was all but Indian having been born to British parents but having spent her entire life in this country. Indira Gandhi knew and liked her. On 10 March, she wrote to the prime minister:

> I am writing to ask if you would do us the great honour of becoming the Chairman of the Indian Board for Wildlife. As a member of this Board, I would most humbly request you to take this on. [...] We desperately need your help to encourage the nation to follow up the efforts to save our forests and wild life from destruction.

Indira Gandhi noted on the letter the same day:

> I should be delighted to accept.

Three days later Anne Wright wrote to Fatehsinghrao Gaekwad, now a Congress MP and the president of WWF-India:

> While in Delhi I asked Yunus if there was any chance of the PM taking on the Chairmanship of the IBWL and he asked her. The message is that if six of us who are members of the IBWL write to her to take it on she might do it. I hope you will be one of the six [...]

Mohammad Yunus was the nephew of Frontier Gandhi, Khan Abdul Gaffar Khan and an intimate part of the Nehru family. Gaekwad did not disappoint Anne Wright and wrote to Indira Gandhi on 16 March:

Although I had every intention of mentioning this topic to you when I met you today, the other topics did not permit me to do so.

As you know, the Indian Board for Wildlife is to be reconstituted and it is my fervent request to you that you take over the Chairmanship of this body. You have been one of the foremost advocates of conservation and it would support the conservation movement in general and in particular in this country if you accede to my request.

Indira Gandhi confessed on the letter on the same day:

I should like to be Chairman. It is a subject after my heart.

Anne Wright managed to get some others—M.Y. Ghorpade, Hari Dang, Billy Arjan Singh, Digvijaysinh and Dr L.M. Nath—to write to Indira Gandhi along similar lines. That her efforts had borne fruit is revealed by a letter she sent the prime minister on 21 April:

Thank you for a most lovely evening. It was very kind of you to ask me to supper [...] It is such good news that you would perhaps agree to be our Chairman of the Indian Board for Wildlife [...] A note on some of our problems in the Eastern Region is attached.

Indira Gandhi replied on 4 May:

We were glad to have you with us but you ate so little, it seemed to me you must have gone home hungry!

[...] I have been so rushed that I could only refer your note to my office. I do hope they are following it up. On my own, I have written to the Chief Ministers concerned.

On 23 May, the IBWL was reconstituted with Indira Gandhi as chairman. Conservation in India had come of age and moved on to the highest gear possible. But there was a slight hitch. It was indeed great to have the prime minister herself chair the IBWL but how much time would she be able to devote to it was the question. Samar Singh reckoned that the full IBWL would meet maximum once a year and so he suggested that a Standing Committee be created to meet more frequently and act as the executive arm of the IBWL. A proposal to set up such a Standing Committee was then submitted to her. She then immediately rang Rao Birendra Singh, the minister concerned, and asked why she could not handle this committee as well. He had no choice but to agree. Then a file suggesting a new Steering Committee for Project Tiger with the minister as chairman was submitted by Samar Singh to Rao Birendra Singh. Once bitten twice shy—the minister marked the file to the prime minister suggesting that she may like to accept the chairmanship, which she did with alacrity. Thus it was that Indira Gandhi became chairman of all the three key wildlife conservation bodies—the first and last time a prime minister held these positions.

Even though Indira Gandhi was to be buffeted by all sorts of political problems, she always found the time for the regular, purposeful meetings of, not only the IBWL, but also the Standing Committee of the IBWL and the Steering Committee of Project Tiger. Moreover, she never held these meetings outside New Delhi. While members would often suggest sanctuaries and national parks as potential venues, Indira Gandhi would turn down these requests saying that VIP visits would only inconvenience and disturb the animals.

The prime minister would get hundreds of letters daily on a variety of subjects. If they concerned wildlife or nature, she would often make it a point to respond.

On 4 October, she received a communication from Eje Lindberg and Ola Lindberg of Stockholm, who went on to compliment her for Project Tiger, and comment that tiger conservation was of vital significance for the world as a whole. Indira Gandhi's office had prepared a routine acknowledgement letter, but the prime minister had other ideas. Although she had no clue who the Lindbergs were, she replied on 4 November:

> 'Project Tiger' is the single largest conservation programme adopted for a single species in any country so far. It is estimated that as a result of protection measures taken under the scheme, the population of tigers in all our game reserves has shown an appreciable increase between 1972 and 1979. We shall continue the efforts to protect the tiger.

Indira Gandhi had made her only visit to the Bharatpur Sanctuary in February 1976 although she would regularly get letters regarding it, especially from Salim Ali. This time, however, it was Peter Scott who complained about the state of affairs there and Indira Gandhi replied to him on 7 February:

> The failure of the monsoon this year has caused great distress to our farmers and also of course to wildlife and birds. Thank you for drawing my attention to the needs of the Bharatpur Sanctuary, especially for the sake of the Siberian cranes. I am getting an urgent report and will see what we can do to help.

Bharatpur was special to her, and Peter Scott was a man she respected. She sent him a letter on 24 March, is mind-boggling level of detail:

> As you have rightly observed, the drought in Western India had created problems in the Bharatpur Sanctuary area also. The irrigation project at Ajan Bund, which normally supplements the supply of water to the Bird Sanctuary, had poor shortage of water. As the usual submergence area tended to be dry, attempts were made to sink surface and artesian wells. The artesian wells did better and additional water was made available by end-December to that part of the area where birds usually alight. Unfortunately, it was too late by then to assure good growth of Sedge Tubers on which the Siberian Cranes thrive. Perhaps, partly because of this, the numbers of these cranes sighted this year were less than usual. Our experts surmise that the cranes may have dispersed to adjacent water-spreads and then left by the end of February on the long return flight to Siberia.
>
> The dry situation in the areas has, however, helped to re-plant trees to provide safe nesting sites which had been seriously depleted over the years. Some extensive mound plantation has been carried out. The money needed for the Sanctuary has been provided.
>
> We ourselves are interested in the preservation of this beautiful bird sanctuary and shall do everything possible to make water available to facilitate the sustenance of the birds at Bharatpur.

I doubt Peter Scott would have ever received such a letter from any other president or prime minister in his long and distinguished career.

☙

Four years earlier, Harsh Vardhan had met Indira Gandhi in Haldighati and convinced her that the Great Indian Bustard required her personal attention. But then, she lost power and nothing much had happened. When she became prime minister again, Harsh Vardhan spotted an opportunity, and organized an International Symposium on Bustards in early November in Jaipur. The symposium would have been just another event but for two happenings: one, the Government of India issued a commemorative stamp; and two, Prime Minister Indira Gandhi sent this message on 1 November:

> A threat to any species of plant and animal life is a threat to Man himself. If the human race we know it is to survive we must curb his rapacity and re-learn the age-old lesson of living in peace and harmony with his fellow-creatures.
>
> My good wishes to all efforts by individuals and by non-officials and official organisations to save the Great Indian Bustard.

With the prime minister now on board, instructions were issued for the establishment of specific sanctuaries and closed areas for the species in various states like Rajasthan, Madhya Pradesh, Gujarat, Maharashtra, Karnataka and Andhra Pradesh. But doubts lingered about hunting and shooting. These fears dimmed when Samar Singh reassured Harsh Vardhan on 6 August 1982: 'Government is not considering any proposal to allow hunting of the Great Indian Bustard anywhere in the country. Hope this sets at rest any doubts on this score.'

India had been a signatory to the Ramsar Convention for the protection of wetlands in February 1971 when Indira Gandhi had sent Salim Ali as one of India's two delegates. But for some reason, India was yet to ratify the convention. Salim Ali, too, did not bother to remind Indira Gandhi about the matter, and it was left to Nagendra Singh, a distinguished civil servant and well-known conservationist,[15] to finally prompt her on 8 September. He wrote: '[…] there was no conceivable reason for India not joining this Convention, specially because we have "Wetlands" of great importance, like the Sunderbans and the Rann of Kutch.'

Nagendra Singh's observation hit home with force. Nothing could be more galling than having been left behind in such a good ecological cause by, of all countries, Pakistan which had joined in 1976 itself. A week later, Indira Gandhi wrote on Nagendra Singh's letter:

We should join. There is no controversy. Pakistan also has joined.

Subsequently, on 25 October, Rajamani sent a note to S.S. Puri, the agriculture secretary: 'PM would like Ministry of Agriculture to take urgent steps to make India party to the Ramsar Convention and inform this office about it.'

India was to join a few months later.

Indira Gandhi, had been present when her father had laid the foundation stone for the Himalayan Mountaineering Institute in Darjeeling on 4 November 1954. Father and daughter had come back to the institute on Christmas Day of 1957. Tenzing Norgay, along with Brigadier Gyan Singh, had been appointed by Nehru to build the Institute.

On 3 October, Indira Gandhi returned, for the third time, for the silver jubilee celebrations. She recalled Tenzing's contributions, honoured Nawang Gombu—the only living Indian to have scaled the Everest twice, and then turned philosophical in her brief remarks:

We should approach the mountains, particularly the Himalayas, with humility and respect, because other things of life which we hold so dear to us look so small before them [...] Mountains are great educators. As you go up a mountain you face dangerous paths and difficulties in breathing. As you progress in life, it becomes more complicated and you face thousand and one problems. There is no escape from life and mountaineering teaches us to scale the peak of life.

Notes

1. I wrote about this key episode in 'How Cement Was Decontrolled', *The Times of India*, 18 August 1982.

2. B.K. Nehru was the first non-American to meet with president-elect Ronald Reagan on what was Indira Gandhi's sixty-third birthday. This is recounted in Nehru (1997).

3. The Travancore Maharajas offered prayers from the *Ottakal Mandapam*—a single granite slab near the sanctum sanctorum. Indira Gandhi was given this rare privilege that day.

4. Kerala was then under President's Rule.

5. I have a feeling that Salim Ali, Zafar Futehally and the IUCN approached the prime minister in a coordinated manner. I found a letter of Salim Ali to Indira Gandhi dated 2 June 1980 on Silent Valley in the IUCN archives.

6. Kochukoshy (1982).

7. In an interview to *The Hindu* published fifteen years later on 18 June 1995, Bahuguna was to say: 'I remember Indira Gandhi intervened to stop the Silent Valley project. In Nainital, there was this old oak tree on a hillock that the Army wanted to uproot. That would have harmed the hill. An SOS was sent to Mrs Gandhi. She intervened and the oak still stands.'

8. 'Indira Gandhi: Fearlessness in the National Interest', Rediff.com, 30 October 2009. Interestingly, like Indira Gandhi, Rajamani also had a deep interest in Indian culture and one of the tasks he embarked upon was to identify the modern-day botanical names of all the tree species mentioned in Varahamihira's *Brihat Samhita*.

9. Gujarat was then under President's Rule.

10. *Sujalaam* (clean water), *Suphalam* (good food), *Malayaja Shithalaam* (wonderful air), *Sasyashyaamalaam* (greenery everywhere).

11. Barbara Ward, British writer, environmental thinker and public figure had written an influential book *India and the West* in 1961. She co-authored *Only One Earth* which set the stage for the Stockholm Conference in 1972. In April 1975, she had urged Indira Gandhi to support Mother Teresa's nomination for a Nobel Peace Prize which the Prime Minister readily did. In January 1977, she wrote to Indira Gandhi regarding Baba Amte. The prime minister's reply on 2 February 1977 had ended by saying 'Just now I myself am down with an attack of herpes'.

12. Actually it is the prime minister's office that drafts every single word of the address with suggestions from different ministries.
13. Singh (1986).
14. Indira Gandhi had been an early convert to solar energy. On 5 July 1976, she had replied to a letter from J.R.D. Tata saying, 'It is not only now but for years before the energy crisis that I have been drawing the attention of our scientists to the importance and urgency of harnessing solar energy.'
15. He was Samar Singh's uncle and had been a judge of the International Court of Justice. Later, in the 1980s, he was to be a member of the Brundtland Commission.

1981

Indira Gandhi collecting shells, Andaman and Nicobar Islands;
June 1981.

Early in the year on 21 February Indira Gandhi wrote to Dorothy Norman in a very reflective mood:

> *I do believe in myself. Perhaps that is what has brought so much trouble. I also seem to have an aptitude to take on the worries and troubles of others. Long ago in my early childhood my grandfather used to joke that if there was a more difficult path, I could be trusted to find it. This was on summer trips to the mountains. I loved them as I do now. Instead of going on the regular road, I preferred to climb straight up the steep side in spite of loose earth and rocks and roots which cropped up unexpectedly all over the place.*
>
> *Sanjay's going has affected me profoundly [...] Basically we do not weep for those who have gone but for ourselves.*

1981 continued to see Assam and Punjab in ferment. Back channel talks were leading nowhere and the agitationists hardened their positions. Ostensibly, the movements in both states were for greater autonomy but there were unmistakable signs of separatism as well. Indira Gandhi herself was convinced that the very 'unity and territorial integrity' of India was at stake and was in no mood for a compromise. The economy was stressed and India had to seek substantial assistance from the IMF, something Indira Gandhi was loath to do given the memories of 1966 but nevertheless she ended up doing. Predictably, there was an uproar but she weathered the storm.

But there were some silver linings also. In February, she gave new shape to her younger son's unfulfilled ambition. A public sector company Maruti Udyog was incorporated and given the task of producing a small car with the help of foreign collaboration. Subsequently, the Japanese company Suzuki was selected as the partner. In June, her elder son contested for Parliament and won handsomely. She travelled abroad quite a bit, including in May to her old school in Switzerland which had given her a sense of attachment with nature when she was just nine years old. In early August she went to Nairobi to address the UN Conference on New and Renewable Sources of Energy. Hers was the keynote speech and she was one of five heads of state or government to attend. She talked eloquently about moving away from a dependence on hydrocarbons and embracing renewable energy, both of which are very much part of the global environmental discourse now. She had taken her two grandchildren long with her and together with the president of Kenya they all went to the Masai Mara, the famous game reserve. They saw a 'pregnant rhinoceros who ran rather fast' and 'lots of wildebeest'. Her granddaughter recalled that the grandmother was most amused by the rhino and by the ivory sceptre the Kenyan president carried around.

This was also the year when a collection of her major speeches appeared for an international audience published in London.[1] In her foreword she talked about the two well-known focal points of global danger—military conflict and the gap between the rich and poor nations. But she added that 'a third confrontation is becoming increasingly visible between human avarice and nature's powers of recuperation and renewal'.

∾

Silent Valley remained a part of the year's preoccupations. The M.G.K. Menon Committee was busy with work and taking its own time. Meanwhile, on 26 December 1980, the Kerala government, in order to establish its environmental credentials, had notified Silent Valley as a national park.

One of those concerned about Silent Valley was K.P.S. Menon—a former foreign secretary living in Kerala, who was often approached by the anti-dam activists to reach the powers-that-be in New Delhi.[2] He wrote to the prime minister on 10 January:

> Just a line to thank you, out of the fullness of my heart, for saving the Silent Valley. And that, in the teeth of almost unanimous opposition from all parties. The episode demonstrates how short-sighted the "demos" in a democracy can be. And how amenable to the pulls of big money. No one could have performed this miracle but you [...]

Three days later, Indira Gandhi noted on his letter: 'There seems to be some doubt in the matter'. A 'Dear KPS' letter followed on 17 January—the salutation reflecting the very warm, three-decade-long friendship she enjoyed with this doyen of the foreign service:

> The Committee of Scientists are looking into the question of the Silent Valley Hydel Project. Perhaps you are referring to the notification said to have been issued by Kerala Government about the National Park in that area. I have yet to receive the details but I hope the whole matter will be solved to the satisfaction of everybody.

K.P.S. Menon's celebrations proved to be hasty, as he himself admitted in another letter to Indira Gandhi on 13 January:

> I fear it was a little premature on my part to have rejoiced over the salvation of Silent Valley. This morning's papers carried a statement from the Chief Minister that the proposed formation of the Silent Valley National Park does not mean the abandonment of the Hydro-electric project [...]
> I do hope that, thanks to you, the Valley will be saved.

The prime minister replied on 31 January: '[...] A copy of the Notification of the Kerala Government has been received and some clarifications have been sought from them. I hope the matter will be resolved satisfactorily.'

Unfortunately, it wasn't. On 4 February, the Kerala government made official what K.P.S. Menon feared—the coverage needed for the Silent Valley Hydroelectric Project was to be excluded from the area to be covered by the national park. When Indira Gandhi was informed about this, she wrote on an internal note on 20 February:

> We must keep close and constant watch. The exclusion of these areas might defeat the whole purpose of the exercise we have been making.

That she was worried was evident even earlier, during an IBWL meeting on 9 February, when she had remarked that

> The situation in regard to Silent Valley is not at all satisfactory.

Then, there was the Lalpur Dam issue. On 2 January, R. Rajamani sent a note to Indira Gandhi, which confirmed that the Gujarat government had agreed to reduce the height of the dam; however, the protesters who had met the prime minister earlier were opposing this.

On Rajamani's note, Indira Gandhi wrote two days later:

> I am told that the entire ashram and Adivasi area will be submerged. This means the work of long years is suddenly wiped out. Is it proposed to settle them somewhere else? In Rajasthan, the Pong Dam oustees are not yet settled.

Indira Gandhi was referring to the well-known Anand Niketan Ashram which was being run for the welfare of tribal communities in the area and whose chairman was Harivallabh Parikh. Parikh wanted a smaller dam in Lalpur so that the impact would be minimized; in addition, he proposed five smaller dams on the main river and its tributaries to benefit tribal families. Lastly, he demanded compensation in the form of irrigated lands for those who had lost their property in the submergence area.

Discussions between the Gujarat government and the agitationists followed, with the Central Water Commission (CWC) and the Union Ministry of Irrigation also getting involved. The Gujarat government did not want to compromise—concerned that this would set a precedent for adjoining projects in the Narmada Valley—but it was willing to keep the Lalpur Dam at a lower height and provide compensation and resettlement on liberal terms.

When Indira Gandhi was informed about the discussion on 4 April, she agreed with the stance of the Gujarat government but she also told her officials by way of a handwritten note:

> We should ensure that any action taken does not lead to any agitation in Gujarat.

That Indira Gandhi was pulled in two directions is evident in Harivallabh Parikh's telegram to her on 28 August:

> YOUR HONOUR TOLD ME THAT LALPUR DAM PROBLEM WILL BE SOLVED. WHEN I TOLD YOU THAT I AM WAITING FOR WORDS FROM RAO BIRENDRA SINGH JI FOR FINAL SETTLEMENT YOUR HONOUR TOLD ME THAT YOU HAVE ADVISED THE CHIEF MINISTER GUJARAT AND THERE IS NO PROBLEM. SINCE I CAME BACK TO GUJARAT HAVE NOT HEARD ANYTHING FROM GUJARAT GOVT [...] PLEASE ADVISE GUJARAT GOVT. TO DO NEEDFUL

Clearly, the prime minister was in two minds. While she was sensitive to what the Gandhian activist was saying, she was also under pressure from the chief minister of Gujarat. To complicate matters, Uttambhai Patel, the tribal MP from Valsad, wrote to the prime minister on 26 November arguing against the Lalpur Dam and reminding her that:

> [...] Sri Harivallabh Parikh and the tribals of this area remained with us during our worst days. Sri Parikh has devoted his whole life for development of this tribal area and is very well known to you. I have got full faith that you will intervene for the sake of poor tribals of the state.

Eventually, Chief Minister Madhavsinh Solanki must have prevailed on the prime minister—for she replied to Patel on 1 December:

> The Chairman, CWC visited the Hiran Dam site in July when officers of the Gujarat Government as well as Shri Hariballabh Parikh and

his associates were present. Thereafter, he has made a number of recommendations keeping in view all aspects including the interests of tribals. The Ministry of Irrigation have been asked to write to the Gujarat Government that these recommendations should be communicated to Shri Parikh for information.

It was little consolation for Harivallabh Parikh that the prime minister wanted the Gujarat government to go ahead with the Lalpur Dam, but *after informing him*. Clearly, the prime minister's final decision went against her better instincts—but this was not to be the end of the story. The Lalpur Dam issue would continue to engage her attention the following year.

The Datardi Dam that was about to be built on the river of the same name would submerge a prime national park area in Gujarat—in and around Gir. Expectedly, the prime minister was worried—doubly so, since various people she respected, including K.T. Satawarala who had been adviser to the governor during President's Rule in Gujarat the previous year, approached her to stop its construction.

Indira Gandhi's second visit to Gir on 21 January helped the issue get sufficient attention. She was there to inaugurate a seminar of Gujarat's conservation strategy, and her remarks began on a light touch:

> It is indeed a pleasure to be here today. I remember my previous visit to the Guest House and to the Gir Forest, when it was much more adventurous to see the lions. They were not so used to human beings and nobody would be quite sure how they would react. In fact we had to be dressed so as to be very inconspicuous. So, this is also a part of development: to have tame lions!

Along the way, she discussed the Datardi Dam issue, and on 9 June, thanks to her persuasiveness, Gujarat's chief minister wrote to her confirming that the project had been abandoned. But Madhavsinh Solanki also made a number of other arguments—that four dams had already been built in the past, touching or slightly encroaching on Gir's territory; that the Datardi Dam would have created a lake which would actually benefit wildlife, particularly in the years of drought which were quite frequent; and that the storage of sweet water in the dam would raise the water levels in the areas near the sea, thereby arresting the ingress of sea water salinity in parts of rain-starved Saurashtra.

His arguments must have sounded credible to Indira Gandhi, because she recorded on his letter on July 2:

> We have to walk on the razor's edge. I agree with the above note. However it would not be advisable to give the impression that environmental conservation is always in conflict with the needs of irrigation and power.

Indira Gandhi's trip to Gir, incidentally, had another fallout. A day before her proposed visit to the national park, a letter went from Rajamani to the chief secretary of Gujarat:

> Prime Minister has received complaints[3] that the damage to the corals in the area of Pirotan Island of Jamnagar continued unabated even after the declaration of the area as a Marine National Park [sic]. A nearby cement company is said to be carrying out large-scale dredging for sand from the seabed in the vicinity of the few remaining corals off Pirotan Island. It is also reported that this is illegal [...]
>
> Prime Minister is anxious that nothing should be done to damage the corals in this area [...] We shall be grateful if expeditious action could be taken to stop illegal mining and damage to the corals.

Because of the great concern she had shown the previous year regarding the destruction of corals, a marine sanctuary had been notified in the Gulf of Kutch on 12 August 1980. But, then, Indira Gandhi highlighted that this was inadequate. In the light of this, the Gulf of Kutch Marine National Park, enjoying the highest level of protection, was to be notified on 20 July 1982.

The Dudhwa National Park was always in the news thanks to the prime minister's good friend Billy Arjan Singh. He had first reared leopard cubs, gifted to him by Indira Gandhi, and had released them into Dudhwa in 1973. Three years later, she had helped him get a tiger cub from London.

He had reared that one too, and let it into the wild. Both episodes had been very controversial but Billy Arjan Singh had survived because of the prime minister's fondness for him.

In 1981, Dudhwa would hit the headlines again, though for a different set of reasons. On 19 August, the Standing Committee of the IBWL chaired by none other than the prime minister herself, decided to translocate a few one-horned rhinoceroses from their only habitat, that is Kaziranga in Assam, to Dudhwa.

Assam of the very early 1980s was radically different from the state Indira Gandhi had visited frequently in the past. Gone was the peace and quiet. Assam was now in ferment, rocked by agitations that often turned violent. The one-horned rhinoceros of Kaziranga was viewed as a symbol of Assam's unique identity, and local newspapers claimed that Indira's decision to translocate a few of them was further proof that she was against the state!

The prime minister was aware of this sentiment—yet if she enthusiastically continued supporting the initiative it was because both Indian and foreign experts in the IUCN had convinced her that there was a substantial risk to the rhino population if it were to be confined to just Kaziranga. Dudhwa had been selected as a second habitat because rhinos had been present there as late as 1878.

Opposition in Assam gathered momentum in response to the prime minister's decision. The governor himself wrote asking for the translocation to be reviewed. The process of bringing the state on board took almost two years. After numerous meetings and extensive discussions, on 9 October 1983, the state government finally gave the green signal. Rhinos were re-introduced to Dudhwa after a gap of over a century in March–April 1984. Given the serious political problems the prime minister confronted in Assam, the decision was extremely bold.

The International Association against Painful Experiments in Animals was a London-based network. It was having its seventh general assembly in late August in Milan to discuss 'practical means of eliminating the appalling pain and misery at present inflicted upon research animals during many biomedical experiments'. Indira Gandhi was asked whether she would send a message, which would, in turn, greatly bolster the movement. She replied on 3 August:

> The truly civilized person is one who has compassion, tolerance and understanding and who uses these in all dealings with fellow humans and also with all creatures.
>
> Experiments to prevent diseases and find remedies may be inevitable but I am sure it is possible to make them in a more humane manner and to lessen the discomfort and the suffering of the animals used.
>
> I gladly give my support to the General Assembly of the International Association against Painful Experiments in Animals.

It was a simple and straightforward message. That she was the only head of state to have been asked for one reflected her standing in the conservation community.

Dehra Dun and Mussoorie were very much on the prime minister's mind in 1981. Earlier in the year she had had a helicopter reconnaissance of the devastation caused to the Doon Valley by mining operations for limestone, marble, dolomite, gypsum and phosphorite by both private and government-owned companies. A number of her friends living in the area had petitioned her about the worsening situation in the area—among them Mady Martyn, widow of a former headmaster of Doon School; and Sita Devi, mother of Rajiv Gandhi's close friend Arun Singh. Her own colleague Dinesh Singh had written to her on 28 April, and she had noted on his letter five days later:

> Mussoorie is being ruined. No one seems to be able to control the contractors.

On 3 November, on a letter she had received from Jai Kishore Handoo, who was obviously a distant relative, she jotted:

> Mussoorie certainly needs attention. It is such a pity that this lovely hill station should go to seed.

Each of these pleas helped strengthen the prime minister's resolve to protect the area. One of her early steps was getting the Department of Environment to set up a 'Board for Doon Valley and Adjacent Watershed Areas of Ganga and Yamuna' on 4 August. The Board had no statutory powers but derived its strength from its membership and the knowledge that it enjoyed the patronage of the prime minister. Besides, it acted as a pressure group to promote environmentally sound proposals for the region.

When the Forest Research Institute at Dehra Dun celebrated its centenary anniversary on 19 December, Indira Gandhi reiterated her anguish over the denudation of the region:

> Time was when Mussoorie was known as the "Queen of the Hills". Dehra Dun blossomed and shared in its glory. She has now been robbed of her garment. Her climate has changed, her beauty has gone.
>
> It is indeed sad how our hillsides in all parts of India are becoming bare and barren.

The prime minister also recalled how trees had been important to her from her childhood; how she hid in their branches to escape grown-ups; and how she later used trees as a refuge for studying and reading. She reiterated her belief that the contractor's axe and human greed were destroying forests, causing great ecological damage, leading to soil erosion and floods—depriving many of their traditional livelihoods. If this speech was important, it was also because it enunciated an idea she had given expression to in her notes to officials:

> [...] foresters must come out of their self-imposed boundaries of reserve forests and think of wood lots, social forestry and other techniques to involve the community itself. We must ensure that social forestry does not replace valuable old forests. I see no conflict between the two [...]
>
> Forests are traditional sources of food, herbs, fuel and other essentials of many unsophisticated people who have lived for generations in and off the forests. These people are now bewildered by the shrinking of the forest area, the depletion of produce and numerous restrictions imposed by officials. The education of the forester and his colleagues in forest sciences should cover the sociology and economics of such communities.

Forestry practices should make the lives of forest dwellers, whether humans or other species, happier not worse. These people should not be driven away from forests.

Indira Gandhi—always vocal that forests were valuable in themselves—came to realize that forests had to exist for the people, too, particularly tribal communities, whose livelihoods depended on them. This explained her call to foresters to be more people-friendly, and sensitive to tribal sentiments. The speech was a landmark and was to re-orient India's thoughts regarding the larger role of forests. In some ways, the historic law passed by Parliament in December 2006 to protect the rights of traditional forest-dwellers can be traced back to the ideas Indira Gandhi first articulated on 19 December 1981. The forest bureaucracy was and continues to be unhappy with this law but ecology, as Indira Gandhi had reminded it, cannot be sustained in a social vacuum.

Much like Indira Gandhi, the indefatigable Sunderlal Bahuguna worried much over the ecological well-being of the hills. He had launched a 4,000-kilometre Kashmir to Kohima padyatra (journey by foot) to heighten public awareness of environmental issues. The padyatra, which started in June, was completed eighteen months later. At some point, during a break in his journey, he must have visited Vienna—for Mira Behn wrote to Indira Gandhi on 4 September: 'Sunderlal Bahuguna, who brings you this letter, has come like a waft of memories from the Himalayas […]'

The prime minister replied on 13 September:

This is just a line to thank you for writing. I was glad to get the latest news about your health from Sunderlal Bahuguna.

Later, Bahuguna must have met the prime minister and requested her for a message for the rest of his march—for on 17 October, Indira Gandhi sent a taped message in Hindi:

We the men, women and children—who live in India—share this country with other species. Trees and animals are also inhabitants of our land.

They perform important functions and have their rights. The thoughtless felling of trees to serve our immediate needs is posing serious problems for the entire nation. The increase in floods and the silting of rivers are the direct consequence of forest denudation. The people must wake up to this danger. We must ensure that the forest area in Himalayas increase. Shri Sunderlal Bahuguna is continuing his journey on foot to spread the message of forest protection and tree plantation. My good wishes are with him.

Sundarlal Bahuguna went on to tell Indira Gandhi in a letter dated 27 October that 'your taped message for the protection of trees and plantation was listened by thousands of people in the remote villages with great interest'.

In the same letter—which had been dispatched from Simla, after the environmentalist had walked across the state of Himachal Pradesh—he made a number of recommendations including banning the private sale of forest products; discontinuing the felling of trees; prohibiting resin tapping; and enforcing a land-use policy in the hills that gave priority to plantation schemes nurturing those species that met the needs of local people.

On 5 November, Indira Gandhi recorded on his letter:

How much of this is possible? Please follow up and reply to Shri Bahuguna on my behalf telling him that I could not do so as I am going out on tour.

The chief minister of Madhya Pradesh Arjun Singh, had received strong letters from Indira Gandhi expressing her extreme displeasure at what his government was proposing to do in the rich forests of Bastar. He had replied but she was clearly in no mood to listen. He remained adamant and sent her a four-page letter on 14 January once again defending the replacement of sal trees by tropical trees like eucalyptus. However, now, he made a concession to the prime minister's sentiments by concluding:

We fully share your feelings and affections for the fast-denuding forest areas and the welfare of the tribals and we shall take up the project only after we are satisfied that it shall be in the larger interests of those who reside in the area. The State Government would welcome any further studies about the effects of the proposed project on environmental or conservation considerations including scrutiny and clearance under the new forest conservation law.

Indira Gandhi was powerful. But as in the case of the Backbay Reclamation issue in 1974—as also this episode—there were limits to her power. If a chief minister set his heart on something, there was little she could do except write letters. In this instance, she was compelled to partially give in to Arjun Singh, and on 24 March her aide R. Rajamani wrote to Inspector General of Forests (IGF) M.K. Dalvi:

> While there may be no objection to take on an experimental plantation on research and pilot schemes in the areas felled before 1980, Prime Minister is of the view that even on these lots monoculture with only tropical trees or similar species should not be attempted without a full and proper evaluation of the monoculture in the long-run. No new areas should be felled and no decision about future projects until after the Tribal Studies and a study by the Group set up under IGF is completed and approval of PM obtained after sending the studies to this Office.

A second letter to the IGF followed on 14 May from another aide, Arvind Pande, who had by then replaced Rajamani:

> Prime Minister has seen and agreed with the suggestion that the pine seedlings should be planted in blocks of 30 ha, with gap in between in which natural forests should be allowed to come up and bamboo and other local species should also be planted.

In May, on Indira Gandhi's instructions, a group was set up under the IGF's chairmanship—its members included Madhav Gadgil; the curator of the BNHS, J.C Daniel; and a tribal Congress MP from Orissa, Giridhar Gomango, who later became chief minister of that state. The group recommended stalling further deforestation for pine plantations; urged that action be taken to make good the loss of sal by planting degraded forests with it; and endorsed the use of bamboo as raw material in paper mills in the area. It also made suggestions for improving the forest cover in Bastar.

The matter that Netam had first raised in October 1980 was concluded with the prime minister formally accepting these recommendations on 7 December.

❧

Indira Gandhi was zealous about tree plantation—a fact that James Brewbaker, a professor of horticulture and genetics at the University of Hawaii, came to appreciate. When he met the prime minister in February on behalf of the Watumull Foundation—which had invited her to Honolulu later in the year—he discussed plants, specifically endorsing kubabul, a small, fast-growing tree from Hawaii. In a letter to the prime minister on 17 March, Brewbaker stated that kubabul could become one of the major fuelwood, fodder, home-building, pulpwood and green manure trees. The prime minister replied on 1 April:

> Our Ministry of Agriculture has kept me in touch with the work being done with regard to this and other trees which do well in dry areas. Some time ago when I went to the drought-affected areas of Rajasthan, I took along seeds of Kubabul. It is indeed a most useful tree. We are encouraging people to plant it.

The prime minister's firm commitment to nurturing tree-cover was evident to her ministerial colleagues and officials, as she urged them to accelerate forestry programmes. On 15 February, she wrote to Minister of Agriculture Rao Birendra Singh:

> [...] We must see that the results of our efforts, particularly in social forestry, become meaningful and visible soon. I do not think enough was done last year to promote the planting of trees on a large scale, perhaps because of drought etc. But this year we should make all the preparations in advance and aim to plant trees on a really massive scale. [...] We should fully utilize the early monsoon to nourish the new plantations.

The information she received was not particularly encouraging. Gujarat, Maharashtra, Madhya Pradesh and Tamil Nadu were expected to do well but in states where the programme was likely to be much more significant like Andhra Pradesh, Bihar, Uttar Pradesh, Orissa, Rajasthan and West Bengal, the increase was not expected to be anything to write home about. Rajamani examined the state-level variations and sent a note to her on 29 April saying, 'If approved, these imbalances will be brought to the notice of IG, Forests, who will be requested to review this immediately [...]' Prompt came the prime minister's response the very same day:

> This is something that <u>must</u> be done. It is not a question of requesting.
> If they default, we shall have to think of curtailing other programmes.

On 1 July, Indira Gandhi launched a massive tree plantation programme to be taken up all over the country by the Youth Congress. The decision was meant to recall the memory of Sanjay Gandhi who had included tree plantation as part of his five-point programme.

Indira Gandhi used the occasion to dwell on her favourite topic—how the merciless felling of trees had already brought about climatic change, led to pollution and caused droughts and floods. She was somewhat critical of the government-run 'vanamahotsava' initiative since she felt it had become a ritual without adequate care being taken to ensure the survival of the tree saplings that got planted. She wanted various kinds of trees to be planted in the name of every newborn child.

It was the first time that the Congress as an organization took up tree plantation in such a gigantic way—some half a million saplings were to be planted all over the country in seven days. Sadly, that momentum would not last for very long, as far as political activities around afforestation was concerned.

જી

17 November marked the first anniversary of the Department of Environment, of which Indira Gandhi herself was a minister. Since the department was still finding its feet, and was yet to achieve anything tangible—although a number of studies had been commissioned and surveys launched—Indira Gandhi decided to offer it a shot in the arm through a public message:

Three days ago we celebrated National Children's Day. For the children's sake we must ensure that the environment is not degraded, that natural resources are not depleted, and that there is a proper ecological balance.

This needs short-term and long-term goals. Over-exploitation and pollution must be avoided [...]

Among nature's most precious gifts are forests. The greatest emphasis must be placed on afforestation and the planting of trees wherever possible. A tree is a symbol of life. Combining our love of children with their concern for trees will broaden our perspectives. A campaign such as "For every child a tree" is a process of education. A tree planted whenever a child is born and nursed to full growth will be an asset to the nation, even as that particular child grows to become a good citizen. Why not plan for a tree on every birthday?

In November last year we set up a Department of Environment. I hope the Department will persuade every parent and child to cooperate with the programmes of environmental management whether they are initiated by Government or non-officials.

A few days later, she broached a new idea before her officials and R. Rajamani, recorded a brief note and dispatched it to Samar Singh.

As I mentioned over the telephone, the Prime Minister would like the need for legislation against indiscriminate cutting of trees to be examined. A note on the legal and practical aspects of this may kindly be sent on priority.

Indira Gandhi's proposal was quite radical. Tired of the complaints she would constantly receive regarding the uprooting of trees in towns and cities, she had wondered aloud if a national law to regulate the felling of trees outside designated 'forest areas', would be of some use. Her officials later told her that such a law would go against the Constitution and it was best to leave such regulation to the states concerned. While the prime minister was less than happy about this, she had no option but to go along. Her eventual request was that the states be asked to pass such a law—and that is where matters stood.

ॐ

The prime minister gave an extended interview to Marianne Lohse of the French newspaper *Madame Figaro*; it was to appear on 16 October—and revealed much about Indira Gandhi's inner world. When asked about the things she liked in life besides politics the prime minister replied:

> [...] I like trees, greenery, flowers, but if I have to choose between having trees and flowers, I would have trees. They are comforting to the eyes. Their colour, especially because of the glare here, may be a reason for that.

When queried further about the flowers she preferred, Indira Gandhi responded:

> Well, I like wild flowers more than garden flowers. But if a flower is very beautiful, one likes it. You know it is so difficult to say what you like. It depends upon the specimen and the environment in which you see it. But I think I like wild flowers because of the qualities which I like in human beings: they grow in such adverse circumstances. You see a wild flower growing where there is tremendous wind and odds against, yet it blossoms on its own, especially in the mountains.

It was in this interview that she had also confessed that she would not write her memoirs as she found it boring to 'write, read or talk about myself'. If she had a free moment she made it clear, 'I really don't want to spend it on myself'.

∾

In 1974, Indira Gandhi had sparred with the chief minister of Maharashtra on the issue of New Bombay and the Backbay Reclamation. She was to have a similar exchange with Maharashtra's new chief minister, A.R. Antulay—who had been with her when the Congress party had split in 1978, and who she went on to hand-pick as the head of the state in the teeth of opposition.

On 20 August, A.R. Antulay wrote to Indira Gandhi about the trans-harbour road link project that was then being studied by a steering group chaired by J.R.D Tata. The BEAG had been writing letters to Tata as well as to the prime minister, raising objections since it believed that the project would violate one of the directives Indira Gandhi herself had issued the previous year while giving clearances for the new port of Nhava-Sheva.

The chief minister, on his part, expressed the hope that the trans-harbour road link project would receive the support of the Government of India. Indira Gandhi replied to him on 13 September that the bridge would 'defeat the objective of decongestion of Bombay' and concluded that:

> I have no objection to the proposal for a discussion at the official and ministerial level, as proposed by you, but we should have an open mind on this keeping in view environmental considerations which are becoming more and more paramount.

That Indira Gandhi was taking the representations of the BEAG seriously even though she may not have been replying to its letters herself is borne out by the fact that she wrote once again to the chief minister on 2 November:

> [...] it was felt that there was need for an in depth study of all the environmental issues including decongestion in Old Bombay and also matters like balanced development of the Bombay Metropolitan region and the need for Nhava-Sheva port to develop as an independent port.

She told the chief minister that the study would take six months. He had no option but to write again nine days later accepting her decision.

As the year drew to a close, Indira Gandhi erected another ecological milestone. After a visit to Orissa—a visit that troubled her deeply—she had written to the chief ministers of the coastal states on 27 November about the degradation and mis-utilization of beaches.

> I have received a number of reports about the degradation and misutilisation of beaches in our coastal states by building and other activity. This is very worrying as the beaches have aesthetic and environmental value as well as other uses. They have to be kept clear of all activities at least upto 500 metres from the water at the maximum high tide. If the area is vulnerable to erosion, suitable trees and plants have to be planted on the beach sands without marring their beauty.

Beaches must be kept free from all kinds of artificial development. Pollution from industrial and town wastes must also be avoided totally.

Please give thought to this matter and ensure that our lovely coastline and its beaches remain unsullied.

Indira Gandhi would come to be criticized for the 500-metre limit she imposed from the high tide line. While there were ecological reasons guiding her decision—as also a genuine desire to protect the livelihoods of fishermen—she had no way of enforcing her pronouncement. The country had to wait for the Environment (Protection) Act, 1986, which would enable the Coastal Regulation Zone (CRZ) Rules to be promulgated in 1991. This would address the concerns that Indira Gandhi had raised a decade earlier.

ॐ

Jawaharlal Nehru had started the tradition of the prime minister heralding the new year by addressing the Indian Science Congress. Indira Gandhi kept this up. This year the conclave was in Varanasi and the theme was something close to her heart—science and the environment. She did not fail to mention this while beginning her address on 3 January, as also the fact that the theme was particularly appropriate with 'Ganga and Varanasi having been symbols of continuity in Nature [...]'

The speech itself may not have been the most memorable, but she did make an announcement—one that is taken for granted these days but that marked a huge step forward back then. She said that a Commission for Alternative Energy was being established and that, in the long run, hydel and solar power, and biogas, would be the principal forms of energy in India. It is often forgotten that this nation was amongst the earliest to seriously start thinking about alternatives to fossil fuels.

Two years later, Indira Gandhi was to establish an Advisory Board on Energy to take forward an integrated energy policy.[4] Sadly, the lead she gave was soon to be lost as oil prices fell and the urgency to diversify the energy mix vanished. It is only in the last decade—with climate change becoming a pressing reality—that solar energy for instance, has come back into the reckoning in a big way.

～

Indira Gandhi had first spoken about a law to control air pollution in 1972 in the run-up to the Stockholm Conference. But for a long time, the idea did not translate into reality. There could be a number of reasons for this—the prime minister had been persuaded by her advisers that existing laws were sufficient; air pollution had not yet emerged as a serious public health concern; and Indira Gandhi had already used her political clout to push for a law to deal with wildlife protection in 1972 and water pollution in 1974.

Nevertheless, it remains a mystery why an environmentally conscious Indira Gandhi failed to pass a law to deal with air pollution during her first tenure as prime minister. It was left to Indira Gandhi's successor government to introduce a Bill for the prevention and control of air pollution in Parliament on 17 April 1978. But it could not be passed during its tenure. On coming back to power, Indira Gandhi picked up the baton and re-introduced the Bill in Parliament on 24 November 1980. The nation finally got a law to control air pollution on 29 March, almost seven years after a law to control water pollution and nine years after she had pointed to its necessity.

～

India hosted the third meeting of the Convention on Trade in Endangered Species, popularly known as CITES, in New Delhi on 25 February. Indira Gandhi threw a reception for the delegates two days later which Peter Scott attended. On 20 March, Scott wrote to her:

> [...] May I congratulate you on the adherence of India to the International Whaling Convention.
>
> You asked me to remind you of the various points we discussed. The first is the proposal by the Indian Board for Wildlife to list the habitats in need of protection in India with proposals for the creation of biosphere reserves, national parks and sanctuaries. [...]

Another point I spoke of briefly was the enforcement of CITES [...]

Finally I would like to mention education which I believe still to be the most important of all human activities. The Education Commission of the IUCN has taken on a new lease of life under the current Chairman Professor Baez [...]

Professor Baez was Albert Baez—a Mexico-born nuclear physicist at Stanford University. While he was a distinguished scientist with a deep interest in education, he is perhaps more famous in history as the father of the singer Joan Baez. That Indira Gandhi was thinking about education in the context of conservation is revealed by the fact that very shortly on receiving Peter Scott's letter, she wrote to him on 25 March: 'I would be grateful for some information on the Commission and in which way the Commission could help us in India'. On 14 April, the professor sent her what she had asked for and suggested the possibility of forming an Indian National Committee for the Education Commission of the IUCN.

The New Delhi conclave of CITES was pertinent for another reason. A forty-five-minute film titled *Birds of the Indian Monsoon*—on Bharatpur—made by a young husband–wife team of Stanley Breeden and Belinda Wright (Anne Wright's daughter) premiered there.

On 11 November, Bharatpur engaged the prime minister's attention once more, when Jeffrey Short, president of the Chicago Academy of Sciences, wrote to her drawing her attention to the threats posed to the sanctuary:

Our two countries have a common interest in trying to preserve two extremely rare species of cranes. These long-distance flyers have been around for some 70 million years and many of them are gravely endangered. [...]

[...] Bharatpur, probably the world's greatest bird reserve, is in danger of human pressures [...It] would be the hope of countless thousands here that somehow Bharatpur is preserved. [...] Siberian cranes migrate an unbelievable distance from the northern Siberian coast in the Soviet

Union, over the Hindu Kush mountains, down through Afghanistan to Bharatpur [...] to spend the winter. Reports indicate that there are fewer than 50 today [...]

As I say Bharatpur is perhaps the greatest of all the world's bird reserves. I have myself seen six species of eagles within a few minutes and it is known for having the largest nesting colony of the beautiful painted stork anywhere. I do hope it is possible to exercise some control to preserve this beautiful area.

Indira Gandhi's reply to Short on 23 December reveals the special place that Bharatpur had in her heart. She wrote:

We regard the Bharatpur sanctuary as one of our natural treasures and I personally share the concern of all bird and wildlife lovers that we should do everything possible to enable birds and especially the rarer varieties to come to it. I have been taking a personal interest in its problems. There are human pressures on all our wildlife sanctuaries. At the same time there is also the beginning of an awareness of the importance of conservation along some of our younger administrators. We are trying to ensure that cattle-grazing and fuelwood gathering does not disturb Bharatpur's tranquility.

All countries must cooperate to preserve the Siberian Crane. I am told last year about 33 were sighted in India. On the 12th November this year arrived the first flock consisting of 35 birds out of which five were this year's chicks. It would be interesting to know more about the other group which goes to the Yangtze region.

Indira Gandhi's interest in the Yangtze region was sparked by Short's reference to it in his letter where he had spoken of a 'second small population which migrates east through far eastern Siberia and then turn south to China, spending the winter on the Yangtze river'. The birdwatcher in her had clearly come alive, even in the midst of all the political chaos.

ॐ

Dillion Ripley would often write to Salim Ali, and Salim Ai would then write on the same subject to Indira Gandhi. At times, Ripley would write directly to the prime minister and then use Ali's good offices to ensure that she personally saw his letter. One good example is an episode involving the visit of the two ornithologists to the sensitive area of Arunachal Pradesh which borders Bhutan, Myanmar and China.

Even for an Indian like Salim Ali to travel to that place would require permission; for Dillon Ripley, a full-blooded American accused in the past of having CIA links, a trip to Arunachal Pradesh would invite the meticulous scrutiny of the Ministry of Home Affairs.

Dillon Ripley wrote to the prime minister on 27 May that Salim Ali and he wanted to travel to a ridge between Tirap and Lohit districts; that this had 'never been visited by naturalists'; and that the area was a 'treasure in India's garland of natural wonders'. He was not above using some emotional blackmail—he said that Salim Ali was keen to accompany him and hoped that 'it might be possible to visit this area before anything happens to our friend'. 'Our friend' was eighty-five years old. Ripley himself was sixty-eight. When Ripley failed to receive a response from Indira Gandhi, he got Salim Ali to forward his letter to the prime minister on 21 June; Ali added the request: 'Both Dr. Ripley and I are most anxious [to go the particular area] before it becomes too late (for me at any rate!)'.

Five days later, Indira Gandhi noted on Salim Ali's letter:

> I should very much like to oblige Shri Salim Ali for whom I have high regard. So far as I know, Dr. Ripley is reliable. But please look into the matter.

A flurry of correspondence followed involving the Intelligence Bureau, the Ministry of Home Affairs, the Department of Forests and Wildlife and the Department of Environment. The bureaucratic recommendation was that Ripley and Ali should be denied permission. But on 12 July, Indira Gandhi wrote to Ali, with a similar letter going to Ripley a little later:

> Last month you wrote for permission for you and Dr. S. Dillon Ripley to resume your field study of birds of the Namdapha area in Arunachal Pradesh's Tirap district.
>
> I am glad to say that all concerned Ministries have given their approval. The Ministry of Home Affairs will send you and the Arunachal Pradesh Government formal intimation of this decision.

There would be a similar episode two years later, but that would come with more serious implications and once again the prime minister would have to overrule her bureaucracy.

ॐ

Porbandar was the birthplace of Mahatma Gandhi—the patron saint of modern environmentalism. Peter Jackson, who had played a key role in protecting Sultanpur's jheels in 1970, made a trip to there early in the year. According to his own account, he 'spotted a small lake where over 4000 Lesser Flamingos were gathered'. When he was told that that the lake's days were numbered and it was soon going to be filled in to construct a park, he approached Indira Gandhi. His last such communication with her had resulted in the creation of the Sultanpur Bird Sanctuary near Delhi. This time, too, the prime minister spoke to Madhavsinh Solanki, Gujarat's chief minister, who assured her that the plan for the park would be abandoned. This paved the way for the notification of the bird sanctuary finally in November 1988 and it continues to thrive. Clearly Solanki was no Bansi Lal, who got the Sultanpur Bird Sanctuary notified in less than two years. Nevertheless, the bird sanctuaries at Porbandar and Sultanpur are a tribute to the Indira Gandhi–Peter Jackson friendship.

ॐ

On the morning of 7 May, Indira Gandhi visited her old school, La Pelouse near Bex in Switzerland. After forty-five years, she was returning to the place that had shaped her love for nature—a place she had described most eloquently in a letter to Nehru way back on 8 August 1936:

> [...] However many beautiful sights and places I may see, I return here to find Switzerland is the most beautiful of all. As I write under the shade of an enormous chestnut tree, on the one side the Dent du Midi (my favourite peak apart from the Matterhorn) peeps from above thin wisps of clouds and on the other in the far distance shines the Lac Leman in this glorious sunshine and the clouds make strange patterns of light and shade on the dark, almost awe-inspiring mountains beyond.

On her return to the school as India's prime minister, Indira Gandhi planted a sapling and spoke to the students about how denuding forests and polluting water were a threat to life itself. Even while praising Switzerland for the manner in which its natural beauty had been preserved, she expressed the hope that the path to progress in India would not weaken its kinship with nature. Her speech was tinged with nostalgia, as she described the 'enchanting surroundings' around Bex which had offered her 'a brief period of calm in a stormy life'.

On 29 December, Indira Gandhi visited the Indian Statistical Institute (ISI), Calcutta for its golden jubilee celebrations. She was nostalgic about its founder P.C. Mahalanobis who had worked intimately with her father in the 1950s. The ISI had provided the intellectual ballast for Indian planning for almost three decades. She had expected to meet statisticians, economists and mathematicians here. She did meet them but she also came across an unusual personality.

R.L. Brahmachary was an expert in statistics but he also was interested in animal behaviour. He had worked with the famous George Schaller in Kanha in the 1960s where the American biologist did his pioneering work on tigers and barasinghas. Through his director B.P. Adhikari, Brahmachary had made a written application for help in getting a tiger cub for his study on pheromones which are bio-chemical footprints of species. Indira Gandhi would have been briefed about this unusual request because when she was introduced to him she remarked with a smile 'so you want a tiger cub?' It took five years for Brahmachary to get the cub but what he got almost immediately was substantial funding for his research project from the newly created Department of Environment of which Indira Gandhi was the minister.

Notes

1. Indira Gandhi (1981).
2. On 8 December 1978, K.P.S. Menon had written to Prime Minister Morarji Desai on behalf of local activists and adding his own voice against the Silent Valley Hydroelectric Project. Eight days later the prime minister had replied that the project should go ahead but with ecological safeguards.

3. Fatehsinghrao Gaekwad, president of WWF-India, had written to the prime minister on 14 January 1981 on this issue.

4. Incidentally, I happened to be amongst the first two persons to join this organization.

1982

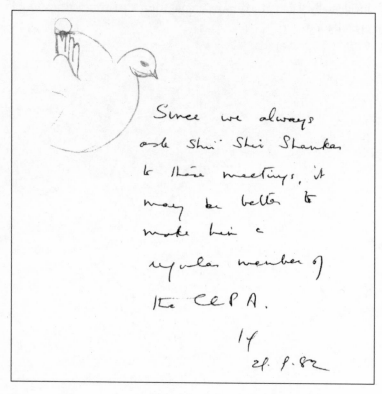

Since we always ask Shri Shiv Shankar to these meetings, it may be better to make her a regular member of the CCPA.

If

2[.] 8.82

Indira Gandhi's sketch of a bird in a note to P.C. Alexander;
August 1982.

Indira Gandhi was engulfed by political problems in Punjab and Assam. She has been charged by her critics for her obduracy but the intransigence of the Akali Dal and the All-Assam Students Union have been conveniently forgotten. Violence and killings in both states showed no sign of any respite with Punjab being particularly bad. There was also more personal anguish—a bitter and public falling out with her younger daughter-in-law who took her two-year-old son away with her. By mid-year the prime minister's mood had become sombre. On 2 August she wrote to Dorothy Norman:

Yes, I am quieter, sadder. Yet is it hardly fair to want more? Life has given of its fullness to me, in happiness and in pain. How can one know one without the other? [...]

[...] Is it because of age that one thinks things everywhere are deteriorating? And this at a time when there is so much excellence and even creativity in people. Yeats said things fall apart, the centre does not hold. What is the centre, and where?

But there were some occasions for cheer as well. Her confidante G. Parthasarathi, was given an extended audience with the Chinese strongman Deng Xiaoping in September. Along with the visit of the Chinese Foreign Minister Huang Hua the previous year, this meeting was a key milestone in the journey of normalization of relations between the two countries that culminated in the historic Deng–Rajiv Gandhi handshake in December 1988. After an interval of eleven years, Indira Gandhi visited the United States, setting the stage for a reorientation of the ties between the world's richest and world's largest democracies ending the estrangement of the 1970s caused in large measure by American policies in the subcontinent.

The year also saw the release of Richard Attenborough's much-acclaimed film Gandhi. *The release led her to write to Dorothy Norman on 2 December:*

The Gandhi film has opened with much fanfare. It is impressive. It is good for the world to know what Gandhiji stood for. Yet for those who lived through those times, the film is a spectacle, grand and powerful, yet lacking some essential quality—the spirit that is India [...] The film makes him a dramatic "super star" type of messiah—not more than he was but rather less by diminishing the other factors.

Rajiv has done a magnificent job with our Asiad. Many have cooperated, working hard and with dedication but watching it all, I have no doubt that it is Rajiv's own effort, his organising capacity, aim at excellence and concern for the minutest detail [...]

∾

On 2 February, in the midst of her confabulations on Punjab and Assam, Indira Gandhi received a note from R. Rajamani:

I have received confidential information about the depredations on the olive ridley turtles in the mangrove swamps of Bhitarkanika Wildlife Sanctuary in Orissa, about 150 K.M. from Cuttack. There is a turtle nesting ground in the Gahirmatha Beach which is reputed to be the largest known turtle rookery for olive ridley turtles. Mass nesting takes place in 2 or 3 spells of 4 to 6 days each any day after February 4th every year. The female turtles come on to the land between 10 P.M. to 5 A.M. to lay eggs (about 100 by each) which are covered by sand and then the turtles slip back to the sea. As they float on the surface, so-called shrimp trawlers from West Bengal catch them, hang them by the flippers and transport them to Digha. Each trawler collects upto 500 to 600 turtles and makes upto Rs 25,000 per night of catch and this is becoming a big vested interest. Though it is a sanctuary, Orissa Forest Department has managed to stop only local fishermen and poaching of eggs by beach combers but the catch of turtles by the trawlers goes on unchecked. This endangers one of Nature's important species [...]

The friend who has sent this information has also sent a fervent plea to P.M. to direct immediate action to check the predatory of the trawlers on the turtles [...][1]

The very same day, Indira Gandhi marked the note as

Urgent

and directed Rajamani to organize

immediate and swift action including pressing the Coast Guard into service.

The next day, Rajamani, both via letter and telephonically, brought the prime minister's instructions to the notice of Samar Singh, with the prime minister's additional message: 'Report compliance within twenty-four hours'. Samar Singh replied on 6 February:

As desired, necessary instructions have been given to the State Government [...] to take all possible measures for extending the fullest protection to the Sea Turtles, particularly the Olive Ridley. It has also been emphasized that, whenever necessary, the help of the Coast Guards of the Indian Navy should be enlisted. The concerned Naval Officer has also been requested in this regard and it has been assured that all possible assistance would be given. In fact, such action has been started already.

A protection programme named Operation Geetur was launched. It encompassed the navy, the coast guard and the state government agencies. On 20 July, Samar Singh was able to report to Rajamani that the prime minister's directives had had a significant impact not just in Orissa but also in other coastal states, especially Tamil Nadu.

The 31 March issue of *India Today* carried a four-page article entitled 'Massacre at Digha' based on the investigations of young herpetologist J. Vijaya. This was brought to the prime minister's attention but she had already been forewarned and had initiated tough action almost six weeks before the article's publication. After the article appeared, her office was inundated with letters from across the world—some 200 in all—orchestrated by the editor of the *Marine Turtle Newsletter,* Nicholas Mrosovsky. What he didn't know was that the prime minister was one step ahead.

Judged by the frequency of her visits there, the Dachigam Sanctuary near Srinagar was undoubtedly one of Indira Gandhi's favourite spots. In February 1981, she had helped Dachigam's status get upgraded from that of a sanctuary to a national park. This was mainly because international conservationists, including those in the IUCN, had been expressing serious concern regarding the rapidly dwindling numbers of the hangul because of poaching and the loss of habitat.

G.M. Oza—a well-known botanist and activist who, along with Fatehsinghrao Gaekwad had launched an Indian Society of Naturalists in Baroda—had been studying the hangul closely. He wrote to Indira Gandhi on 26 September and a preoccupied prime minister replied four days later. His request to her was to release a special postage stamp depicting the hangul, Indira Gandhi, did so on 1 October, at a meeting of the IBWL. She added:

> I am delighted that we have a postage stamp on the Hangul. But this is not sufficient. I agree that we must focus attention on the need to

protect the Hangul, its habitat and the floristic elements necessary for the Hangul's conservation.

Soon after, the newly appointed Chief Minister of Jammu and Kashmir Farooq Abdullah, with whom she was to have a bitter political falling-out a year later, sent a very encouraging message. On 7 October, she thanked him for his assurance that 'the Hangul shall never die' and added:

> We know of the interest which Sheikh Sahib [Sheikh Abdullah] took in wildlife conservation. I hope that these efforts will be further strengthened under your stewardship.

In late October, Indira Gandhi received a letter from a woman in London who introduced herself as Mrs A.K. Commander. The prime minister did not know her but when she saw Billy Arjan Singh's name in the body of the letter—and the writer's request to acknowledge his contribution—she must have taken her seriously.

Mrs Commander called the re-introduction of big cats into the wild—which Billy Arjan Singh had accomplished at Dudhwa with more than a little help from the prime minister—as one India's most original and spectacular achievements. Yet after reading his *Prince of Cats,* she told Indira Gandhi that she felt compelled to bemoan the fact that in India 'a prophet hath no honour'. She was at pains to point out that Billy Arjan Singh himself had no idea that she was writing to the prime minister on his behalf. What Mrs Commander did not mention was that she was Billy Arjan Singh's sister.[2] If Indira Gandhi knew of that connection, she did not let it out, and replied on 7 November:

> I know Mr. Arjan Singh and support him and his efforts to save wildlife. Unfortunately he managed to rub a lot of people the wrong way and there is strong opposition to his ideas even within the wildlife movement.

Billy Arjan Singh was a hugely colourful and controversial personality. That the prime minister backed him wholeheartedly throughout her tenure is a sign of her commitment to his work as a conservationist.

M.Y. Ghorpade was one of the prime minister's party colleagues in Karnataka. He came from the princely family of Sandur and had been finance minister of the state in the 1970s. He was also a well-known conservationist and had been a member of the IBWL.

In the early months of 1982, he approached Indira Gandhi, requesting her to write a foreword to his book, *Sunlight and Shadows*[3] which would include sixty to seventy of the best wildlife photographs he had taken over the preceding two decades. Indira Gandhi could not refuse him, and on 1 November wrote as a part of the foreword:

> Some of my own most pleasurable moments are when I was able to see animals free in the wild, with their rippling muscles and astonishing grace—two images engraved in my memory are those of a magnificent tiger on a pucca highway in broad daylight near a village on the way to the Jog Falls in Karnataka; and in quite another part of India, in Dachigam, Kashmir, a black panther stretched lazily across the jeepable road, his coat shining in the soft evening light. I have enjoyed the lions in Gir before the government took in hand their preservation and made them so tame, approachable and uninteresting, and many other animals. But we in India have nothing to compare with the vast stretches of land with the huge herds of many species roaming and migrating undisturbed in the Game Parks of Africa.

Every sentence echoed with her love for the wild.

Indira Gandhi had found herself in the middle of a huge storm in 1980 for selecting an Italian–Danish combine for supplying ammonia technology for a new generation of gas-based fertilizer factories. Now, another controversy erupted and this time it revolved around the location of one of these factories in Rajasthan. The expert committee on site selection had identified Sawai Madhopur—around 20 kilometres away from the Ranthambore Tiger Reserve. In June–July, conservationists—led by no less a person than Kailash Sankhala himself—objected to this site vehemently since the factory would disturb the big cats.

Those who wished to retain Sawai Madhopur as the location had powerful arguments in their favour. The Planning Commission had sanctioned this site and so had the Ministry of Chemicals and Fertilizers. The state government supported the decision. The industry lobbyists also recalled that Asia's largest cement plant had been set up at Sawai Madhopur years earlier and that had not damaged Ranthambore.

Both sides had direct access to Indira Gandhi and both made their arguments before her. The debate remained inconclusive as long as she was alive. Finally, in 1985, the private company, Chambal Fertilizers, incorporated itself, with Sawai Madhopur as the plant location.

But this was not to be the end of the story. The new prime minister, Rajiv Gandhi, was also not entirely convinced about the plant site, and referred the matter to expert committees. Between November 1987 and June 1988, two such committees—one of them chaired by the noted environmentalist Anil Agarwal—rejected the proposed location citing environmental considerations and the plant's proximity to Ranthambore. On the basis of this committee's recommendations, the company was finally directed to shift to the adjacent district of Kotah. The country had come a long way from the Mathura refinery episode a decade-and-a-half earlier.

Over the previous year Indira Gandhi had somewhat reluctantly agreed to the construction of the Lalpur Dam on the Heran river, Gujarat. But opposition to it, led by Harivallabh Parikh, continued unabated and the construction of the dam got stalled. On 18 August, Rajamani suggested in a note to the prime minister that work on the dam could start with clear instructions that its actual height would not exceed 122 metres until all conditions presented by Parikh and his colleagues were fulfilled. On this note, Indira Gandhi wrote a day later:

Yes, but will they [Gujarat government] stick to this?

Later, on an internal note she queried on 17 November:

If the ashram is being inundated, is any alternative arrangement being made?

340

In the meantime, on 22 November, Harivallabh Parikh wrote a long, six-page plea; he begged the prime minister to prevent the dam from being built, for its construction would spell disaster for hundreds of tribal families. He added that the promises being made by Indira Gandhi's own government in Gujarat did not amount to much. In response, a week later, the prime minister wrote on his letter:

> I did my best to save the area but there seems to be no way out.

Despite her belief that there was little she could do to help Parikh, she directed her officials to urge the Ministry of Irrigation to give the opponents of the project one more hearing; she said that the alternatives they were proposing had to be studied again.

On 6 December, the prime minister received a telegram from MP Ramsingh Rathwa, a Congress member, and two other state legislators that the Gujarat government was trying to start work on the Lalpur Dam and that Harivallabh Parikh was being harassed unnecessarily. They, too, wanted her to speak to the chief minister and have the project scrapped. She wrote on the telegram the same day:

> I am worried about this and have tried to do something.

The Lalpur Dam saga would rage throughout the following year.

One of the resolutions passed at the historic IUCN General Assembly held in New Delhi in November–December 1969 concerned the protection of wetlands of Calcutta. George Archibald, who had been in touch with Indira Gandhi regarding Siberian cranes, wrote on 20 July: '[…] the salt lakes and marshes east of Calcutta [must] be protected as a nature reserve for birds, including the migratory cranes, which used to visit the area and are expected to reappear before long'.

Indira Gandhi had an excellent personal rapport with Chief Minister of West Bengal Jyoti Basu—their association stretched back to the late 1930s when both were in England. But politically, the centre and the state government were daggers-drawn—which explains the nature of Indira Gandhi's reply to Archibald ten days later:

As you probably know, we have a Marxist Government in West Bengal. It is strongly opposed to me and my party and they regard conservation as a gimmick of capitalists. I can certainly convey your views to them but I doubt whether it would have much effect.

Indira Gandhi wasn't wrong. Her communication with Jyoti Basu regarding the protection of wetlands had no impact whatsoever.

�∾

Dillon Ripley had met Indira Gandhi in January to offer her a first-hand report of his expedition to Namdapha in the company of Dillon Ripley. On 3 February, he wrote:

On our return to the austere and unsmiling snows and bitter cold of Washington, I cannot begin to tell you how warm and pleasant our stay in India has been, made even more so by your friendly reception of us in Delhi. We loved our chat and talk about birds and old days [...]

Four months later, on 15 June, Dillon Ripley wrote to Indira Gandhi again. After thanking her for making the Arunachal Pradesh trip a possibility, he requested her to declare Namdapha a biosphere reserve. This was, in any case, an idea that was being debated at that time. But it was not to translate into reality; instead Namdapha was to be notified as a national park and a tiger reserve in March 1983.

Another suggestion by Ripley in the same letter did have an impact, though. He had brought to Indira Gandhi's attention that a proposed hydel project in the area would attract multiple human inhabitants; this would have a deleterious impact on Namdapha in the long run. Indira Gandhi did not reply to Ripley directly—but it is obvious that she acted on his petition because Rajamani sent a note with the prime minister's approval to T.R. Satishchandran, the secretary of the Department of Power on 31 August:

The Department of Environment is taking action for preserving the area [Namdapha] as a biosphere reserve. In this context, they do not see any justification for the Arunachal Pradesh Government in constructing a hydel project on Barmah Nala within the proposed Reserve as the area is uninhabited and the nearest town is about 28 miles away. The project itself cannot generate more than 3 to 7 MW and its purpose seems to be to provide power for saw mills, etc., to exploit the rich tropical rain forest of Namdapha. This would destroy the character of its environment. It is, therefore, requested that Secretary, Deptt. of Power, may kindly stop the investigation of the hydel project within Namdapha Sanctuary [...]

On 27 August, Ripley wrote to Indira Gandhi, conveying his regret that they had been unable to meet at the Smithsonian during her visit to Washington. He did, however, see her at a White House dinner and complimented her on 'how well you looked and how positively your address and other remarks and speeches were received'. He told her that the press coverage of her trip had been excellent and paid tribute to his long-time collaborator:

> All of who have had any contact or connection with Salim Ali owe him the greatest debt of gratitude for his pioneering work which has done so much to heighten the consciousness of the citizens of the Indian sub-continent of their natural surroundings.

Indira Gandhi replied on 9 September. She said she was sorry that 'the constant rush did not enable me to do a lot of things I would otherwise have done' and shared his sentiments regarding their common friend:

> I entirely agree with you about Salim Ali. Apart from his scholarship and dedication, he is a delightful person.

This statement is the key to understanding why and how Salim Ali came to enjoy Indira Gandhi's complete trust and confidence when she was prime minister. She knew he would never misuse his friendship with her. She also knew his concerns were genuine and legitimate. A few months earlier, for instance, Salim Ali had been very worried over the fact that a private company was about to be given permission by the Andhra Pradesh government to manufacture salt and other marine chemicals right in the middle of a lake in the well-known Pulicat Lake Bird Sanctuary that straddled Andhra Pradesh and Tamil Nadu. In a matter of a few days, Salim Ali's fears were laid to rest; word was sent to him on behalf of the prime minister that the state (Andhra Pradesh) had been 'ordered' to shelve the chemicals project.

Salim Ali's letters to Indira Gandhi were dead serious, and so were her replies. But there were informal exchanges as well. On 8 August, for instance, Indira Gandhi sent Salim Ali a clipping from *The New York Times* titled 'Worldwide Tributes to the Beauties of Nature'. She wrote on the copy of the news item: 'Dr. Salim Ali may be interested in this'. The article mentioned four recent stamps in India that had been issued depicting unusual Himalayan flowers—blue poppy, showy inula, cobra lily and Brahma Kamal.

Now and again, though, there were also some light-hearted moments in the correspondence between the prime minister and the ornithologist— as is evident in a letter from Salim Ali to Indira Gandhi on 15 January, which also carried an interview of his in *The Statesman*. Salim Ali wittily described the interviewer Gopal Gandhi as a 'double distilled' grandson. Gopal Gandhi's paternal grandfather was the Mahatma and his maternal grandfather was C. Rajagopalachari, popularly known as Rajaji.

In the interview itself Salim Ali mentioned the fact that he had deliberately kept away from Jawaharlal Nehru—a leader he had known from the early 1940s—'lest it be suspected that I had axes to grind'. He added that 'this was a tactical blunder because with his [Nehru's] sympathetic backing much could have been done to conserve wildlife and forests'. He confessed that the error in judgement had made him wiser, and that he had found in Indira Gandhi 'a knowledgeable bird watcher in her own right' and an ecologist who, like her father, was deeply concerned about the environment.

❧

Early 1982 saw Jeffrey Short back in Indira Gandhi's life, discussing Siberian cranes. On 11 January—in response to her query on Siberian cranes migrating to China—he wrote:

The Siberian cranes of Eastern Asia breed in the Yakutia area of the Soviet Union and migrate to China. This is in the northern part of the Jiantxi Province, north of the city of Nanchang, along the middle courses of the Yangtze River. Approximately 100 cranes were found in a large swamp area similar to the Bharatpur bird sanctuary.

Short introduced George Archibald to Indira Gandhi as a 'Canadian resident of the United States [...] one of the world's outstanding Authorities on cranes', who was to visit Delhi soon. Then, he added: '[...] if you are interested in seeing pictures of the birds from China or Iran, he would be honoured to show them to you while he is in Delhi'. To conclude, he wrote: 'Americans will drive hundreds of miles to see a small colony of our national bird, the bald eagle. However, on my visit to Bharatpur we saw seven species of eagle [...]'

Indira Gandhi's reply on 23 January showed that the exchange fascinated her no end:

> Your letter of the 11th of January is interesting giving information on Siberian cranes. What attractive birds they are! We are glad to welcome them to Bharatpur.
>
> I should be delighted to see the pictures. But this depends on the time available during Dr. Archibald's stay in Delhi.

Short had perhaps rarely communicated in this manner with a head of state; he wasted no time in giving India Gandhi more information in another letter dated 8 February. He also recalled the uniqueness of Bharatpur and appreciated her work 'to preserve it against encroachment, very difficult things to do'.

In early March, George Archibald did get to show Indira Gandhi a photographic album of Siberian cranes. But the meeting was quite a disaster as he recalled later in his communication to me:

> Maneka Gandhi, Mrs. Gandhi's daughter-in-law, was the first to arrive [...] Eventually the Prime Minister, encased in a light blue veil-like sari arrived [...] The presentation went without a hitch [...] After mentioning that she had another appointment, she disappeared into the night [...] But I was not pleased with the meeting. Mrs. Gandhi had said very little

345

and she seemed remote. Three weeks later big news broke that Maneka would be heading an opposition party to Mrs. Gandhi's Congress Party and that Mrs. Gandhi had asked Maneka to move from the residence of the Prime Minister. The separate arrivals of Maneka and Mrs. Gandhi on the evening of our meeting, and the tensions we felt, were perhaps in part a consequence of the conflict between the two leaders.

George Archibald's fears notwithstanding, Indira Gandhi's letter to Jeffrey Short on 8 March suggested that she had liked what Archibald had shown her:

> [...] Dr. Archibald has been here and shown us his interesting film. We also discussed the difficulties in the way of preserving the Siberian cranes.
> You probably know how difficult it is to keep our sanctuaries intact. The pressure of population and development is tremendous, and it is not easy to persuade the local people.

On 2 June, she wrote to George Archibald himself:

> I am delighted to hear of your success in breeding Siberian cranes and the survival of the little ones.
> I wish I could come to your Foundation. It would have been a relaxing change from the routine of State visits. But my schedule is so rushed that it is not possible to add to it or to go to another town.

She was referring to the news that the second Siberian crane to be bred in captivity had hatched on the night of 13 May in Baraboo, Wisconsin, USA. She is certain to have been doubly delighted to learn that the chick was named after her.

The Keoladeo Ghana National Park at Bharatpur was to witness a human tragedy later in the year on 7 November. Approximately three thousand villagers began protesting against the ban on cattle grazing in the park. The previous month itself, the IBWL under Indira Gandhi's chairmanship had reiterated the government's resolve to ensure that the ban was enforced strictly, for which a boundary wall had also been constructed. The protests soon turned violent and the police resorted to open firing; reportedly seven villagers lost their lives.

ॐ

Indira Gandhi addressed a conference of state forest ministers on 18 October—the only time she did so as prime minister. She used the occasion for some plain speaking. Her two visits to Gir prompted her to say:

> Wildlife has to be wild and it has to survive. I would like to say that I am quite unhappy at the way, for instance, the Gir lions are now treated. They have become quite tame and are no longer wild. They are fed and now they have got no capacity to hunt for themselves.

Above all else, the focus of the prime minister's speech remained on forestry practices:

> This Conference is not really called for enabling you to know my views. I think my views are very well-known but it is to emphasise once again the importance of this subject [...]
>
> [...] I have been writing repeatedly to Chief Ministers on different facets of forestry in these last three years. This was to convey our collective anxiety on the rapid depletion of our forests and the ill-effects that this would have on our climate—it is already having—or economic development and our future itself [...] The Minister was pleased to say that I was a saviour of forestry and wildlife but I will be a saviour only if they are actually saved.

Mahatma Gandhi had exhorted Indians to think of the 'last man' while taking decisions. This call was—in his own words—his talisman. Indira Gandhi gave it an ecological spin by saying:

> [...] when any decision about the felling of trees or allowing wildlife to be over-run is taken, we have to think of the life of the tree and the lives of wild animals and how intimately these are bound up with human living.

The prime minister came down heavily against the system of leasing forests on a contractual basis, the clear felling of trees and monoculture plantations.

> It has caused me great unhappiness to hear the lifestyles of tribals being affected by forestry programmes and practices [...] The Forester should be a friend of the tribals [...]

ॐ

In 1982, Indira Gandhi was to write two letters in quick succession to all the chief ministers. The first, on 30 August, spoke of the 'importance of preserving our forests [that] is being increasingly highlighted by the behaviour of the monsoons, the severe soil erosion leading to depletion of productivity, silting of rivers, etc'. She wanted the chief ministers to give more attention to the 'afforestation of catchment areas, hill slopes [and] vacant land, within or outside the forest and even in our urban areas'. She also called for a moratorium on tree felling in all catchment areas, hill slopes and tank beds, and asked the chief ministers to ensure that the Forest Department at various levels maintained high standards of probity and efficiency. She gave the chief ministers a six-point action agenda and reminded them once again that 'this matter cannot be allowed to drift [and has] to be dealt [with] urgently'.

She followed it up with another letter on 14 September, expressing her frustration that the states were not doing enough for wildlife protection and for bringing in specialization to the field of wildlife management. This time she was more elaborate in her analysis, identifying thirteen 'deficiencies' in the working of wildlife wings in different states by the IBWL. Clearly, even after a decade, she was very unhappy with the way the national law for wildlife protection was being enforced.

The two letters were expressions not just of what Indira Gandhi felt but also of what she expected the chief ministers to do in specific terms. Great thought would have gone into the finalization of such communications, for they avoided generalities and pinpointed the actions that had to be taken by the states.

From time to time—as indeed the letters to the chief ministers highlight—the prime minister would express her unhappiness at the attitude and approach of the forest bureaucracy towards wildlife protection. She emphasized the need for specialization and continuity when it came to wildlife management, and expressed her concerns, even frustrations, at meetings of the IBWL, and in notes—an example being a handwritten internal memo dated 18 January 1981:

> The Department of Forestry is singularly unaware of the needs of the
> environment and much of our current environmental problems are due
> to their shortsightedness.

Eventually, Indira Gandhi adopted a new approach. In September, she
transferred the responsibility for wildlife management from the Ministry
of Agriculture to the Department of Environment. This meant that wildlife
issues were no longer the sole preserve of the forest establishment. But it
also created a tricky situation for Samar Singh who had been looking after
forests and wildlife in the Ministry of Agriculture—Indira Gandhi's move
meant that Samar Singh would report on forest matters to the agriculture
minister and on wildlife matters to the environment minister. While the
prime minister was the environment minister, she had a deputy minister to
whom Samar Singh would have to report first in the hierarchy—and that
deputy, Digvijay Sinh, the elder brother of M.K. Ranjitsinh, was a cousin of
Samar Singh. When Indira Gandhi was told about this, she laughed it off.

In January 1985, Indira Gandhi's successor would combine forests
and wildlife once again and make it one department, distinct from the
Department of Environment but under the same minister. In September
1985, the two departments would be merged to form an integrated Ministry
of Environment and Forests (including wildlife).

The Dalvi Committee had been set up to examine the Bastar pine plantation
issue. This was to result in a report on the larger issue of forest management
by Madhav Gadgil and two others—one of whom, Rauf Ali, was Salim Ali's
grandnephew. The report had been commissioned by the new Department
of Environment in view of the concerns voiced repeatedly by the prime
minister that forest management practices were alienating tribals and not
paying adequate attention to the regeneration of natural vegetation cover.

The manner in which Gadgil's report got to Indira Gandhi reveals
much. In this case, Zafar Futehally sent a handwritten 'Dear Salim Bhai'
note to Salim Ali on 31 August; it says it all:

> At the meeting of the N.C.E.P [National Committee on Environmental
> Planning] Madhav Gadgil's paper on Alternate Approaches to Forestry was

discussed and approved. The Chairman B.B. Vohra has been requested to send it to the Cabinet Secretariat for early action.

It was also decided that you should be requested to write to the Prime Minister suggesting that she should initiate early action to get the new policy approved.

Salim Ali followed Zafar Futehally's instructions and wrote to Indira Gandhi on 4 September. Nine days later, on an internal three-page note sent to her by R. Rajamani, she made two observations in her own hand. Against one of the main conclusions as summarized by Rajamani that read—'Forestry sector should cease to be treated as a revenue-generating sector. The Planning Commission should not urge the States to raise resources through forests'—Indira Gandhi observed, 'This is most important'. And at the very end she scribbled:

I am told that water hyacinth is quite good for paper and might do for cardboard, etc. Our scientists should go into the question of substitutes for wood.

On the same day she replied to Salim Ali's 4 September letter:

Many of Dr. Gadgil's excellent suggestions [...] have already been exercising our mind and some thought has been given to translating them into action plans.

It is worth mentioning that Gadgil's report on forest management was to be the starting point for preparing a National Forest Policy—which Indira Gandhi was very keen to initiate. The draft of the policy, prepared by Jayal and Gadgil, got Indira Gandhi's initial approval but she wanted a larger consultation regarding it before it became final. These consultations were completed by August–September 1984 and India would have had a National Forest Policy, 1984 had she not been killed. Thereafter, the momentum was lost; competing interest groups once again got active; and the policy, diluted in some respects, would see the light of day only four years later.

ॐ

Fourteen months earlier, Parliament had enacted a new, tough law for forest conservation. This had been entirely because of Indira Gandhi. But she was not satisfied since this law applied only to officially designated 'forest areas'. She would get complaints frequently from different parts of the country—such as, for example, cities and towns like Delhi, Bombay, Guwahati and Manali—that trees outside forest areas were being cut recklessly. In early January, Indira Gandhi asked her officials to examine whether there could be a separate national law to deal with—in her view—such calamities. But she was soon told that Parliament had no competence to legislate on trees which were not situated in forest areas and that the states had to pass such a law if they considered it necessary.

The Ministry of Law also overruled the other option she was contemplating—that of making such a regulation part of the Forest (Conservation) Act, 1980. They pointed out that the Act had been passed because forests were the 'concurrent' responsibility of the centre and states in the Constitution; trees outside forest areas were fairly and squarely in the jurisdiction of states and municipal authorities.

The prime minister did not press the point further but asked her officials to, at the very least, make sure that state legislatures passed resolutions that would bring about some regulation to deal with the indiscriminate felling of trees in urban and rural areas. Most states ignored these requests—even those ruled by her own party.

So much for her overweening powers and authority.

ॐ

Mehroo Boga, Indira Gandhi's friend, had written to her from Bombay on 13 June. Along the way, she mentioned the 'desecration of the Panchgani–Mahabaleshwar plateau area, through the depredations of commercial developers'. She appealed to the prime minister to save this 'jewel of the Konkan'. Three days later, Indira Gandhi—who was familiar with the area, having holidayed there for the first time in March 1932 and subsequently in July 1943—wrote on the letter:

Please see. This is tragic—inspite of all our efforts.

351

The prime minister's note triggered a flurry of letters between her office and the Department of Environment on the one hand and between the Department of Environment and the Maharashtra government on the other. Nalni Jayal visited the hill stations and submitted an eyewitness account, which the prime minister went through. Finally, Indira Gandhi herself wrote to Chief Minister Babasaheb Bhosale on 7 December:

> I have been receiving representations about the ecological and environmental harm being caused to Hill Stations in the Western Ghats particularly in Matheran and the Panchgani–Mahabaleshwar plateau area. I understand that commercial developers have moved in and caused a great deal of harm to the unique beauty of these Hill Stations. Recently, our Department of Environment had discussed these matters with your authorities and have suggested that there should be a strict check on commercial building activity, notification of the whole area for implementing a regional ecologically-based plan, freezing any further land development in the area till this plan is ready, control over unauthorized thinning and felling of trees in the area [...], afforestation of the escarpments of the plateau, etc. This is necessary to preserve the fragile eco-system of the area.
>
> These measures can be more effectively implemented if the matter is seen in its total perspective and remedies entrusted to a devoted team of administrators, planners, scientists and non-officials who are sincerely interested in the preservation of these hill areas. Please look into this matter personally.

The state government constituted a Mahabaleshwar–Panchgani Regional Planning Board on 29 April 1983. A few residents of the area were also included as a part of the board, at Indira Gandhi's behest. This was the first significant step taken to regulate construction activity in the two towns and also address the environmental issues that the prime minister herself had highlighted.

The board had its first meeting in Mahabaleshwar in mid-1983 and after this Indira Gandhi got 'fan mail' from someone named Molly Vakharia from Bombay who thanked her for 'your recent interest in arresting the ruination of this beautiful hill station'. She went on:

I would not have taken the liberty to approach you in this matter if it were not for a mutual friend and a great admirer of yours Mrs Lucille Kyle who always stressed that there was nothing too small for your interest or attention. [...]

May I add that this old Canadian lady has taught me to love and appreciate my Prime Minister.

Sometime during the year Indira Gandhi authored an unusual article in a professional journal called *Environmental Conservation*. The article had been intended for the Third International Conference on Environmental Future organized by Nicholas Polunin, who happened to admire her immensely. The conference was rescheduled and ultimately took place in Edinburgh in 1987 by which time Indira Gandhi was no more. *Environmental Conservation* was to publish her article in its winter 1995 issue with the title: 'A Politician's Views on Why We Are Not Saving Our World'. The byline read: 'By Indira Gandhi. Twice Prime Minister of India'.

The article is noteworthy for many reasons. For one, she anticipated the debates currently taking place:

> Some free-marketers view the concern for 'ecology' as a conspiracy of radicals to interfere with prosperity and progress, while in developing countries it is described as a whim of foreign capitalists who wish to thwart our development. In my own country, development projects have become emotional and political issues, and there is resistance even to give an ear to conservation. This ignores the permanent harm, caused by deforestation and pollution, to the economy and the people. There is no conflict between economic development and environmental conservation but reconciling the two does need greater effort, more attention to detail and a heavier financial burden [...]

Indira Gandhi spoke of Chipko and Silent Valley; of how India was trying to balance development and conservation; and how 'now as never before, no matter what their profession or interest, people cannot remain neutral as regards peace, poverty or pollution'. In many ways, this was a hark-back to her Stockholm address. She ended by talking of the 'interconnected issues of our one world' and answered Polunin's poser by saying:

[...] the responsibility to mould the future to use our increasing knowledge with wisdom and to good purpose lies not only with politicians but also widely with scientists and technologists, with industrialists and organized labour, with journalists and parents and teachers—in short with all citizens. Apart from their own positions, theirs are the voices and votes which most influence politicians.

Indira Gandhi very rarely spoke of what she had personally done for conservation. She allowed her actions to speak for themselves. But on 1 March, while replying to a debate in the Lok Sabha, she let her defences down in response to critical comments by a MP who claimed that her government was not paying adequate attention to environmental problems. She allowed herself a rare moment of self-congratulation:

> I am glad that one Honourable Member spoke on environment and forest, even though he did so only to criticize us. I can legitimately take some credit for making the country environment-conscious and I am most anxious to make environment conservation an integral part of development. Environmentalists all over the world consider me as one of themselves and come to me when they have a problem or a suggestion. Countless are the instances in which I have personally intervened. [...] I shall not willingly sacrifice the nation's long-term good for immediate gain but for this I do need people's cooperation. The pressure of population and of development is very great on the States and on the local people and frankly I am finding it exceedingly difficult to convince them that if today they do not look after their forests or wildlife and so on, later on it is those very people living in those areas who will suffer the most.

In her last years, Indira Gandhi spoke frequently on the need to build up public support for nature conservation. She was concerned that the movement to safeguard the environment had a small constituency and that if it did not expand, the battle for ecological security would be lost. The debates in Parliament in 1980 helped her increase awareness among lawmakers themselves.

The prime minister, in the meantime, encouraged a few of her colleagues to organize a larger forum for championing the cause for the environment. Thus it was that on 30 April, she spoke at the first ever national conference of legislators on the environment. She dwelt on the problems already being caused by water and air pollution; by deforestation in ecologically sensitive areas; and by the loss of precious biodiversity in the name of economic progress. Conscious of the criticism that conservation confronted—it was viewed as an abstract principle or worse, as the preservation of status quo—she redefined the term as an attitude that gave precedence to prudence over greed.

Her message was political—that legislators as people's representatives had to take a more serious interest in environmental issues; act as responsible advocates for the protection of flora and fauna; and put pressure on governments to be more environmentally conscious. Her desire was not just to educate people but also to ensure that legislators put pressure on governments to become more sensitive to ecological considerations. In her words:

> A good parliamentarian must be concerned with today but also with tomorrow. Conservation links today with tomorrow. It teaches us the importance of ensuring that development should reconcile immediate needs with long-term social interests.

On 17 August, Indira Gandhi received a letter from Minister of State of Tourism and Civil Aviation Khurshed Alam Khan, along with photographs of a dilapidated Fatehpur Sikri. This triggered a handwritten note from the prime minister to her officials two days later:

> It is truly distressing to find that in spite of all the stress we are laying on the preservation of the environment and our heritage, the denudation of forests is not only continuing but at a much faster pace. Our priceless monuments are being destroyed. Please see the note and photographs of Fatehpur Sikri. The same is, I am told, happening in Khajuraho.
>
> Gisela Bonn told me the other day about the old Alchi monastery in Ladakh.
>
> Drastic and immediate action is called [...]

A month later, on 18 September, Jayal, now joint secretary in the Department of Environment, sent out a letter to various ministries that showed Indira Gandhi's deep-seated belief that nature and culture were two sides of the same coin. The letter began thus:

> The Prime Minister has desired a Committee to be constituted under the Chairmanship of Dr. T.N. Khoshoo, Secretary (Environment), to consider measures necessary for conserving the environment and improving the aesthetic quality of such national heritage areas as Fatehpur Sikri, Kushinagar, Sravasti, Brajbhoomi Parikrama Complex, Agra Fort and the Red Fort in Delhi. The Union Department of Tourism has recently prepared master-plans which [...] reveal the kind of environmental degradation that is taking place in these areas [...]
>
> The Prime Minister has also received a letter from the former President of the National Trust of Australia offering any assistance that we may need [...] The Committee mentioned above could also consider the possibility of establishing a comparable National Trust in India, modeled on the U.K. or Australian experience [...] for integrated environmental conservation of our national heritage which might cover such other complexes as Jaisalmer, Khajuraho, Mahabalipuram, Konarak, Bhubaneshwar, etc.

In December, Indira Gandhi sent Jayal to study the National Trust, UK to see how it could be replicated in India.[4] One direct outcome of this visit was that the director of the UK National Trust, Sir Angus Stirling, came to India between 6 and 17 May 1983, interacted with various officials, and travelled around the country. He met Indira Gandhi and later submitted a fairly lengthy report on what could be done in India. Finally, on 25 July 1983, the highest committee of officials in the government recommended that a National Heritage Trust be set up by an Act of Parliament. Sadly, nothing came of this bold idea—but a variant of it, known as the Indian National Trust for Art and Cultural Heritage (INTACH), got created in early 1984. It must be admitted, this was but a pale shadow of what Indira Gandhi had envisaged.

Fritjof Capra, the author of well-known books on science and mysticism, travelled to India for the first time in 1982. On 25 February, he met Indira Gandhi for about an hour—an encounter he has described in his *Uncommon Wisdom*.[5] The prime minister told him that she had always been close to flora and fauna, and had grown up with a strong sense of kinship with 'the whole of living nature'. She recalled a childhood where plants, animals and trees were constant companions. She reminded Capra that India had an ancient tradition of environmental protection going back to the reign of Ashoka—a king who considered it his duty to not only protect his citizens but also preserve forests and wildlife. Throughout India, she said, 'edicts carved on rocks and stone pillars twenty-two centuries ago could still be seen and they foreshadowed today's environmental concerns'.

Ashoka had been one of Nehru's favourite historical figures, along with the Buddha; his admiration for them was conveyed to Indira through his letters. It is not a surprise, therefore, that thanks largely to Nehru's exertions, the Sarnath Lion Capital with four lions, a horse, an elephant and a bull became the national emblem when India became a Republic on 26 January 1950.

If Nehru prized the political values of Ashoka—movingly articulated in *The Discovery of India*—for Indira Gandhi, it was the fact that Ashoka was a pioneer of early environmentalism that made him truly remarkable. Evidently, she had first-hand knowledge of his edicts—especially of jottings on the fifth pillar, inscribed in many places, including Delhi, Allahabad, Lauriya Araraj, Lauriya-Nandangarh and Rampurva—where Ashoka listed every variety of cruelty to living creatures in order to express his loathing for non-violence.

In Indira Gandhi's conversation with Capra, it is clear that she drew on ancient India's wisdom while articulating her concern for the environment.

On 3 January, Indira Gandhi delivered her usual annual address to the Indian Science Congress that was having its sixty-ninth session in Mysore. She offered no hint whatsoever regarding the sensational news that was to invigorate the country seven days later.

In the early hours of 9 January, India's first Antarctic expedition reached its destination; Indira Gandhi commented that the news was 'thrilling' and that one of her long-standing wishes had been fulfilled.

Operation Gangotri—as the expedition was christened—had been a hush-hush exercise. Planning had started as soon as Indira Gandhi had taken over for a second time as prime minister, and gained momentum when she appointed the marine biologist, S.Z. Qasim as secretary of the Department of Environment in April 1981. In July 1981, a separate Department of Ocean Development was created.

The prime minister was well aware of the political impact such an expedition would have since India was not a member of the Antarctic Treaty signed in December 1959 and no other Asian country, China included, had a presence in that continent. Rather tellingly, the well-known British science magazine *New Scientist* reported India's expedition under the headline: 'Indians quietly invade Antarctica'.

Yet, beyond politics, there was another impulse compelling the prime minister to back the expedition. Well aware of Antarctica's mineral wealth, Indira Gandhi was drawn equally—I would venture to suggest even more— to the ecological dimensions of Operation Gangotri—greater knowledge of the Indian Ocean and the monsoons, life in ice-bound regions, and marine biodiversity. It was therefore no coincidence that the leader of the team was S.Z. Qasim.[6] C.P. Vohra, who had been a member of the successful Indian Everest expedition of 1965, was Qasim's deputy.

A second expedition led by one of India's top geologists, V.K. Raina, followed soon after; this team landed in Antarctica later in the year on 10 December. Incidentally, Raina was to capture the headlines in 2009 when I was environment minister—he challenged the assertion of the Intergovernmental Panel on Climate Change (IPCC) that the Himalayan glaciers would become extinct by 2035. It was his critique that compelled the IPCC to revamp the manner in which it carried out peer reviews of climate science literature.

With two expeditions successfully completed, Indira Gandhi gave the go-ahead to India becoming a member of the Antarctic Treaty in August 1983. A few months before her demise she had the satisfaction of knowing that India had set up its own unmanned Antarctic research base—named by her as Dakshin Gangotri. She would also have the satisfaction of seeing India's first Antarctic team start wintering there from 1 March 1984.[7] A seabed mountain in the Antarctic Ocean is named after Indira Gandhi in recognition of the bold decision she took in July 1981 to launch Operation Gangotri.

༄

The J. Paul Getty Wildlife Conservation Prize—named after a businessman who had made his money in oil—had been instituted in 1974. Salim Ali had been the second recipient. In 1982, after having accepted his place on the jury, he wrote to Dillon Ripley on 17 November:

> For some time now I have been seriously thinking of nominating Mrs Indira Gandhi for the Paul Getty Prize. I feel that within recent years no one known to me has done more for Nature Conservation in India (and indirectly elsewhere in the world) than Mrs Gandhi [...] The resounding success of Project Tiger in India has demonstrated in a graphic way how the complete protection of a habitat, ostensibly for a single endangered species, can bring about a total resuscitation and rehabilitation of the entire ecosystem and the entire biota [...] Mrs Gandhi has followed this up with other measures for the protection of the environment through enactment by Parliament of the Forest (Conservation) Act, 1980 [...] Her creating a Department of Environment is itself an expression of her deep concern for conservation of Nature. All in all, I think here we have a highly deserving case.

This is as good a summary of her accomplishments in the field of ecology as any. However, Salim Ali told Ripley that if there was any chance of her nomination not being unanimous, then the most dignified approach was not nominating her at all.

Duleep Matthai also made a similar plea to Dillon Ripley a few months later. Ripley was to inform Salim Ali in early 1983 that the earliest her nomination could be considered, if at all, was 1984. But for reasons I have not been able to fathom, Ripley kept procrastinating, even though he had

359

promised his long-time collaborator that he would speak to other jury members and assess if Indira Gandhi's nomination would be unanimous. Sadly, he never got around to doing that.

ᖇ

Yet there were other awards. On 18 May, the Government of Netherlands recognized Indira's Gandhi's contribution to the cause of the environment by conferring the Order of the Gold Ark on her. Prince Bernhard, who had been president of the WWF and had helped launch Project Tiger, flew into New Delhi to do the honours. The prime minister's acceptance speech was short and had a quotation from D.H. Lawrence's work:[8]

> My own involvement with flora and fauna preceded any ideas of conservation. As a child I felt closeness to the earth. When I began to read I found an echo in D.H. Lawrence's words: 'I am part of the Sun as my eye is part of me. That I am part of the earth my feet know perfect and my blood is part of the Sea [...] My soul is an organic part of the great human soul as my spirit is part of my nation [...] I am part of that great hole and I can never escape' [...] In my world animals and plants played an important part [...]

Indira Gandhi went on to summarize her basic ecological philosophy:

> [...the] immediate pressures of economic development, of [a] growing population and the understandable and increasing demands of the people who have long been denied equality and justice are in conflict with the need for preservation and conservation. We must find ways of reconciling these different aspects.

On 26 May, she replied to her old friend Billy Arjan Singh's note of congratulations:

> I am not interested in such Awards but they help to focus attention on particular subjects—in this case the protection of the environment and wildlife. This issue is not a luxury but a must for our future.

Four years earlier, Billy Arjan Singh had got the same award. But his rank was that of a 'knight'. While Indira Gandhi had followed him on the honour roll, her rank was the most distinguished—that of a 'commander'. Salim Ali had been given exactly this status in 1973.

ॐ

Indira Gandhi remained in touch with Albert Baez and met him on 2 December. Some days later, in the midst of a frenzied election campaign, she sent him a foreword for a booklet he was bringing out titled 'World Conservation Strategy':

> [...] There is no real conflict between development and conservation. Enduring development needs a clean environment, more thoughtful and thrifty use of non-renewable and renewable resources, greater care in the planning and siting of industrial and other projects, the bettering, rather than replacing, of existing life styles and local materials.
>
> [...] The various movements for the conservation of nature and the redressing of the balance which has been grievously upset are not impractically idealistic [...]
>
> The movement for conservation is working against great odds, facing criticism and sometimes ridicule. Its numbers grow but not sufficiently [...]
>
> We must enable the earth to renew its riches [...] Our ancients believed in the unity of all living beings, and even of life and non-life. We must rediscover this sense of identity with and responsibility for fellow humans, other species and future generations.

The foreword dwelt on themes which she had spoken about earlier—in other words, it was not entirely earth-shattering. But it led to some interesting developments as her letter of 11 January 1983 was to highlight:

> I have your letter of 3rd January. I am glad you like the foreword I have sent [...]
>
> If you think my becoming Honorary Chairman of the IUCN Commission on Education will help the cause, I shall be delighted to accept the position.

No head of government had ever been recognized by the IUCN in this manner and none has been since then. The IUCN made the announcement some months later but within a year of that happening she was killed. Given that this was a subject that had preoccupied Indira Gandhi's attention, and had she lived she may well have used the IUCN forum creatively to launch educational programmes in the field of conservation *and* development.

∾

The Governing Council of the UNEP held a special session in May in Nairobi to mark the tenth anniversary of the Stockholm Environment Conference as well as that of the establishment of the UNEP. Indira Gandhi had been invited along with twenty-five other world leaders but her officials advised her against accepting the invitation because she was not a 'keynote speaker'. Besides, she had been to Nairobi just the previous year. Indira Gandhi agreed with her officials, noting on 6 December 1981:

> Enough of such conferences.

The president of Kenya opened the eight-day conference on 10 May, following which messages from dignitaries were read out. Only two prime ministers sent messages—the premier of China and Indira Gandhi. The Indian prime minister's communication was short but recalled one of the central themes of her Stockholm speech—namely, the link between the peace movement and the ecological movement. It read:

> The problems of peace, development and conservation are inter-related. We must curb the growing sense of fear and doubt in humanity's ability to solve problems. The only way is for people of faith and vision to get together and reiterate their views. In all countries the voices for peace are now more numerous and louder. They want to check the arms race and advocate greater cooperation among nations to reduce disparity. The environmental movement will gain by allying itself with these related causes.

This theme had also appeared in her address to the Pugwash Conference on Science and World Affairs in Madras in January 1976, in which the Chemistry Nobel Laureate Dorothy Hodgkin took over as that movement's president. That day, on the dais, there were two eminent women who had studied at the same college in Oxford. In February 1967, India's President S. Radhakrishnan had somewhat condescendingly told the one who had actually graduated—when she was going to meet her college mate who was prime minister—'Not perhaps a very good student but I believe she is making a good Prime Minister.'[9] From an environmental perspective, that was to be a grand understatement.

∾

Indira Gandhi made a trip to the USA in the last week of July. She and Ronald Reagan—an unlikely duo—got along quite well. Despite Indira Gandhi's best intentions, she could not make it to Baraboo in Wisconsin to the breeding centre for Siberian cranes. But she did indulge the naturalist in her, as is evident in her letter to Horace Alexander from Washington DC on 29 July:

> Although I cannot do any regular bird-watching I do occasionally see interesting ones. The other day just driving from the Airport I saw two beautiful Oreoles.

On her way back from Washington, on 4 August, the prime minister stopped over at Honolulu and gifted an Indian elephant 'Mari' to the zoo. This was a female captive-bred elephant from Hyderabad. Speaking on the occasion, Indira Gandhi said that

> elephants [are] a symbol of strength and hard work and in India of good fortune and good luck.

The Hyderabad Zoo would be getting a giraffe and a bison in exchange; referring to the giraffe, Indira Gandhi added that

> it is for all those who stick their necks out for good causes.

Today, there is a plaque in Honolulu commemorating her visit.[10]

Indira Gandhi's remarks at the Honolulu Zoo had a deep impact on a New Zealander named Elma Aitken, who on 19 September, wrote to the prime minister that her husband and she had been present that day and on returning home to Auckland had come to learn that an elephant had died of a heart attack at the city's zoo. Aitken wanted the prime minister's help to get a replacement. Indira Gandhi replied nine days later:

> I am sorry that the Auckland Zoo elephant has died. Our own elephant population is declining, so our people are not happy about any being sent out but I shall find out if anything can be done for Auckland.

Notes

1. Rajamani's 'informant' was R.K. Rao, a forest service officer then working at the Crocodile Breeding and Management Institute at Hyderabad. He was pleasantly surprised to see the Rajamani–Indira Gandhi exchange when I sent it to him through Rajamani's daughter.

2. Amar Commander was a distinguished archivist in the India Office Library and wrote a well-researched book, *The Himalayan Triangle* on British India's relations with Tibet, Sikkim and Bhutan.

3. Ghorpade (1983).

4. B.G. Verghese was her information adviser from February 1966 to December 1968. A few months before leaving he had gone to Jaisalmer and sent the prime minister a long report on what he had seen and what needed to be done to restore and revive that city's glory. One of the broader points he had made in that note was that there should be a National Trust for the preservation of India's cultural heritage. Indira Gandhi had asked her ministerial colleagues to think about that suggestion but nothing had happened.

5. Capra (1989).

6. Earlier he had been director of the National Institute of Oceanography in Goa.

7. This is described in Satya S. Sharma (2001). He led India's first wintering expedition.

8. She had a fondness for quoting from D.H. Lawrence. Writing to her father from Switzerland on 13 April 1940 she recalled Lawrence saying, 'one's mind has no existence by itself, it is only the glitter of the sun on the surface of the waters' and went on to say 'what we want is […] to reestablish the living organic connections with the cosmos, the sun and earth, with mankind and nation and family. But how? How, when all our sense of values has gone crooked, when life is dominated not by the living organic connection but

by the false inorganic connections, not by the sun and earth but by money and the like—How?'

9. Dorothy Hodgkin in G. Parthasarathi and H.Y. Sharada Prasad (eds) (1985).

10. It was on landing from this visit that she air-dashed to Bombay to be with the son of her close friends since 1942—Amitabh Bachchan who had suffered a near-fatal accident during the shooting of the film *Coolie*.

1983

Indira Gandhi with H.Y. Sharada Prasad; August 1983.

Nothing seemed to be going right for Indira Gandhi this year. Assam was to see a horrific ethnic massacre on the morning of 18 February. Ironically, just eight days earlier she had written to Dorothy Norman while flying from New Delhi to Assam:

> What has moved me to write now is the truly magnificent view of the snow covered Himalayan range. We are close enough to identify many of the most famous peaks which are the world's highest mountains. This is a sight that never fails to thrill me. It is like Wordsworth's daffodils, an ever refreshing memory picture [...] I am on a flight to Assam. It is not going to be a pleasant trip [...] Had the Opposition parties not encouraged the agitation, I am sure a solution would have been found by now, as at several meetings we were on the brink of an agreement, which the students refuted within a few hours of their return to Assam.

On 9 May, she wrote to A.C.N. Nambiar about the worsening situation in Punjab:

> *Situations seem to be changing fast and not always for the better. America's short-sighted policy is doing a great deal of harm, and coming in the way of solutions that are otherwise not out of reach. India seems to be a special target. Yesterday a Women's Delegation of different parties went to the Golden Temple in Amritsar to appeal to the Akali leadership. They report that the whole place is swarming with American Sikhs and on all the balconies there were men with guns.*

Politics in Jammu and Kashmir had become very murky and non-Congress chief ministers were to come together to form a broad front. The Congress citadels in Karnataka and Andhra Pradesh were badly shaken in the assembly elections there. In just three years, like what had happened in the early 1970s, a huge mandate seemed to have been frittered away by some events she could have controlled better and others well beyond her control.

It was also a year where India hosted, for the first time, the summit of non-aligned countries as well as that of the Commonwealth heads of government. She was very much in charge of both these high-profile events. Fidel Castro's bear hug of Indira Gandhi at the inaugural of the Non-Aligned Movement (NAM) Summit in March was immortalized in a photograph but what is generally not known that the Cuban leader was also responsible for her meeting an author she greatly admired. The author had come as part of the Cuban delegation and later mentioned this encounter in his memoirs. His name— Gabriel Garcia Marquez.

As the year progressed, her mood became more introspective. On 11 October, Indira Gandhi wrote one of her last letters to Dorothy Norman while travelling from Visakhapatnam to Delhi saying:

> *[...] Perhaps because I have been so far removed from [...] leisure and quiet in my life, that I have got quietness within myself. As I am dictating, a line from an old Indian film comes to mind, "What has he to do with flowers, whose fate is shaped amongst thorns"! But there is hardly a flower without thorns.*

By the year-end, the first Maruti-Suzuki car was on the road, ushering in a revolution not just in the Indian engineering industry but also in consumer culture.

෨

Unlike her father, Indira Gandhi never wrote long letters or sent detailed memos. She was normally brief, even terse. On 21 February, three days after she was stunned by the ethnic massacre in Assam, she sent one of her longer notes—at least on environmental issues—to the newly appointed secretary in the Department of Environment, T.N. Khoshoo:

> In spite of all our efforts and the legislation that has been passed with regard to the pollution of air and water, wherever I have travelled I have seen and breathed a great deal of pollution caused by factories, power plants and so on. There is no visible evidence of any effort on the part of the Central and State Governments or other interested groups to take effective steps. The same is true of our rivers.
>
> A debate is going on about wildlife. Secretaries feel strongly that this Department should be separated from Forests. Up to now our forest policy has been dictated entirely by financial considerations. Unfortunately, contractors have managed to get the upper hand, with the result that the depletion of forests continues at rapid pace. Those in charge of this programme, as we noticed at the meeting of Wildlife held last year, were not even willing to accept the fact that our forest cover is wholly inadequate and that further depletion would be disastrous for our economy. Obviously this outlook has little sympathy for wildlife which is already pressurized by the growth of population, the need for more land for cultivation and so on. I can appreciate the point of view of our Secretaries that it may not be administratively possible to separate wildlife from forestry. Yet keeping it there means the end of the programme and the erosion of our efforts for the protection of our environment.
>
> Please give urgent thought to these questions. It might be useful for you to talk this over with someone like Duleep Matthai or any of the others who feel deeply concerned. I should like to have your comments as soon as possible.

Duleep Matthai—the son of John Matthai who had resigned as finance minister in April 1950 while protesting against Nehru's decision to set up a Planning Commission—was an active conservationist associated with WWF-India. Indira Gandhi had been in touch with him for well over a decade-and-a-half on wildlife and forestry matters. He was to later get involved in the government's wasteland development programme when her son became prime minister.

The note to Khoshoo was vintage Indira Gandhi and it continues to have relevance over three decades later. Amidst all her other preoccupations, she found time to express her frustration regarding the administration's disregard for the environment in a pointed manner. It was, to be honest, an admission of failure almost at the end of her life.

ॐ

Anne Wright and Indira Gandhi were in regular touch in 1983.

On 21 February, Anne Wright wrote to the prime minister for a message on the occasion of a ten-day exhibition, film festival and fun fair being organized to raise funds for WWF-India. Indira Gandhi responded quickly and positively on 2 March:

> Our earth supports many forms of life. In the past century thoughtless exploitation of its resources has decimated several species and threatens to extinguish more. We must bestir ourselves to prevent further damage. The extinction of our wildlife inevitably leads to the degeneration of the environment which in turn affects humankind.
>
> The World Wildlife Fund has done a great deal for the identification and preservation of endangered species.

On 5 and 6 February, Bharatpur hosted an international workshop, organized by Anne Wright and George Archibald, on Siberian cranes. Indira Gandhi could not attend the event but sent Digvijay Sinh instead to get a commemorative stamp issued—a painting presented to her by the American artist, Diane Pierce, on 27 February 1981 when Indira Gandhi had thrown a farewell tea party for the delegates attending the CITES meeting in Delhi. The *Brolga Bugle*, a quarterly newsletter of the

International Crane Foundation, while writing about this presentation, had reported on 19 April 1981:

> With Diane Pierce at the presentation was Sir Peter Scott, world famous conservationist [...] who lauded Mrs. Gandhi's past record of interest and concern for wildlife. Mrs. Gandhi was completely surprised by the gift but charmed her audience with an impromptu account of her life-long love for animals and her continued support for wildlife preservation.

If ever incontrovertible proof were needed of Indira Gandhi's ecological credentials, what she did in March 1983 was it. On 5 March, even as she was busy with the Seventh Non-Aligned Summit in New Delhi she wrote to Anne Wright:

> I have written to the President of Pakistan and the Prime Minister of Afghanistan for the Non-Aligned Conference, conveying the points you have made about Siberian Crane and other migratory birds. However, I must confess that, preoccupied as they are with difficulties in their own countries and without any special interest in wildlife or its preservation, there may not be a very positive response.

Her fears provided unfounded. For on 7 May, she wrote again to Anne Wright in what must be a remarkable letter by any yardstick:

> I have received good responses to my letters to the President of Pakistan and the Prime Minister of Afghanistan regarding Siberian Cranes and other migratory birds.
>
> The Afghans have decided that the Ab-i-Estoda lake and other lakes in and around the Ghazni province would be a protected area for Siberian crane in their migratory flights. More wardens will be posted at the lake during the Siberian cranes' stopping periods. They have also strictly prohibited hunting or other interfering activities to ensure that these lakes remain a protected area.
>
> The President of Pakistan has informed me that as a signatory to the Ramsar Convention on Wetlands of international importance, Pakistan has designated 9 water-fowl habitats of international importance to promote the conservation of various types of flora and fauna on which these birds are dependent, and for the protection of the birds. Crane

hunting and trapping is already banned in Pakistan and while there is no evidence of Siberian Cranes actually stopping over in Pakistan, they will consider ways or protecting and conserving them if they do stop-over in Pakistan before they fly to India.

An ecstatic Anne Wright replied to the prime minister on 13 May:

> This letter is a letter of congratulations and thanks twice over—because I have just got the message from your office to say you would be taking in the matter of tapping the Teesta river for water for Kalimpong, thus saving the Neora Valley.

Anne Wright was to reach out once more to the prime minister on 16 October. Her letter is untraceable but Indira Gandhi's reply the very next day is:

> I know of the good work of the World Wildlife Fund Eastern region and how it is dedicating itself to the preservation of our national heritage. Such an endeavour needs the widest support from Governments as well as other citizens. All have to be made keenly aware of the benefits of conservation and the dangers in any imbalance of the environment. Voluntary organisations have a special responsibility in working for such projects.
>
> I am glad to learn that the World Wildlife Fund India is involving the children of Calcutta in the programme.
>
> You have my good wishes for your project.

That was the last of the letters exchanged between these two dedicated conservationists.

On getting to know that she was going to be in New York in late September, Horace Alexander wrote to Indira Gandhi suggesting that she take a break while she was there. She replied to him on 26 May while she was flying from Madras to Ahmedabad and revealed that the birdwatcher in her was very much alive:

> How I should love to get away from New York and look at American birds! This time my trip has nothing to do with the American government.

It is as Chairperson of the Non-Aligned Movement and may therefore keep me busier than an official visit!

What do parakeets do at night? They all fly together at almost exactly the same time in one direction between 6.15 and 7.15 p.m. and back in the morning. It is quite a spectacle. The Canadian High Commissioner invited me to watch it from his garden one evening and this evening I saw the mass fly over in Ahmedabad.

Indira Gandhi went to New York in her capacity as chairman of the Non-Aligned Summit but, as she had feared, had no time whatsoever to see American birds. However, she had dinner with a small group of intellectuals organized by her friend Ralph Buultjens. The guest list included the Nobel Laureate in Economics Wassily Leontief; lawyer and author Louis Nizer; famous science-fiction writer Isaac Asimov; Roxane Witkem, author of a book on Mao Zedong's widow; and well-known historian Bruce Mazlish. The dinner, held in her suite at the Helmsley Palace, got reported in *The New York Times* on 1 October, but what was not reported was that Indira Gandhi's desire to meet Barry Commoner, the well-known ecologist whose 1971 book *The Closing Circle* had appealed to her.

Commoner could not attend the dinner but the prime minister made it a point to speak to him over the phone before the guests arrived and invited him to India. Buultjens recalls that she had asked him whether he knew Commoner's four laws of ecology. When Buultjens feigned ignorance she rattled them off: *one*, everything is related to everything else; *two*, everything must go somewhere; *three*, nature knows best; and *four*, there is no such thing as a free lunch.

Indira Gandhi had last visited the BNHS in December 1978. She came back for its centenary on 15 September. Before that, however, she did something she would never have done for any other individual—except perhaps Mother Teresa or Baba Amte, or in this instance, Salim Ali. She wrote to Chief Minister of Maharashtra Vasantdada Patil on 5 July, asking him to allot land to the BNHS:

Dr. Salim Ali wrote to me that the Bombay Natural History Society has asked you to release a plot of land for a Field Research Centre on the outskirts of the Sanjay Gandhi National Park in Bombay when they celebrate their centenary on the 15th of September, 1983. I believe a 30-acre plot has been identified for this purpose.

The Bombay Natural History Society has done good work, so I hope it will be possible for you to help them in this request.

A day before she was to arrive for the centenary celebrations, the Maharashtra government, having completed the paperwork in record time, made the official sanction of the land valued at about Rs 40 lakh to the BNHS at a nominal rate of one rupee per year. She handed over the sanction letter to Salim Ali the next day.

In her speech during the centenary celebrations, she returned to the theme of conservation and development:

Basically, there is no conflict between conservation and economic development or between the immediate and the enduring. Indeed, in the long run neither can survive without the other. But we cannot wish away the problem.

Earlier in the year, on 3 March, Salim Ali had written to the prime minister, drawing her attention to the environmental damage being caused by high-rise buildings in cities, and citing Poona as an example. He wanted her to intervene to ensure that the Maharashtra government did not buckle under the pressure coming from the builders. The prime minister's reply, uncharacteristically delayed till 1 July, was a somewhat weary one. Perhaps she had begun to recognize the limits to which even a leader like her could accomplish in the Indian scheme of things. She ended her letter by observing:

Saving the environment is a constant battle. The States resent what they consider interference and ideas of beautification also do not always favour nature.

But her weariness was a passing phase. By September, she was back to being optimistic. Perhaps, the centenary celebrations of the BNHS offered the intellectual tonic she needed. Two days before she went to Bombay, she wrote a foreword to a book on Indian wildlife by two well-known naturalists Romesh Bedi and Rajesh Bedi. She liked this book and commended it:[1]

> [...] because many photographs are being published for the first time. They show the beauty and grace of the denizens of our forests and something of the high drama of life itself. In these pages will be found many lesser known animals, the pangolin, the thamin, the marbled and leopard cat, the slender loris and others photographed in their natural surroundings.

In her foreword, she expressed her worry yet again on the shrinking forest cover and on species being endangered by growing towns and cultivation regarding shrinking forest cover, but ended with a message of hope:

> We have saved the tiger, the lion, the rhinoceros and the bustard. Across the country larger numbers of people are making it their business to come to the rescue of animals. [...] It is important that the animals are allowed to live naturally, not as showpieces for tourists.

She had, however, forgotten to add the crocodile to the list of species saved from the very brink of extinction. She was singularly responsible for each of the conservation success stories.

Two years earlier, Indira Gandhi had overruled her national security bureaucracy and approved a field trip to Arunachal Pradesh by Salim Ali and Dillon Ripley. On 26 January Ripley wrote to the prime minister again, saying that a third trip to Arunachal Pradesh was being planned for later in the year because sightings of bird species in the second trip had been hampered by inclement weather.

Indira Gandhi asked her officials to process the letter. Thereafter, once again all hell broke loose. This time it was worse than ever—for it wasn't just the security administration but also the scientific bureaucracy that was opposed to the duo's trip. R. Rajamani, supported these objections, as did T.N. Khoshoo. The lieutenant governor of Arunachal Pradesh (it was to become a full-fledged state in 1987), T.V. Rajeswar—a former director of the Intelligence Bureau who had been in charge of Indira Gandhi's security a few years earlier—also remained suspicious of Ripley and Ali.

Rajamani sent a long note to Indira Gandhi on 31 March. On the same day, against his observation that Ali and Ripley had visited Arunachal Pradesh twice but no report had been submitted, Indira Gandhi noted on 13 April:

Why not ask Dr. Salim Ali?

Further, against his comment that over the last trip Ripley fired at an animal from a vehicle at dusk time, the prime minister noted:

I am sure this cannot be an ordinary gun. Various types of guns (which do not injure or kill) are used by scientists for scientific research.

Investigations continued and it was revealed that Ripley who had been charged with firing at a clouded leopard had actually shot at a civet cat. Ripley had also been charged with smuggling a large number of birds, small animals and reptiles out of the country—to this, the counter-argument presented by Jayal was that the Wildlife (Protection) Act, 1972 had provisions predominantly for controlling hunting for sport but had rather weak provisions for the scientific study of wildlife.

It took almost four months for Ripley's letter seeking permission to visit Arunachal Pradesh to be processed. The consensus that had emerged was that his request ought to be denied.

Yet, after all this huffing and puffing in different government departments, on 21 May, Arvind Pande, an aide of Indira Gandhi, informed the Department of Environment that the prime minister had approved Salim Ali and Dillon Ripley's visit to Arunachal Pradesh later in the year. The caveat was that 'an official of the Wildlife Department should accompany them but not as a monitor of their activities'.

As it turned out, the trip never took place.

ॐ

Prince Bernhard of the Netherlands had helped launch Project Tiger in 1973. Ten years later, his successor at WWF-International, Prince Phillip of the UK, was present in New Delhi at a 22 November function to mark that milestone.[2] Indira Gandhi lauded the success of Project Tiger and wondered aloud: 'Is man important or the tiger?' She went on to answer the poser by saying:

> There is no conflict between the two. In fact, there is a close linkage between man and nature. We are but one of the several thousand species of living beings.

She pointed out that the tiger was really not to blame for the problem of cattle-lifting—which was a sore point in the neighbourhood of tiger reserves. She asserted that it was because of the 'damage to its habitat [...] that the tiger was forced to move to distant places'.

Indira Gandhi had been growing increasingly concerned that local communities were hostile to the conservation efforts of the government. In September 1982, she had set up a task force on this subject with her young colleague Madhavrao Scindia as the chairman. At the 22 November function, after praising Project Tiger, she released the task force's report titled 'Eliciting Public Support for Wildlife Conservation'. Successive governments were to implement many of its recommendations. The function was significant for another reason. At her instance, the IBWL had instituted a national award for wildlife conservation. The first recipient was her friend and someone she was genuinely fond of—Salim Ali.

Elizabeth Kemf, the editor of *World Wildlife Fund News*, was in India to learn more about the country's conservation efforts and collate a longish feature on this. Project Tiger was naturally her focus but she wanted the larger picture, too, and wrote to Indira Gandhi on 6 April. Eight days later an 'in flight' reply was sent by the prime minister:

> [...] I spoke of the need to protect the environment and ecology in my address to the Group of Non-Aligned Nations as I do in all forums, national and international. Most countries in the Non-aligned Group are struggling hard to overcome poverty and economic backwardness, so

their pre-occupation will understandably be for the acceleration of their rate of economic development. But I shall try my best not to repeat the mistakes made by the developed world at a similar stage of development.

Women [...] must also take active interest. Without their participation, no cause can succeed in a big way.

As Chairperson of the IUCN Commission on Education, I shall continue to encourage a widening of awareness in individuals and societies, and make them more conscious of the urgency to educate people, particularly children, on ideas of conservation, which is not an isolated subject but part of all aspects of our lives. All problems are inter-related. We must, above all, learn to see the world as a whole.

The inter-relatedness of issues was something that had been on her mind for quite some time. A little earlier, T.N. Khoshoo had sent her a copy of a lecture on environmental management he had delivered at the Indian Institute of Technology (IIT), Bombay and she had sent it back on 21 February with a handwritten note:

I have read your article with great interest. Your points are well taken and deserve immediate attention. Much of our troubles with the economy and other matters are caused by compartmentalization and fragmentation in dealing with issues. We must take a holistic view. It is unfortunately true that the more laws we have the less effective they seem to be. [...]

The prime minister had been receiving a barrage of letters from across the world regarding the protection of sea turtles off the coast of Orissa. Archie Carr of the University of Florida, a world authority on the subject, wrote to her on 11 March:

I am writing to you to beg you to instigate an inquiry into the status of the olive ridley sea turtle, Lepidochelys olivacea, in India. After being almost obliterated by overexploitation on the Mexican coast, formerly believed to be the main breeding ground of this species, other huge nesting assemblies were discovered in India, on the Orissa coast and in West Bengal. No sooner had this welcome news reached us, however, than word came that heavy overuse was in progress there. [...]

Now, as Chairman of the Marine Turtles Specialist Group of the IUCN, I am writing to express concern of the members of our Group over the survival outlook of the olive ridley and our hope that your government will endeavour to bring out reliable information regarding the alleged inroads into Indian populations. [...] The line between rational use and degradation can be very fine, however, and should be drawn only after a careful assessment of the populations to be used.

Indira Gandhi replied a month later on 28 April:

I have received your letter of the 11th March. There have been other similar letters about the protection of marine turtles. *Even before these reports were received last year* [emphasis mine], I called for immediate action through the Orissa State Government and the Coast Guard of the Indian Navy to prevent the hunting of these turtles or for collection of eggs by beachcombers. All coastal States have been asked to be vigilant in this matter [...] We are aware of the importance of the endangered species to our ecosystems. Our concerned Ministries here and in the State Governments have been asked to take the required measures to see that the olive ridley turtle, which is an endangered species, is looked after.

The International Whaling Commission (IWC) had been set up as part of the International Convention on the Regulation of Whaling—signed in Washington DC in December 1946. Peter Scott had written to Indira Gandhi on 12 June 1980, asking that India became a member of the convention, and she had replied on 9 July 1980:

I have always been greatly interested in animals and the conservation of nature. I share your concern about the preservation of the whale. Hence, we agree to the International Whaling Convention and also to participate in the International Whaling Commission.

Indira Gandhi readily agreed even though India was not a whaling country and despite being keenly aware that two of India's closest political allies—the USSR and Japan—were the worst offenders.

The thirty-fifth annual meeting of the IWC was to take place at Brighton, UK in July and Indira Gandhi was asked to send a special message. She did so on 9 July. Even while recalling that she grew up 'with a sense of kinship with nature in all its manifestations', she described her feelings for the largest mammal:

> I have found whales fascinating since I first saw one in childhood: their size, their habits, how they raise their young, and the recent findings about their intelligence, their relationships with each other, with other sea creatures and with humans.

She expressed her commitment to the conservation of marine mammals in the Indian Ocean, particularly the smaller cetaceans, and strongly supported a complete ban on all commercial whaling activities by 1986—a deadline that was to be kept. She wrote to her counterpart in Mauritius regarding this in early 1983—unfortunately the letter cannot be traced, despite there being a note by her on a file that such a plea had indeed been sent.

Indira Gandhi had for long worried about cities and the environmental consequences of urbanization. She had written to the chief ministers earlier on this subject and she wrote again in August expressing her concern regarding the proliferation of slums that brought 'increasing squalor and shabbiness'. She urged state governments and civic authorities to develop green areas in cities through strict regulation; she argued for space for parks, gardens and playgrounds; she called for movement to 'inculcate in all citizens the realization that it is part of their responsibility to keep the environment clean and healthy'.

Three years earlier she had catalyzed the creation of a Legislators' Forum in Parliament to strengthen environmental advocacy. Now she wanted the states to form similar forums within civic bodies to provide a political push to the environmental upkeep of cities. She recalled with some pride how the nation's capital had been cleaned up for the Asian Games in 1982 and for the Non-Aligned Summit in 1983, and wanted state capitals to witness such drives regularly.[3]

Indira Gandhi sent a steady barrage of letters to individual chief ministers on issues of heritage conservation. She sent one to the chief minister of Haryana, Bhajan Lal, on 20 May expressing her distress regarding construction activity by the state government in the vicinity of Surajkund:

> We must preserve our ancient monuments and particularly ensure that their environment is not ruined by constructions which are out of character and not in tune with the old architecture and surroundings. The preservation of monuments is incomplete if the entire area around them is not given equal attention.

The chief minister of Himachal Pradesh, Virbhadra Singh, was next to receive such a letter; on 23 July the prime minister wrote to him in the context of what she had been told about the art and antiquities of Chamba:

> I am rather anxious about the gradual destruction of the beautiful old things which are our heritage and are today regarded as art treasures. These are not only the known ancient monuments but even the small hill houses and temples and what is [in] them.

Two months later, on 14 September, Indira Gandhi wrote to the chief minister of the hill state again:

> I feel that very often decisions are taken by officials and agencies who do not have an overall view and perspective. This is a great pity. Because in the process many prominent features which mar the beauty of the environment. Even more tragic, many old and beautiful buildings and areas are destroyed or modified without realizing their inherent beauty, function, value or tourist attraction.

Thanks to the flurry of letters, the state government formed an Advisory Group on 25 December, comprising officials and outside experts, for the 'preservation of [the] environment and historically important buildings of Chamba'. Two years earlier, a similar Advisory Group had been set up at her behest for the preservation of Kulu Valley.

With the commissioning of the Mathura refinery, the issue of its pollution impact on the Taj Mahal resurfaced. The Indian media carried reports on the matter frequently. Indira Gandhi herself had reviewed the situation the previous year in July. On 2 February, she received a letter from the UK from a 'group of explorers including several notable and well reputed experts on the subject who have just returned from a fact finding tour of Taj Mahal'. She replied a week later to A.J. Malik and others who had written from Wolverhampton:

> I myself am deeply concerned about the beauty and environment of the Taj Mahal. A number of steps have been taken, such as minimizing air pollution around the Taj and for regular monitoring of the air quality [...]

The prime minister had been, from time to time, watching over what was happening in Agra–Mathura. As a result of her constant prodding, the steam locomotives in the Agra shuntyard had been replaced by diesel engines by end-March 1981. Two coal-based power plants in Agra run by the state government had also been forced to close down. Indeed, one half of the sulphur dioxide emissions came from the power plants and the shunting yard.

But the threat of pollution loomed large because of the inability to shift the 250-odd foundries in the city—these accounted for a third of the emissions of sulphur dioxide. The state government was dragging its feet although an alternative location for the foundries outside the city had been identified. Indira Gandhi asked the Department of Environment which was under her direct charge to set up an expert committee to monitor the pollution abatement measures at Agra–Mathura, including the creation of a green belt around the area. She recorded on a note prepared by her officials on 7 April:

> We should not allow any industry with pollution potential near Agra.

The National Environmental Engineering Research Institute, Nagpur and the Central Building Research Institute, Roorkee had, during the year, carried out an investigation of the condition of the Taj Mahal; this had been reviewed by the ASI. When she was informed by Rajamani that the investigation had revealed that the marble in the Taj Mahal faced no danger, and that the situation was under control, she recorded on 12 October:

I am afraid I am unable to accept the veracity of this report. I myself have noticed damage in 1978.

It wasn't just Agra's pollution levels that concerned the prime minister in 1983. Kashmir, undoubtedly her favourite state for a quick holiday, had been getting increasingly polluted, and the prime minister mentioned this to her officials. The chief minister of the state was close to her personally—but at that point, he had been making common cause with her political rivals. Even so, she wrote a 'Dear Farooq' letter on 15 March:

> The increasing air pollution in Srinagar has been worrying me for a long time. I understand that the problem is compounded by road transport vehicles which are not well maintained. There are some long-term measures [...] which would bring about significant improvement in lessening the emission of pollutants of these vehicles. But in the short run it would help if these vehicles are checked by road transport authorities [...] At some stage you should also think of legislation in this regard which is suited to local conditions. I understand that army vehicles in Srinagar are well maintained and do not add to pollution.
>
> Please let me know what action you propose to take in this regard.

A month later the chief minister replied to her, promising a series of steps that he would take to address her concerns.

In April, Indira Gandhi confronted a rather tricky situation—it concerned an irrigation project that India had proposed the previous year in Bhutan. The aim had been to build two dams on the Manas and Sankosh rivers there, to increase the discharge in the Hooghly and maintain the viability of the Calcutta port—a port that was being threatened by high salinity from the back-waters of the Bay of Bengal. Power was also to be generated at both the dams.

Indira Gandhi was well aware of the environmental impacts of these dams. The previous July itself it had been brought to her notice that the Manas Sanctuary in Assam, home to a number of endangered species including the tiger, would be badly affected. The Department of

Environment had been asked to carry out a detailed study on the issue but, at the same time, the irrigation engineers were allowed to pursue their technical investigations.

Now, it had become clear that the Government of Bhutan was not very enthusiastic about the project because it would inundate the only low-land forest area of that nation and affect a considerable population of wild buffaloes, swamp deer and rhinoceroses. When Indira Gandhi was made aware of the situation on 19 April, she observed on file:

> Surveys can take place. But we shall invite the world's wrath if we inundate areas in Bhutan which are regarded as important from an environmental point of view.

Her observations were unexceptionable.

Strangely, she allowed the technical surveys to continue. Her reason may well have been: 'Let the engineering design and environmental impact studies continue side-by-side and we can always take a decision later'. As it turned out, the project was aborted. But it baffles one why a committed conservationist would issue a 'have your cake and eat it too' type of directive.

❧

The Silent Valley issue continued to engage her attention during the year.

A year ago, in mid-1982, M.G.K. Menon had submitted his committee's report. Its final summary was a masterpiece of equivocation:

> The Committee would like to stress that the decision as to whether the Silent Valley Hydroelectric Project is to be implemented or not, involves questions of a political, techno-economic and social nature, apart from ecological considerations. The view of the Committee relates only to the latter aspect. It is clear that there will be an ecological impact to the extent of reduction or loss of habitat area and accompanying changes in physical factors, and species diversity, as also of an important riparian ecosystem. This will be in areas of tropical evergreen forest, the magnitude of which had diminished by alarming proportions. However, the importance of this aspect has to be judged against the other aspects mentioned earlier which would govern a final decision on the issue.

Menon's foreword itself was equally evasive. The maximum he was willing to say was:

> The implementation of the project will result in the submergence of 830 hectares. [...] It is the view of many that this submergence as well as the activities needed for the construction of the project [...] will result in serious loss of biological diversity and irreparable damage to the area as a whole. The other viewpoint is that disturbance will be only to the extent of submergence. It has not been possible for the Committee to reach an unambiguous conclusion. It is clear that if one were to exercise caution, the former view must prevail.

So, when 1983 began, the ball was in Indira Gandhi's court. She had to balance various factors. The Menon Committee had confirmed her fears concerning ecological damage but its recommendations were not clear-cut. The state government wanted the project, as did her own party colleagues. On 9 February, in response to an appeal from someone who was unknown to her but to whom she nevertheless replied—Professor Devraj Sarkar of the Univerity of Mysore—she wrote:

> I entirely agree with what you say about Silent Valley. But you know how jealous the States are of their rights. We are trying our best to save the Valley.

In the meantime, as late as 24 June, her own party MP from the area, V.S. Vijayaraghavan, wrote to her on behalf of the Silent Valley Scheme Protection Committee, begging that the hydel project be approved. Indira Gandhi replied a week later:

> The various points you have mentioned will be kept in view while taking a decision on the recommendations of the [MGK Menon] Committee.

While Indira Gandhi was clear that Silent Valley had to be protected, she was worried about how the electricity needs of the Malabar region would be met, especially since the alternatives were tied up in disputes over the Cauvery. Finally, on 17 October the prime minister decided against the project, and two days later Arvind Pande wrote to S. Venkitaramanan, secretary, Department of Power, that

The Prime Minister has seen the recommendations of the Menon Committee on the Silent Valley Project in Kerala [...] Prime Minister agrees that for valid ecological reasons, the Silent Valley Project cannot be approved. You are requested [...] to examine the possibilities of starting alternative hydel projects in North Kerala.[4]

&

The Lalpur Dam issue continued to preoccupy Indira Gandhi in the year. On the one hand, the Gujarat government was growing increasingly impatient that the construction of the dam had not begun, even though the prime minister had broadly given her the go-ahead two years earlier. On the other hand, the noted Gandhian Harivallabh Parikh kept successfully stalling the project.

On 23 August, Indira Gandhi was reminded that the Gujarat government was seeking categorical instructions from her; all clearances and approvals had been obtained. Her joint secretary, G.K. Arora, presented a note to her on 23 August which ended thus:

[...] the opposition may have its origin in the unhappy experience of the Ukai Dam where adivasis were deprived of their land but did not get rehabilitation benefits. The approach of Shri Parikh does not look unreasonable and it should be possible to get his cooperation for starting work on the Heran dam.

Indira Gandhi observed on the note two days later:

One more effort to convince Shri Parikh might be made by other people. Their other complaint is that the adivasis will not benefit from the irrigation.

Clearly, the prime minister was sympathetic to Parikh's arguments against the dam.

&

By September 1982, the Doon Valley Board set up by Indira Gandhi the previous August suggested that no new mining leases should be granted in the Mussoorie–Dehra Dun area and that the renewal of leases should not be permitted. But it lacked the legal and executive authority to enforce these recommendations.

Indira Gandhi therefore, continued putting pressure on the state government. One letter to her from Shripati Misra, the chief minister of Uttar Pradesh, on 21 January began by recalling: 'While recently in Dehra Dun, you had expressed your concern about the ill-effects of limestone quarrying operations on the environment and ecology of the Doon Valley [...]'

This concern got reflected in the constitution of a working group on 21 February to 'examine the question of whether the existing leases need to be terminated and also suggest steps for scientific exploitation of mines causing minimum ecological imbalances'. This group was given three months to submit its report.

The local environmental community, in the meantime, was getting frustrated by the wait. The Save Mussoorie Society told her on 20 June that the 'damage to the entrance of Mussoorie is much worse than the previous year. The quarrying is most indiscriminate and wanton [...]'. The prime minister replied to Sita Devi on 14 July:

> I am terribly worried by the continued quarrying operations in the Doon area. I know of the extensive damage caused. The Uttar Pradesh Government tried to prevent this by cancelling 4 leases prematurely and also by not renewing 18 leases which were ending in December, 1982. The lessees, however, appealed to the Courts and have obtained stay orders from the District/High Courts, Uttar Pradesh. I have asked the C.M. of U.P. to look into the matter and ensure urgent action to have the stay vacated [...] On longer term measures for the area we are awaiting the recommendations of a Working Group [...]
>
> I hope you are well.

On the same day, she wrote to Shripati Misra:

> I am told that damage continues to be caused by quarrying operations in the Dehra Dun area [...] Could you not take urgent action to have the stay orders vacated and immediately suspend quarrying operations in the mines which are not conforming to mining laws?

Two days later, she asked one of her aides, Arvind Pande, to send a note to the cabinet secretary (dictating parts of it herself) showing her deep concern on the subject:

> A Committee of Secretaries has discussed the whole question of mining leases in the Dun area in December 1982 and also considered necessary changes in the MMRD [Mines and Minerals Regulation and Development] Act, 1957 which would permit cancellation of mining leases on environmental considerations and make it obligatory for the lessees to restore mined areas after exploitation of the mineral resources. A Study Group has been formed with the Controller-General Indian Bureau of Mines as Convenor to look into several aspects of the problem.
>
> Cabinet Secretary is requested to expedite consideration of this report and take an overall view in the matter. Basically, the approach has to be one of limiting and controlling the mining effort to the minimum required and also to ensure simultaneously that either the mine-owners themselves or the State Government can get the mine area fully rehabilitated and restored to as much of its original condition as possible through appropriate measures by mud-filling, tree plantations, etc. If this requires legislative changes, they should be considered.

The problem was clearly that while on paper the state government appeared to be at the same wavelength as the prime minister, in actual practice it was not enforcing the laws strictly. This became apparent a few weeks later, on 9 August, when Indira Gandhi again wrote to Shripati Misra:

> [...] you wrote that the cement plants being set up near Dehra Dun were cleared after imposing stringent pollution control measures.
>
> I have now been informed that the air pollution abatement equipment has not yet been installed and that the plant has been set up in violation of the existing land use in an area which formed part of an agricultural belt near Malsi Deer Park.
>
> Please direct the existing cement plants to immediately install adequate pollution abatement equipment in the absence of which they could also be asked to stop production [...]

It looks like Indira Gandhi's communication was not having its desired impact—for, on 16 November, Mady Martyn, on behalf of the Friends of the Doon, and Prem Thadani, on behalf of the Save Mussoorie Society, wrote to Arvind Pande:

> We are reliably informed that in 1982 a letter was addressed by the Prime Minister to the Chief Minister of U.P., asking him to instruct the concerned departments not to licence any industries in the Doon Valley without prior clearance from the Department of the Environment.
>
> If such a letter was issued, you will be shocked to know that it seems to have been totally ignored. Industry is being sanctioned without any concern for its damaging effect. In fact, land is being acquired by the U.P. Government for further industry and many plans are afoot without a care for the Dehra Dun Master Plan which is still not finalized.

Thadani was absolutely right. The prime minister was livid when she got to know of the letter's contents. Meanwhile, the activists adopted a fresh strategy. On 2 July, Avdesh Kaushal of the Rural Litigation and Entitlement Kendra, Dehra Dun filed a public interest writ petition in the Supreme Court. Instructions from New Delhi had not worked. For some reason, amendments of the law had not been carried forward. It was now left to the judiciary to take a firm stand, and Indira Gandhi may well have felt that this was the best option. The final judgement was announced on 30 August 1988, and all mines were closed, save three.

One offshoot of the prime minister's concern for the Doon Valley was the formation of an eco-development task force by the Ministry of Defence. It comprised 243 officers and jawans—all of them ex-servicemen. The Doon Valley Board was to use this force in 1983 and later for the reforestation in the area—the impact of which became visible in the 1990s. Indira Gandhi was keen that such eco-development task forces be used not just in the Shivaliks but also in other areas like Rajasthan and the hill states. She had, in fact, written on a file on 24 June 1981:

> I am all for this [ex-servicemen for afforestation]. In fact, we have publicly invited ex-servicemen to get involved.

Barring an odd instance here and there, however, the success in the Doon Valley could not be replicated on a larger scale.

ॐ

India hosted the Seventh Conference of Heads of State or Government of Non-Aligned Countries, and Indira Gandhi gave the inaugural speech on 7 March. She dwelt at length on the real meaning and significance of non-alignment and of its continued relevance. She spoke of global political and economic issues—emphasizing the threat posed by nuclear weapons, the need for disarmament and how such a move would propel development. Palestine, South Africa, Namibia, Diego Garcia all figured in her speech, as did a tribute to Fidel Castro, the out-going chairman of the non-aligned collective, a position she was now assuming.

Indira Gandhi did not let go of this opportunity to talk on her favourite subject, despite being aware that many in her audience would not agree with her. This paragraph was added at the last minute:

> Some people consider concern for the environment an expensive and perhaps unnecessary luxury. But the preservation of the environment is an economic consideration since it is closely related to the depletion, restoration and increase of resources. In any policy decision and its implementation, we must balance present gains with likely damage in the not-too-distant future. Human ecology needs a more comprehensive approach.

In June, Indira Gandhi went to Belgrade to deliver two lectures. Josip Tito and her father had been good friends, and she herself had met the Yugoslav leader many times—she went on to recall this association in her speech to the Federal Assembly on 9 June.

But what stood out was her Raul Prebisch Lecture, delivered the day before, and organized by the United Nations Conference on Trade and Development (UNCTAD). Indira Gandhi presented a scholarly survey of global economic and financial issues. She famously described developing countries as 'the step-children of the Industrial Revolution', and discussed debt crises, reforms in the World Bank and the IMF, and how growing military expenses diverted resources from essential social needs.

But the speech was notable for another theme she had first hinted at earlier in the year at the Non-Aligned Summit:

On this small planet of ours, there is not room for permanent enmities and irreversible alienations. We have to live side-by-side. As Buckminster Fuller puts it, either war is obsolete or man is. We must recognize the interrelation of security, development and environment. Nuclear and chemical weaponry is genocidal and ecocidal. True security is not the defence of this country or that country but of the world as a whole. Not merely military security but the saving of life—our lives, of humans and all species.

On 30 September, Indira Gandhi accepted the first UN Population Award in New York. Her co-recipient was Qian Xinzhong, the minister in charge of family planning in China. Her acceptance speech was a pointed summary of India's past and ongoing efforts to control the growth of its population. Reiterating that the family planning programme in a democracy like India has to be voluntary, she reminded her audience that 'agricultural growth in India is ahead of our population'.

This was not the first time she was rebutting the neo-Malthusians. In the 1960s, the dominant view in the global environmental discourse was that the population explosion in developing countries was the main cause of all ecological imbalances. 1968 saw the publication of two works that advocated this view forcefully—Paul Ehrlich's best-selling book *The Population Bomb* and Gareth Hardin's less sensational and more academic *The Tragedy of the Commons*. The previous year, *Famine-1975!* by the Paddock brothers had dominated the headlines. All three books used India as an example of unbridled population growth and its devastating environmental consequences. Indira Gandhi had challenged such doomsday views before global audiences—most notably in her Stockholm speech of June 1972. She could do so because of the success of the Green Revolution for which she herself had provided determined leadership.

She had always been an active proponent of family planning. She had created a Ministry of Health and Family Planning and set up a Cabinet Committee on Family Planning. She had taken the bold step of making abortions legal with the passage of the Medical Termination Pregnancy Act in 1971. But she preferred caution and prudence and her pre-Emergency approach to family planning was summarized by Karan Singh at the UN Population Conference in Bucharest in August 1974. He had, by then, become the health and family planning minister, even as he continued to be the chairman of the IBWL. Just as Stockholm came to be known for Indira Gandhi's 'poverty is the worst form of pollution' misquote of sorts, Bucharest became famous for Singh's 'development is the best contraceptive' motto.[5]

The Emergency was to change all that. On 1 January 1976, while speaking to her party colleagues at Chandigarh, Indira Gandhi had announced that the 'government would have to take some strong steps which may not be liked by all to promote family planning.' Three weeks later, while addressing the Association of Physicians, she had declared:

> We must now act decisively to bring down the birth rate speedily [...] We should not hesitate to take steps which might be described as "drastic". Some personal rights have to be kept in abeyance for the human right of the nation—the right to live, the right to progress [...] We cannot accept the habit of people of affluent countries lecturing to us about our improvidence and describing the population growth of India and some other countries as the greatest threat to the future of the human race.

The number of sterilizations went up almost three-fold in 1976–77—from a previous peak of 3.1 million to almost 8.3 million. This did contribute heavily to her electoral debacle of 1977 in north India especially. This may well have led her to categorically and unequivocally reject any element of coercion—gentle or forced—in family planning.

Indira Gandhi had retained a keen interest in mountaineering. After speaking, in 1968, at the tenth anniversary celebrations of the Indian Mountaineering Foundation, she returned for its silver jubilee function on 29 August. Many noted mountaineers from all over the world had turned up for the occasion and the prime minister got emotional:

> I myself have not had the overpowering desire to scale the top. I am content to be on the mountains or near them, or if this is not possible, as

is usually the case, then see the snow from a distance. The sight never fails to touch the core of my being. Each time I feel as if it was the first view. Each time it brings a feeling of being cleansed from inside and renewed. One seems to inhale something of the strength of the mountains as well as their repose. My father loved the mountains and in his autobiography, he quotes the poet Li Tao Po: "we never grow tired with each other, the mountain and I". That is how I feel too. John Ruskin described the mountains as being full of expression, passion and strength.

Nehru used to call jail 'his other home' since he spent considerable time in prison. While flying from Gorakhpur to Guwahati on 11 November, Indira Gandhi, in a letter to her grandson, called the Boeing 'my second home'. She continued;

> We have been flying alongside the magnificent Himalayan range which has such famous mountains as Everest, Kanchenjunga and so on. Somehow the sight of such mountains gives me a special feeling. I feel aglow from inside.

Incidentally, in this letter to a thirteen-year-old, the prime minister was in an unusually reflective mood. She had been accused by one of her bitterest political foes, Dr Ram Manohar Lohia, of being a *'ghoongi gudia'*—a 'dumb doll'—for remaining silent in Parliament. Many people who met her came away wondering whether what they had said had registered with her at all. She explained this to her grandson as a lesson in life:

> Because I was not talkative, some thought I was stupid or uninteresting. The reason for not talking was actually shyness. Also I had very definite views of my own, so either I had to get into an argument or was considered peculiar! Much later when I was older I found a lot of very interesting and well-known people agreed with my ideas and shared some of my thoughts.

Notes

1. Bedi and Bedi (1984).
2. Earlier, on 1 March 1982, Indira Gandhi had hosted a lunch for Prince Philip who was on a short tour of India as president of WWF-International.

A month later while writing to a conservationist, he said that he had discussed conservation issues with Indira Gandhi. He wrote that he had found her personally interested and that was something.

3. The letter itself was untraceable but a longish report on it was published in *The Times of India*, Bombay edition of 11 November 1983.

4. A very large number of books and articles have been written over the years on the Silent Valley issue. D'Monte (1985) is an early informed account based on conversations with all those who took part in the movement.

5. His exact words were: 'We are quite clear that fertility levels can be effectively lowered only if family planning becomes an integral part of a broader strategy to deal with problems of poverty and underdevelopment. It has truly been said that the best contraceptive is development.'

1984

Indira Gandhi in Kanha National Park; January 1984.

This was to be Indira Gandhi's last year. The agitation in Punjab was moving towards its tragic denouement that took place in early June when the Indian army moved into the holy Golden Temple complex in Amritsar undertaking what was called 'Operation Blue Star'. The operation did achieve its objectives but the prime minister had signed her death warrant. On 14 June she wrote to Margaret Thatcher giving her a run-down on what had happened in Punjab. She explained why the army operations had become essential to rid the holy Golden Temple complex of terrorists whose objective was secession. She told her British counterpart that talks in the early 1980s with the Akali Dal had failed because that party kept changing its demands and in the end hardened its attitude considerably. She ended by saying 'Although the hard core of the terrorists within have been liquidated, we have a difficult period ahead of us. Many in the Sikh community have been shaken by the traumatic event. The process of healing and conciliation will take time but we shall persevere'.

Retribution was to come in less than six months' time. Negotiations to bring back peace in Assam and Mizoram continued and these negotiations were to lead to a settlement in the former a year later and in the latter in early 1986. In the region, Sri Lanka had continued to engage her attention especially after the bloody ethnic riots in Colombo in July 1983 in which thousands of Tamils had lost their lives. This had led her, at the insistence of the Tamil Nadu chief minister, to support groups claiming to be protectors of the interests of Tamils—and one of these groups was to blow up her son and successor as prime minister in 1991.[1]

While Operation Blue Star had sealed her fate, another less-written-about initiative, Operation Meghdoot to which she gave the go-ahead in April secured India's frontiers. This had been launched by the Indian army on the barren and icy heights of the strategically located Siachen glacier. After it had been firmly secured, Indira Gandhi flew over the glacier on 23 June. She saw the Indian tricolour flying at a post and immediately ordered that the officer manning the post should go to Europe for a fortnight as part of the team that was being sent to buy specialized equipment, snow clothing, and other items. Nobody was more surprised than the captain in question himself who never imagined that he would be given this responsibility.[2]

During the year, Indira Gandhi wrote six letters in eight months to her close family friend A.C.N. Nambiar—prolific even by her father's standards. These letters are warm and personal but also reveal her thinking on burning national issues, particularly Punjab, in an unrestrained manner. Writing from Bangalore on 15 September and after giving him an account of happenings in Punjab and Andhra Pradesh, she lamented:

> *The Opposition, the press and self-styled liberals seem to have a yardstick to measure democracy and that is, 'Anything said or done against Indira Gandhi and the Congress is right.'*

∾

395

For someone acknowledged as a champion of tiger conservation, Indira Gandhi hardly ever visited the tiger reserves she had helped create. She had been to Gir twice, and once to Kaziranga. Despite her long association with Billy Arjan Singh, she had never visited Dudhwa. In May 1978 she had spent an evening at the Nagarhole Sanctuary in Karnataka but there, too, all she had seen were deer and bisons. Therefore the desire to see a tiger in the wild lingered—perhaps fuelled by her two sightings around the Jog Falls area in Karnataka.

On the morning of 17 January, she went to Kanha, which had been declared a wildlife sanctuary in 1933 and a national park in 1955. Subsequently, it was one in the first list of nine tiger reserves created under Project Tiger in April 1973. Indira Gandhi was very lucky. Within two hours of her safari, around mid-day, while seated on an elephant, she saw a young male tiger on a hillock with the remains of a chital by his side. The elephant took her within ten feet of the tiger where she spent roughly fifteen minutes; she remarked to H.S. Panwar, the then director of Project Tiger who was with her, that 'that was a real tiger in its truly wild perch'. She noted in the visitors' book before leaving in the afternoon:

> I am delighted to have this brief respite in one of our best known and best kept national parks. I hope such efforts will enthuse others to take a greater interest in conservation.

ॐ

Indira Gandhi had a packed tour of Assam and Arunachal Pradesh in the early days of February. She was mainly fulfilling party duties and on the flight back to the capital on 4 February, she found time to write to her granddaughter, Priyanka:

> The last stop was Itanagar (I hope you remember that it is the capital of Arunachal!). Amongst other things, I met the smallest elephant I have ever seen. He was a few months old and was called Mayamurti. I was to give him bananas and he seemed eager to eat but he didn't seem to like them and ate only one, throwing all the others around. At Raj Niwas

Itanagar they also have a hornbill, three years old. I fed him a banana too although I was worried he might snap my fingers off.

❧

From 1956, the nation had been observing the first week of October as wildlife week. Ever since she had returned as prime minister in January 1980, Indira Gandhi had started giving a public message to mark the occasion. Her very last message which had been prepared on 3 July itself reinforced what she had been emphasizing for quite some time—that growth and conservation needed to be reconciled. While drawing attention to India's past and how our ancestors had learned to live with a magnificent array of wild creatures, she urged the country to 'hold this heritage in trust for future generations'.

It was akin to a farewell message—and indeed it turned out to be just that.

❧

The 1972 Stockholm United Nations Environment Conference had decided to mark 5 June every year as World Environment Day—this was to mark the date when the conference had opened. As always, Indira Gandhi gave a message to the country. This year she called for a massive effort by farmers and craftsmen in villages, managers and workers in the public and private sectors, teachers and students, parents and children to make barren lands, denuded hillsides and eroded water sheds come alive with trees and plants.

But the nation's attention was elsewhere. Operation Blue Star had begun. Maybe Indira Gandhi, too, was similarly preoccupied—for her message carried interesting phraseology—vegetation formed a 'green security blanket' that protected the fertile yet fragile soil.

❧

The battle over preserving Silent Valley had been won, and Salim Ali had played an important role in this victory.

But he hungered for more. On 26 March, while congratulating Indira Gandhi for her stance on Silent Valley and expressing his regret over inflicting on her 'this tiresome screed', he pleaded strongly for quickly establishing India's first biosphere reserve as a model for 'ecologically sound and sustainable development of the people while safeguarding the threatened genetic diversity of the country'.

Salim Ali did not need to convince Indira Gandhi. Since the mid-1970s, she had been trying to propagate this concept—first put forward by UNESCO—and ensure that it was accepted by her colleagues. Her efforts had resulted in Madhav Gadgil starting serious preparatory work on a Nilgiri Biosphere Reserve in 1980.

She did not live to see this notified. On 1 August 1986, the reserve was to spread across the three states of Tamil Nadu, Karnataka and Kerala, and span an area of over half a million hectares. Subsequently, by the end of the 1980s, four more such reserves were to be notified, all of which owed their creation to her—particularly the Nanda Devi Biosphere Reserve in the Himalayas.

∾

It was way back in November 1973 that Indira Gandhi had first evinced interest in having a convention with the USSR for the protection of migratory birds—of which the most well-known were the Siberian cranes that made Bharatpur their home in winter. A draft of the convention had been prepared by mid-1974 with the approval of Salim Ali. It lay dormant till Indira Gandhi revived interest in it in the run-up to her visit to the Soviet Union in September 1982. However, some last-minute objections were raised by the USSR and the convention could not be signed.

Correspondence resumed upon the prime minister's return to India and ultimately, the Convention on the Protection of Migratory Birds was signed on 8 October. It listed 303 migratory birds by name.

While the delay was inexplicable, it was some consolation that the convention could be signed before Indira Gandhi's demise just twenty-three days later.

∾

Amongst the very last letters she received was one from Peter Scott who wrote to her on 23 October. It was on a species becoming extinct. Scott wrote:

I am happy to see that Sam Mackenzie's visit to India is now going ahead and, when he arrives in December, he will be able to present four pairs of White-Winged Wood Duck to the State Ministers of Assam and Arunachal Pradesh.

I would also like to take this opportunity of thanking you most cordially for your interest and support of this scheme. I believe that added public awareness is being generated by the production of a commemorative stamp depicting this species.

Had she lived longer, Indira Gandhi would definitely have met Sam Mackenzie.

As it turned out, the ducks came in June 1986 and were received at Calcutta's Dum Dum Airport by Anne Wright. They were kept in her daughter Belinda Wright's bathroom for a few days before being taken to Assam. Sadly, the initiative did not prove to be a success because conservation centres had been started in tea gardens and not in their natural habitat! Even today, this critically endangered species survives in extremely small numbers in a few protected areas of Assam.

∾

Indira Gandhi paid her third visit to the Andaman and Nicobar Islands on 18 and 19 February.

A well-known Indian ecologist S.C. Nair had toured the islands extensively; he submitted his report in June 1983. The report, propped by meticulous research, reinforced the view that the tropical rainforests of the Andaman and Nicobar Islands were unique and had to be preserved. This chimed with Indira Gandhi's own views. She took the report with her on her third and final trip.

Upon her return, while she was sitting in her office in Parliament, she was handed a letter that had come from her thirteen-year-old granddaughter who was then studying in Dehra Dun. Gone were the cares of governance for a few minutes as the grandmother dictated her reply. It was a two-page Nehru-like letter offering the youngster a social history of the place she had just been to:

The Andaman and Nicobar Islands are very beautiful. They have some of the few really old forests in the world and the sea around is in lovely shades of blue. There is coral and lots more to be seen if one goes farther out in a glass-bottomed boat. [...This is] the first time that I could go down to the southernmost part—Pygmalion Point. I have brought back some shells which I picked up on the shore there.

Indira Gandhi's desire, all along, had been to preserve the ecological wealth of the Andaman and Nicobar Islands. Her visit in 1983 had been timely. There were pressing demands for increasing resettlement, starting oil palm plantations, establishing defence facilities and building trunk roads. As long as she was prime minister, most of these demands—barring those relating to India's strategic installations—were resisted. It must be admitted that even the armed forces did not have it easy.

That she cast a long shadow can be judged from the fact that by May 1983, a large Mahatma Gandhi Marine National Park was created near Wandoor on the Andamans, and in 1987, *ninety-six* wildlife sanctuaries were notified in the islands. These account for around a fifth of the country's total.

A highlight of this trip was her visit to the southernmost tip of India, known then as Pygmalion Point in Nicobar district. Eighteen months later it was to be renamed Indira Point as a tribute to her consistent efforts to protect the unique heritage of the archipelago.

Indira Gandhi's position on the Tehri and Silent Valley projects must have emboldened the anti-dam community. The prime minister kept receiving petitions against dams.

The widely respected activist Baba Amte had first written to her on 12 July 1983 seeking her intervention to stop the construction of the Inchampalli Hydroelectric Project on the Godavari and the Bhopalpatnam Hydel Project on the Indravati. He had highlighted the submergence of large swathes of prime forest land, the loss of many endangered species, and the displacement of over 40,000 Madia-Gond tribal people. Indira Gandhi responded on 30 August 1983:

My own views are well-known. But it is a very difficult battle. We shall pursue the matter. I am asking the Planning Commission to look very carefully into the aspects you have mentioned.

Baba Amte took up the cudgels again and on 26 June wrote to Indira Gandhi: 'It is a difficult battle—surely it is, but not an impossible one'. He reiterated his demand that the Inchampalli and Bhopalpatnam projects, which involved the states of Maharashtra, Madhya Pradesh and Andhra Pradesh, ought to be abandoned, and went on to express his admiration for her: '[…] when you espouse a cause and get involved in it, success is always with you and will always be with you'.

Indira Gandhi replied on 18 July that she had already asked the Ministry of Irrigation to examine alternative sites, as also consider his suggestion to construct a series of small dams instead of two big dams. She added:

> I am most unhappy that development projects displace tribal people from their habitat, especially as project authorities do not always take care to properly rehabilitate the affected population. But sometimes there is no alternative and we have to go ahead in the larger interest. All concerned should ensure that development and tribal welfare are harmonized.

Thanks to Baba Amte and Indira Gandhi, these two projects—which would have led to the destruction of thick, moist deciduous forests in the Gadchiroli and Bastar districts, and the displacement of thousands of tribal families—were aborted.

For quite some time, Indira Gandhi had been expressing her concerns regarding the pollution of India's holiest river—a river that also found the most eloquent expression in Jawaharlal Nehru's last will and testament.

On 13 March 1982, the prime minister had written to the chief minister of Rajasthan, Shiv Charan Mathur, that 'in some stretches of the Ganga water quality is below desirable levels'; she stated that she had asked the Department of Environment to set up 'an administrative arrangement to coordinate the entire work [of cleaning the Ganga]'. In February 1983,

Veer Bhadra Mishra, the well-known engineer-environmentalist and head priest of the Varanasi-based Sankat Mochan Foundation, was in touch with Indira Gandhi to launch a major initiative to cleanse the Ganga of all its pollution.

Forty days before she died, Indira Gandhi wrote to the chief ministers of Uttar Pradesh, Bihar and West Bengal, informing them that she had directed the Department of Environment to prepare an integrated action plan to clean the Ganga. She drew the attention of the chief ministers to the fact that the water quality in the river had deteriorated significantly and pollution levels in some stretches had become alarmingly high because of untreated sewage being discharged into it. Reminding them of the sanctity of the Ganga, she said that 'we can no longer afford to abuse the great and famous river'.

In his first broadcast to the nation on 5 January 1985, after being swept into power, her successor Rajiv Gandhi announced a national initiative to clean the Ganga. He set up a committee of the three chief ministers under his chairmanship to prepare a detailed plan. One of them, Jyoti Basu, the chief minister of West Bengal, paid Indira Gandhi a compliment later in the year: 'I had a lot of differences with Mrs Gandhi but I must pay tributes to her for her concerns for the environment and wildlife'. On 14 June 1986, Rajiv Gandhi launched the very first Ganga Action Plan at Varanasi.

In June 1983, the IUCN had announced that Indira Gandhi was to receive its highest accolade—the John C. Phillips Memorial Medal—at the Sixteenth General Assembly of the IUCN scheduled to begin in Madrid on 5 November. The citation called her a 'gifted naturalist from her earliest years' and concluded that 'no other political leader or statesman of modern times has had a greater influence on world conservation'. It was a fitting tribute from an organization which had played a key role supporting her over a period of fifteen years.

But fate had other plans; the award was to be received by her son in Geneva in June 1985.

Indira Gandhi has started her prime ministerial innings by visiting the Nehru Institute of Mountaineering in Uttarkashi in June 1966. A month before her final innings were cut short, she chaired the executive council meeting of the Himalayan Mountaineering Institute. She spent nearly two hours with people she had long known and admired. Captain M.S. Kohli suggested that the next meeting scheduled for 15 May 1985 be held in Darjeeling. Indira Gandhi simply smiled. Perhaps she had a premonition that this was not to be.

Just three days before she was shot, the prime minister wrote her last foreword—this time for a book by her ministerial colleague Digvijay Sinh, titled *The Eco-Vote: Peoples' Representatives and Global Environment*:[3]

> This book's title might suggest that the aim is political gain. However, conservation has to be seen in a much larger perspective. Whether or not the human race and all that lives on our beautiful Earth survive depends on peace and conservation.

∾

After Indira Gandhi's murder on 31 October, eulogies poured in from all over world. Tributes were paid. Resolutions were passed. Obituaries were written. Six eulogies stand out for the reason that they dwelt on her special relationship with nature.

The Sixteenth General Assembly of the IUCN started on 5 November in Madrid; it began with silence, in memory of Indira Gandhi. In the opening ceremony attended by the king and queen of Spain and the Duke of Edinburgh, tributes were paid to her by various people including Dr Mostafa Tolba, the executive director of UNEP. The president-elect of IUCN was none other than Dr M.S. Swaminathan, one of the key architects of the Green Revolution and very appropriately he drew attention to the fact that Indira Gandhi was 'not only one of the greatest environmentalists of our time' but also 'one of this century's most successful and dedicated campaigners against hunger'.

Then, there was a tribute by Captain M.S. Kohli, who spoke on behalf of the entire mountaineering community. Writing in *The Times of India* on the day Indira Gandhi would have turned sixty-seven, he recalled his association with her, going back to 1956 when he had first met her after the Saser Kangri expedition in Ladakh.

> We were invited to the PM's house. Panditji was out of station and Indira Gandhi wanted to hear about our expedition and see the film of our venture. She inquired about the difficulties we encountered, about the scenic views of the Karakorams and about the charming people of Ladakh.

He gave a number of vivid examples of how mountains stirred her and how she would make it a point to meet any mountaineering team, howsoever busy she was. He reminisced that she had been present on 15 May 1968 at the release of a ninety-minute film on the first successful Indian Everest expedition. She had been so excited by what she saw that she presented it to her Australian counterpart in Canberra a week later. He recalled the inauguration of the new headquarters complex of the Indian Mountaineering Foundation in New Delhi on 24 December 1980, which she had described as a 'beacon of adventure'; she dedicated the Indian Mountaineering Foundation to the 'Indian resurgence and the sense of adventure and the confidence we have in our future'.

The IFS had come into being in July 1966, five months into Indira Gandhi's first stint as prime minister; recruitment started two years later. Foresters worshipped her. They felt orphaned by her death. The IFS Association met in end-November, issued a twenty-seven-page booklet highlighting her contributions to forestry and wildlife, and adopted this resolution:

> The community of foresters in the country mourns the tragic and sudden demise of our beloved Prime Minister Shrimati Indira Gandhi, with deep anguish.
>
> She was the first and foremost among the world leaders to focus global attention on conservation of living natural resources as an essential aspect of human survival. The feelings of our bereavement of foresters are therefore intense. It was Shrimati Indira Gandhi whose keen foresight brought about the translation of the hitherto lip-concern for forests and wildlife into concerted governmental action.

Not often do professional publications mourn political leaders. But *Environmental Conservation* did and the tribute and was authored by its editor Nicholas Polunin and A.P Venkateswaran, then India's ambassador in China and later to be foreign secretary.[4] It appeared in the November 1984 issue under the title 'Indira Priyadarshini Gandhi, 1917–84':

> With the dastardly assassination on 31 October 1984 the environmental movement has lost one of its most powerful-ever allies [...] For not only did Mrs. Gandhi love wild things and all Nature but she had a deep appreciation of their importance for Mankind and steadfastly preserved a strong conservationist attitude regardless of political expediency. [...]

Nature is among the most prestigious scientific journals in the world. Eight days after her demise, John Maddox, its editor, captured his meeting with 'a sharp-witted democrat' eight months earlier:

> [She] was reading and signing her mail while keeping command of the conversation [...] There was an awkward moment at the beginning, when it seemed as if the Prime Minister thought that *Nature* is a magazine devoted to environmental causes; she launched on an eloquent speech about the beauty of the Indian landscape that threatened to use up the 45 minutes available. But, when prompted, she changed the course of the conversation without batting an eyelid.
>
> Quite apart from her belief (taken over from her father) in the importance of research and development in India, she exuded affection for the field and its practitioners—"my scientists" she called them. Her gratitude to people like Professor M.G.K. Menon [...] was evident. So was her pleasure at having colleagues such as Dr T. Khoshoo, now Secretary at the Department of Environment, whom she had inveigled to Delhi over a period of two years [...]

Finally, there was the eulogy by Nikhil Chakravarty, a noted journalist and left intellectual whom Indira Gandhi had first met at Oxford. He had subsequently become close to her husband. But after Haksar's exit he had distanced himself from Indira Gandhi. In the last two years of her life, he and Indira Gandhi met a couple of times, and on 1 October, on learning that he had just come back from Kabul, she called him for a chat. She herself had been to Kabul fifteen years earlier and clearly, Afghanistan interested her greatly. In an article published in *The Times of India* on 19 November, Nikhil Chakravarthy dwelt on that last encounter:

With child-like simplicity, she listened to my impressions about Kabul Bazar, about the dry-fruit lobby. And then when I talked about my flight crossing the Hindu Kush, she was curious to know how it looked from the air. We talked about the varying shades of different mountains—the Himalayas, the Karakoram, the Hindu Kush. One could sense her intense love for those majestic sentinels.

∾

On 30 November, a book published for the Smithsonian Institution titled *Our Green and Living World: The Wisdom to Save it* was released. It was written by four leading conservation scientists,[5] and had an epilogue by Indira Gandhi, penned the previous July. In fact, when Edward Ayensu— one of the authors and the main force behind the book—had sent Indira Gandhi a draft foreword, she had penciled:

> It is my Foreword. I have to write it myself.

What she wrote deserves mention:

> For countless centuries, Indian civilization has proclaimed the oneness of all existence and the unity of life and non-life. [...] It is ironical that [...] when this ancient tenet of Indian philosophy is being recognized by the world, our own people are allowing deforestation and the extinction of various species. The compulsions of development, the pressures of population and the greed for profit have all combined to threaten our forests, our animals and the very air we breathe.
>
> [...] Already the whole world and my own country have lost a great deal by neglecting the ecological equilibrium. Little time is now left to us [...] Human beings can thrive only in a green and living world. The problems of the environment have to be faced by the world as one [...]

While concluding the book, the authors wrote

> Finally the authors gratefully acknowledge the source of the title of the book. During a long search, several titles were tried. Finally in Mrs. Gandhi's epilogue, the perfect words appeared. Though now used elsewhere in the book, the phrase "green and living world" originated with Mrs Indira Gandhi.

Sadly, she was not around when the book was released.

On 25 March 1985, Prakash Narain, the secretary of the Union Ministry of Shipping and Transport announced in Madras that the Government of India had decided not to establish the National Institute of Port Management on the shore near the city's Adyar estuary and would identify an alternative location. This was a victory for the environmental activists of Madras who had been agitating for quite some time to protect the ecologically fragile area with its mangroves and which was home to a wide variety of avian visitors. A few weeks before she was killed, Indira Gandhi had, in fact, bowed to the demands of the activists but the formal announcement to shift the institute to another site had not been made. Nanditha Krishna, a key player in that episode recalled to me what had happened:

> Out of sheer desperation I wrote to Mrs. Indira Gandhi and followed it with a telegram. The response was startling. Within two days, the local Director of the Port Management Institute came home to apologise and said that they had decided to shift the location [away from the Adyar estuary] and asked me whether I had any objection to Uthandi on the East Coast Road! I told him I was nobody to approve or object; but I was concerned with the ecology of the Adyar estuary and wanted it to remain sacrosanct. The Port Management Institute was shifted out of Adyar immediately and went to Uthandi. Later it became the Indian Maritime University, through an Act of Parliament.

Dillon Ripley came to Delhi on 3 November as part of the official US delegation to Indira Gandhi's funeral. He wrote to Salim Ali from the Maurya Sheraton where he was staying: 'What a way to come to India! We are all so shocked and horrified.' Salim Ali replied eight days later in words that could not be bettered:

> I was surprised to get a note from your Delhi hotel [...] Though we were watching the whole dismal affair on TV all day, I did not notice anything that could be suspected to be you! I still find it hard to believe this dreadful catastrophe that has left us all stunned. It was the vilest and

most despicable act of treachery one can imagine, and that it should have been perpetrated by her own security guards makes it more heinous and abominable […]

On 9 December, en route to London from New York, Ripley scribbled a letter to Salim Ali: 'I had an extremely poignant but interesting time […] The ceremonies were most moving'. Referring to mankind's worst industrial disaster—the Union Carbide plant catastrophe in Bhopal on the night of 2 December—he added: 'What a ghastly business in Bhopal […] I have a menacing feeling this is the beginning of a world-wide Pandora's Box. What to do?'

On 2 January 1985, Salim Ali congratulated Rajiv Gandhi for his landslide electoral victory and went on to recall Indira Gandhi:

> It was her deep personal concern for nature and environmental conservation that is responsible for whatever little we have been able to achieve in saving our fast vanishing wildlife and forests and we shall look to you to help in carrying on the good work patronized by her all through her stewardship of the country.

On 28 August 1985, the eighty-nine-year-old Salim Ali met the forty-one-year-old prime minister; the former wrote to the latter four days later:

> I feel honoured at having being considered for nomination by you to the Rajya Sabha. As I tried to explain to you, my disqualifications for the responsibility at this stage of 'senile decay' are many and real. However, if you really feel that I may occasionally be of some help, especially in matters concerning environment and wildlife conservation I am willing to give myself a trial. *It would give me the greatest satisfaction if I could be sure—as I was with your mother—that any environmental issue that I wished to bring to your attention would reach you directly and as quickly as possible* [italics mine].

Salim Ali continued the barrage of letters to Rajiv, and these covered a range of topics—Silent Valley, Forest Development Corporations, the Andaman and Nicobar Islands, to name just three. He continued to get quick responses from the son of his friend.

On 7 January 1986, Indira Gandhi was posthumously awarded the Smithsonian Institution's First Medal for Conservation. The medal was presented by Dillon Ripley to Rajiv Gandhi in New Delhi. Ripley had known Indira Gandhi for over three decades. She was very well aware of his great fondness for India and his close professional association with Salim Ali. In one of her last acts, she had made him co-chair, along with Pupul Jayakar, of the Festival of India in the USA to be held in 1985.

On 9 March 1987, Salim Ali wrote to Rajiv Gandhi to tell him that he was delighted that the latter had agreed to attend a seminar being organized thirty-five days hence in the nation's capital on the BNHS's research and conservation activities. Twelve days later, he wrote again saying that he would be happy if Rajiv's wife Sonia and the children could also attend because they, too, would find it of interest.

On the morning of 13 April 1987, Salim Ali fell ill and was hospitalized. But the show went on and Rajiv was present along with his family. He complimented Salim Ali handsomely and wished him a speedy recovery. Alas, two months and a week later, Salim Ali passed away.

Notes

1. Indira Gandhi had written to Margaret Thatcher on 9 June 1984 asking the British PM to use her good offices to convince Sri Lankan President J.R. Jayewardene about the need for a political settlement through negotiations to the ethnic problem in that country. This letter was in the background of reports that the UK was assisting the Sri Lankan army.
2. Interview with (then) Captain Sanjay Kulkarni in Gokhale (2014).
3. Digvijay Sinh (1985).
4. He had been with her in Stockholm in June 1972 and retained a keen interest in environmental issues.
5. Ayensu, Heywood, Lucas and Defillips (1984).

VII. A Final Word

Thus ended the life of a committed conservationist; a courageous political leader who had seen triumph and tragedy; and a remarkable personality who never flinched from taking decisions—some of which were magnificent, while others did injustice to her.

I DID NOT SET OUT TO ASSESS OR JUDGE INDIRA GANDHI. WHAT I SOUGHT TO do was paint a fresh portrait of a much-written about but little-understood personality—a leader who was complex and contradictory on the one hand, and charismatic and compelling on the other. I sought to discover and elucidate an aspect of who she was and what she did—an aspect that has not received the attention it deserves in the volumes that have been written about her.

Indira Gandhi's institutionalized educational journey followed a zig-zag route. She went to college without actually ever getting a formal degree. But she graduated with the highest distinction, *summa cum laude,* from the University of Nature.[1]

Who was the real Indira Gandhi? Historians have grappled, and will continue to grapple, with this question. She has hordes of admirers, awed by her spectacular achievements. She also has a large number of critics who cannot see beyond her errors of judgement and action—some of which were of her own making, while some others forced on her by circumstances.

There were, to be sure, poignant paradoxes in her personality. But what should be beyond any doubt from this chronicle is her commitment to the environment. Her tryst with nature inspired and refreshed her throughout turbulent personal upheavals and a tumultuous political career. Her love for all things ecological was an inheritance and a part of her disposition, which she nurtured into an abiding passion.

Critics of Indira Gandhi may well say: 'So what, how does her concern for the environment make any difference?' Such a reaction would be churlish. There was nothing private about her passion for nature to make it irrelevant in a balance sheet of her record in office. Her passion became a public calling, defining who she was and driving what she did as prime minister. That is why any assessment of her work must necessarily take into full account her accomplishments as an environmental advocate and leader.

ᐁ

Throughout her career as head of a nation, buffeted as she was by a series of crises, Indira Gandhi revealed her true self through her abiding concern for nature. This is what makes her fascinating—that she found the time to pursue environmental causes despite the numerous weighty preoccupations that asked for all her attention during some of the most difficult years of our Republic. The greater the political pressure, the more she reached out to the natural world. It was as though she considered politics ephemeral and nature the true significant constant in her life.

When with visitors or in meetings, it was well-known that she would appear distant and distracted, continue reading her files, or indulge in her favourite pastime—doodling. But this was decidedly not the case when she was with naturalists or in meetings concerning wildlife or forests or environmental conservation in general. At such points, she was intensely focused, engaged and in charge.

Today, heads of state or governments across the world wax eloquent about climate change and sustainable development. But over four decades ago, Indira Gandhi was amongst the small handful of political leaders who took environmental issues seriously and gave them the importance they deserved in matters of day-to-day governance. It needs to be recalled that apart from the host prime minister, she was the only other head of government or state to speak at the very first United Nations Conference on the Human Environment in Stockholm in June 1972. Similarly, she was among the five heads of state or government to speak at the very first United Nations Conference on New and Renewable Sources of Energy at Nairobi in August 1976. Compare this with the famed Rio Earth Summit Conference in 1992, where there were over a hundred heads of state or government present!

Without question, Indira Gandhi was a trailblazer on environmental issues not just within India but on the world stage as well.

Indira Gandhi is very often portrayed as an authoritarian figure. Her life in nature shows that while she did have her say, she did not always have her way. There were undoubtedly a few occasions when she laid down clearly what ought to be done, and how. But, on the whole, her life in nature as a prime minister was an odyssey in suggestion and persuasion. This approach was guided by two facts. First, she was acutely conscious that in India paramount importance had always to be given to improving the living standards and the quality of life of people through economic development. Second, many of the actions she would have wanted taken to preserve nature and protect the environment were the primary responsibility of state governments. Had she been the bulldozer she was purported to be, she actually would have ended up accomplishing much more than she did as an environmentalist.

Equally, Indira Gandhi's life in nature reminds us that she agonized over several of her decisions. She knew, for instance, that the Silent Valley needed to be saved from a hydel project but it took her almost three years to finally decide, allowing discussion and debate to take place in the meantime. On occasion, she allowed herself to be persuaded to take a particular decision against her own ecological convictions on account of larger economic and political considerations. Then, there were times when she sought the opinions of those she liked and trusted—Salim Ali being the most famous example within India, and Peter Scott and Peter Jackson being two examples internationally.

Indira Gandhi's own views evolved as she grappled with new situations. While, to begin with, she was an environmental purist, over time she became convinced that without the full involvement and participation of local communities neither wildlife nor forest conservation would ever succeed on an enduring basis.

No doubt enigmatic, the *essential* Indira Gandhi was the committed conservationist, who saw the protection of India's rich natural heritage, along with its diverse cultural legacy, fundamental to its economic advance. Indeed, for her, development without conservation was unsustainable, just as conservation without development was unacceptable. Further, for her, conservation, respect for biodiversity and concern for ecological balance were all derived from the India's civilizational ethos. She often referred to the chief lesson that 'our ancients' taught us—to revere and live in harmony with nature.

Her environmental legacy comes with no qualifiers, no caveats. It is a legacy that continues to resonate and is really for the ages.

∾

Shakti Sthal—the abode of energy—is the memorial to Indira Gandhi in the nation's capital and reveals her kinship with nature in its myriad forms. It is set in a square space of open earth where her last rites and cremation rituals were conducted, and captures dramatically her fascination with stones.[2] The central spot is marked by a gigantic rock of jasper haematite, one of the hardest substances known to man. The memorial—set as a geological park—comes with nearly a thousand rocks from every part of the country representing the four major geological eras. A small collection of stones from Antarctica has also been placed, in view of her role in establishing India's presence in that icy continent.

The landscape has a rolling topography as generally seen in the Himalayan foothills. And, of course, the trees are those she loved, especially the laburnum with its yellow blossoms; the *Chorisia speciosa* or the silk floss tree with pink flowers which she had planted in her home garden; alstonia, with its white florets, that she had popularized in the nation's capital; the yellow-flowered putranjiva or Indian kusum, with its beautiful bronze-coloured leaves; and the historically and culturally significant kadamba.

Indira Gandhi had once described Rabindranath Tagore as an 'ecological man'. Undoubtedly, the Santiniketan student did the Great Sentinel[3] proud by herself evolving into an ecological woman.

Notes

1. A felicitous phrase first used in Masani (1975). This is quite a fine biography but Indira Gandhi had this to say to A.C.N. Nambiar on 29 May 1983 while flying from Delhi to Chandigarh. 'Masani's biography is quite terrible, I am told. I never read anything on it myself, but his articles on me are really vicious. I hope you don't mind if we do not spend money on such a book.'

2. She used to pick up interesting stone specimens on her many travels and kept them in her home and enjoyed their feel and touch. Writing to her

father from Moscow on 17 July 1953 after three days at the Black Sea Resort of Sochi, she recalled: 'The Black Sea was very calm and like a lake or the Mediterranean. She must have sensed my disappointment because the very next day there arose a storm and then she was changing her dress every five minutes and nobody could decide which was the most beautiful. It was fascinating to watch. We swam and lay on the pebbly beach—uncomfortable but quite lovely because of the different coloured stones.'

3. Mahatma Gandhi's description of Rabindranath Tagore, *Young India*, 13 October 1921.

A Note on Sources

Indira Gandhi's letters to her ministerial colleagues and chief ministers, her notings on files and observations on letters received by her have been taken from recently declassified files available at the National Archives, New Delhi.

Her correspondence with Salim Ali has been taken from the latter's archives at the Nehru Memorial Museum and Library (NMML), New Delhi. The P.N. Haksar papers also at NMML have been used. Similarly, her exchanges with Dillon Ripley are from his archives at the Smithsonian Institution, Washington DC. Her letters to T.N. Kaul and Mira Behn are from their respective archives at NMML.

Indira Gandhi had a fairly long correspondence with Billy Arjan Singh. His niece has made these letters available to me. Similarly, her letters to Anne Wright have been made available to me by Anne Wright herself.

A number of messages that Indira Gandhi sent on various occasions and forewords that she wrote to some books have not been included in the official five-volume compendium of her speeches and writings. These have been taken from the repository in the National Archives.

Indira Gandhi's letters to Lucile Kyle have been taken from the latter's archives at Cornell University, UK. The archives of the WWF and the IUCN in Switzerland have been used for material related to the interactions of these two organizations with Indira Gandhi. Her letters to Rajni Patel are from the Penn State University Archives while Alice Prochaska, Principal of Somerville College has made available her letter to Kathleen Davies.

Other archives that have been tapped and that have yielded useful material are those at the Bombay Natural History Society, Mumbai, Cambridge University, UK, Friends House, UK, Durham University,

UK, Swarthmore College, USA, Johns Hopkins University USA, Stanford University, USA, Harvard University USA, and Georgetown University, USA.

Letters exchanged between Indira Gandhi and Jawaharlal Nehru are from Sonia Gandhi (editor) *Two Alone, Two Together* (Penguin Books, 2004). Indira Gandhi's letters to Dorothy Norman are from the latter's *Indira Gandhi: Letters to an American Friend*, to Phyllis Cartwright from P.D. Tandon's *Indira: Lingering Echoes* (Allied Publishers, 1990), to Gertrude Emerson Sen from Girish N. Mehra's *Nearer Heaven than Earth* (Rupa Publications, 2007) and to A.C.N. Nambiar from Vappala Balachandran's *A Life in Shadow* (Roli Books, 2016). Letters and notes of Jawaharlal Nehru are from different volumes of *Selected Works of Jawaharlal Nehru* (Oxford University Press).

All photographs are from the NMML, IGMT and the UN. Indira Gandhi's surrender of her rice ration in 1966 is from P.D. Tandon's *Indira: Lingering Echoes* (Allied Publishers, 1990). The bird doodle in 1982 is from Alexander (2004).

Her last trip to Kashmir with which the book opens is described best in M.L. Fotedar's *The Chinar Leaves: A Political Memoir* (HarperCollins, 2015).

A Note of Thanks

Without Jaya Ravindran's enthusiastic assistance I would not have been able to access recently declassified material from the National Archives for the period 1966–84. I should also thank the staff of the reading room of the National Archives for their ready help in locating old records.

Natwar Singh and Moni Malhoutra who were Indira Gandhi's key aides in the prime minister's secretariat deserve special gratitude for many extended conservations. Both were gold mines of information and Natwar Singh permitted me to use H.Y. Sharada Prasad's letter to him.

A few people, who worked closely with Indira Gandhi and are still active, have been generous with their time and recollections. They include M.S. Swaminathan, Sunderlal Bahuguna, Karan Singh, Salman Haidar, Ashok Parthasarathi, M.K. Ranjitsinh, N.D. Jayal, Samar Singh and H.S. Panwar. Samar Singh was particularly helpful. I also spent hours with Ashok Khosla and C.K. Varshney and they gave me much valuable material from their files.

Anne Wright was wonderful especially because she had maintained a written record of her association with Indira Gandhi which she gladly shared with me. Belinda Wright, too, was exceedingly helpful on many subjects, ranging from tigers to white-winged wood ducks.

Deepak Apte and Nirmala Dhotre of the Bombay Natural History Society (BNHS) were available at all times and facilitated my research in the BHNS Library. Dilnavaz Variava and Asad Rahmani, close associates of Salim Ali, shared their recollections of Indira Gandhi's association with him.

Neelam Vats at the Nehru Memorial Museum and Library (NMML) helped me access the papers of Salim Ali, Madhav Gadgil, S. Varadarajan, M.G.K. Menon and Shekhar Singh that are in the archives there. D. Ramesh of the Parliament Library tracked down interventions of Indira Gandhi in Parliament.

Tad Banicoff at the Smithsonian Archives, George Clarke at the Harvard University Archives, Stephen Ross at the Yale University Archives, Jim Stimpert at the Johns Hopkins University Archives, Mark Harkness at the Durham University Archives, Irfan Noorduddin of Georgetown University and Ron Herring of Cornell University readily sent me the material related to Indira Gandhi that I had asked for. Other archivists who have been helpful are those at Stanford University and the University of Toledo.

Shubhobrato Ghosh was always prepared with references most of which I had not seen before. Prerna Bindra replied to my email queries promptly, as did Valmik Thapar. Lee Durrell responded immediately on my queries regarding her late husband Gerald Durrell and pygmy hogs.

Rashid Raza of the Wildlife Institute of India answered all my queries speedily and came up with more material I had bargained for. I also thank V.B. Mathur and Y.V. Jhala of the Institute for their courtesies and conversations. Karthik Shankar was very helpful locating correspondence between Indira Gandhi and Archie Carr on sea turtles. Rom Whitaker answered my questions on snakes and crocodiles cheerfully.

Bob Bustard, B.C. Choudhury and Lala A.K. Singh provided me details of the crocodile conservation programme. Hari Singh and Dinesh Misra dug out old reports on the Gir Lion Project and Kartikeya Sarabhai sent papers of his father Vikram Sarabhai. Amit Sankhala was a valuable source for some of his father Kailash Sankhala's papers, as was Chandrasekhar Pant whose father Pitambar Pant's papers are archived at the NMML.

H.Y. Mohan Ram, Sanjiva Prasad and Ravi V. Prasad educated me on H.Y. Sharada Prasad and his love for nature both before and during his long association with Indira Gandhi. Radhika Rajamani assisted in unearthing material related to her father R. Rajamani's stint with Indira Gandhi.

Brinda Dubey was very gracious with her time and gave me the letters that Indira Gandhi had written to her uncle Billy Arjan Singh. Sheetal Amte sent me the correspondence between Indira Gandhi and her grandfather Baba Amte. Radhika Herzberger shared material related to Indira Gandhi from her mother Pupul Jayakar's archives. Vappala Balachandran allowed me to use Indira Gandhi's letters to A.C.N. Nambiar which were first published in his book.

Amrita Patel handed over some useful papers of Duleep Matthai's association with Indira Gandhi as did R.S. Dharmakumar Sinhji's daughter regarding her father's large volume of writings. Tusna Park and Shahnaz Slater helped me get Nari Rustomji's photograph of Indira Gandhi on a yak on her way to Bhutan in 1958 as well as her letter to him.

Chris Halls unearthed a treasure trove of papers in the WWF archives related to the lion and tiger conservation projects. Ravi Singh was the person I would contact on all matters related to Indira Gandhi and WWF-India. Inger Anderson was most helpful in locating correspondence between Indira Gandhi and the IUCN.

George Archibald shared his memories on Indira Gandhi and Siberian cranes and his assistant Karen Becker helped me get hold of the correspondence between Indira Gandhi and Jeffrey Short. Harsh Vardhan of the Wildlife and Tourism Society of India was a mine of information on Indira Gandhi and the Great Indian Bustard, as also on her trip to Bharatpur in February 1976.

Cyrus Guzder, Navroz Mody and Hema Ramani, colleagues of Shyam Chainani, opened up the old files of the Bombay Environment Action Group which was very useful.

Sugatakumari, V.S. Vijayan and M.K. Prasad sent me material on Silent Valley based on their personal experience. S. Satis shared a copy of the M.G.K. Menon Committee report that is now not easily available.

Madhav Gadgil, Ramchandra Guha and Mahesh Rangarajan gave me a number of useful leads and suggestions. Ullas Karanth and Shiv Someshwar of Columbia University were similarly helpful. Ralph Buultjens was very forthcoming with his recollections of Indira Gandhi.

I wouldn't have been able to access the Cambridge University archives and online journals but for Shruti Kapila. Lisa Randell provided assistance regarding the archives of Horace Alexander and Prince Philip. Wendy Chmielewski tracked down Indira Gandhi's letters to Horace Alexander in a matter of hours.

India's high commissioner in Kenya, Suchitra Durai, and India's former ambassador in Sweden, Banashree Bose Harrison, went out of their way to respond to my requests.

Gautam Kaul happily shared a note he prepared for me on his father Kailas Nath Kaul. Sudhir Vohra took the trouble of locating the papers written by his father B.B. Vohra in the early 1970s, as did Raj Khoshoo for his father T.N. Khoshoo's papers in the 1980s when he worked with Indira Gandhi.

Madhavan Palat, Geeta Kudaisya, Rajendra Prasad and N. Balakrishnan of the Jawaharlal Nehru Memorial Fund were always there to answer my queries. Nilanjan Banerjee was my 'go to man' for Indira Gandhi and Santiniketan.

Dharini Bhaskar, my editor at Simon and Schuster India, who had also worked on an earlier book of mine, vastly improved the structure of this narrative, along with Sayantan Ghosh. Rajinder Ganju chose an excellent font and carefully designed the inside pages of the book.

Ritu Vajpeyi Mohan who had worked on two of my recent books was a valuable sounding board. Suman Dubey was, along with M.S. Kohli, my guide on all matters related to mountaineering and Nayanjot Lahiri on all matters related to the built heritage.

Priyanka Gandhi Vadra readily shared her memories of her grandmother as a nature lover as well as some of the letters she had received from the late prime minister. Sonia Gandhi reminded me of her mother-in-law and Anne Wright and gave me access to some of Indira Gandhi's letters to her son and grandchildren, as well as some of the books in her personal library.

Bibliography

Ahluwalia, H.P.S., *Higher than Everest*, Vikas Publishing House, 1973.

Alam, Jawaid, (ed.), *Kashmir and Beyond 1966–84: Select Correspondence between Indira Gandhi and Karan Singh*, Viking by Penguin, 2011.

Alexander, P.C., *My Years with Indira Gandhi*, Orient Paperbacks, 1991.

———, *Through the Corridors of Power*, HarperCollins, 2004.

Ali, Salim, *The Fall of a Sparrow*, Oxford University Press, 1985.

Austin, Granville, *Working a Democratic Constitution*, Oxford University Press, 1999.

Ayensu, Edward, Heywood, Vernon H., Lucas, Grenville L. and Defillips, Robert A., *Our Green and Living World: The Wisdom to Save It*, Cambridge University Press, 1984.

Balachandran, Vappala, *A Life in Shadow: The Secret Story of ACN Nambiar: A Forgotten Anti-Colonial Warrior*, Lotus/Roli, 2016.

Bedi, Romesh, with pictures by Bedi, Rajesh, *Indian Wildlife*, Brijbasi Printers, 1984.

Berwick, Stephen and Saharia, V.B., *The Development of International Principles and Practices of Wildlife Research and Management: Asian and American Approaches*, Oxford University Press, 1995.

Bhagat, Usha, *Indiraji Through My Eyes*, Viking by Penguin, 2005.

Bhatia, Krishan, *Indira: A Biography of Prime Minister Gandhi*, Praeger, 1974.

Brahmachary, R.L., *My Tryst with Big Cats*, Naturism, 2013.

Capra, Fritjof, *Uncommon Wisdom: Conversations with Remarkable People*, Flamingo, 1989.

D'Monte, Darryl, *Temples or Tombs? Industry Versus Environment: Three Controversies*, Centre for Science and Environment, 1985.

Davies, Anne, 'Women's Overland Himalayan Expedition, 1958', *Alpine Journal*, 1959.

Deacock, Antonia, *No Purdah in Padam*, Harrap and Co., 1960.

Dhar, P.N., *Indira Gandhi: The 'Emergency' and Indian Democracy*, Oxford University Press, 2000.

Divyabhanusinh, *The Story of Asia's Lions*, Marg Publications, 2005.

Durrell, Gerald, *The Ark's Anniversary*, Westland, 2007.

Engfeldt, Lars-Goran, *From Stockholm to Johannesburg & Beyond*, Ministry of Foreign Affairs, Sweden, 2009.

Fotedar, M.L., *The Chinar Leaves: A Political Memoir*, HarperCollins, 2015.

Frank, Katherine, *Indira: The Life of Indira Nehru Gandhi*, HarperCollins, 2001.

Futehally, Zafar with Chandola, Shanti and Chandola, Ashish, *The Song of the Magpie Robin: A Memoir*, Rainlight/Rupa, 2014.

Gandhi, Indira, *Eternal India*, Vendome Press, 1980.

———, *Problems and Prospects*, Hodder and Stroughton, 1981.

———, *My Truth*, Vision Books, 1982.

———, *Selected Speeches and Writings (in five volumes)*, Publications Division, Ministry of I&B, Government of India, 1986.

Gandhi, Sonia (ed.), *Two Alone, Two Together: Letters between Indira Gandhi and Jawaharlal Nehru 1922–1964*, Penguin, 2004.

Ganguli, Usha, *A Guide to the Birds of the Delhi Area*, Indian Council of Agricultural Research, 1975.

Gee, E.P., *The Wild Life of India*, E.P. Dutton, 1964.

Ghorpade, M.Y., *Sunlight and Shadows*, Gollancz, 1983.

Ghosh, D.N., *No Regrets*, Rupa, 2015.

Gill, Manohar Singh, *Himalayan Wonderland*, Vikas Publishing House, 1972.

Gokhale, Nitin, *Beyond NJ 9842: The Siachen Saga*, Bloomsbury India, 2014.

Guha, Ramachandra, *India After Gandhi*, Picador, 2002.

Gundevia, Y.D., *In the Districts of the Raj*, Orient Longman, 1992.

Gupte, Pranay, *Mother India: A Political Biography of Indira Gandhi*, Penguin/ Viking, 2009.

Harper, Kristine, *Make it Rain: State Control of the Atmosphere in Twentieth-Century America*, University of Chicago Press, 2017.

Hart-Davis, Duff, *Honorary Tigers: The Life of Billy Arjan Singh*, Roli, 2005.

Holdgate, Martin, *The Green Web: A Union for World Conservation*, Routledge, 2013.

Indira Gandhi Memorial Trust, *What I Am: Indira Gandhi in Conversation with Pupul Jayakar*, 1986.

———, *Remembered Moments: Some Autobiographical Writings of Indira Gandhi*, 1987.

Jayakar, Pupul, *Indira Gandhi: A Biography*, Viking, 1992.

Kalhan, Promilla (ed.), *Indira Gandhi Writes*, Arnold–Heinemann, 1976.

Kochukoshy, C.K., *Into an Hour Glass*, published by Mrs G.K. Koshy, 1982.

Kohli, M.S., *Nine Atop Everest*, Orient Longmans, 1969.

Khagram, Sanjeev, *Dams and Development: Transnational Struggles for Water and Power*, Cornell University Press, 2004.

Kumar, Ravinder and Prasad, H.Y. Sharada, *Selected Works of Jawaharlal Nehru*, Second Series, Volume 23, Oxford University Press, 1998.

Kurien, Verghese as told to Gouri Salvi, *I Too Had a Dream*, Roli Books, 2005.

Lewis, Michael, *Inventing Global Ecology: Tracking the Biodiversity Ideal in India 1945–1997*, Orient Longman, 2003.

Lutyens, Mary, *The Life and Death of Krishnamurti*, John Murray, 1990.

MacDonald, Malcolm, *Birds in My Indian Garden*, Jonathan Cape, 1960.

Malhotra, Inder, *Indira Gandhi: A Personal and Political Biography*, Hay House India, 2014.

Manoharan, T.M., Biju, S.D., Nayar, T.S. and Easa, P.S., *Silent Valley: Whispers of Reason*, Kerala Forest Department, 1999.

Masani, Zareer, *Indira Gandhi: A Biography*, Oxford University Press, 1975.

Mathur, Dr K.P., *The Unseen Indira Gandhi through Her Physician's Eyes*, Konark Publishers, 2016.

Mehra, Girish, *Nearer Heaven than Earth: The Life and Times of Boshi Sen and Gertrude Emerson Sen*, Rupa Publications, 2007.

Mitra, Ashok, *A Prattler's Tale*, Samya, 2006.

Mohan, Anand, *Indira Gandhi: A Personal and Political Biography*, Meredith, 1967.

Moraes, Dom, *Indira Gandhi*, Little, Brown and Company, 1980.

Nehru, B.K., *Nice Guys Finish Second: Memoirs*, Penguin, 1997.

Nehru, Jawaharlal, *Letters from a Father to His Daughter*, Puffin by Penguin, 2004.

Norman, Dorothy, *Indira Gandhi: Letters to an American Friend*, Harcourt Brace Jovanovich, 1985.

Pant, Apa B., *A Moment in Time*, University of Nevada Press, 1974.

Parthasarathi, Ashok, *Technology at the Core: Science and Technology with Indira Gandhi*, Pearson Longman, 2007.

Parthasarathi, G. and Prasad, H.Y. Sharada (eds), *Indira Gandhi: Statesmen, Scholars, Scientists and Friends Remember*, Vikas, 1985.

Prasad, H.Y. Sharada and Damodaran, A.K. (eds), *Selected Works of Jawaharlal Nehru*, Second Series, Volume 30, Oxford University Press, 2002.

Prasad, H.Y. Sharada, *The Book I Won't Be Writing and Other Essays*, Chronicle Books, 2003.

Raghavan, Srinath (ed.), Sarvepalli Gopal, *Imperialists, Nationalists, Democrats: The Collected Essays*, Permanent Black, 2013.

Ramesh, Jairam, *Green Signals: Ecology, Growth and Democracy in India*, Oxford University Press, 2015a.

———, *To the Brink and Back: India's 1991 Story*, Rupa, 2015b.

———, *Old History New Geography: Bifurcating Andhra Pradesh*, Rupa, 2016.

Randhawa, M.S., *Flowering Trees in India*, ICAR, 1957.

Rangarajan, Mahesh, *Nature and Nation: Essays in Environmental History*, Permanent Black, 2015.

Rustomji, Nari, *Enchanted Frontiers*, Oxford University Press, 1971.

Sahgal, Bittu (ed.), *Lest We Forget: Kailash Sankhala's India,* Sanctuary Asia, 2008.

Sahgal, Nayantara, *Indira Gandhi: Tryst with Power*, Penguin, 2012.

Santapau, H., *Common Trees*, National Book Trust, 1966.

Shankar, Kartik, *From Soup to Superstar: The Story of Sea Turtle Conservation along the Indian Coast*, Litmus/HarperCollins, 2015.

Sharma, Satya S., *Breaking the Ice in Antarctica*, New Age International, 2001.

Singh, K. Natwar, *Yours Sincerely*, Rupa, 2010.

Singh, Samar, *Conserving India's Natural Heritage*, Natraj, 1986.

Sinh, Digvijay, *The Eco-Vote: Peoples' Representatives and Global Environment*, Prentice Hall of India, 1985.

Sinha, R.P.N., *Our Birds*, Publications Division, Ministry of I&B, Government of India, 1959.

Strong, Maurice, *Where on Earth Are We Going*, Vintage Canada, 2001.

Tandon, P.D., *Indira: Lingering Echoes (Letters and Reminscences)*, Allied Publishers, 1990.

Thapar, Valmik, *The Last Tiger: Struggling for Survival*, Oxford University Press, 2011.

Vasudev, Uma, *Indira Gandhi: Revolution in Restraint*, Vikas Publishing House, 1974.

Ward, Barbara, *India and the West*, Norton, 1961.

Ward, Barbara and Dubos, Rene, *Only One Earth*, W.W. Norton & Company, 1972.

Index

Abdulali, Humayun, 46
Abdullah, Farooq, 338
Abdullah, Sheikh, 144
Adams, Alvin P., 81–82
Adhikari, B.P., 332
Agarwal, Anil, 291, 340
Ahluwalia, H.P.S., 176
Aitken, Elma, 363–364
Alexander, Horace, 34–35, 51n3, 57, 58, 62n1, 65, 73, 250–251, 363, 371
Alexander, P.C., 334
Ali, Aruna Asaf, 24
Ali, Salim, 21–22, 46, 58, 61, 73–74, 74, 79, 80, 95, 96, 97, 113, 129, 130, 131, 171, 175, 181–182, 183, 208, 228–229, 231, 233, 234, 240, 254, 256, 260–261, 262, 271, 273, 280, 296, 303, 329, 343–344, 350–351, 359, 372–373, 397–398, 408–409, 415
Alkazi, Ebrahim, 166
All India Congress Committee (AICC), 239
All India Services Act, 1951, 59
Amte, Baba, 401
Anand Bhawan, 12, 25
Andaman and Nicobar Islands, preservation of, 182–183, 282–283, 308, 399–400
Antarctic expedition, 358–359
Antarctic Treaty, 358–359
Antulay, A.R., 324
Appleby, Humphrey, 113
Archibald, George, 341–342, 345–346, 369
Arora, G.K., 385
Arundale, Rukmini Devi, 162, 163, 225
Asimov, Isaac, 372
Attenborough, Richard, 335
Ayensu, Edward, 406

Backbay Reclamation Scheme, 147–148, 194, 320, 324–325
Baez, Albert, 328, 362
Bahuguna, H.N., 156, 211, 238, 274, 278
Bahuguna, Sunderlal, 259, 273, 285, 289, 318–319
Baker, Richard St. Barbe, 275–276
Bandipur Sanctuary, 162
Banerjee, Purnima, 24
Banuri, Tariq, 138
Bastar forest, 319–321
    pine plantation issue, 349–350
Basu, Jyoti, 341–342
Bazaz, M.L., 46
Bedi, Rajesh, 374
Bedi, Romesh, 374
Behn, Mira, 132, 133
Bendliner, Robert, 135
Bernhard, Prince, 112, 122, 360, 375
Betla Sanctuary, 191
Bhabha, Homi, 55, 242, 273
Bhagat, Usha, 37
Bhakra Nangal Dam, 274
Bhattacharjea, Ajit, 148
Bhitarkanika Wildlife Sanctuary, 336
Bhopal gas tragedy, 298, 408
Bhopalpatnam Hydel Project, 400
Bhosale, Babasaheb, 352
Bhutan, 40–41, 81, 120, 198, 330, 382–383
Bhutto, Zulfikar Ali, 142, 247
Billner, Borje, 69
Bird Migration Study, 183
Bird Migration Treaty, 175
Blake, William, 153
Board for Doon Valley and Adjacent Watershed Areas of Ganga and Yamuna, 317
Bolt, Robert, 132

Bombay Burmah Trading Corporation, 205

Bombay Environment Action Group (BEAG), 278–279, 324–325

Bombay Metropolitan Regional Development Authority, 148

Bombay Natural History Society (BNHS), 16, 46, 89–90, 107, 130, 174, 183–185, 229, 230, 372–373, 409

Bombay Wild Birds and Wild Animals Protection Act, 1951, 46

Borivali National Park, 208

Borlaug, Norman, 139

Bowles, Chester, 68

Boys Training Establishment (BTE), 97–98, 131–132, 172, 173

Brahmachary, R.L., 332

Breeden, Stanley, 328

Brewbaker, James, 321

Buddha Jayanti Park, 166

Bustard, Robert, 224

Buultjens, Ralph, 372

Calcutta Zoological Gardens, 208–209

Capra, Fritjof, 357

Carson, Rachel, 138

Central Pollution Control Board (CPCB), 193

Central Public Health Engineering Research Institute, 192

Centre for Science and Environment, 291

Chainani, Shyam, 278, 280–281

Chakravarty, Nikhil, 405

Chamba, preservation of, 380

Chandola, Ashish, 221

Chandrasekhar, S., 63

Chandra Shekhar Azad University of Agricultural Sciences and Technology, 15

Chatterjee, Admiral A.K., 97

Chattopadhyay, Bankim Chandra, 284

Chaudhary, B.D. Nag, 204

Chavan, S.B., 208, 237

Chavan, Y.B., 95, 167

Chidananda, Swami, 288–289

Chilka Lake, 97–98, 131–132, 172–174

Chipko Movement, 291–292, 353

Chogyal of Sikkim, 252

Choudhury, Moinul Haq, 133

Clean Cities Week, 165–166

Coastal Regulation Zone (CRZ) Rules, 1991, 326

Commander, Mrs A.K., 338

Commoner, Barry, 372

Convention on Trade in Endangered Species (CITES), 327–328, 369

Corbett, Jim, 45

Corbett National Park, 151, 191

cow slaughter ban, 68

Crocodile and Sea Turtle Conservation Programme, 224–225

Dachigam Sanctuary, 100, 337

Dalvi, M.K., 320

Dang, Hari, 301

Daniel, J.C., 90, 320

Das, Biswanath, 131

Das, Premvir, 77n1

Datardi Dam, 313–314

Daulatram, Jairamdas, 51n3

Dave, P.K., 206, 226

David, Reuben, 243n5

Davis, Kathleen, 18

Delhi Bird Watching Society, 35, 50n2

Delhi Ridge area, 293

Delhi Urban Art Commission (DUAC), 166

Deoras, P.J., 170

Desai, Bhadra, 48

Desai, Morarji, 279

Devi, Sita, 316, 386

Dhar, D.P., 147, 158, 159, 197

Dhar, P.N., 52n14, 175, 197

Dharmakumar Sinhji, R.S., 36, 95, 260, 285

Divine Life Society, 288

Divyabhanusinh, 43
Dixit, J.N., 112
Doon Valley, mining operation in, 316–317, 388
Dudhwa National Park, 155, 157, 206–207, 222, 314, 396
Durrell, Gerald, 226–227

Ehrlich, Paul, 138
Engfeldt, Lars-Goran, 142
Environment (Protection) Act, 1986, 298, 326
ethnic massacre in Assam, 366, 368

family planning, 58, 63–64, 76–77, 240
Fertilizer Corporation of India (FCI), 194–196
Forest (Conservation) Act, 1980, 295
forest farming, 241
Forest Research Institute, Dehra Dun, 317
Foundation for Environmental Conservation, 251
Friends of Trees, 20
Fuller, Buckminster, 39, 40, 85–86, 115
Futehally, Zafar, 46, 61, 68, 112, 116, 122, 123, 174, 233, 234, 285, 297

Gadgil, D.R., 66, 320
Gadgil, Madhav, 66, 273, 285, 290, 295, 297, 398
Gaekwad, Fatehsinghrao, 164, 236, 300
Gandhi, Feroze, 29n19
Gandhi, Gopal, 344
Gandhi, Mahatma, 11, 33
Gandhi, Priyanka, 396
Gandhi, Rajiv, 37, 45, 47, 109, 219, 232, 340, 408–409
Gandhi, Sanjay, 37, 47, 57, 72, 95, 109, 111, 116, 120, 180, 254, 268
    five-point national programme, 219–220

Ganga Action Plan, 402
'Garibi Hatao', 109
Gee, E.P., 44
Ghorpade, M.Y., 301, 339
Ghosh, D.N., 78
Ghosh, Niren, 120
Gill, Manohar Singh, 148
Gir forest, 42, 188, 255, 347
Gir Lion Sanctuary Project, 105
Godrej, S.P., 210, 236
Gomango, Giridhar, 320
Gombu, Nawang, 305
Green, Steven, 203–205
Green Revolution, 79–80, 139–141, 143
Guha, Ramachandra, 58, 295
Guindy Deer Park, 88
Gujral, I.K., 138, 220
Gulf of Kutch Marine National Park, 314

Haes, Charles de, 123
Haidar, Salman, 116, 181, 186–187, 204–205, 211, 222, 224, 226, 235, 279
Haksar, P.N., 64, 78, 105, 108, 120, 134, 137, 141
Haldighati, 232, 304
Handoo, Jai Kishore, 316
Hangul, conservation, 337–338
Harper, Kristine, 61
Harrison, Agatha, 25
Hasan, Prof. S. Nurul, 168, 214
Hatch, Alden, 39
Hillary, Edmund, 98
Himalayan Mountaineering Institute, 252, 403
Hodgkin, Dorothy, 362
Holdgate, Martin, 135
Holloway, Colin, 221
Honolulu Zoo, 363
Hornbill House, 174
Huang Hua, 335
Hyderabad Zoo, 363

Inchampalli Hydroelectric Project, 400
Indian Board for Wild Life (IBWL), 45, 78, 83–85, 91, 92n4, 95, 102–103, 125, 162, 167, 231–232, 243n7, 300–302, 311, 315, 337, 339, 346, 348, 376, 391
Indian Forest Service (IFS), 59
Indian Hotels Company Limited, 115
Indian Mountaineering Foundation, 65, 75, 391, 404
Indian National Trust for Art and Cultural Heritage (INTACH), 356
Indian Society for Conservation of Nature (ISCON), 106–107
Indian Society of Naturalists, Baroda, 337
Indian Statistical Institute (ISI), 332
Indian Wildlife Conservation and Management Bill, 1972, 125–127
Indira Paryavaran Bhawan, 289
Indo–Pak War, 1971, 121
Indo–Soviet Treaty, 1971, 64
Intergovernmental Panel on Climate Change (IPCC), 358
International Association against Painful Experiments in Animals, 315
International Council for Bird Preservation, 231
International Crane Foundation, 370
International Monetary Fund (IMF), 75
International Union for the Conservation of Nature and Natural Resources (IUCN), 60, 89, 91, 233, 285, 315, 361–362
International Whaling Commission (IWC), 378
International Wildfowl Research Bureau, 113
Interstate River Water Disputes Act, 1956, 92
Iranian Revolution, 1979, 216, 299
Iyer, V.R. Krishna, 244n12

J. Paul Getty Wildlife Conservation Prize, 359

Jackson, Lady, 292
Jackson, Peter, 98, 99, 284, 331, 415
Jaisalmer, 75, 213
Jatti, B.D., 173
Jayakar, Pupul, 20, 248, 250
Jayal, N.D. 'Nalni', 199, 225, 230, 232–233, 296, 298, 352, 356
Jersey project, 227
Jha, L.K., 61, 268
Jog Falls, 45, 257
Johnson, Lyndon, 56, 61
Joshi, Harideo, 161, 189, 207
Joslin, Paul, 88
Jung, Ali Yavar, 147, 165

Kalakkadu Reserve Forest, 206
Kanchenjunga, 252
Kanha National Park, 88, 100, 101, 394, 396
Kanvinde, Achyut, 166
Kao, R.N., 109
Karunanidhi, M., 163
Karve, Maharshi, 58
Kaul, Kailas Nath, 15, 16, 290
Kaul, T.N., 56
Kaushal, Avdesh, 388
Kaziranga, 44, 315
Kemf, Elizabeth, 376
Kenya, 141–142
Kenyatta, Jomo, 49, 141–142
Keoladeo Ghana Bird Sanctuary (also see Bharatpur Bird Sanctuary), 34–35, 65, 73, 79, 95–96, 162, 170, 188–189, 207–208, 229–230, 255, 303, 329
Kerala State Forest Corporation, 232
Kerkar, Ajit, 116
Khan, Khan Abdul Gaffar, 300
Khan, Barkatullah, 145, 161
Khan, Khurshed Alam, 355
Khoshoo, T.N., 297, 368, 374, 377
Khosla, Ashok, 117, 172, 234, 284
Kochukoshy, C.K., 272

Kohli, M.S., 176, 403
Kramer, Karl-Heinz, 209
Krishna, Nanditha, 407
Krishnan, M., 38, 87, 163, 233, 297
Krishnatry, S.M., 222
Kudremukh project, 215–216
Kulu Valley, 380
Kumar, Narinder, 251–252
Kumaramangalam, Mohan, 150
Kurien, V., 68, 70n3
Kyle, Lucile, 72, 110, 120, 151, 180, 198, 247, 248, 255

Lal, Bansi, 99
Lal, Bhajan, 380
Lalpur Dam project, 276–277, 311–313, 340, 341, 385
Lawrence, D.H., 360, 364n8
L'Ecole Nouvelle, 16
Leontief, Wassily, 372
Leyhausen, Paul, 221, 249
Limaye, Madhu, 188, 255, 259
Lindberg, Eje, 302
Lindberg, Ola, 302
Linduska, Joseph, 231
Lohia, Ram Manohar, 392
Lohse, Marianne, 324

MacDonald, Malcolm, 36–37, 51n5
Mackenzie, Sam, 399
Maddox, John, 405
Madras Snake Park, 225
Mahabaleshwar–Panchgani Regional Planning Board, 352–353
Mahalanobis, P.C., 332
Mahatma Gandhi Marine National Park, 400
Malaviya, K.D., 274
Malhoutra, Manmohan 'Moni', 60, 97, 99, 100, 101, 106, 108, 110, 114, 115, 116, 131, 143, 146, 153, 163, 172, 174, 181, 279
Malik, A.J., 381

Manali, 38, 180
Manas National Park (formerly Sanctuary), 47, 227, 382–383
Manekshaw, General Sam, 121–122
Marquez, Gabriel Garcia, 367
Martyn, Mady, 387
Maruti project, 120, 309
Masai Mara Reserve, 309
Mashobra, 37, 180
Mathias, Charles 'Mac,' 184
Mathiesen, Karl, 138
Mathur, K.P., 213
Mathur, Shiv Charan, 401
Mathura refinery, issue of pollution, 169–172, 215, 340, 380–381
    Agra's pollution levels, 381–382
Matthai, Duleep, 124, 263, 359, 369
Matthews, G.V.T., 113
Mazlish, Bruce, 372
McNamara, Robert, 61
McVean, D.N., 182
Mehrotra, Phyllis, 48
Mehta, Jagat, 40
Menon, C. Achuta, 233
Menon, K.P.S., 310–311
Menon, Krishna, 64
Menon, M.G.K., 273, 297, 310, 383–385
Menon, V.P., 96
Miller, Harry, 226
Milligan, Spike, 223–224, 243n2
Minkowski, Karen, 203–204
Mishra, Veer Bhadra, 402
Misra, Shripati, 386–387
Mitra, Ashok, 68
Mitra, Swapna, 66
Mountbatten, Edwina, 43
Mountfort, Guy, 104, 123, 220
Mrosovsky, Nicholas, 337
Mudumalai Sanctuary, 162
Mukherjee, Pranab, 262
Mukherjee, Sharada, 281
Mukherji, S.P., 290
Munro, David, 270

Naidu, Padmaja, 83, 93n7, 94, 152, 166
Naik, V.P., 147, 190
Nair, S.C., 399
Nalaban, 97
Nambiar, A.C.N., 268, 367, 395
Namdapha Biosphere Reserve, 342–343
Nanda, Admiral S.M., 172
Nanda Devi Biosphere Reserve, 398
Narain, Prakash, 407
Narain, Raj, 197
Narayan, Jayaprakash, 179, 197–198, 259
Narmada Bachao Andolan, 217
Narmada river
  dispute over sharing of the water of,
  92, 216–218
Narmada river, master plan for the
  development of, 91–92
Nath, L.M., 301
Nathu La Pass, 40
National Audubon Society, 231
National Botanical Research Institute
  (NBRI), 15
National Committee for Environmental
  Planning and Coordination (NCEPC),
  127–129, 163, 173, 191, 204, 234
Navagam Dam, 216–218
Naxalite movement, 64
Nayanar, E.K., 270, 272
neem tree planting programmes, 285
Nehru, B.K., 61, 268
Nehru, Jawaharlal, 12, 26, 34, 36, 43,
  49–50, 344
Nehru, Kamala, 15, 18
Nehru Institute of Mountaineering, 60,
  66, 403
Netam, Arvind, 287
New Bombay project, 194
Nilgiri Biosphere Reserve, 398
Nizer, Louis, 372
Non-Aligned Summit, 370, 372, 379, 389
Norgay, Tenzing, 98, 305
Norlin, Anne, 137
Norman, Dorothy, 39, 79, 85, 119, 150,
  198, 308, 334, 335, 366, 367

Oates, John, 205
Operation Blue Star, 394–396
Operation Gangotri, 358, 359
Operation Geetur, 337
Operation Popeye, 62n3
Oza, G.M., 337

Pahlavi, Abdorezza, 199
Pal, Bachendri, 66, 70n1
Pal, B.P., 143, 285
Palamau National Park, 191
Palme, Olaf, 180, 220
Panchgani–Mahabaleshwar plateau area,
  351–353
Pande, Arvind, 70n2, 320, 375, 384,
  387–388
Pande, Kedar, 142
Pande B.D., 196
Pandit, Vijaya Lakshmi, 16, 40
Pant, Govind Ballabh, 59
Pant, K.C., 191
Pant, Pitambar, 50, 66, 106, 114, 118,
  127, 132, 149n2, 172
Panwar, H.S., 396
Parekh, Kirit, 163
Parikh, Harivallabh, 312–313, 340–341,
  385
Parmar, Y.S., 180, 211
Parthasarathi, Ashok, 105
Parthasarathi, G., 335
Patel, Rajni, 18
Patel, Sardar Vallabhbhai, 96
Patel, Shirish, 148
Patel, Uttambhai, 312
Pathak, G.S., 186
Patil, Vasantdada, 278, 372
Pawar, Sharad, 278
Periyar Sanctuary, 88
Pierce, Diane, 369
Pipli Reserve Forest, 185
Plage, Dieter, 221–222
Polunin, Nicholas, 251, 353, 405
Porbandar, 331

Pouchepadass, Jacques, 28n10
Prasad, H.Y. Sharada, 50, 106, 134, 148, 198, 294, 366
Prevention of Cruelty to Animals Act, 1960, 162
Project Crocodile, 201–202
Project Gromet, 61
Project Lion, 223, 283
Project Tiger, 4, 151–155, 200, 220, 233, 249, 284, 302, 360, 375–377, 396
Pugwash Conference on Science and World Affairs, 362
Pulicat Lake Bird Sanctuary, 343
Purple Martins, 110
Pygmalion Point (Indira Point), 400
pygmy hog episode, 226–227

Qasim, S.Z., 297, 358
Qasim, Syed Mir, 160, 165

Radhakrishnan, S., 363
Rahman, Habib, 86
Rahman, Sheikh Mujibur, 198
Raina, V.K., 358
Rajagopalachari, C., 260
Rajamani, R., 279–281, 283, 311, 320, 322, 323, 335–337, 340, 342, 351, 364n1, 374–375
Rajeswar, T.V., 374
Ram, Jagjivan, 82, 83, 91, 131, 202, 204, 207
Ramachandran, A., 242
Ramachandran, V., 217
Raman, Radha, 145
Ranebennur Blackbuck Sanctuary, 158
Rangarajan, Mahesh, 293
Ranjitsinh, M.K., 100, 116, 117, 125, 298, 349
Ranthambore Tiger Reserve, 339
Rao, K.L., 63, 91, 92
Rao, P.V. Narasimha, 262, 263
Rao, V.K.R.V., 63
Rathwa, Ramsingh, 341

Reagan, Ronald, 268, 363
Reddy, Sanjeeva, 297
Revelle, Roger, 117
Rio Earth Summit, 138
Ripley, Dillon, 35, 68–69, 175, 183, 329–330, 342, 359, 374, 375, 407–408, 409
Roy, Sunil, 275
Royal Botanic Gardens, 15
Rustomji, Nari, 41

Sadiq, G.M., 100
Sahay, Bhagwan, 166
Sahni, Birbal, 15
Sankat Mochan Foundation, 402
Sankhala, Kailash, 86, 88, 116, 177n1, 339
Santapau, H., 235
Santiniketan, 17, 62
Sarabhai, Mridula, 144
Sarabhai, Vikram, 61, 106, 117–118
Sardar Sarovar Dam, 91
Sarin, H.C., 65, 216
Sariska Tiger Reserve, 80, 81, 162, 185, 207
Sarkar, A.K., 68
Sarkar, Devraj, 384
Saser Kangri expedition, 404
Satishchandran, T.R., 342
Satkosia Gorge Sanctuary, 225
Satpathy, Nandini, 224
Save Mussoorie Society, 386–387
Saxena, V.S., 229
Schaller, George, 88, 332
Scindia, Madhavrao, 376
Scott, Peter, 284, 303, 327, 378, 398, 415
Sen, Boshi, 252
Sen, Gertrude Emerson, 252–253, 259, 285
Sen, P.C., 65
Sen, Triguna, 63, 75–76
Seshan, N.K., 80
Sethi, P.C., 186, 216
Shah, K.K., 164

Shakti Sthal, 416
Sharma, K.K., 148
Shastri, Lal Bahadur, 50, 57
Sherathang, 40
Short, Jeffrey, 328, 344
Shreemati Nathibai Damodar Thackersey (SNDT) University, 58
Shukla, Shyama Charan, 92, 101, 104, 111
Shukla, V.C., 111, 288
Siberian cranes, 344–346
Silent Valley, 261, 269–273, 310, 353, 383–385, 397
Simla Accord, 64, 119
Simla Summit, 142
Simon, Noel, 88
Singh, Arjun, 316, 319
Singh, Billy Arjan, 95, 116–117, 151–155, 156–157, 206, 222, 240, 261, 285, 296, 297, 301, 314–315, 361–362, 396
    Order of the Golden Ark award, 256–257
Singh, Brigadier Gyan, 60, 66, 305
Singh, Charan, 255, 260, 274
Singh, C.P.N., 280
Singh, Dinesh, 95
Singh, Dorendra, 201
Singh, Hari, 61
Singh, Jai, 80
Singh, Karan, 67, 75, 78, 83–84, 89, 110, 116, 124, 125, 138, 139, 153, 157, 162, 167, 200, 221, 292, 300, 391
Singh, Karni, 145
Singh, K.P., 115
Singh, L.P., 81, 201
Singh, Dr Manmohan, 80
Singh, Nagendra, 305
Singh, K. Natwar, 65, 74, 82, 95, 198, 230
Singh, Rao Birendra, 296, 302, 321
Singh, R.K. Dorendra, 200
Singh, Samar, 295–296, 298, 304, 323, 336–337, 349

Singh, Satyanarayan, 72
Singh, Swaran, 219
Singh, Virbhadra, 380
Sinh, Digvijay, 292, 301, 349, 369
Sinh, Ranjit, 100
Sinha, Deepali, 65
Sinha, Sarat Chandra, 212, 249
Sivaraman, B., 79, 103
Solanki, Madhavsinh, 312, 331
Soni, R.C., 116
South Luangwa National Park, 220
Sreeraman, N.S., 282
Srinivasan, T.N., 128
Stephens-Holmberg, Loucia, 101–102
Stirling, Angus, 356
Strong, Maurice, 114, 135
Subramaniam, C., 134, 138
Subramaniam, T.N., 64
Sudhir, N., 232
Sukhadia, Mohanlal, 80, 213
Sultanpur Bird Sanctuary, 331
Sunderbans Tiger Reserve, 250
Swaran Singh Committee, 239

Tagore, Rabindranath, 17, 258, 416
Taj Mahal, 170, 171, 380–381
Taronga Zoo, 71
Tata, J.R.D., 307n14, 324
Tehri Dam project, 273–276
Thal-Vaishet Fertilizer Project, 277, 278, 281
Thimayya, K.S., 44
Tiger Haven Wildlife Trust, 157
Tito, Josip Broz, 389
Tiwari, N.D., 238
Train, Russell, 135
Twycross Zoo, 222

United Nations Conference on Trade and Development (UNCTAD), 389
United Nations Conference on the Human Environment, Stockholm, 4, 12, 69, 106, 113, 114, 119, 128, 129,

133, 134, 136–139, 138, 141, 142, 362, 397
United Nations Environment Programme (UNEP), 141
Urs, Devraj, 190, 257

Valley of Flowers National Park, 298
vanamahotsava initiative, 322
Varadarajan, S., 171
Vardhan, Harsh, 229, 232, 244n8, 304
Varshney, C.K., 172, 177n3
Velavadar Blackbuck National Park, 158
Venkateswaran, A.P., 405
Venkitaramanan, S., 384
Verghese, B.G., 364n4
Verma, M.C., 242
Vidyasagar, Ishwar Chandra, 58
Vijaya, J., 337
Vijayaraghavan, V.S., 384
Visva-Bharati University, 62
Vohra, B.B., 146–147
Vohra, C.P., 358

Ward, Barbara, 292
Water (Prevention and Control of) Pollution Act, 1974, 193
Watumull Foundation, 321
White Revolution, 70n3
Wildlife Institute of India, 228
Wildlife (Protection) Act, 1972, 159, 199, 212, 271, 375
Williams, General Harold, 65
Witkem, Roxane, 372
Women's Himalayan Expedition, 51n7
World Conservation Strategy (WCS), 284, 361
World Wildlife Fund-India, 112, 154, 210, 230, 233, 236, 369
World Wildlife Fund-International, 112, 122
Wright, Anne, 116, 124, 236, 300, 369, 370–371, 399
Wright, Belinda, 328

Yusufzai, M.W.K., 143

Zakaria, Rafiq, 148